Billie Holiday

Stuart Nicholson has written extensively on jazz for a variety of magazines and newspapers. His first book, *Jazz: the Modern Resurgence* (now republished as *Jazz: the 1980s Resurgence*), was described as 'the definitive guide to jazz during the eighties'. His biography of Ella Fitzgerald was widely acclaimed on publication in 1993 and has been translated into several European languages. *Ella Fitzgerald* and *Billie Holiday* were named 'Notable Book of the Year' by the *New York Times* in 1994 and 1995 respectively.

'Stuart Nicholson's *Billie Holiday* is intelligent, well written . . . His remarks are often original, putting order into her chaos by dissecting every artistic move . . . Where Mr Nicholson excels is in describing song after song after song with their interjected cooings and adulatory supportings by this or that instrumental soloist'
Ned Rorem, *New York Times Book Review*

'With perhaps more success than any other biographer so far, Nicholson illuminates complexities in [Holiday's] personality, her art and her times that made the singer a phenomenon of American culture. As good as he is in biographical detail, his greatest contribution is perspective on the singer's creative process'
Jazz Times

'Thoroughly readable, linking nitty-gritty facts, gee-whizz flourishes and well-evaluated opinion in a manner guaranteed to keep you flicking pages'
Fred Dellar, *Vox*

STUART NICHOLSON

Billie Holiday

From the Library of Suzanne

BPP-03697 © Antioch Pub.

INDIGO

First published in Great Britain 1995
by Victor Gollancz

This Indigo edition published 1996
Indigo is an imprint of the Cassell Group
Wellington House, 125 Strand, London WC2R 0BB

A catalogue record for this book is
available from the British Library.

ISBN 0 575 40016 1

Printed and bound in Great Britain by
Cox & Wyman Ltd, Reading, Berkshire

96 97 98 99 10 9 8 7 6 5 4 3 2 1

For Talc

Contents

Preface

The polarities of life and art, once carefully separated by T. S. Eliot and the New Critics, collided with such violence during the forty-four years of singer Billie Holiday's life that they became bonded into one immutable whole. Together they gave force to the Billie Holiday legend, a legend that has grown with increasing definition since her death in 1959. Although a sense of sadness and waste provide the backdrop for her troubled yet colourful life, that life is ultimately redeemed by the joy, passion and, in her final years, the pathos of her music.

Listening to Billie Holiday can be as profoundly moving as it can be profoundly exhilarating. Her singing has such great humanity that it reaches beyond the arbitrary boundaries of jazz or pop to touch people who do not care much about either. She is an icon of twentieth-century music who has influenced, both directly and indirectly, vernacular singing as we know it today. Yet in many ways it was the extreme contradictions to be found in her character that created the tensions that gave rise to her genius.

Even if her life was like a long tortuous sentence struggling to express itself, to attempt to reconstruct it as that of an ordinary woman beset by trial and tribulation is to misunderstand Holiday with a degree of perversity equal to her own. Billie Holiday most certainly was no ordinary woman. People who knew her were frequently in awe of not only her talent but also what is now the stuff of her legend: a voracious appetite for living, for sex, for alcohol and drugs.

Legend, however, tends to have scant respect for fact. A life of swirling, stark imagery has, I discovered, left many a tall tale in its wake and many pitfalls for a potential biographer. The problem, as always, is to sort fact from fiction. That there was a very real possibility of achieving this slowly became clear to me when I was researching my biography of Ella Fitzgerald in 1991–2. Ella's career and that of Billie Holiday ran parallel in the 1930s and 1940s. As I was looking into Ella's now legendary Apollo debut in November 1934 on Ralph Cooper's 'Amateur

Night in Harlem', I discovered that Billie Holiday played the Apollo just two days later, for the week commencing Friday, 23 November, with pianist Bobbie Henderson.

This seemed to me to be a historical snippet of some importance since every history book, biography, album-liner note and magazine article places Billie's Apollo debut in 1935. When I then found the details of that 1935 appearance, I discovered that it was in very different circumstances to received wisdom. My interest aroused, I kept a weather eye open during my Ella research for further references to Billie Holiday and soon accumulated enough new material to convince my publishers that her full story was yet to be told.

This may seem a surprising claim since there have been at least six Billie Holiday biographies of various shapes and sizes over the years. However, all systematically touched base with John Chilton's pioneering *Billie's Blues* (Quartet, 1975) for their historical information. But while it is a foolhardy biographer who criticizes his predecessors, I had from the start discovered flaws and omissions in Chilton's account, flaws and omissions that were in turn perpetuated in each of the subsequent five biographies. Indeed, the more new, previously unresearched material I discovered, the more I found them lacking; so much goes unmentioned, unexplained and uncorroborated that I decided to put them to one side and rely on my own research.

Equally, I had come to regard Billie Holiday's autobiography, *Lady Sings the Blues*, with suspicion. When writer and critic Francis Davis charitably wrote it off as 'none-too-reliable'[1] not a voice was raised in protest, certainly not my own. Yet, to my surprise, it became clear that it hit major episodes in her life square in the face. For example, her childhood rape, an episode treated with much caution and caveats by commentators through the years and even written off in one biography as being 'hard to believe' because 'documentary evidence' pointed to the contrary, actually took place with consequences exactly as Billie had described.

As months of research passed, the inconsistencies and guesswork that had hitherto comprised Billie's life story were replaced by hard fact. Several significant episodes, such as her relationship to attorney Earle Warren Zaidins, and countless small details, such as the date of her marriage to Louis McKay, always given as 1956 but in fact 1957, were corroborated from official records.

Here I am grateful to my dear friend Marsha Saron Dennis who made so much possible. Her kindness and generosity have been an inspiration to me as much as her sharp, perceptive insights into the human condition. Equally, the warmth of my welcome from her and

6

her husband Bob and their sons on my visits to New York is something I treasure. As I finished each chapter I passed copies to Loren Schoenberg and Norman Granz whose comments and perceptive insights enabled me to make countless timely revisions. I sincerely hope that they will consider their time and trouble was worthwhile.

Loren also made room in his busy schedule as a tenor saxophonist, bandleader, musicologist, broadcaster and jazz lecturer at Manhattan's New School on Fifth Avenue to encourage and help me with research work in New York, setting up interviews as well as contributing a dozen pages of closely typed manuscript on the Billie Holiday/Lester Young sides. My text is gratefully based on his outline. Also thanks to Artie Shaw, who gave of his time in an interview and also read, checked and appropriately amended the chapter that deals with his involvement in Billie Holiday's career.

Tracing someone's footprints through time is at its most exciting and rewarding when it takes you in new and unexpected directions. Professor John Morgan, MD, who heads the Department of Pharmacology at the City University of New York Medical School, kindly acted as consultant on all drug-related matters. Not only did he find time to give me two detailed and extensive interviews which provided a fascinating insight into addiction and the drug dependency culture, he also scrutinized Billie's medical records to provide valuable insight into her treatment at the Federal Reformatory for Women, Alderston, West Virginia. In addition he kindly checked my text to make sure I heard him right; even if we do disagree over the matter of crop-circles, his company is as absorbing as it is stimulating and he has my utmost gratitude for his help. Also thanks to John's daughter, Jennifer L. Morgan, for her research work on my behalf in Baltimore.

Professor David Courtwright of the Department of History, University of North Florida, Jacksonville patiently explained the sociological history of narcotics addiction in Harlem and New York during the 1930s and 1940s, and the relevance this would have had to Billie Holiday's pattern of addiction. The whole subject of addiction in these years is dealt with in considerable detail in the valuable and fascinating *Addicts Who Survived (An Oral History of Narcotics Use in America 1923–65)* (University of Tennessee Press, Knoxville, 1989) which he co-authored with Herman Joseph and Don Des Jarlais. David graciously allowed me to quote freely from its text.

Once again I am indebted to Dan Morgenstern at the Institute of Jazz Studies, Rutgers University, Newark, New Jersey, both for granting me untrammelled access to the Institute's vast resources and for allowing me shamelessly to pick his encyclopedic brain for ideas and inspiration.

Particular thanks are due to Sister Mary Rosaria Baxter of the Good Shepherd Center, Baltimore who finally resolved the details of Billie Holiday's association with the institution which are published here for the first time. In our interviews she also gave me a valuable historical perspective on the Center's untiring efforts over the decades on behalf of young girls with emotional and behavioural problems.

I would also like to acknowledge the kind help and assistance of Janice Blackwell, Dave Bennett, George Haslam, Stanley Crouch, Jane and Martin Samuel, Daphne Dennis, Kenneth R. Cobb who is the Director of New York City Municipal Archives and tracked down details of Billie Holiday's incarceration in 1929, Arthur Martinez, Mark H. Tanenbaum and Frank Braile of New York County Surrogate's Court, Carl Schoettler of *The Baltimore Sun*, Paul Wilson of the British Library's National Sound Archive, Ken Jones of the National Jazz Foundation Archive at Loughton Central Library, Graham Langley of the British Institute of Jazz Studies, Pim Gras and Herman Oppenner of Stichting National Jazz Archief in the Netherlands, Cees Schrama of Polygram Jazz International Music B.V. of the Netherlands, Richard Cook of Polygram Jazz UK, Laurie Staff of Harmonia Mundi UK, Dr Wolfram Knauer of the Jazz-Institut Darmstadt in Germany, Kendall Crilly of the Music Library at Yale University, Ellen Cordes of the Beinecke Rare Book and Manuscript Library, also at Yale University, The Library of Congress Music Division, Martha Minor of the Free Library of Philadelphia, Temple University Libraries in Philadelphia, the Enoch Pratt Free Library in Baltimore, The New York Public Library Schomburg Center for Research in Black Culture in Harlem and The New York Public Library Performing Arts Research Center at Lincoln Center.

The list of interviewees is long and since they are credited in the text I will not list them here. But I am sincerely grateful to them all for the insights they were able to share with me and the courtesy they afforded me. Thanks also to Phil Schaap, dubbed the 'Dean of jazz radio' by the *New York Times* and the winner of a Grammy award for his work on the monumental *The Complete Billie Holiday on Verve 1945–59* CD set, for his suggestions, encouragement, details from his archives and a fascinating discography. Also thanks to Max Harrison for providing the epigraph.

Once again my editor Richard Wigmore has been a model of support and patience and when finally confronted with what I fondly imagined was the final text was the source of countless helpful suggestions to pull everything together into this, its final form. Throughout, my family have given me all the encouragement and more that I could ever need. My dear wife Kath has made everything possible. My mother and the in-laws, Jim and Eileen, have kept me smiling, while my brother Malcolm, to whom this book is dedicated, has debated every critical opinion and musical observation I make here. His astute judgements and unfailing good humour have, I hope, kept me on course and my spirits up. A psychology graduate of the University of Wales Institute of Science and Technology, he compiled a psychological profile of Billie Holiday which helped steer me through alien territory. He also provided the analysis of tempos and live recordings to be found in the appendices, both valuable resources which I believe contribute a little more to our under-standing of Billie Holiday the artist. For the last word I return to Kath with heartfelt thanks for her love and encouragement which make it all worthwhile.

Stuart Nicholson
Woodlands St Mary, Berkshire
August 1994

'No people sing with such pure voices as those who live in deepest hell; what we take for the song of angels is their song.'

Kafka, *Letters to Milena*

Billie Holiday

Prologue

The rue Saint-Benoît in Paris begins at the rue Marbeuf and ends a block away in a cul-de-sac. Situated at the end of this little Montmartre street used to be the Mars Club, a popular jazz hang-out for fans and musicians until it was closed down because of complaints about noise during the 1960s. In its heyday it had that special kind of ambiance that clicked with the public and was appreciated by musicians. It is still remembered with affection, but those who went there during the week of 24 November 1958 have a particularly good reason to remember it. It was the week Billie Holiday played there.

As she stood alongside her pianist Mal Waldron, the incandescence of her great talent seemed to light up the whole club. Her voice was dry and parched but somehow found a way of getting to the end of each song without revealing too many fault-lines. Her wine-coloured eyes, clouded by addiction and drink, looked into the middle distance. Her face, scarred by a thousand morning-afters, was dominated by her sensual mouth, a mouth that from time to time seemed to toy with the idea of a smile. Barely moving, she held her arms in front of her, bent at the elbows, her left hand occasionally snapping to the rhythm. Her concentration was intense: this was maximum minimalism.

Her head twitching imperceptibly to the beat, Billie appeared relaxed. Yet the week before she had been given the bird by the crowds in the Olympia Theatre who thought her voice was shot. But here, in the intimate surroundings of the club, her delicate one-to-one art spoke to everyone present. Using elision, paraphrase and a sure sense of rhythmic placement, she seemed to pare a song down to the very essence of its meaning. The audience loved it.

Few present realized that she was working for a percentage of the door money. Her European tour, organized by Bruno Coquatrix for a fee of $10,000 plus transportation, had been cancelled from under her. She had been paid only a tiny proportion of what she was owed when Coquatrix left her stranded in Paris without funds to get back to the

United States. Even though the tour was bonded with the American Guild of Variety Artists (AGVA) for the full amount, her lawyer in New York, Earle Warren Zaidins, had failed to recover a single dollar on her behalf. Billie Holiday was singing to raise the cost of an airplane ticket home.

The pianist Hazel Scott, then visiting Europe, remembers how the depressing grey chill of Paris in early winter had descended on her. She sat in the club drinking, brooding and weeping about a broken romance as Billie Holiday sang. 'It was a real bitter blues,' she recalls, 'and on top of the problems I was having with my own life at the time, I began thinking of what was happening to Lady Day. Brilliant artist, beautiful person – you could pin all the superlatives on her, but there she was, having been misused again by somebody who didn't give a damn about her.'[1]

Far from home and in a foreign country, Billie Holiday was feeling the sickening pain of loneliness. Back in her hotel room, her whole life seemed to stretch out in front of her, the good times, the bad times and the in-between times. But through the ups and downs of those crowded, hectic years, most of all she missed her mother, who had died unexpectedly at the age of fifty on 6 October 1945. It was a blow from which she never really recovered.

Chapter One

1915–28

Sarah Julia Harris was born out of wedlock on Sunday, 16 August 1895 in Baltimore, Maryland. It was the year the city employed black labour in municipal jobs for the first time. When the ruling was approved by the city elders, the Republican administration reassured its white constituents that black workers would never work alongside white. And while some blacks were employed as messengers, cleaners and janitors, the great majority worked on the sewage wagons. At the time, Baltimore could claim the dubious distinction of being the largest unsewered city in the United States.

For its 67,000-strong black community, then the largest in the United States outside Washington, DC, Baltimore was a grim place to live. Its only attraction was the promise of employment in its heavy industries or along the wharves of its docklands. For Sarah Harris, born on the wrong side of the tracks, life was always going to be difficult. Disowned by her father, Charles Fagan, she was brought up by her mother, Sussie, and her elder half-sister by nine years, Eva.

About eighteen months after Sarah was born, Sussie married James Harris, a labourer, and moved into 1356 Carroll Street, Baltimore, taking her husband's name for herself and her two illegitimate daughters. Within three years she and James had two children of their own, George and Maggie.[1] From an early age all Sussie's children had to learn to fend for themselves. Sarah spent little time in school and could barely read and write.

Her mother and half-sister worked as domestic cleaners by day and took in laundry by night. To help them make ends meet, Sarah had joined their daily struggle before she was ten. As she progressed into her teens Sadie, as she liked to be called, developed into a promiscuous, pleasantly plump girl who loved cooking. At eighteen she took the seventy-minute train journey to Philadelphia on a 'transportation' job with a white employer; they provided transport and employment and she provided her labour.

In February 1915, very obviously pregnant and as a single woman an embarrassment to her employers, she was told to leave. With little money and no place to go, she was admitted into Philadelphia General Hospital at 34th and Pine Street where she waited on patients and scrubbed floors in exchange for care during her imminent confinement. At 2.30 a.m. on 7 April 1915 she gave birth to an illegitimate daughter. When she registered the birth on 24 April, she gave the child's name as 'Elinore' and the father's name as Frank 'DeViese', a twenty-year-old waiter then living at 1131 South Street. The couple were not living together; Sadie gave her address as 331 South Broad Street and her occupation as 'Housework'.[2]

Whether or not DeVeazy was Eleanora's true father will never be known. But what is known is that Sadie always told her daughter that her father was Clarence Holiday and that she was born in Philadelphia.[3] If Clarence Holiday was the father, there could be any number of reasons why Sadie refused to acknowledge his paternity at the time she registered her daughter's birth.[4] In the Southern States they have a saying, 'Mother's baby; Father's, maybe!'

However, there would never be any doubt in Eleanora's mind who her father was. She would go to the grave believing he was Clarence Earnest Holliday, the fourth child of Nelson Holliday and Mary Johnson, a hospital labourer and laundress of 1617 Walker Street, Baltimore.[5]

Two years after Eleanora was born, America declared war on Germany and on 5 June 1917 Clarence Holiday registered with the Draft Board, signing his Draft Registration in neat, educated handwriting (using the one-1 version of his surname). He gave his date of birth as 23 July 1895. The year was crucial; since Clarence was in fact born on 23 July 1898 he was not required to register, as the first draft was for all males between twenty-one and thirty-one years of age.

Through error, impulse or misplaced patriotism, Clarence had set in progress a chain of events that resulted in his call-up papers arriving five months later. At the time he was living at 790 North Franklin Street and working as an 'elevator conductor' for Hutzler Bros. in the Howard & Clay Building, Baltimore.[6] When he reported for duty he was posted to the National Army as a Private on 25 November 1917 and assigned to the Stevedore Regiment in Washington, DC. Two days later he deserted.

He was again inducted on 21 August 1918 'under a misapprehension of status', having resolved the confusion over his year of birth. He was assigned to the 54th Company, 153rd Depot Brigade as a member of

Company I, 811 Pion Infantry on 11 September 1918 and became a bugler on 1 October 1918.

Although he was sent to France on 20 October 1918, there is nothing on his war record to indicate that, as has often been claimed, he was a victim of a poison-gas attack. Indeed, Armistice Day was 11 November 1918, exactly twenty-two days after Clarence's ship left port in America to engage in hostilities. He remained in France until 28 June 1919 and received an Honourable Discharge on 7 July 1919, promptly returning to Baltimore.[7]

With the arrival of her unplanned daughter, Sadie sent word to her half-sister Eva back in Baltimore asking if she would take care of Eleanora for a while. By then Eva had left home and had recently married Robert Miller, a labourer who lived at 803 North Somerset Street.[8] Whether Sadie was in a relationship, maybe with Frank DeVeazy[9] or someone else, or she had found work, is uncertain. In the event, Robert Miller made the journey to Philadelphia to pick up the babe-in-arms. It marked the beginning of a pattern of being hived off to relations and friends that would recur with increasing regularity throughout Eleanora's formative years.

On his return from Philadelphia, Robert placed her in the care of his mother, Martha Miller, and for the first eighteen months of her life, Eleanora was brought up by the woman she would later come to call Grandmother.[10] Martha Miller took the baby into care because Robert and Eva were about to start a family of their own. Their son Charles was born on 6 October 1916, followed on 5 April 1919 by a daughter, Dorothy.

However, Robert Miller had another daughter, Evelyn, from his previous wife Jenny, who had died in 1909. Evelyn Miller, who became Evelyn Conway when she married in 1924, was born in 1906 and was raised by Robert's mother when Jenny Miller died. Evelyn was a ten-year-old when Eleanora suddenly arrived in their midst. 'My mother died when I was three years old,' she recalled. 'My grandmother, Martha Miller, raised me. It was an open house, my grandmother was always taking in neighbourhood kids who had fallen on hard times or had been abandoned. It was her who partly raised Eleanora.'[11]

It is not known when Sadie returned from Philadelphia, but it was certainly prior to Clarence Holiday's conscription. For a while Sadie stayed at Martha Miller's. 'Once in a while Clarence Holiday would visit,' recalled Evelyn Conway. 'He sort of helped out whenever he could. They were never married; Sadie had the baby on the outside.'[12]

By 1920, however, Sadie and Eleanora had moved in with Robert

19

and Eva Miller's family at 432 Colvin Street in downtown Baltimore,[13] not far from Orleans Street, one of the main routes in and out of the city. Sadie, who by then had taken her father's surname, Fagan, had found a job as operator in a shirt factory, and when she was at work Eleanora was tended by Eva, who stayed at home caring for Charles and Dorothy and taking in laundry.

Sadie was a staunch Catholic and frequently played host to her parish priest for Sunday lunch. Later in life, Eleanora recalled those early years: 'One preacher . . . used to come every Sunday and Momma said, "Oh, go on. Eat all you like, Reverend so and so," I can't even think of his name . . . I have a cousin Charlie and a cousin Dorothy, and the two of them had to wait. And he would bring his wife and his whole family sometimes and we'd wait and wonder about the gravy, so one Sunday I made a booboo, I said, "Mama, you know there's no more in the pot!" '[14]

Despite the certainties of religion, however, Sadie was a pragmatist who looked approvingly on God as the dispenser of good and ill alike; in the same spirit Eleanora readily accepted the teachings of Catholicism and regularly attended church with her mother. For the rest of her life religion provided something to kick against without her ever being able to kick away entirely.

When she reached maturity, Eleanora's attitude towards religion would appear perfunctory, although she often wore a crucifix as a young woman.[15] However, while a core of belief always remained, for her the concept of the Holy Father would remain illusory. Discipline from within her conscience was never truly within her grasp. Yet throughout her life she desperately sought a father-figure, someone to exert the discipline she sought from the outside, a discipline which unaided she was incapable of providing for herself.

Her yearning for a father-figure was a deep desire she kept sealed as a block of time in the never-never land of her imagination. Such a desire was not easy to bury; later it emerged from her dreams and from the hallucinatory world she came to inhabit as a manifestation of reality; this surreal world, while untrue as to fact, was inseparable from Eleanora's psyche. In 1945, for example, when registering her mother's death, she gave Sadie's surname as Holiday, stating she was the widow of Clarence, although the two had never married. Two years later she told a social worker that she was the only child of 'Clarence and Sadie Holiday' and spoke of a 'happy childhood' when they were a 'family'.[16] And, finally, in the pages of her autobiography, *Lady Sings the Blues*, she again metaphorically joins Sadie and Clarence in marriage.

These profound, troubled desires were an imaginary tapestry woven to cover a deep scar. When Clarence returned from military service in the summer of 1919, when Eleanora was four, Sadie was involved with another man. There was never any family life with Clarence, who went alone into lodgings at 1109 McCullough Street.[17]

Sadie was dating Philip Gough, a twenty-six-year-old driver who lived at 233 Spring Street.[18] On 20 September 1920, the couple applied to the Circuit Court of Baltimore City for a marriage licence and on 20 October were duly married according to the articles of the Roman Catholic faith by Father Joseph F. Murphy, Sadie's parish priest.

During the same month Sadie got married, Eleanora began her education at Public School 102, the Thomas E. Hayes Elementary School at 601 Central Avenue. The five-year-old was taken there by Eva Miller on behalf of Sadie, who was away working. Eva was incorrectly registered as Eleanora's mother, but gave their address as 609 Bond Street, in the Fells Point district of the city.[19] The *Baltimore City Directory* shows this was the home of Mrs Viola Green,[20] who lived on the ground floor with her son Freddie. He soon struck up a friendship with Eleanora, recalling: 'She was an only child, her mother worked as a servant over in Roland Park and that area. I knew her mother as Sadie Gough, that was her name then . . . I never did see the man who was her father, not even once. She was basically a loner. She spent most of her time playing softball (she was pitcher), stickball and roller skating with the boys in the neighbourhood. Often she would scrape for a dime and go to the Dunbar Theater to see a movie.'[21]

At school, Eleanora soon picked up 'naughty' songs from other kids in the playground and loved to annoy her Aunt Eva, or Miss Eva as she was known, by singing a blues over and over again about 'my man this, and my man that'; at the time many black households considered the blues too vulgar for polite society and banned such music from their households.[22] However, in November 1920, Eleanora began attending a Catholic school; her school records indicate that she was taken out of the public school system after only a month and sent to a 'Parish School'.

By 1922 Sadie had set up home with Philip Gough at 209 East Street, where they appear as Philip and Sadie Gough in the *Baltimore City Directory*. The following year there is no entry for either of them, but in 1924 Philip Gough appears on his own at 2130 Brunt Street, his marriage with Sadie over. *Lady Sings the Blues* made little of Sadie's marriage to Gough. 'I was happy for a little bit,' said the Eleanora figure. 'He was a good step-daddy to me as long as he lived, which was only a little while.' But Philip Gough was still appearing in the *Baltimore City*

21

Directory as late as 1929, after Sadie and Eleanora had left the city for good.[23]

Ever since Sadie had returned to Baltimore from Philadelphia her father, Charles Fagan, had little to do with her; Sadie's mother Sussie, it seems, was not the only woman who had succumbed to his charms.[24] Contact between Charles and Sadie was intermittent but even so, a piece of family lore was passed on to her, which she in turn passed to Eleanora: Charles claimed that his mother, Rebecca Fagan, had been brought up as a slave. This is certainly possible, but Rebecca was hardly in a position to have mothered some sixteen children during her enslavement, as is claimed in *Lady Sings the Blues*, since she was only thirteen when Congress passed the 13th Amendment to the Constitution ending slavery once and for all. The only thing she took from 'the handsome Irish plantation owner' was his surname.

Rebecca, who in 1880 gave her occupation as 'works at washing',[25] did, however, have a number of children – at least eight and all out of wedlock – of whom Charles was the eldest. He entered domestic service and in 1905 married Martha Dixon, a strong, prim, devoutly religious woman who promptly converted her husband to Roman Catholicism. However, Martha, or Mattie as she was known, disdained Charles's family. When he visited his sisters Rosie and Margerite, she refused to accompany him. And when he died on 8 July 1931, she failed to inform either of his death.[26] Dominated as he was by Mattie, it is hardly surprising that Sadie saw little of her father. The most profound influence he ever had on her was to reinforce her religious belief with that of his own.

After the break-up of her marriage to Philip Gough, Sadie left her young and impressionable eight-year-old daughter back in the care of Martha Miller who now lived in the 600 block of North Barnes Street, Baltimore. 'I was ten years older and went around with girls of my own age,' recalled Evelyn Conway. 'The child Eleanora was left with my grandmother whenever her mother had to go away, off working and whatever, in a sense like being neglected, her going from place to place and my grandmother, Martha Miller, would keep her. Eleanora called her grandmother and she spent so much time with us, my grandmother really raised her. Her mother would be off working, or with other men. She was neglected by her mother, it all stems from them early days.'[27]

Being shunted from household to household and the gradual realization that she was not the most important person in her mother's world began to have a profound effect on Eleanora's psychological well-being.

Her sense of security, already profoundly undermined by being split up from her mother for long periods, was exacerbated by the domestic strife that accompanied the break-up of her mother's marriage with Philip Gough. Perhaps inevitably, there were serious repercussions in the girl's behavioural patterns as she tried to focus the attention she felt she was being denied on to herself. 'Her mother was the worst to her if anything,' observed Evelyn Conway. 'She left her all the time and that was the problem. The child had an attitude, I guess from being neglected.'[28]

Eleanora's cry for help was expressed by cutting school on such a spectacular scale that a probation officer, Anna M. Dawson, was forced to intervene, but to no avail. On 5 January 1925 Eleanora was brought before the Juvenile Court. Sadie Gough, who gave her address as 1421 North Freemont Avenue, and Anna Dawson were called as witnesses.

Magistrate T. J. Williams declared Eleanora 'a minor without proper care and guardianship' and sent her to Baltimore's Catholic-run House of Good Shepherd for Colored Girls at Calverton Road and Franklin Street for one year.[29] The institution was opened in 1894 for troubled adolescent girls who needed guardianship and care and was run by the Sisters of Good Shepherd. The chaplains were priests of the Josephite order from the parish of St Peter Clavier Church in Baltimore.[30]

In the disciplined environment of the House of Good Shepherd, Eleanora found the guidance and security that were missing in her life. Like all the girls, she was given a pseudonym for both protection and confidentiality. Hers was 'Madge'.[31] She picked up her education at Fourth Grade and was taken under the wing of Sister Margaret Touhe, with whom she subsequently kept in touch throughout her life. In later years she often visited the institution when in Baltimore and on one occasion in the 1950s, Sister Margaret persuaded her to sing for the girls. Indeed, throughout her life Sister Margaret, who died on 5 December 1984, retained a great affection for 'Madge'.[32]

Although the Eleanora figure in *Lady Sings the Blues* paints a rather harsh picture of the House of Good Shepherd, one event she describes does have a basis in fact. Occasionally a disadvantaged girl would develop tuberculosis, which was still prevalent in the slum tenements of Baltimore. In the event of a death it was a practice of the institution that one or perhaps two Sisters would sit through the night with the deceased praying for the salvation of her soul. It was a religious gesture on behalf of the departed that was taken seriously by the nuns, and must have given rise to all sorts of lurid stories invented by the young inmates. This is surely the basis of Eleanora's terrifying tale of spending

State of Maryland, Baltimore City, to wit:

To the _____ Sister in Charge - HOUSE OF GOOD SHEPHERD FOR

COLORED GIRLS * BALTIMORE

Whereas it has been duly adjudged after hearing by the subscriber, an additional Justice of the Peace for said City, designated Magistrate for Juvenile Causes, that.

ELENORE GOUGH

is a minor without proper care and guardianship in Baltimore City and that____she____ stand committed to said institution for care and guardianship:

You are, therefore, hereby empowered and directed to receive said

ELENORE GOUGH

to be kept and detained under your care and custody, until discharged by due course of law.

Given under my hand and seal, this 5th day of January, 1925, sitting at the Court House in Baltimore City.

T. J. O'Williams [SEAL]

Magistrate for Juvenile Causes

Figure 1: On the evidence of Anna M. Dawson, a Baltimore probation officer, Eleanora Gough, then aged nine, was declared a 'minor without proper care and guardianship' and on 5 January 1925 placed for one year in the care of the 'House of Good Shepherd for Colored Girls'.

a night locked up with a corpse as punishment for an infraction of the rules and beating the door until her hands bled. In reality it would be inconceivable that any of the girls would be allowed to intrude on the Sister's act of devotion.

While in care, Eleanora was baptized by Father Edward V. Casserly on 19 March 1925. On her baptismal certificate, her parents are given as 'Sara Harris (Mrs Sara Gough)' and 'Clarence Holiday' and her place of birth as Philadelphia.[33] The Good Shepherd records also reveal a further 'conditional baptism' on 14 August 1925 by the Rev. Joseph J. Winc, when her birthplace was shown as Baltimore.[34]

After nine months in care, Eleanora was 'paroled' to her mother on 3 October 1925[35]; still only ten years old, she was shy, and kept herself to herself. 'Shortly afterwards they went to East Baltimore,' continued Evelyn Conway. 'Sadie got a place of her own. There was no such thing for us people as cars in those days; when she went there she might just as well have been out of town as far as my grandmother and I was concerned.'[36]

Sadie had opened a new venture called the East Side Grill at 1325 Argyle Avenue,[37] some two blocks east of North Freemont Avenue where she had been living. Sadie and Eleanora worked long hours into the night since the heart of the black community's night-life was a stone's throw away, on Pennsylvania Avenue. 'Always working at some job or other, I never had a chance to play with dolls like other kids,' Eleanora reflected later.[38] At eleven she dropped out of fifth grade. 'School never appealed to me,' she said. 'About the only thing I learnt in school was how to play hooky. Instead of going to school . . . sometimes I would go into the five and dime store and steal silk stockings.'[39]

At some point towards the end of 1926, Sadie and Eleanora moved into 219 South Durham Street.[40] The *Baltimore City Directory* for that year shows that this was the home of William and Mary Hill and that William Hill's occupation was that of labourer. But during 1926 Mary left when Sadie began an affair with William, or 'Wee Wee' as he was known. Several years her junior, Wee Wee liked to have a good time, and Sadie often went out on the town with him when they were in funds. On their return in the small hours of the morning of 24 December 1926, Sadie discovered a neighbour, Wilbert Rich, in the act of having sex with her daughter.

She immediately called the police and Officer John Arnold of the Northwestern District arrived at a scene of domestic turmoil. Sadie, backed up by her friend Mary Walker of Bond Street, made her accusation, and Rich was arrested. At the station house, two doctors, Dr Mary Waters and Dr H. D. McCarty, examined Eleanora, and on their evidence and Sadie's sworn statement, later that day Rich was formally charged with rape and held in custody pending his arraignment.[41]

The charges made, the question of Sadie's care and control of her daughter once again became an issue. While the matter was being looked into, Eleanora was sent that same day to the House of Good Shepherd where she was to be held in protective custody as a 'State Witness in the case of State of Maryland vs Wilbert Rich, charged with Rape'.[42] Clarence Holiday was informed in New York; the House of Good Shepherd shows his address as 219 135th Street, New York City.[43]

Wilbert Rich was indicted on six counts of rape on 29 December 1926 and brought to trial on 18 January 1927. The sixth count of rape was dropped and he was found not guilty on counts 1–4, 'Rape – Carnal Knowledge of Under 14 year old (Code 1953, Article 27, Section 350)', but guilty of the fifth count, 'Rape – Carnal Knowledge of 14–16 year old (Code 1203, Section 351)'.[44] This was despite the fact that Eleanora

State of Maryland, City of Baltimore, to wit:

To the Warden of the Baltimore City Jail, Greeting:

YOU ARE HEREBY COMMANDED To Receive from any officer the body of
Wilbert Rich (C)

who is charged on the oath of Sadie Gough (C)
with Rape by carnally knowing and abusing one Elenora Gough (C) a
woman child age 11 years.

in Baltimore City, State of Maryland, on or about the 24th day of December, 192 6

Hearing had, and...he was in default of Without Bail

COMMITTED for the action of the Criminal Court of Baltimore City,
and h.e., the said Wilbert Rich(C) safely keep in your jail
and custody until ....he shall be thence delivered according to law. Hereof fail not at your peril.

WITNESS, The subscriber, a Police Justice of said State, in and for the city aforesaid, who hath hereto
set his hand and seal this 24th day of December, 192 6

.... J. P. (Seal)

Northwestern District.

Form 8 to be used for "Partial Hearings" and "Commitment for Further Hearings."

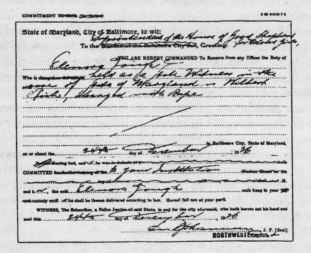

Figure 2: On 24 December 1926 Wilbert Rich was held in custody pending arraignment for the rape of Eleanora Gough, aged eleven. The victim was immediately placed in protective custody as a State Witness for the Prosecution at Baltimore's 'House of Good Shepherd for Colored Girls'. A reminder of the racial climate of the time is the letter 'C' that appears on each committal form denoting 'Coloured'.

was only eleven at the time of the incident and both the court and the House of Good Shepherd held her correct date of birth. Rich was committed to three months in a 'House of Correction'.[45]

Eleanora's fate was not decided until the following month. During this her second stay at the House of Good Shepherd another baptism was recorded, seemingly to reinforce her sense of 'belonging', this time by the Rev. Charles B. Carroll who was pastor of St Peter Clavier Church: her birthplace is shown as Philadelphia.[46] Sadie finally secured her daughter's release by appealing to Charles Fagan, the only person she knew with any money, to get a lawyer on the case. The court order was finally reversed and Eleanora was released on the grounds of 'Habeas Corpus' to Sadie Gough on 2 February 1927. The House of Good Shepherd marked her file, 'Did not return to us'.[47]

Eleanora went back to sharing her mother's long hours, helping with the cooking, waiting on tables and washing dishes. The busy milieu of her mother's restaurant brought her into contact with the people of the night and perhaps it was here she got to know, as she put it in a 1956 interview, the 'lady that had a little sportin' house'.[48] The Madame gave her tips for running errands and chores around the whorehouse – washing basins and toilets, changing towels and putting out soap.

Once again Sadie seemed glad to have Eleanora out of her hair as she continued her affair with Wee Wee Hill. In 1927 he moved next door, to 217 South Durham Street, and Sadie and Eleanora followed. But once again Sadie's love-life seemed doomed. By 1928 they had gone their separate ways: Sadie had returned to Argyle Avenue and by 1929 Hill was living on Bond Street in Fells Point.[49]

Left to her own devices, Eleanora soon discovered that the principal attraction of working for the Madame was not so much the extra money as listening to the wind-up Victrola left in a downstairs room for the use of patrons. It provided the defining moment of her life. It was here, she says, that she was bitten by the jazz bug. In countless interviews[50] she named the record that turned her on as 'West End Blues' by Louis Armstrong and his Hot Five. It was recorded on 28 June 1928 and would have been released about six weeks later, towards the end of August 1928, when Eleanora was thirteen.

In later years she would often speak of what she learned trying to imitate Armstrong from the records in the bordello: 'I heard a record by, as we call him, Pops, and it was called "West End Blues" and . . . he sang "Ooh be doo", and I would wonder why he didn't sing any words and he had this most beautiful feeling.'[51]

What she says about Armstrong's 'beautiful feeling' is of enormous significance. Four years earlier he had turned New York musicians on their collective ears with his sensational trumpet-playing. His superb sense of time and syncopation heralded the modern concept of 'swing', while his New Orleans heritage left his style deep in the shadows of the blues. Armstrong somehow transferred the stately, moving quality he brought to his blues performances to non-blues material, which had the effect of transcending sentiment, creating heartfelt and often moving musical statements.

Armstrong's melodic and rhythmic logic was such that it seemed to release music from the shackles of the stave to float free with imperious disdain over the printed page. Quite simply, he transformed jazz during the 1920s and the phonograph record played a key role in this process. It enabled his playing to be examined, copied and imitated by musicians throughout the world in a way that would have been impossible just twenty years before. Now musicians did not have to attend his every performance to absorb his style; trumpeter Freddie Keppard, who had a formidable reputation in the early days of jazz, was reluctant to record for precisely that reason. He felt that as soon as he committed himself to wax the secret of his playing would be revealed, and he would put himself out of work.

Armstrong's musical persona was expressed with equal ease vocally or instrumentally. On his 1928 'West End Blues', for example, he sings as he plays, exchanging question-and-answer patterns with Jimmy Strong on clarinet, answering not with his trumpet but with his voice, and gradually elaborating his answers to Strong's insistent questions into an obbligato. With vocals like 'Basin Street Blues', almost an abstraction of W. C. Handy's lyrics, or 'Squeeze Me', with its voice-as-instrument vocal that blends into the ensemble as an equal member, Armstrong was revolutionizing the vernacular vocal just as surely as his trumpet-playing was revolutionizing instrumental jazz.

During the next couple of years Eleanora would spend a lot of time listening to records, and Armstrong would provide the key influence: 'I copied my style from Louis Armstrong,' she would say later.[52] Many of his OKeh recordings of this period, where his use of syncopation released lyrics from the underlying groundbeat, provide the basic ingredient of her whole rhythmical approach to singing. Armstrong's 1931 version of 'Them There Eyes', for example, includes several phrases that she lifted, almost note for note, in her own 1939 version of the song.

Another formative influence was Bessie Smith, the 'Empress of the Blues'. Most early blues were often simple pentatonic pieces, sometimes no more than three tones chanted in constant petatonicism, and Bessie's blues were frequently no exception. A singer with a narrow range, probably no more than about a fifth or a sixth, she would often reduce her line to perhaps two or three tones with no loss of emotional intensity, something that was thrown into stark and dramatic relief when she sang non-blues material. It was this ability to reduce a melodic line to its barest essentials that became a feature of Eleanora's subsequent singing style, as in her twenty-six repeated As on her recording of 'I'll Get By' from 1937.

However, the transition from imitation to developing a personal voice in jazz is a complex process and with Eleanora, as with many artists, involved more than just two key influences. Her 1956 rehearsal tapes show that she listened to Sophie Tucker and in 1935 she told guitarist Lawrence Lucie she was an Ethel Waters fan,[53] and there would certainly have been other singers who caught her ear. However, beyond listening and singing along with recordings, her other source of musical experience came from her regular attendances at church.

The Catholic Church in Maryland was strict in its religious conventions which have always remained true to Rome. During the most formative years of her life Eleanora learned the Latin Mass with its signs and symbolism, the litany, Gregorian chants and *missa cantata* that were both accompaniment and stimulant to Catholic worship. It was in stark contrast to the 'shake-rattle-and-roll' services of the Sanctified or Holiness Churches which took to heart the 150th Psalm of David and used instruments and vigorous hand-clapping to stir hearts in praise of the Lord. The Baptist 'holy-roller' tradition produced extrovert singers like Mahalia Jackson, Sarah Vaughan, Dinah Washington and later Aretha Franklin, Sam Cooke, Patti LaBelle and Whitney Houston. In contrast, the tradition of religious music Eleanora came from was very conservative, an important consideration in defining what would ultimately become her undemonstrative style.

The Catholic Church, with its ecclesiastical chants in Latin where vowels are more important and frequent than consonants, places great stress on pronunciation. This would certainly have provided a foundation for Eleanora's remarkable diction when singing, quite different from her speaking voice. The litany and Gregorian chants embodied two other equally important factors that helped shape her style; they were performed *sotto voce* and utilized a minimum of melodic movement.

As Eleanora struggled within the bonds of selfhood she gradually came to realize that there might be a way to escape her difficult life. She began dreaming of becoming a star, like the glamorous sirens with their long gowns and elaborate make-up she saw at the five-cent matinees at the local movie-house. In her imagination she saw herself in dazzling screen sets, earning thousands of dollars and pursued by dashing leading men. Every week she watched with rapt and breathless interest until she finally resolved that one day she would get her name in lights too. She would be a singer.

Chapter Two

1928-33

At the end of 1928, Sadie Gough decided to try her luck in Harlem.[1] Stories were rife amongst the black community of better housing and employment prospects there, while its vibrant night-life and cultural renaissance were attracting international acclaim. There was a new spirit in the air inspired by Marcus Garvey and his Universal Negro Improvement Association, adding to the momentum begun in 1910 by the National Association for the Advancement of Colored People. Co-founded by W. E. B. Du Bois, it is still the most powerful civil rights group in America. Harlem was in vogue, with a rich surge of arts, music and letters that in 1925 prompted the *New York Herald Times* to observe that 'We are on the edge, if not in the midst, of what might not improperly be called a "Negro Renaissance".' As 'Negro Renaissance' gave way to 'Harlem Renaissance', black people suddenly found prominent figures of their own colour they could at last look up to.

Perhaps the most passionate writer of the renaissance, W. E. B. Du Bois, called on the negro (his chosen word) to 'demand his social rights: his rights to be treated as a gentleman when he acts like one, to marry any sane, grown person who wants to marry him'. If that view sounds commonplace now, it was viewed as radical then, and was often attacked. Yet for a black person living outside New York, such stories made it seem as if Harlem's streets were paved with gold; they flocked there in their thousands. In 1910 the population of Harlem was 91,000; by 1930 it had more than doubled.

When Sadie went to Harlem, she left her daughter in the care of Martha Miller. But Eleanora's 'attitude' made it difficult for the woman she called Grandmother to control her. Left to come and go as she pleased, she was drawn to the fast life like a moth to the flame; she was fascinated by the whores and the pimps and the good-times crowd. Buoyed by their company, she tried her luck singing in public.

Monday night was an off-night in the entertainment business in Baltimore and that included the whorehouses. To attract clients the house-party custom had grown up. In those days the phonograph was a popular entertainer; a fixture at private parties in Waugh's London, Brecht's Berlin and Van Vechten's New York as much as speakeasies and whorehouses which were also places of music. The chances are that Eleanora began her singing career singing along with hits of the day on a wind-up gramophone in a whorehouse parlour.[2]

Borrowing from the omnipotence of Louis Armstrong and Bessie Smith, she had developed a small repertoire of songs from listening to recordings. She had a remarkable ear and almost certainly possessed relative pitch – the ability on hearing a note to discern the relationship of every other note of the song to the note sounded and hit them perfectly in tune. She also had a knack of picking up lyrics after hearing them just two or three times.

Soon she was looking for other places to perform her half-dozen or so favourite hits of the day. On nearby Pennsylvania Avenue there were countless small clubs and speakeasies. She may have tried her hand on the amateur hour of the nearby Harlem Theater or even sung and danced for tips in the streets, along with countless other kids. In any event, by the end of 1928 she had begun singing in a speakeasy called Club Paradise on Lafayette Avenue, between Pennsylvania and Druid Hall Avenues.[3] Her apprenticeship as a jazz singer had begun.

Her burgeoning career in Baltimore was brief, however. In early 1929, Sadie sent for her daughter and Eleanora was packed off to New York. Sadie was living in Harlem at 151 West 140th Street, between Lenox and Seventh Avenues. Her landlady was a sharply dressed, handsome woman called Florence Williams. She ran a whorehouse. In order to live, Sadie had become a prostitute. Within a matter of days Eleanora was also turning tricks for clients at $5 a time. Maybe she had already tried her hand at prostitution in the bordellos of Baltimore. One thing was certain, however. She had just turned fourteen.

But within weeks, on the night of Thursday, 2 May 1929, the Police Department in 19th District had a big round-up of prostitutes. In all twenty-three arrests were made, with Eleanora and Sadie among ten girls rounded up by Officer Emanuel Howard. All were black and five gave their address as 151 West 140th Street: Florence Williams, thirty-two; Inez Allen, twenty-seven; and Gladys Johnson, twenty-three. Sadie used her middle name, calling herself Julia Harris, age thirty-four, while Eleanora gave her surname as Fagan, not Gough, and said she was twenty-one. All the women were detained overnight and appeared the following evening in the Women's Night Court of the Magistrates' Court, 9th District of Manhattan, charged with Vagrancy (Sub-division 4A, Section 887, Code of Criminal Proceedings), in front of Judge Jean

Norris. Of the five girls from 151 West 140th Street, Inez and 'Julia' were discharged, Florence was sent to the workhouse for five days, and Gladys for 100 days, while Eleanora was sent to hospital to be followed by 100 days in the workhouse.[4]

Judge Jean Hortense Norris was New York City's first woman magistrate and was appointed on 27 October 1919, the beginning of a career that led to the leadership of many civic and legal organizations and honours from all over the world. Yet on 22 June 1931 she was brought before five justices of the Appellate Division on six charges for her removal as a city magistrate brought by Judge Samuel Seabury.

On Thursday, 25 June she was found guilty on five counts by unanimous vote: 'taken together they show unfitness for judicial service and constitute cause for removal,' said the court.[5] All the charges related to women defendants. Judge Norris was conducting a campaign to rid the streets of what she considered 'wayward minors'. As Justice Seabury pointed out in his summing up: 'This court knows what has been happening to wayward minors in New York. For years they have been packed off to reformatories without trial and no respect for the legal demands of the cases.'[6]

The hospital and workhouse where Eleanora and Gladys Johnson were sent was situated on Blackwell's Island on the East River, later called Welfare Island. It was established in 1849 and was supposed to house 'vagrant and dissipated adults'; many people committed to the workhouse were actually sent to the Island Hospital for treatment. On 9 July Eleanora was discharged from hospital and appeared in front of Magistrate Jesse Silbermann (later also disbarred by Samuel Seabury) who confirmed that she was fit to complete the balance of her sentence in the workhouse.

When Eleanora was released in October 1929, Sadie was waiting for her. She had found accommodation in Brooklyn, at 7 Glenada Avenue, and was determined it should represent a fresh start for them both. Living nearby was Kenneth Hollon, then twenty and starting out on tenor saxophone, who remembered Sadie and Eleanora when they first arrived in the area. 'They explained they had just arrived from Baltimore,' he said. Sadie had found work as a domestic, but Eleanora announced she would 'never scrub floors or keep house for white folks', all she wanted to do was sing. As Hollon practised his sax, Eleanora sang along with him, beginning a lifelong affinity with the saxophone and saxophone players. 'I took her on her first singing job in this city in 1930 or 1931,' Hollon continued.[7] Billie sang 'How Am I to Know' and Fats Waller's 'My Fate is in Your Hands' with the Hat Hunter band at the Grey Dawn, a small cabaret-bar on Jamaica Avenue and

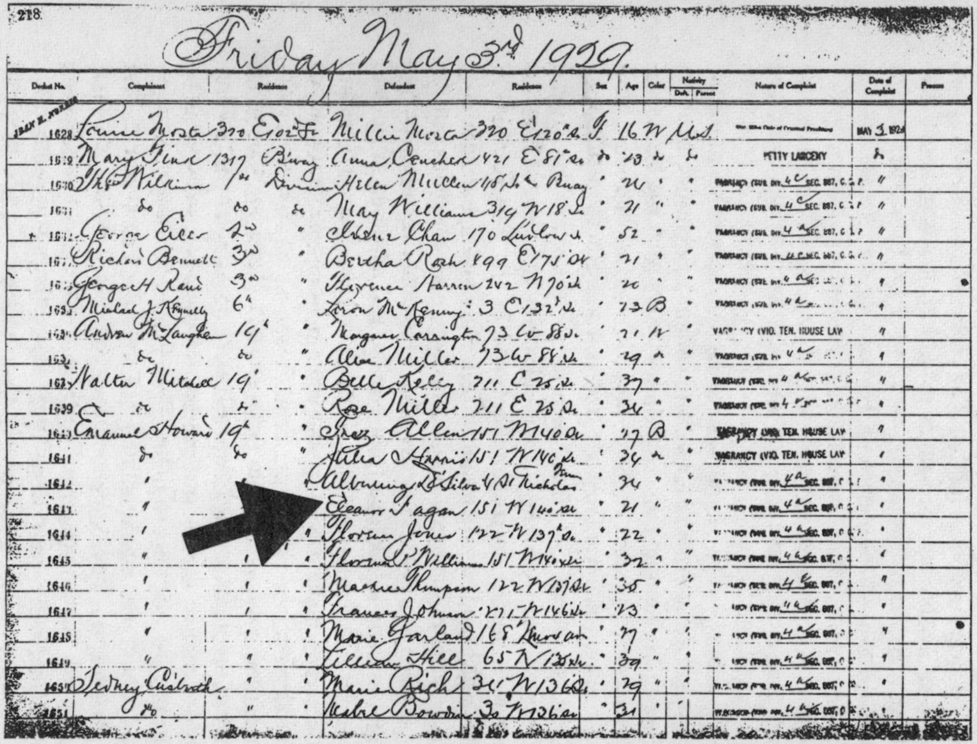

Figure 3: Extract from the court records of the Magistrates' Court, 9th District of Manhattan (Women's Night Court) for Friday, 3 May 1929. Eleanora Fagan is held, along with her mother who gave her name as 'Julia Harris', for 'Vagrancy (Sub. Div. 4A, Sec. 887 CCP)', the prostitution rap. Note the presence of Florence Williams, referred to in *Lady Sings the Blues* as 'one of the biggest madams in Harlem' and that the judge presiding (see top left hand corner) was Jean H. Norris, who was described as a 'tough, hard faced old dame'.

South Street in Jamaica, Queens, for tips thrown on the floor by the audience.

The name Eleanora Gough, however, did not suit the image she had of herself as a singer. Taking the Christian name of the movie star Billie Dove and, like her mother before her, appropriating her father's surname, she became Billie Holiday. The informal duo of Hollon and Holiday began looking out for venues to work in Brooklyn and finally managed to hold down a regular spot at the local Elks Club, which put on dances and entertainment on Saturday nights as fund-raisers. However, when Sadie found work in the kitchen of Mexico's on 133rd Street, Harlem in spring 1930,[8] these gigs ended abruptly. Mother and daughter moved into a tiny room on West 127th Street between Fifth and Lenox Avenues.

Sadie's new job in the kitchens of Mexico's lasted into the early hours. Benny Carter remembers it as a small club popular with musicians, run by a character whose nickname was 'Mexico'.[9] (Mexico's real name was Gomez and he came from South Carolina. He got his nickname from his service as a machine-gunner with General Funston against Pancho Villa.) While Sadie cooked, Billie helped in the kitchen and started waiting on table. Here she began the practice of singing at tables for tips, going from one to another like 'a gypsy fiddler in a Budapest café'.[10] This was valuable on-the-job training, forcing her to sing the same song with different variations as she went around the tables. In so doing she was learning the essence of the jazz singer's art, that of reshaping her material into something personal, interesting and individual.

Mexico ran the 'hottest gin-mill in town', and musicians and entertainers, including Duke Ellington who was a regular, spent hours at his place drinking his 'ninety-nine per cent'. It was one of over 125 nightspots situated in an area of intense musical activity, between West 125th and 135th Streets bounded by Lenox and Seventh Avenues. Billie Holiday was soon making friends and contacts while singing and waiting on tables, and as a result, opportunities began coming her way. One night Marge Johnson,[11] who was headlining at Ed Small's Paradise at 2294½ Seventh Avenue, was sufficiently impressed by Billie's singing to wangle an audition for the youngster with Charlie Johnson, who had been running Small's house-band since 1925, when the club opened.

It was Billie's first taste of the big time. Small's had a capacity of 1500 and had caught on big with whites from downtown. There were waiters who danced the Charleston, several floor-shows a night with spectacular dance routines, all with Charlie Johnson's orchestra at the hub of things; 'Johnson's band is hot and it makes [everyone] dance,' reported *Variety*.[12] But up to now Billie's experience had been very much small-time and she had much to learn. 'I get in there,' she recalled in 1955, 'and I'm all ready to sing and this cat asks me, "What key you singin' in?" I said, "I don't know, man, you just play." They shooed me out of there so fast it wasn't even funny . . . From then on I'd start remembering and I would pitch my keys.'[13]

Despite this disappointment, other job opportunities followed. Benny Carter remembers hearing Billie sing in 1930 or 1931: 'It was at the Bright Spot at Seventh Avenue and West 139th Street. It was a small club, she was there with just a pianist as accompanist. She was not the typical blues singer, like Mamie Smith or somebody like that; all I can say is that she was definitely not just another singer. Great is a big word. Maybe she was great even then; I don't know if I ever heard anything like that prior to hearing her for the first time, or indeed since.'[14]

As she gradually became known in musicians' circles, Billie began to move into the fast lane of Harlem night-life. At the time smoking marijuana was the craze in Harlem and at two sticks for 25 cents, many musicians indulged the habit. Smoking marijuana was hip, and Billie Holiday was well on the way to becoming a very hip chick. Within weeks of starting work in Mexico's, she went around briefly with the drummer Hal Austin, who was six years her senior, sharing her birthday. 'When she came in from Baltimore we used to smoke a lot of pot. We had a reefer-pad in 133rd Street. Kaiser's [Marshall], place in the basement. It was gorgeous,' he said.[15]

In those days most white people never realized that 'reefer', 'weed', 'muggles', 'tea', 'gauge' or 'grass' was the Harlemites' name for marijuana or that marijuana smokers were known as 'vipers'. It had become so much a part of the entertainment culture that many songs by Harlem bands actually celebrated what today would be called the drug problem. Bandleader Cab Calloway's 'Minnie the Moocher' and her playmate, the cocaine-happy Smokey Joe, were two reefer-smoking characters who cropped up in the lyrics of songs like 'Kickin' the Gong Around', 'Hotcha Razz-Ma-Tazz', 'Ya Gotta Hi-de-Ho', 'Minnie the Moocher's Wedding Day', 'Swing for Minnie', and 'Ghost of Smokey Joe'. Louis Armstrong, throughout his life a recreational marijuana smoker, recorded 'Muggles' in 1928 and 'Song of the Vipers' in 1934. There were many other examples; some of the better-known include Fats Waller's 'Viper's Drag', Don Redman's 'Chant of the Weed', Benny Goodman's 'Texas Tea Party', while Charlie Johnson (with whom Billie unsuccessfully auditioned) recorded 'Viper's Dream'. One title, 'Reefer Man' was recorded by several bands, including top performers like Cab Calloway and Don Redman.

Billie hung out with musicians whenever she could; she drank with them, she smoked pot with them and she sat in with them. She was seldom, if ever, pushy. Musicians say she was quiet, even shy, but if there was a chance to sing she would take it. She was comfortable just listening. Every night became a lesson in the art of jazz. She listened hard; to how the instrumentalists swung, how they negotiated chord progressions during their improvisations, how they used nuances of tone and, most important of all, how individuality was prized above all else. She learned everything by ear; her attitude to musical theory took the drastic form of complete indifference. By doing, by trying out ideas – her own and other people's – rejecting those with which she felt uncomfortable and memorizing those which sounded good, she began to develop her own individual style.

Gradually she began to build a small reputation for herself. From the occasional gig here and there she was getting return bookings, and some of the most popular bars and grills started using her. In 1932, Charles Linton, who within a year would become a vocalist in the Chick Webb band, was working at the Hollywood Cabaret near West 122nd Street: 'At the time she was working on the corner of West 126th Street and Seventh Avenue, a place called the Alhambra Bar and Grill. I didn't go in that much, I wasn't earning that much at the Hollywood, I used to watch her from the street. She was a lovely girl. Very beautiful. She had a small band, it was a night-club thing and she sang from table to table.'[16]

Linton soon got to know her from hanging around outside. They shared the problem of earning very little and although he never smoked or drank, while she most certainly did, he got on well with her. She was, he said, easy to talk to and loved laughing.

With so much music and so many musicians in such a small area, it was inevitable that Billie would be reunited with the man she was told was her father. Clarence Holiday had worked hard at the guitar and banjo on his return from the army. After gigging around Baltimore he moved to New York and found an apartment at 219 West 135th Street. In September 1926 he was with saxophonist Billy Fowler's band in the Cameo Club on West 52nd Street near Broadway where he began dating Fannie Lee Taylor. Clarence, a ladies' man, fell for Fannie, who was born in 1898 in Fredricksburgh, VA. She soon moved in with him and on 5 July 1927 they were married in the Municipal Building in Manhattan by J. J. McCormick, the Deputy City Clerk.

In November the following year Fletcher Henderson reorganized his orchestra and brought in Clarence to replace banjoist Charles Dixon. He was now in the pre-eminent jazz orchestra of its day, alongside such greats as Coleman Hawkins, Rex Stewart, Jimmy Harrison and Benny Carter. 'I knew Clarence from Fletcher's band,' said Carter. 'We never had a drink together or shared lunch, but he was a very nice man as I remember. Very pleasant and very quiet.'[17]

By 1929 Clarence was doubling on both banjo and guitar in Henderson's orchestra, his playing admired by peers. 'I knew him very well. A very good rhythm player,' confirmed guitarist Lawrence Lucie. 'I liked his salesmanship with his playing with Fletcher's band, different kind of strokes. The circle stroke we called it. Nice personality, not a tall man but a handsome type of person.'[18] Between early 1929 and 1930 Clarence spent a lot of time on the road with Henderson, but by 1932 he could often be seen in Bert Hall's Rhythm Club on 132nd Street and Seventh Avenue. 'It was a place where musicians hung out,' continued Lucie, 'it was a place for socializing. That's where I got to know Clarence well. They had a piano if a guy wanted to play for himself; Jelly Roll Morton often did. They had a blackboard up there for jobs.'[19]

In the summer of 1932, Lawrence Lucie was invited to join a rehearsal orchestra formed by the twenty-five-year-old Benny Carter who wanted to become a leader in his own right after stints as musical director of the Wilberforce Collegians and McKinney's Cotton Pickers. In July Carter's new band landed their first gig, accompanying a tabloid version of Connie's Inn revue at the Central Theater on Broadway and West 47th Street. Among those watching the progress of the band was John Hammond, who filed an enthusiastic report to England's *Melody Maker*. Hammond, who came from a wealthy, socially prominent family, was three years Carter's junior and had dropped out of Yale the previous year. He was already deeply involved in jazz, as a writer and producer of records. A great proselytizer for the music, he was fast getting a reputation as a remarkable talent scout.

Midway through their Connie's Inn engagement, Lawrence Lucie was jamming with a few musicians from the band in an after-hours club. It was late into the night when Billie Holiday walked in. Lucie barely gave her a second glance. 'We didn't know anything about her,' he recalled. 'She was singing someplace and came in late. And she got up and sang with the band. Everybody thought she was so great; we hadn't heard her before. The guys backed her up and when we came off the bandstand, people were saying, "That's Billie Holiday." We hadn't heard anything like that, a natural *jazz* feeling. She was very well developed as a singer, but hadn't reached the star quality of a few years later. We were all amazed, the guys in the band.

'Some of the guys knew her and some didn't. She was like an innocent girl and came to talk to us, that was my first meeting with her, when I had just joined Benny Carter's band playing for the Connie's Inn revue. But a funny thing, I had never heard Clarence talk about his daughter, it was always the guitar, music and other things, but never Billie. Now isn't that funny? Later I saw them talking together at the Rhythm Club; once in a while she would come up, she loved being around musicians, she'd sit down and talk with us.'[20] The relationship between Billie and her father remained at arm's length. In 1932 he was just thirty-four and embarrassed by this striking young woman who claimed to be a part of his past.

Towards the end of the year Billie opened at a small club called Covan's on West 132nd Street, right behind the stage entrance to the Lafayette Theater, accompanied by pianist Dot Hill. 'I first saw her at Covan's,' said pianist Roger 'Ram' Ramirez. 'This girl, she had a gingham gown on her and she was vivacious and young and nice, and she was singing to the tables, and she said, "How are you doing? Sit down." Oh, she was so *vivacious* and she was like sunshine. I didn't know her then.'[21]

Billie had been brought in to replace Monette Moore, who in 1932 had all but made Covan's her own, backed by Garland Wilson on piano with Mae Barnes doing dancing and singing routines as relief. It was there that producer Leonard Sillman caught one of Moore's powerful performances and brought the writer Howard Deitz to see her. As a result Deitz offered her a part in his show *Flying Colours* with Buddy Ebsen, Patsy Kelly, Tamara Geva, Larry Adler and Clifton Webb. 'I stayed at Covan's until rehearsals started for the Broadway opening,' recalled Moore. 'This was 1932. It was in this show I introduced the tune "Shine on your Shoes".'[22]

John Hammond loved Moore's singing with her infectious low-down growl and enjoyed Garland Wilson's piano-playing even more, paying the costs involved to record him on four twelve-inch 78s for the Columbia Phonograph Company. 'Monette Moore was very popular,' recalled Ramirez. 'I didn't know how popular she was until a young fellow named John Hammond from Yale used to sit [listening to her], he was very enthusiastic.'[23]

Expecting to see Moore and Garland at work in what had become their usual haunt, Hammond called into Covan's one night in early 1933. To his surprise he was confronted with an unknown singer called Billie Holiday.[24] Immediately he realized he was listening to something quite unique in contemporary music, later saying she almost changed his musical taste and his musical life. 'The way she sang around a melody, her uncanny harmonic sense and her sense of lyric content were almost unbelievable in a girl of seventeen,' he reflected later.[25]

But whatever his gut feeling, Hammond was careful to get a second opinion. He turned to his close friends Red Norvo and his wife Mildred Bailey. Both were exceptional musicians: Bailey, the 'Rocking Chair Lady', was a featured vocalist with Paul Whiteman and his orchestra, the most popular band of its day, while Norvo, a featured xylophone soloist with Whiteman (he later took up the vibraphone), would launch a solo career in 1936. In the late 1930s Norvo led an innovative group of his own and went on to perform alongside the likes of Benny Goodman, Woody Herman and Charlie Parker. Hammond valued the council of Mr and Mrs Swing, as they were later known, and both frequently accompanied him on his club-hopping visits in Harlem. Hammond was especially keen to hear what Bailey, one of the great, although today sadly underrated, singers in jazz, thought of his new find.

'John Hammond, Mildred, myself and three others went up to the different clubs,' recalled Norvo. 'And we went to a little place where John said the daughter of Fletcher Henderson's former guitar player, Clarence Holiday, was singing. So we went into this club and when she started to sing Mildred leaned over to John and I and said, "This girl can sing!" and John got up and went right over to her after she got over and that's what started her. He respected Mildred's judgement.'[26]

Hammond immediately went to work on Billie's behalf as her unofficial publicity agent; in the April 1933 *Melody Maker* he wrote, '[She] sings as well as anybody I ever heard. Something must be done about her for gramophone records', and he took musicians uptown to hear her – 'I had found a star,' he said.[27] But in the middle of the recession record companies were not interested in signing talented unknowns. For the time being there was little Hammond could do to advance her career on records.

From Covan's Billie returned to Mexico's where she met up-and-coming songwriter Bernie Hanighen. He demonstrated a few of his songs for her, and she was quite taken by 'If the Moon Turns Green', which she featured every night for years; later she would regularly feature his 'When a Woman Loves a Man'. Hanighen also persuaded Billie to cut some paper audition discs for him, which he took to bandleader and raconteur Eddie Condon. A month later Condon booked her to appear with his band for a fee of $10.

Hanighen had attended Hackley Preparatory School in Tarrytown, New York before attending Harvard, from where he had recently graduated. There he had written several musicals for the Hasty Pudding and Pi Eta clubs and had been an officer of the Instrumental Clubs and President of the Harvard Dramatic Club. He also ran a collegiate jazz band called the Crimson Ramblers which frequently recruited ringers such as trombonist Jerry Colonna and trumpeter Max Kaminsky. When he moved to New York to try his luck as a songwriter, he had already made several contacts in musical circles. Promoter Ernie Anderson has suggested that Hanighen may even have spoken to John Hammond about Billie's singing, providing further confirmation, if indeed Hammond needed this, of her remarkable talent.[28]

During this period of Harlem's history its major clubs and speakeasics had become the playground of the rich and famous who called their club-hopping visits 'slumming'. Within a few years of Prohibition, a number of prosperous clubs catering to white sightseers had opened in Harlem. They provided the opportunity to watch exotic entertainment and to listen to jazz, as well as drink plenty of bootleg liquor. Some clubs actively barred blacks while others were willing to serve whoever could pay, 'Throughout the speakeasy era, and for years after, the pleasure-lovers rarely considered the evening's excitement exhausted unless the night, or rather the early post-midnight hours, were topped off with an evening in Harlem,' said Louis Sobol in *The Longest Street*.[29]

Among Billie's early admirers were the actors Paul Muni and Charles Laughton. '[Her] appeal to theatrical people ... was tremendous,' observed Hammond.[30] Laughton, who was appearing in his first Broadway play, *Payment Deferred*, became a nightly visitor, often with his wife Elsa Lanchaster and at other times with his manservant. 'I had no idea that he was a movie actor,' recalled Billie in 1956, '... and I said, "Who is that man there who's asking for me?" That's how we got acquainted.'[31]

Perhaps not the flashiest Harlem nightspot, but certainly one of the most popular, was the Catagonia Club at 168 West 133rd Street, or, as it was more familiarly known to its patrons, Pod's and Jerry's. It was one of many hot spots located in the basements of New York's brownstone and greystone buildings, row after row of identical four- to ten-storey apartment buildings. Every night smart limousines would pull up outside Pod's to drop their passengers off. They would ask for George Woods, the headman, who would show them to their seats. The resident piano player and informal master of ceremonies was Willie 'The Lion' Smith. 'The piano had the right kind of vibrations,' he said. 'Every night mink coats would wind up on top of it.'[32]

In 1930/1, the big attraction had been Mattie Hite who slunk from table to table singing ribald but sensuous numbers like 'Stop It, Joe', 'My Daddy Rocks Me with One Steady Roll' and 'Salty Dog', picking up tips afterwards by lifting her dress and taking rolled-up dollar bills between her legs. From two until seven in the morning, Pod's and Jerry's cooked: music, singing, dancing, with waiters and bartenders

41

working flat out through the night. 'Everybody who cares for night-life always visits Jerry Preston at the Log Cabin Grill in the wee hours of the morning,' reported *New York Age*.[33]

For a while 'The Lion' took a young Artie Shaw under his wing for a crash course in jazz improvisation. 'When I was a kid I came up to New York and I was going through a very bad phase,' recalled Shaw. 'At that time I saw a lot of people in Harlem, one of them was Billie. I knew her, everybody knew everybody, it was a small world the jazz community at that time . . . Billie was one of the people around.'[34]

Shaw described Billie as a young, healthy seventeen-year-old, already on her way to developing a distinctive style. She had an excellent ear, he said, and a remarkable sense of timing. When he first saw her at Pod's and Jerry's she was not one of the 'entertainers' at the club. Within a few months, however, she would land a job there when ownership of Mexico's abruptly changed hands and Billie and the new boss failed to see eye to eye. 'The proprietor of Mexico's sold out one day with two weeks' salary coming to me,' she recalled. 'The new owner was a very mean man . . . He said, "I don't give a damn . . . that's your problem," and walked off.'[35] Her temper flared and her job ended there and then. Sadie followed.

Out of work, they began to struggle to make ends meet. Billie started making the rounds of clubs and after-hours joints to find a regular singing spot, and after a day of rejections, she tried Pod's and Jerry's. Jerry Preston auditioned her and offered her $2 a night plus tips. She accepted. Within weeks Sadie followed, working in the kitchens.

Billie did not like Willie 'The Lion' Smith's style of accompaniment, considering it 'old-fashioned'. She preferred the modern playing of Garnett Clark, who was in turn followed by Bobbie Henderson. Robert 'Bobbie' Henderson was reputed to be a distant relative of Fats Waller but achieved only neighbourhood fame as a pianist, despite a considerable talent. Born in 1910, by the age of fifteen he was good enough to play in a supporting act to the Fletcher Henderson Orchestra when they played the annual dinner of the West 135th Branch of the YMCA in January 1925; he accompanied Edgar Sampson on violin. Although he had the opportunity to record, he mysteriously failed to appear on sessions set up by John Hammond, offering only feeble excuses in return. However, he was a great stride pianist with a considerable technique and played the Newport Jazz Festival on 4 July 1957, where his solo piano work sparkled in a set devoted to the music of Fats Waller.[36] With Henderson, Billie's apprenticeship was almost complete. Hammond, who saw them perform together frequently, said the better the pianist, the better was Billie's singing. Henderson was a good pianist.[37]

At Pod's and Jerry's, Billie alternated with a singer called Jazzbo Jimmy, who although short, hunchbacked and effeminate, had an engaging smile that displayed a mouthful of gold teeth. More importantly, he was a good enough singer to hold his own when it came to tips. The singers would sing a chorus at each table in the hope of picking up a billfold. These would be folded through their fingers in such a way that there would be a cluster of bills sticking out of each fist as they made their way among the 125 or so tables of the club. By now Billie was a master at varying the same chorus as she made her way around the house. It was here that Ernie Anderson first heard her: 'She was marvellous,' he said, 'I never heard her in better voice in all the years I knew her.'[38]

After her stint at Pod's and Jerry's Billie was booked by the Hot-Cha Restaurant at 2280 Seventh Avenue at the corner of 134th Street with Bobbie Henderson. Throughout 1933 they worked the 'bar and grill circuit' together: the New Woodside Grill, The Lafayette Grill, The Poosepahtuck Club at 773 Nicholas Avenue which specialized in Southern fried chicken, and the Jarvena Tavern & Grill. They lived on whatever salary they could pick up, plus tips. The white 'slummers' spent their money lavishly, much to the glee of the waiters and entertainers. Waiters, for example, hardly ever considered their $1 per night salary when they spoke of their gross earnings per week. But with Billie it was easy come, easy go, with no thought for tomorrow. 'You saw Billie and all these fast-moving young people around all night in joints,' said guitarist Danny Barker. 'At 3 a.m. . . . they went into after-hour joints. At nine o'clock they went back into the opening bars, cafés and clubs for breakfast. Twelve o'clock noon, off to the many vaudeville theatres . . . Their attitude? Who the hell wants to sleep? You might miss something. On to the reefer joints to smoke, get high.'[39]

The round of clubs and dine-and-dance spots was exhausting; Tillie's, the Nest, the Stable, the Mad House, the Yeah Man, the Hot-Cha Restaurant, the Silver Dollar, the Golden Grill, the Renaissance Tavern, Jimmie Ashe's New Thrill, the Big Apple, the Brittwood Café, the Cavalcade and the Alhambra Grill where the theatre people hung out. Often Billie sat in for a few numbers before moving on. At dawn she usually ended up in the Clam House at 131 West 133rd Street, a favourite early morning eating spot, where Gladys Bently, dressed in male attire, entertained with 'naughty' songs. Most Sunday mornings, after Billie finished work at 4 a.m., she and the fast crowd, including Audrey Thompson who worked at the Silver Dollar, went up by car to the White Castle night-club in Westchester County for breakfast.

Billie had talent, but her career had no pattern, no direction. She was unknown below 125th Street. As she continued her round of obscure Harlem night-clubs she was enjoying the happiest time of her life. Whenever she was short of money she was to be seen drinking at the Moulin Rouge Café, known as Mike's. A true character of the night-life of Harlem, Mike had made the place famous during Prohibition and it was always crowded. Once he knew his clients, he would let them run up a tab when times were tough. Almost any night Mike's was full of celebrities: Cab Calloway, Ethel Waters, Leonard Harper, Monette Moore, Duke Ellington, Willie Bryant, Bill Robinson, Aida Ward, Adelaide Hall, Ted Blackmon, Lucky Millinder, Jack Carter, Earl (Snakehips) Tucker and countless girls from the theatres.[40] To those who knew Billie, it was clear that the girl just wanted to have fun. The trouble was, as Willie 'The Lion' Smith confided to Artie Shaw, she was good, but was beginning to drink too much and had already got fired from some jobs.[41]

Chapter Three

1933–35

For almost two years, John Hammond had tried in vain to break into the record business. As the country bumped along at the bottom of the Depression, record sales in 1932 had plunged to a sixth of those for 1927. Companies were laying off employees rather than taking them on. Even though American Columbia was tottering on the verge of bankruptcy, Hammond saw that one of the ways the company met the demands of a reduced market-place was to import titles from English Columbia, who from time to time set up recording sessions in America for their own domestic market.

In July 1933 he visited London. When he returned to the States he had a commitment from English Columbia to record eight sides by the Benny Carter Orchestra, eight by the Fletcher Henderson Orchestra, six by a group led by Joe Venuti and four by a group led by Benny Goodman. Within two months he had produced fourteen record sessions using some of the most important musicians in jazz.

When it came to record the Goodman sides, things did not go entirely as Hammond had planned. However, while they were not quite what he had hoped for, they were, he felt, not bad either. A coupling of 'Ain't-cha Glad?' and 'I Got a Right to Sing the Blues' had been named by *Metronome* magazine as one of the best records of the month when it was released in November. But more importantly, record boss Ben Selvin liked what he heard and decided to let Hammond record Goodman again, this time for American Columbia.

The success of 'Ain't-cha Glad?' was a key point in the career of both John Hammond and Benny Goodman. For Goodman it increased his involvement in jazz after drifting increasingly into commercial music following Wall Street's infamous 1929 egg. For Hammond it gave him an opportunity to establish himself in record production for an American company. They agreed a date of 27 November 1933 at Columbia's studios at 55 Fifth Avenue where the entire company was housed on two floors. Goodman booked the complete 'Ain't-cha Glad?' band with

45

just one change at Hammond's urging. In came trumpeter Shirley Clay for Mannie Klein.

Clay was a capable trumpeter who had joined Don Redman's band in 1931 from Hardy's Alabamians. Hammond liked his playing, he had seen him with Redman at Connie's Inn, but musically there was no need to drop an experienced studio musician like Klein. The reason was as significant as it was simple. It was to continue Hammond's pioneering policy of integrating black and white musicians at recording sessions.[1] While white bands backing black singers did not seem to offend racial taboos of the time (singers were considered 'apart' from the band), black and white musicians sitting alongside one another in the studios was still a rarity. Jelly Roll Morton had done two sessions with the New Orleans Rhythm Kings in 1923, and there had been occasional integrated sessions since, but they had been few and far between.

Hammond's practice was trail-blazing; just three days before Goodman's date he had recorded Bessie Smith in the same Fifth Avenue studios with an integrated backing band that included Goodman, Jack Teagarden, Frankie Newton, Chu Berry and pianist Buck Washington, the nominal leader. It was Goodman's only date with the greatest of the blues singers, who, though no one knew it at the time, was making her final appearance in a recording studio. Yet within seventy-two hours Goodman was to sample a unique distillation of the past, present and future of female vernacular singing. The first two sides of his own session, 'I Just Couldn't Take It, Baby' and 'A Hundred Years from Today', were cut in two takes each with Ethel Waters taking the vocals. On the final two sides (sessions typically produced four or five) Billie Holiday was set to make her recording debut.

Goodman and Hammond had been frequent visitors to hear Billie perform uptown, which culminated in Goodman dating Billie for a while.[2] Goodman seems to have taken her on some of his broadcast and recording sessions with commercial bands, but an interracial liaison in those days was always going to be difficult. Even Benny's sister Ethel resisted the idea. She need not have worried; within eighteen months Goodman had formed his first band and had fallen for his girl vocalist Helen Ward.

Billie had Goodman and Hammond in her corner willing her to do well but she was desperately nervous at the recording session.[3] Although a veteran of the bar-and-grill circuits, a recording session was quite a different proposition. Her composure was not helped by the presence of Ethel Waters, twice her age and with a decade of success already behind her, who stayed on to hear Hammond's much-touted discovery.

Billie's anxiety was made worse by the prospect of having to sing into the large microphone, something she had never done before: 'I says, "Why do I have to sing in *that* thing? Why can't I sing like I do at the club?" I was scared to death of it.'[4]

As if to compound her problems, the first song she was given to sing, 'Your Mother's Son-in-Law', was not only in an uncomfortable key, but Goodman wanted a slightly brighter tempo than she felt comfortable with. There were several run-throughs before she felt ready to go. Eventually she took three takes to settle and by then the session was over.

Billie's singing, despite the nerve-racking circumstances of the session, is far better than she has been given credit for. Her own feelings about it were mixed, later saying that while she got a kick out of it, her voice sounded funny and high.[5] But this is no helium-laugh of a raw beginner. There are specific pointers that show the basic elements of her style were most assuredly in place.

The form of 'Your Mother's Son-in-Law', although simple, is not straightforward. An eight-bar introduction leads into the thirty-two-bar ternary AABA song, followed by a four-bar modulation into the minor and a sixteen-bar transition of two eight-bar sections before Billie's thirty-two-bar AABA vocal. Although the melody line is never explicitly stated, we do get a good idea of what it might be from the initial A sections through Kincaide's crafty writing. Goodman and the band toss fragments and phrases of the melody between them, although the middle eight is improvised by Jack Teagarden and is not stated until Billie's vocal, when it is sung more or less 'as written'.

Compared to the exposition of the melody, shared between Goodman and the band in the A sections, Billie's entry is positively minimalistic. Singing near the top of her range, she essentially reduces the A theme to two semi-tones, which are repeated a third down and back in the tonic key again, with only the lyrics 'Your mother's son-in-law' following the shape of Goodman's original melodic outline. Joe Sullivan's piano accompaniment for Billie is excellent, incidentally, particularly in the second eight bars of the A section.

Billie's pared-down vocal on the A section creates an inherent tension which is resolved by singing the B section, or middle eight, and the final eight bars of the A section, which begins 'You don't have to sing like Bledsoe', a reference to the then popular black classical baritone singer Jules Bledsoe, in an arpeggiated manner which we take to be the song as written. It would be a formula she would use countless times throughout her career. But it is the first sixteen bars of her vocal that are of most interest. Here Billie draws more on Bessie Smith's influence

47

in simplifying the melodic line to just one of two notes rather than Armstrong's freedom within form.

Her diction, for an eighteen-year-old with a rudimentary education and who had been living on the fringes of society, is crystal-clear, even at the bright clip chosen by Goodman. There is no trace of a Baltimore accent, in fact her singing throughout her career remained largely accent-neutral, something she clearly must have worked hard to achieve, surely following the example of Ethel Waters's precise enunciation. There are also hints of the Holiday rasp, perhaps inspired by Armstrong, that would become more pronounced as her career progressed; a kind of vocal multiphonic that brings to mind trombonist Albert Mangelsdorff's use of 'chords' on the trombone, emulated vocally (and astonishingly) by fellow-trombonist Ray Anderson.[6]

A week later Billie and the Goodman ensemble returned to the Fifth Avenue studios. The guitarist on the date, Dick McDonough, had come up with an original theme, unusually of eighteen bars length, intended for Billie. He called it 'Riffin' the Scotch' but couldn't come up with the right lyrics. He contacted Johnny Mercer who produced a simple but uncredited line:

> I jumped out of the frying pan right into the fire,
> When I lost me a cheatin' man and got a no-count liar,
> Swipe the old one for the new one,
> Now the new one's breaking my heart,
> I jumped out of the frying pan, right into the fire, Lord, right into the fire.

The lyrics are interesting because they had nothing to do with the song title, neither riffing a Scots tune, as the sixteen-bar introduction implies, nor the pleasures (or otherwise) of Scotch whisky. Instead, they were tailor-made for Billie who was beginning to define the subject matter of her repertoire by adding a third element to Armstrong's improvisatory freedom and Bessie Smith's note economies by drawing on the theme of being unlucky in love favoured by the torch singers. 'Don't forget,' observed Benny Carter, 'that particular kind of singing was popular then. There were also a lot of white singers they called torch singers: Libby Holman, Helen Morgan.'[7]

A torch singer is primarily a mood singer specializing in love songs, who, through a combination of stylization and repertoire, evokes the sadness and pain that love can bring. And while 'Riffin' the Scotch' was by no stretch of the imagination a torch song, the lyrics described the kind of experiences in love a torch singer dealt with. 'When I met Billie in 1933 ... there was something about ... the torchy quality of her voice,' Mercer later reflected.[8] That 'torchy quality' had a bearing on the direction his lyrics took, reflecting Billie's night-club style that, as will be seen, consistently led her to being labelled a torch singer for the first few years of her career.

Reaching out to popular culture, incorporating aspects of torch singing into her style, raises the age-old question of the 'purity' of the jazz singer. A large grey area exists between the popular vocal and the jazz vocal in much the same way as Hegel's beach is neither land nor sea. The modulation from one to the other is, on occasion, imperceptible, so that to draw a definitive boundary is impossible. But that does not mean that beaches do not exist or that the jazz vocal and the popular vocal are the same thing. Almost as soon as Louis Armstrong placed jazz singing on the map, he listened to Bing Crosby and vice versa, a process of free exchange that can be traced throughout the history of the jazz vocal.

However, on the 4 December session things did not gel; both Billie's takes of 'Riffin' the Scotch' along with 'Keep on Doin' What You're Doin'' with a Jack Teagarden vocal were rejected from a session that produced just three numbers. The problem, so far as Billie was concerned at least, seems to have been arranger Deane Kincaide's strange modulation from G minor to E minor based on the 'Bugle Call Rag' motif that precedes her vocal. Four bars in length, it is impossible to predict what key it is heading for.

At the subsequent 18 December session she tries a further two takes of the tune. There is a slight delay to her entry as she momentarily establishes tonality after the confusing modulation, forcing her to syncopate her entry, making 'I jumped' into 'I-jumped,' creating a precedent she follows with the subsequent 'When-I' and the final 'I-jumped'; the 'I' and 'When' would properly be written as an anacrusis, or pick-up.

In the event, the session produced the usual four sides, with the second take of 'Riffin' the Scotch' chosen for release. Billie's vocal, sandwiched between trumpet solos by Charlie Teagarden and Shirley Clay, gives a more accurate snapshot of her style in 1933 than 'Your Mother's-Son-in-Law', simply because the tempo allows her a degree of improvisatory manoeuvrability that enables her to stretch and contract lyrics in a way that would become a hallmark of her style, such as between bars thirteen and fifteen of her vocal.

Although these recordings have been largely dismissed by the critics, they do, in fact, stand up quite well today. The arrangements are fairly sophisticated by 1933 standards and the ensembles are generally well executed and display a modern sense of swing. They are not, however, big-band performances of the sort that would become popular some two or three years hence, but a balance of improvised and written sections for an unusual instrumental combination of clarinet, two trumpets, trombone and tenor sax plus rhythm. Both songs have a rhythmical snap and crackle that is due, in no small measure, to Joe Sullivan on piano, Dick McDonough on guitar, Artie Bernstein on bass and Gene Krupa on drums.

During the 1980s, in the years leading up to his death in 1986, Benny Goodman came to regard his work with Jack Teagarden in the early 1930s as among the best from his long and distinguished career.[9] It is perhaps easy to see why; the pressures of leading a big band were ahead of him and these loose, free-wheeling performances come from a time in his life when he was looking to the future with optimism as he strived to establish himself.

Taken together, 'Your Mother's Son-in-Law' and 'Riffin' the Scotch' clearly show that Billie's style was all but fully formed by 1933, when she was just eighteen years of age. Since she always maintained that her interest in jazz first began when she heard Armstrong's recording of 'West End Blues', her style from that point seems to have coalesced with surprising speed. As a thirteen-year-old feeling her way into jazz in 1928, the year 'West End Blues' was released, she was hardly in a position to be defining her approach to jazz singing. With most of 1929 lost through her run-in with the law, it meant that effectively she put together a style of originality and invention in just three years, from 1930 to 1933. By any standards this was a remarkable achievement.

However, Billie was not to cut another record for two years. The next time the Benny Goodman 'orchestra' was reconvened in the recording studios, in February 1934, Billie and Benny's fling was over, so he and Hammond turned to their mutual friend Mildred Bailey. For that session Goodman hired Coleman Hawkins, considered the pre-eminent tenor saxophonist in jazz and at the time a member of the Fletcher Henderson Orchestra. Within eight weeks, however, Hawkins would leave Henderson to join the English bandleader Jack Hylton in London.

Hawkins's replacement in Henderson's band was Lester Young, then with the Count Basie band in Kansas City, who joined Henderson around 25 March 1934 for an engagement at the Cotton Club on Lenox Avenue that ran until the end of the month. New to New York City, Young initially roomed at Fletcher Henderson's home where he came under pressure from Henderson's wife to play in his predecessor's style. In fact, the whole band felt that Henderson should have chosen Chu

50

Berry, a saxophonist in the Hawkins mould, who had been given a brief run before Young. Consequently there was such strong support for Berry fermenting in the band that Young felt desperately uncomfortable.

Even so, he decided to stick it out, hoping to win the band around to his individual approach to improvisation. Where Hawkins's tone was heavy and muscular, Young's was light and graceful; where Hawkins signalled each chord change by flashing arpeggios, Young skimmed over the chord tops with conversational melodic logic. Young and Hawkins were like chalk and cheese and the talk among musicians was about who was best.

When they finished work, Young and trumpet player Jack Wilson, also new to the Henderson band, usually went out to jam. It was not long before they met Billie Holiday. From their first meeting there was no doubt in Billie's mind who was best tenor saxophonist in jazz. Around this time, as Billie recalled in her autobiography, Benny Carter and Lester Young were jamming at a club where she was singing. When Chu Berry entered, everyone wanted to see a contest, expecting Young to come off second-best. Berry did not have his saxophone with him, but 'Benny Carter wouldn't let that stop him,' Billie claimed in this frequently quoted story, 'he was like me, he had faith in Lester. So he volunteered to go and pick up Chu's horn.' Inevitably, Lester Young subsequently cut Berry. The only problem is that Carter does not think the story holds together: 'Of course I admired Lester,' he said later, 'but I thought very highly also of Chu, who was in my band for a time and a close friend. I doubt that I'd want to set them against each other or to humiliate anyone – least of all Chu.'[10]

By now Young had found cheap accommodation that was not the best. When Billie heard of his circumstances she invited him to move in with her and her mother. 'I came to New York in 1934,' said Young. 'I used to live at her house, with her mother, 'cause I didn't know my way around. She taught me a lot of things.'[11] Equally, this early exposure to Young's playing must have taught Billie 'a lot of things' too. Whenever he could, Young sat in with her on the bar-and-grill circuit. For Billie there could be no better finishing-school in the whole of jazz.

Billie's association with Young marked the beginning of a deep, platonic love affair that would stretch across decades. They were linked spiritually by their music. Billie had reached a similar musical conception to Young's by a mixture of quite specific musical influences, intuition and inspiration, and was now privy to the innermost musical thoughts of a musician who would become one of the most important influences in jazz. It would be over two years before Young would make his

51

first recordings, in October 1936, but he was already twenty-seven and taking the jazz world by storm. In April 1934 the *Chicago Defender* said that he was 'rated by many to be the equal' of Coleman Hawkins,[12] while in June that year John Hammond wrote that he had heard from several sources that Young 'had actually "cut" the master', Coleman Hawkins.[13]

In contrast to Billie, Young had arrived at his style as a result of a thorough, disciplined musical training that had begun as a child in his father's band, a professional unit with which he worked well into his teens. Musically he had much in common with Billie; he spurned the superfluous, using one well-chosen note in place of many, he loved to syncopate notes temptingly behind the groundbeat, he preferred medium and slow tempos and, just like Billie, loved marijuana. Although Young's playing did not match the complexity of Hawkins, his melodic ideas were at least as advanced. One aspect of his style was his ability to play against chord changes instead of through them, often with a restraint that made what he played seem like an integral part of a musical composition. Certainly these aspects were at their most apparent in Billie's singing during the 1930s and 1940s and it is impossible not to think Young's influence played a part in this. But equally, they were two separate musical personalities and it seems clear from the great mutual respect they had for each other that each reinforced the other's belief in what they were doing.

By mid-July, however, pressure from the Henderson band had grown too much for Young to bear. A sensitive man, he resigned his chair to join the Andy Kirk band back in Kansas City. Before he went, Henderson is reputed to have told the carpers in his ensemble that Young could outplay all of them, and that they would hear from him again.[14]

Throughout 1934, however, Billie's career failed to gather momentum. In terms of publicity, her sides with Goodman turned out to be something of an anti-climax since they were not released until the autumn; 'Billie Holiday is making records for Columbia,' reported *New York Age* in September, without mentioning the song titles or saying with whom she recorded.[15]

Professionally, Billie still had a long way to go to establish her career. It is often forgotten what hot competition there was among girl vocalists in Harlem's night-spots during this period; Sallie Simmons was becoming a favourite at the Harlem dawn-spots, Anna Brady was 'turning on the heat' in a variety of bar-and-grill joints, Elizabeth Harrison was featuring at the Alhambra Grill, Amanda Robinson was drawing crowds in the Old Restaurant on Lenox Avenue, 'charming' Avis Andrews was impressing audiences with her appearances at the Apollo, Marion

Hairstron, 'the good-looking song stylist', was 'in her eighth month at Small's Paradise', Dotty Johnson was 'wowing nitelifers at Johnson's Grill', Nina Mae McKinney, described as 'one of Harlem's finest entertainers', was pulling in crowds wherever she appeared, and Cora LaRedd was featuring at the Cotton Club. And these were just a few of the better-known Harlem singers of the day.[16]

Seemingly oblivious to the number and variety of singers, all vying to make the big time, Billie allowed her career to drift as she became seriously involved with pianist Bobbie Henderson. This had begun with a flirtation during their gig together at Pod's and Jerry's and quickly grew into the first major love affair of Billie's life. For a while she spent as much time as she could in his company.

It is quite possible that it was Henderson's reputation as a pianist, rather than Billie's as a singer, which brought them to the attention of the Apollo Theater management on 125th Street. Billie's Apollo debut was for the week commencing Friday, 23 November 1934 as a duo with Bobbie Henderson. Billie's surname was given as Halliday, although not too much should be read into the spelling; some writers have assumed she wanted to distance herself from her father's reputation to prove she could make it on her own. In reality, artists' names were frequently wrongly spelt on the weekly Apollo advertisements.[17] The only problem was that once the Apollo printed a name incorrectly, artists were often stuck with the wrong spelling for some while afterwards.

Legend has it that Billie's Apollo debut was marked by encores that in turn prompted a repeat booking the following week. Neither was true. Billie failed to get a mention when *New York Age* and *New York Amsterdam News* reviewed the show, although *Amsterdam News* listed her and Henderson among the weekly cast list. The big news was of compere Ralph Cooper's 'grippe and nervous breakdown' and the ovation he received when he made his only appearance of the week to host the Wednesday night talent show, broadcast on Radio WMCA.[18]

Had there been any encores for Billie 'Halliday', the *Age* and *Amsterdam News* would have leapt at the chance to report the fact; both were struggling to register anything beyond faint praise for the acts featured that week – in fact it was the Dick Powell movie *Happiness Ahead* that got the compliments – '[it] provides a really bright spot in a somewhat dull programme,' said the *Age* wearily.[19] The following week the Luis Russell Orchestra was the main feature. Billie was not among the support acts.

One bit of show-biz apocrypha about Billie's Apollo debut is probably true, however. It has always been said that she was so nervous she had to be pushed onstage by Pigmeat Markham. Billie was frequently

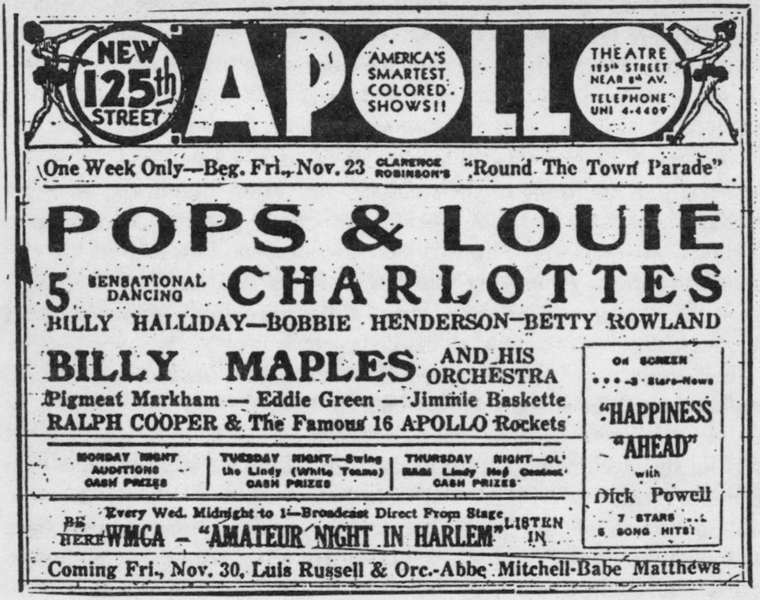

Figure 4: The Apollo bill for the week commencing Friday, 23 November 1934. 'Billy Halliday' makes her major Harlem debut a year earlier than is recorded in the history books.

troubled by performance anxiety and Pigmeat was definitely on the bill during the week of 23 November 1934. And certainly an encouraging shove into the spotlight was one way of ensuring a nervous youngster made it on stage. '[I was] scared to death,' recalled Billie. 'I waited until the last minute, I said I wasn't going to go on. So somebody gave me a push and when I stopped running I was almost in front of the mike ... Then I couldn't control my knees – and I had on a satin dress and you could see my knees is going – people didn't know whether I was going to dance or sing.'[20]

Shortly after their Apollo appearance, the romance between Billie and Henderson came to an abrupt end when Billie discovered he was a bigamist.[21] 'Now that the engagement between Bobbie Henderson, the pianist, and herself has gone the way of many,' said the *New York Age*, 'Billie Halliday (sic), the blues singer, is stepping up the pulses of Sugar Hill debs ... at the Sunset.'[22] On 5 January 1935 Billie moved from the Sunset to the Hot-Cha Restaurant at 2280 Seventh Avenue at West 134th Street. 'It was in the back room I first heard her,' said columnist Bill Chase. 'Even then one felt an unusual sensation in listen-

54

ing to her peculiarly styled rendition of songs like "Painting the Town Red" and "If the Moon Turns Green".[23]

However, while still at the Sunset Billie offended Marcus Wright, the entertainment columnist of *New York Age*, during one of her final performances there. Wright responded with Hedda Hopper-esque bitchiness: 'Billie Halliday (sic), when you think you are playing sophisticated, take a look in the mirror before you make your appearance at the Hot-Cha, then you will find you are not so hot after all, you are just an entertainer.'[24] But Billie was indeed 'playing sophisticated' to the slummers, as Ted Yates, another *New York Age* columnist, would recall three years later: 'Night after night the performances of that torch-singing lady while at the Hot-Cha Restaurant delighted Park Avenue's elite and uptown Seventh Avenue's smart set. No more . . . swanky doings this side of Manhattan.'[25]

In late 1934, John Hammond was working for the office of Irving Mills, a leading impresario who represented several top bands including Duke Ellington and Cab Calloway. He convinced Mills that Billie was a star in the making and that he should represent her. Mills's first step was to increase her exposure by including her in a forthcoming Ellington film short called *Symphony in Black*. Work on the film began in December at Paramount's Eastern Service Studios at Astoria, Long Island while Ellington was in New York after several months on the road. Produced by Adolph Zukor and directed by Fred Waller, it was just nine minutes fifteen seconds long. But despite its brevity, over the years the film has acquired an almost mystic aura, heightened by its symphonic title, arty set lighting and elaborate compositions by Ellington, plus Billie Holiday's cameo role, one of the few times she appeared on film.[26]

Surprisingly for a short, it took ten months to complete and was finally released on 13 September 1935, the *New York Amsterdam News* reporting that 'Duke Ellington's Paramount short, *Symphony in Black*, is scoring largely everywhere it is shown.'[27] The soundtrack was recorded in December 1934, while the majority of the filming took place in March 1935. The fact that the film was completed in two segments is borne out by a report in the *Pittsburgh Courier* from January 1935: 'The music for this piece has been finished and awaits photographing of the acting to fit the mood of the compositions.'[28]

Ellington treated Billie's feature just as he did when he featured his own star instrumentalists; he chose the accompaniment to suit the individual characteristics of her style. He adapted a number he had previously recorded on 12 September 1934 called 'Saddest Tale',[29] where he himself had solemnly intoned a brief four-bar interlude:

Saddest Tale told on land 'nd sea,[30]
Was the tale they told when they told the truth on me.

Ellington retained this for Billie's feature, albeit amending the second stanza to:

Was when my man walked out on me

This immediately staked out the emotional territory which her subsequent vocal, after a chorus by trombonist Joe 'Tricky Sam' Nanton, would deal. In *Lady Sings the Blues* Billie remembered correctly singing a slow blues but was wrong in recalling her role as that of a whore. The lyrics followed the theme of being unlucky in love, the same theme that had been hastily adapted for her on 'Riffin' the Scotch'. This time it was about a girl's battle to secure a boy against the treachery of a female peer and failing:

My man's gone I feels a lull[31]
I've got those lost my man blues
He didn't treat me fair
It's more than I can bear
I've got those lost my man blues
I've got those lost my man, can't get him back again, blues.

Ellington and his director Fred Waller could have easily chosen a fast tempo or even a medium bounce for Billie, and the subject matter could have been about sunshine, happiness and bluebirds. Significantly it was none of these things. Both Ellington's music and Waller's tableau were shaped with Billie's personal style specifically in mind. Ivie Anderson, then Ellington's regular vocalist, said that when she joined him in 1931, Ellington told her to find a 'character' part as a singer and maintain it. 'He's a leader who takes a lot of time and trouble to find the right background for a singer,' she said, 'he's always supplied me with ideal accompaniment, one which suited the "character" which I adopted.'[32] Equally, Ellington recognized the 'character' role Billie had adopted for herself and sought to project this in her tableau.

'Blues' was performed at a slow tempo,[33] and Billie rose to the challenge with an impressive visual and musical performance, acting out a minidrama in which the emotional theme described by the lyrics was less important than the way in which they were sang and portrayed. It would be interesting to know who came up with the words, since Billie moulds them as if they were her own. Again she uses the minimum of notes to maximum effect; there are only three notes that are neither tonic, mediant nor dominant of the home key of B flat in the whole vocal. The pervading mood is one of melancholia, heightened by the 'Ellington effect', and was Billie Holiday's first important statement as an artist.

Her appeal in this performance is how she shares her feelings, expressed in the first person, both visually and vocally. As the story unfolds it becomes a kind of novelette in the way it describes the eternal triangle of love. It is a conventional story, familiar to the listener, where the basic idea is set out in the four-bar 'Saddest Tale' introduction and elaborated (she is thrown to the ground from where she sings) over twelve bars in such a way that we feel sympathy, perhaps even empathy, for her plight. It is a simple 'story' reflecting the opposition between those who are lucky in love and those who are not. Once again it is the kind of theme favoured by torch singers, but Billie's handling of it is far removed from the heart-on-the-sleeve emotionalism of the torchers.

What Billie Holiday did in 'Blues' eventually became central to her art. She was constructing an image that would become central to the songs she sang, creating a link between lyrics, music and singer. Still only nineteen years old, she presented a 'character' whose life's experiences appeared to be mirrored in the text of her songs. This would later become commonplace in popular music; Sinatra with his barstool performances, Piaf as the sparrow unbroken by life, and Garland who was. Today, in rock music, we take 'image' for granted, something that embraces non-musical factors such as lifestyle, fashion and sex-appeal that become bound up in the stage presence of an artist. These are elements that contribute to the authenticity of a singer which ultimately decides the public's desire to identify with him or her, the so-called 'star' appeal. Yet in 1935 all this was unheard of, and even today the way the Billie Holiday 'image' interacts with her music remains the least understood aspect of her art.

Following her role in *Symphony in Black*, Irving Mills offered Billie a try-out with the Mills Blue Rhythm Band at the Lincoln Theater in Philadelphia for the week of 15 February 1935. The Blue Rhythm Band had been taken over by Mills in 1930 mainly to fulfil engagements when his main clients, Ellington and Calloway, were tied up elsewhere. It was highly regarded by the dancers in Harlem and a successful audition meant a key opportunity for Billie in one of Harlem's top bands bankrolled by the leading entrepreneur in jazz. However, the engagement ended before it actually began because of a dispute with the theatre's management. Just as Billie's great talent was coalescing, so too, it seems, were traits in her character that seemed to prevent her making the most out of opportunities that came her way.

Chapter Four

1935

In April 1935, Ralph Cooper, the master of ceremonies at the Apollo Theater, decided to try his luck as a bandleader. In the early 1930s he had fronted a group called Ralph Cooper's Kongo Knights, but then went on to become Harlem's most successful MC. He built his reputation at the Lafayette Theater, where in 1933 he was acknowledged as the audience's favourite by *New York Amsterdam News*.[1] By February 1934 he had moved to the new 125th Street Apollo and became widely recognized as a key figure in the theatre's success, hailed as 'the best man on the boards today' by *New York Age*.[2]

But despite his popularity, Cooper still had the bandleading bug. At the end of March 1935 he began rehearsing a line-up which included saxophonists Emmett Mathews and Louis Jordan and was set to debut at the Apollo for the week commencing Friday, 12 April. Booked as 'Ralph Cooper with his 18 Kings of Melody', he was going straight into the slot coveted by all the top big bands in Harlem.

A matter of days before opening, Cooper called into the Hot-Cha for a plate of its renowned spaghetti. As he was eating, a tall girl came out to sing on the small two-by-four stage. Initially, Cooper did not pay much attention as he spent all day around show people. 'Then she started singing,' he recalled later. 'That's when I noticed she was young and pretty, with a lovely smile, and she had a voice like I never heard before. She sang with a crying style.'[3] After years of compering weekly amateur night competitions at the Lafayette and the Apollo, he quickly recognized talent when he saw it. As soon as she finished, he offered the girl a job as a featured vocalist with his new band.

Billie Holiday was elated. Cooper was one of the most popular celebrities in Harlem and any big band he was set to lead seemed a sure bet for success. It was the break she had been waiting for. Cooper immediately talked to the restaurant manager and promised to mention the Hot-Cha over the radio hook-up at the Apollo in exchange for her release. But when Billie turned up for rehearsals on the morning of

12 April, things did not go well from the start. She had no stage costume and was sent away to get one. Then, as she ran through her material with the band, 'They didn't know whether she could cut it,' said Cooper. 'Still, I had a gut feeling. I knew I never heard singing so slow, so lazy, so sexy.'[4]

Cooper's band, with Billie as featured vocalist, opened the show after the first picture that afternoon. But there was no great Apollo roar when she was through singing her songs. 'Billie Halliday (sic), whose singing may be likened to that of Helen Morgan, falls short of Cooper's flattering introduction,' said *New York Age*.[5] Helen Morgan was a popular torch singer of the day; once again a reference emerges that suggests that Billie's style, in live performance at least, was continuing to incorporate elements associated with torching. But even though she was not a great success with the Apollo crowd, she found herself held over for a second week along with the rest of the bill who had been doing standing-room-only business every night.

Cooper, however, had severe misgivings about Billie's second week. He persuaded her to drop several of her slower numbers in favour of some new uptempo material. And just in case this was not enough to click with the crowds, he brought in Herb Jeffries from Chicago to share the vocal duties. 'Herb Jeffries Steals Show at Apollo Theater,' enthused *New York Age*, 'Ralph Cooper has pulled a fast one on the theater world . . . by producing . . . Herb Jeffries to sing with his newly formed orchestra . . . Ralph's boys are working themselves into an aggregation which should go places before many weeks have passed. Even Billie Halliday (sic), with a week's performance under her belt, steps into the spirit of the theater and sings numbers better suited to her voice than those she chose last week.'[6]

But Cooper's foray into bandleading did not last long. During the first week, Jimmy Baskette had taken over as the Apollo master of ceremonies. The public wanted Cooper back, though: 'As just another Harlem baton-wielder he loses his individuality,' observed the *Age*.[7] Eventually the demand was such that when, during the second week, he finished his big band spot and returned to share MC duties with Jimmy Baskette, there was a huge cheer from the crowd. The writing was on the wall.

Within a week, Cooper had decided to forget bandleading as a career. 'What has become of Ralph Cooper's highly touted orchestra?' inquired *New York Amsterdam News* a few weeks later. 'There was much ado about nothing as Mr Cooper was supposed to have welded a new orchestra together and it appeared for a week or two at the Apollo and then passed out without a word of explanation to the boys [in the band] who

Figure 5: Billie Holiday's second Apollo appearance was for the week commencing Friday, 12 April 1935. Hired at short notice and too late to be included on the bill posters for that week, she was added on 19 April, when the whole cast was held over for doing standing-room-only business.

have been hollering about it.'[8] Once again Billie found herself back at the Hot-Cha.

Meanwhile, a young girl who had just turned eighteen was establishing herself as the new vocalist with the Chick Webb Orchestra. After an initial two-week try-out in March, she had become a regular up at the Savoy, a second-storey ballroom that stretched the length of the block between 140th and 141st Streets on the east side of Lenox Avenue. Remarkably, the sum total of her professional experience before joining Webb was a week in February at the Harlem Opera House with the Tiny Bradshaw band as a prize for winning their weekly amateur night competition.

Curious and bitter, Billie decided to check out Ella Fitzgerald for herself. 'Billie Holiday used to come into the Savoy and I'd look from the bandstand, she'd have a big coat on and she would walk in and just look,' said Charles Linton, Webb's male vocalist. 'What I figured was that she was surprised to see Ella with Chick Webb's band. "A great band like that with Ella," she used to say, "that bitch!" turn around and walk out."[9]

Why, then, did Webb, the foremost jazz drummer of his day and a leader of one of the finest big bands in the history of jazz, not even consider Billie as a girl vocalist? The answer was simple: 'I did the classics and the ballad tunes,' explained Linton, 'they wanted someone who could do the swing tunes.'[10] According to Linton, Billie had become known for singing slow tunes, 'Tunes that were like, you know, torchy. We would call those particular kind of tunes ballads today,' he said.[11] Ella, on the other hand, immediately displayed an infectious finger-snapping, foot-tapping gift which was just what Webb wanted. 'She could swing,' said the drummer Hal Austin, who witnessed Ella's first performances at the Savoy, 'she came into this business swinging.'[12]

Around this time Billie was dating tenor saxophonist Ben Webster, a strikingly handsome man but who, after a few drinks, had an explosive temper. Like a moth to a flame, Billie seemed strangely fascinated by Webster's dark side. She would deliberately provoke him when he was in his cups and from time to time she could be seen with facial bruising. The situation deteriorated to such an extent that on one occasion when Webster came around to pick Billie up from the apartment she now shared with Sadie at 9 West 99th Street, her mother, upset at what was happening to her daughter, attacked Webster with a wooden umbrella by way of retribution. But although Billie was discovering a new kind of excitement in this romance, her career once again seemed to be heading nowhere. Back on the bar-and-grill circuit, she went from the Hot-Cha to Clark Monroe's Uptown House. While she was there, John Hammond contacted her quite unexpectedly in June 1935. He had worked out a deal with Brunswick Records and wanted to record her again.

In 1930 Benny Carter was playing alto sax in the Fletcher Henderson Orchestra. While the band was on tour in Providence, the trumpet player Roy Eldridge persuaded Carter to go with him to see the Speed Webb band in Woonsocket. He wanted Carter to hear their pianist, Teddy Wilson. Carter was impressed. When he formed his own band in 1933 he thought of Wilson, as did John Hammond who had recently heard him on the radio playing the Grand Terrace with the Eddie Moore band. Hammond lent Carter the money to drive to Chicago to persuade Wilson to join him. Carter went with his friend George Rich, who owned the club where Carter's new band was about to debut. By the time Carter arrived in Chicago, Wilson had moved on to Jimmie Noone's band and after some persuasion succumbed to Carter's offer,

61

as did trombonist Keg Johnson. Both men moved to New York.

Carter, who repaid the loan to Hammond in 1961, was in the recording studios with Wilson on a Hammond-produced Chocolate Dandies session on 10 October 1933, when Wilson made his recording debut. His playing on 'Krazy Kapers' and 'I Never Knew' is astonishingly mature for a twenty-one-year-old, as is his solo on 'Blue Lou' with Carter's big band later in the month, and contains the stamp of a master.

Wilson refined Earl Hines's extrovert, sometimes harsh, approach to the piano with crisp, intricate right-hand figures of great balance and symmetry. He rejected an implicit time-keeping role for the left hand, the norm in jazz until then, using instead a more subtle pattern of moving tenths which became something of a trade-mark. But although Wilson's linear approach to improvisation was genuinely innovative, his playing none the less remained within the technical grasp of the more advanced players. Perhaps this was why it was he, and not Art Tatum, who became one of the most imitated pianists of the 1930s.

After the Carter band broke up Wilson joined the Willie Bryant Orchestra, a band which despite its workaday arrangements had, at the time, an extraordinary personnel including Ben Webster, Cozy Cole and, for a while, even Carter himself. Here Wilson tried his hand at arranging, producing an excellent chart of George Gershwin's 'Liza' which the band subsequently recorded. By now Wilson had been in New York for almost two years and was establishing a formidable reputation as a brilliantly inventive pianist. All the while, John Hammond continued to do what he could to promote Wilson's career; he helped him get record dates with Mezz Mezzrow in 1933 and Red Norvo's Swing Septet and Swing Octet in 1934 and was the conduit between Wilson's historic association with Benny Goodman that began on record on 14 May 1934.

Getting a recording contract for Wilson, rather than ad hoc dates as a sideman, proved to be more difficult, however. In 1935 Hammond had approached the newly formed Decca Record Company, but its energetic head, thirty-two-year-old Jack Kapp, was not interested since Hammond wished to retain production duties. Kapp had also declined Duke Ellington's manager Irving Mills for much the same reasons. Writer George Frazier was another who tried to persuade Kapp to sign Wilson: 'Jack . . . is so damn pigheaded he won't listen to any opinion that fails to fit in with his own scheme of things,' he said.[13] But with the record industry now showing definite signs of recovery, Hammond contacted other record companies.

In June 1935 he approached the American Record Company and secured a commitment from Brunswick's Harry Grey to produce a jazz series built around Wilson with an eye to the fast-expanding coin-operated music-machine business, which was already accounting for some 40 per cent of Decca's output to some 150,000 jukeboxes. In July 1935 Grey signed an exclusive twelve-month contract with Wilson, guaranteeing a session a month, either with small ad hoc bands or just Wilson's solo piano. It was a remarkable deal; 'I don't know what Brunswick were thinking of when they took us on,' said Wilson.[14]

Hammond's role of producer was enormously influential. His enthusiasm and persuasiveness were such that he was able to have the say when it came to hiring the band. Quite simply, Hammond made sure he got the best and because of the Depression, top musicians were prepared to accept union scale. But his small budget meant no money for arrangements, so he had Wilson write skeleton charts. 'They were not really arrangements,' said Wilson. 'They were just little sketches . . . what was written would be an introduction or a simple harmony behind the soloist. We might sometimes write out a little ending.'[15]

The first session was lined up for 2 July 1935 at Brunswick's studios at 1776 Broadway. The Brunswick executives were particularly interested to see what their investment was about to yield and Hammond was well aware of this. He picked some of the finest musicians available, including Benny Goodman on clarinet, Roy Eldridge on trumpet, Ben Webster on saxophone and for the vocals he chose Billie Holiday.

Wilson had first heard Billie with his wife Irene at the Hot Shot Club on Seventh Avenue. 'It wasn't much of a spot,' said Irene Wilson, 'I remember Billie wearing a lavender skirt and a pink shirt and looking like an overgrown child . . . [Then] she started coming up to the house to rehearse for records.'[16]

Wilson selected the numbers and ran through them with Billie at his apartment the day before the recording session. This would become a feature of his sessions with Billie; sometimes he had the whole band around, despite occasional protests from neighbours who finally resorted to complaining to the police. As Billie's accompanist for recordings Wilson played a key role in helping her focus her ideas and realize her style. Their first session together went with hardly any hitches, although Goodman, who was to open in Pittsburgh's Stanley Theater three days later on his first out-of-town booking with his new big band, had called a rehearsal for 5 p.m. that day and wanted to pull out. Hammond persuaded him to turn up: 'I put on a greater burst of temperament than the New York Telephone Company has ever before had to suffer,' he later recalled. 'Result: in ten minutes Benny Goodman was sitting and playing in the studio.'[17]

Hammond did agree to let Goodman get away early, so he is on only three of the four sides that went down that afternoon, but his performance was so inspired that his contribution was significant in making this session one of the finest of all the Billie Holiday–Teddy Wilson collaborations. 'That session was never, never surpassed,' asserted Wilson later. 'It may have been equalled, but never surpassed.'[18]

Two key titles emerged from this record date, 'What a Little Moonlight Can Do' and 'Miss Brown to You', and so profound is Billie's treatment of them that they became indelibly associated with her for the rest of her life. The striking thing about Billie's vocals on this session is her confidence, which borders on exuberance in places. It is 'What a Little Moonlight Can Do' that sees her best singing of the session. After Wilson's four-bar introduction, Goodman begins the thirty-two-bar theme in the chalumeau register of his clarinet and follows it with a stunning solo where caution is thrown to the wind.

Here Goodman plays with the sort of abandon that would later characterize his brilliant live performances with his own small groups and big band in 1937–8.[19] Indeed, 'Moonlight' effectively opens as a Benny Goodman small group performance featuring remarkable interplay between clarinettist and pianist that had been developing out of the public gaze and would culminate in the first of the legendary Goodman trio recordings just eleven days later. As with all the greatest jazz soloists, there is a sense of danger in what Goodman played; at times sounding a little wild, particularly in the last eight bars, he creates here a genuinely 'hot' chorus.

Goodman's creative heat is perfectly balanced by Billie's cool and sensuous entry that follows. It announces an inherent tension between the rhythm of the song and the metre of the lyrics which she manages to sustain throughout her vocal; the melody line, with its large note values, appears to pass by at a slower pace than the brisk groundbeat. As the rhythm remains a jaunty four beats to the bar, both Wilson and bassist John Kirby play *alla breve* and it is over their 'cut time' feel that Billie's teasing, behind-the-beat delivery shows up in sharp relief. As in her past recordings, she reduces the melody line as much as possible; for example, the first three notes of the song are written as D-B-D but Billie sings them all as D.

The other highlight of the afternoon session was 'Miss Brown to You'; after Goodman's *a capella* introduction he states the melody in the chalumeau register before launching into an improvised middle eight. Here, during the first bar, on beat four, and the second bar, on beat one, there is the unmistakable sound of an impatient car horn from the hot street below. Billie's vocal is playful, yet swings profoundly. The Holiday 'rasp', that semi-growl with harmonic overtones, can be heard on the second eight bars of the A section, on the word 'Tennessee' and during the middle eight on 'wait' and 'you'll see'. Totally immersed in her vocal, she is reluctant to part company with the song, and during Wilson's solo joins in with a 'yes, YES' that perfectly suits the tight, cohesive swing generated by Wilson, John Kirby, John Trueheart and Cozy Cole.

It was ironic that in spite of these two superlative performances, after attending the recording session the Brunswick executives viewed Billie's singing with no great favour, one of them even telling Hammond that she did not sound enough like Cleo Brown. They began to change their minds, however, when 'What a Little Moonlight' (the B side was 'A Sunbonnet Blue' from the same date) went into the record chart at twelve on 3 October. When the recordings appeared in England later in the year, *The Gramophone* was hardly more enthusiastic than the Brunswick executives. 'The truth is that they can never rank among the greatest things in jazz,' wrote Edgar Jackson, '. . . to appreciate Billie Holiday one has to be very much in sympathy with the Negro mode.'[20]

In fact, what Billie Holiday had done was to conceptualize a role for a jazz singer at a time when such a role could scarcely be said to exist. The transition from megaphone to electric microphone was still a relatively new development in the mid-1930s. Just six or seven years before the use of a megaphone was a commonplace, but this left no room for subtlety; singers were functional, there to deliver the song's lyrics and melody with no regard to the subjective weight of their material. Men sang girls' songs and girls sang men's songs without bothering to change nouns or pronouns and without regard to how strange they sounded.

The early popularity of radio ushered in singers who sang the melody more or less straight, based on the precedent of European operatic singing; there was 'The Songbird of the South' (Kate Smith), 'The Red-Headed Music-Maker' (Arthur Godfrey) and, most popular of all, 'The Street Singer' (Arthur Tracy). There were the Irish tenors, Italian tenors, and there were crooners with high falsetto voices, like Jack Fulton with the Paul Whiteman Orchestra or Charles Linton with the Chick Webb band. Since it was sales of sheet music that decided a song's popularity, singers attempted to render songs accurately with little emotional immediacy.

All that changed with Louis Armstrong and Bing Crosby who were the prime movers in introducing a swinging approach to melodic organization. They were not alone; both Ethel Waters and Al Jolson deserve credit for taking rhythmic liberties with songs and moving towards a 'swinging' vocal line during the 1920s. But ultimately, it was Armstrong and Crosby, singing with an intimacy made possible by the electronic microphone (contrast the megaphone Crosby of the Rhythm Boys to the one-to-one crooner of the Decca days), who ushered in the notion that singers could be objects of the microphone in the same way that movie actors on the silver screen were becoming objects of the camera.

Just as on the screen a faint smile could replace a grand gesture on stage, the electronic microphone favoured a relaxed style of singing which heightened nuances of personality. It transformed the recording process; now recordings really came into their own. For the first time the stylistic integrity of the singer made hearing the record more important than seeing the sheet music. It released vernacular singing from the rigorous techniques of the operatic tradition and made Billie Holiday's art possible.

Looking back on the Brunswick recording session, Teddy Wilson reflected: 'I was much more excited by the musicians we had on those dates than I was about Billie . . . [she] was not a particular favorite of mine. In those days for jazz singing . . . I just fell in love with Baby White . . . But John Hammond, he didn't hear anything in Baby White. He was crazy about Billie Holiday.'[21] Without Hammond's patronage, it is very unlikely that Wilson would have turned to Billie to provide the 'vocal refrain' on his sessions, and as a consequence Billie Holiday could well have remained another obscure Harlem singer, much like Baby White today.

Beverley 'Baby' White was a popular attraction at the time. She later joined the Claude Hopkins Orchestra where she played 'second' piano in addition to being the featured vocalist. Her recorded legacy is just six vocal sides with Hopkins on the Decca label in 1937. If they are typical of her style it is impossible to see what Wilson saw in her singing. Yet for Billie, still with only a tenuous grip on her career, Baby White represented strong competition.

Exactly a month after recording with Wilson, Billie was booked into the Apollo on a bill headlined by the Willie Bryant band, coincidentally with Wilson at the piano. Also appearing that week, but not advertised, was Baby White. After the Friday night show, *New York Age* reported: 'Billie Holliday (sic), still singing in her dragging way, should stick to the faster-timed numbers, such as "Living in a Great Big Way", rather than the slow draggy tunes which she has been doing. Her renditions of songs don't quite fit in with personality and voice type. Baby White, on the other hand, can get the most out of the songs she sings as evidenced by the insistent demand for encores.'[22] Once again, contrary to legend, Billie was still unable to knock them dead at the Apollo.

Yet what Billie did on the Apollo stage that week took both artistic integrity and courage. The Apollo crowd was well known for their shared belief of what constituted a good performance. Even established artists were not immune from the audience's wrath if they suspected a below par performance. Consequently to appear on the stage of the Apollo, even in the 1990s, remains a nerve-racking experience for any performer, whether seasoned pro or newcomer. Billie stuck to her repertoire of largely 'slow, draggy tunes', tunes that appeared to drag because of her behind-the-beat syncopations, although her experience with Ralph Cooper's band in April would have told her that the Apollo audience wanted 'faster-timed' numbers. Faced with one of the most demanding audiences in the world, she was not prepared to compromise her style. She would later say it took about ten years for people to catch on to what she was doing,[23] and she was right. In contrast, it was the more easily accessible style of singers like Baby White that was getting the encores.

Baby White's style was simple and straightforward. 'She had that lyrical sound,' said Teddy Wilson, 'tell you the story and yet the beautiful phrasing of this clear voice was spellbinding singing straight melody . . . to me Billie was like a girl doing a take-off on Louis Armstrong. It was novel, no one else had thought to do it, but I didn't think it was original.'[24] When the choice of vocalist was left to Wilson on later sessions, he chose girls who, like White, had clear voices and sang the melody largely straight: Helen Ward, Ella Fitzgerald, Frances Hunt, Sally Gooding and Nan Wynn. 'I was not a Billie Holiday fan,' he said.[25]

Wilson was back in the studios with another pick-up group at the end of July with much the same line-up except for the addition of Hilton Jefferson on alto, with Cecil Scott replacing Goodman, and Lawrence Lucie instead of Trueheart on guitar. 'I can remember getting the call,' said Lucie. 'Teddy told me to meet at the session. Teddy had already coached Billie on the songs – I found this out later. It all went very smoothly. When John Hammond walked in he was smiling, as though "This business will be a thrill for me, I know everything's going to be all right!" The people he hired to do it, they had sold themselves before they had got into the studio, that's really the point.'[26]

There is not quite the quasi-jam-session informality of the 2 July date on these sides; Wilson's sketch arrangements here are much more tightly written, albeit interpreted loosely rather than accurately, so that it is Billie's role that assumes central interest. The session contains one uptempo number, 'What a Night, What a Moon, What a Girl', amended by Billie to 'What a Night, What a Moon, What a Boy'. Just as in 'What

67

a Little Moonlight Can Do', the rhythm is fast, but the metre of the lyrics is not, so once again Billie is able to prise the words away from the groundbeat and syncopate them tantalizingly behind the beat. The sturdy simplicity of Bessie Smith's note economies is again apparent, but Billie's application of the science is both sophisticated and subtle, rejigging the songwriter's basic model with a more aero-dynamic scheme that allows her vocal to take flight.

This process of Holidizing a lyric is applied with precision to 'I'm Painting the Town Red', a song she had been singing in live performance for some time, but on 'It's Too Hot for Words' the tempo is bright and the melody line is crammed with words. There is no chance to trade off metre and rhythm here, although she tries during the first six bars; of more interest is how she incorporates the conversational *sprechgesang*-like delivery of Don Redman at points during her vocal. Redman, a fixture at Connie's Inn with his band during the early 1930s, was among the first jazz vocalists with his 'My Papa Doesn't Two Time No Time' with Fletcher Henderson in 1925. His 'How'm I Doin' Hey, Hey' from 1933 was enormously popular in Harlem, a song-title that became a figure of speech, much like Bobby McFerrin's wonderfully ironic 1988 hit, 'Don't Worry, Be Happy'.

Redman's style would be well known to Billie, who produced a good jive-vocal that, like Redman, concentrates more on the riffish melody than the lyrics. Here she is concerned less with the song's meaning than evolving a conversational directness, making tune and lyric sound like an extension of speech and in so doing putting into place the final piece of the jigsaw that comprised her fast-evolving style. This Redmanesque delivery surfaces again in parts of 'Yankee Doodle Never Went to Town' from October, while December's 'Spreadin' Rhythm Around' is almost pure Redman. What she was doing on these numbers in 1935 would later be slowed down and projected more intimately on to a bigger screen as she later linked her concern for the song's meaning with conversational directness.

Certainly she was well on the way to achieving this on 'If You Were Mine'. Here she scoops into the bottom of her range with a rasp, but in contrast it is her delicate phrasing of 'Yes, even my heart' that lingers in the memory; it certainly had an effect on trumpeter Roy Eldridge who echoes it in his beautifully sculpted solo.

Even though she is still polishing and refining her technique, it is impossible not to think of her work as being touched with genius. Such creativity has led many commentators to conclude that had she been given 'better' material, the results would somehow be proportionally improved. Much has been written[27] about how she turned 'base metal into gold', how the songs she sang on the Wilson sessions over the ensuing few years, and later, those under her own name, often had lyrics 'unworthy' of her talents.

Yet it is almost meaningless to say the lyrics of a popular song are either good or bad; they are only one piece of a jigsaw that must fit in with other pieces, each dependent on the others. Lyrics are not poetry, so it makes little sense to judge them apart from a song. They are just one component in a song's inherent drama that also embodies melodic, harmonic and rhythmic elements. For example, to separate the lyrics of Little Richard's 'Tutti Frutti, All Rootie!' and make them an object of criticism out of the context of the song would be to make both lyrics and criticism look ridiculous. The only full explanation is to hear the song as a whole. Part of the singer's art is to reveal subtleties in the most commonplace of words, which has more to do with the *sound* of the singer's voice than lyrics. 'Words,' said Greil Marcus, 'are sounds we feel before they are statements to understand.'[28]

And Billie's voice was fast becoming one of the most recognizable sounds in jazz. 'One thing about Billie,' conceded Teddy Wilson, 'was that she had a very strong gift in that she could sing five seconds and her name was written all over the music.'[29] Billie's sound was at once interesting and attracted attention; both the grain of her voice and her style of expression were immediately recognizable and, even at twenty, she sounded astonishingly mature; for example, her vocal on 'I Wished on the Moon', from her very first session with Teddy Wilson, takes very few harmonic or rhythmic liberties, relying less on syncopation than ironic enunciation – the sound of her voice – for its success. But if the lyrics of a song are less important than the way a singer is able to give real, personal meaning to them, what of the songs in themselves?

Conventional wisdom has it that as a black artist Wilson was being fobbed off with second-rate material, yet one glance at the discography shows this is not so. But, so the reasoning goes, how else did he end up with numbers like 'Eeny Meeny Miney Mo' or 'Yankee Doodle Never Went to Town'? The answer was that these were 'plug' songs and Wilson succumbed to the song pluggers, just like any other band-leader of the period, including the fastest-rising name in music, Benny Goodman, who also recorded these 'second-rate songs' that 'were not number-one plugs' in November 1935, a month *after* Wilson.

In reality, almost all the Wilson–Holiday discography is anything but second-rate songs. Every one was selected by Teddy Wilson himself: 'I always picked them,' he explained. 'We would put in some standards of the day and some brand-new tunes. I was given a stack of new music by Jack Higgins who was the head of this department . . . Each month he'd get a stack of music from all the publishers – all the new music that was published. He'd give me the stack to go through and pick out.'[30]

Wilson recorded a mixture of plug songs and 'covered' other artist's songs, a standard practice of the day based on the hope of cashing in on someone else's success; for example, 'I Wished on the Moon' was recorded by Bing Crosby on Decca, Ray Noble on Victor and Henry 'Red' Allen on Vocalion. Wilson also chose songs that he thought might have hit parade potential as much as numbers that, quite simply, he liked. What he did not know, of course, was which tunes would become hits and which would not. Today, it is the hit songs that are remembered, somewhat simplistically, as 'gems from the golden age of popular music', while the misses are rather uncharitably dismissed as 'the work of Tin Pan Alley hacks'. But it is worth remembering that a 'great' standard, such as 'I Can't Get Started', which Billie recorded in September 1938, did not guarantee a great performance; it was the singer who gave personality to the songs, not the songs that gave personality to the singer.

Little credit has gone to Wilson for his consistently fine taste and integrity in his choice of material. Many of his less well-known choices are often denigrated by critics but actually stand up well today. In fact the Billie Holiday–Teddy Wilson repertoire of these years has provided inspiration and a treasure trove of well-known and not-so-well-known standards for jazz singers to sift through for decades. 'Almost every jazz singer in the world today . . . sings "What a Little Moonlight Can Do",' and Wilson, 'that one we made the first recording of. Another we made the first recording that all singers do is "Easy Living".'[31]

On Sunday, 15 September 1935,[32] Billie opened at the Famous Door on 52nd Street with Teddy Wilson. Wilson had just left the Willie Bryant band and was hired as intermission pianist and to accompany Billie on what was her first job downtown. Her engagement was scheduled to last until 1 November. They shared the bill with a band led by trombonist George Brunis, with Max Kaminsky on trumpet, teenager Joe Bushkin on piano, Pete Peterson on guitar and Harlod Seder on bass. All were part of a package represented by Irving Mills. After playing the first set on the first night, trumpeter Max Kaminsky headed for the washroom. 'A stately young coloured girl in a white evening dress sitting alone in the deserted foyer threw me a half-timid, half-scornful look,' he recalled. 'She told me her name was Billie Holiday and that she was working there too.'[33]

Billie was required to spend her off-stand time sitting in the upstairs foyer because of the non-integrationist policy of the club's management, a musicians' cooperative including Mannie Klein, Jimmy Dorsey and Glenn Miller. But from the very first night it was clear the new bill was not working out. Neither Billie's singing nor Kaminsky's horn-playing related to the flamboyant entertainment the Door's clientele had been used to. It was novelty music that drew the patrons, played by bands like Jerry Colonna, who had preceded them.

Within a week Kaminsky was replaced by Cy Baker and Billie by Arnie Freeman, brother of saxophonist Bud. 'She was taken off the stand . . . after four nights and probably won't be back,' predicted *Downbeat*.[34] Arnie Freeman had been singing with the Floyd Town band in Chicago and was in New York on a visit to see his brother and assess the chances of a career on the Broadway stage.

At short notice the Mills office found Billie an engagement in Montreal, Canada from 29 September to 7 October.[35] On her return she sat in at the Yeah Man Club. 'Gladys "Chickadee" Dorsay, that irresistible songstress of the club, was double-burning last dawning because Mac, in charge of affairs, decided to let Billy Holliday (sic) do a number for the guests,' reported *New York Age*. 'Many people were wondering why "Chickadee" was sore . . . because of jealousy, one or two of the patrons whispered.'[36]

Billie Holiday was back in Harlem. She may have been down, but she was far from out.

Chapter Five

1935–37

Joeseph G. Glaser left Chicago in controversial circumstances in 1933. Although he came from a wealthy, property-owning middle-class Chicago family, he dropped out of polite society and became, as Earl Hines put it, 'a man about town'. His mother owned the Sunset Café at 35th and Calumet, the scene of some of Louis Armstrong's great triumphs in the late 1920s. Although it was leased to Ed Fox and Sam Dreyfus, several musicians confirm that Glaser was involved in booking the bands and musicians who performed there.[1] While Armstrong was resident at the Sunset, Glaser claimed to be the first to bill him as 'The World's Greatest Trumpet Player'.

Glaser was also involved in an automobile agency, probably involved in the fight game, and almost certainly owned a whorehouse. Irresistibly drawn to the characters at the fringes of society, the bootleggers, whores and cheap criminals, he eventually became peripherally involved in organized crime, even affecting the mannerisms of a B-movie hood. A brush with the law in 1933 made it expedient for him to leave town and move to New York. He was down on his luck when Louis Armstrong disembarked from the liner *Champlain* in early 1935 after almost two years in England and Continental Europe, disastrously handled by his manager John Collins.

Soured and weary, Armstrong well remembered the brash Glaser from his Sunset Café days and turned to him to act on his behalf. It was the beginning of an enduring relationship that lasted until Glaser's death in 1969. Glaser quickly bought out Armstrong's contract with the disgraced Collins and set about bringing order to the trumpeter's chaotic financial affairs. During the spring he asked Zilner Randolph to put together a band for a theatre tour with Armstrong in July. Glaser went on the road with them, not only to intercede on Armstrong's behalf, but to get a better understanding of the music business.

In so doing he quickly realized that few whites were prepared to represent black artists and that there was a hole in the market he could plug. Within weeks of taking over Armstrong's affairs he was determined to become the biggest agency representing black talent. What was remarkable was that he almost succeeded. On his return to New York he began renting space in the office of Tommy Rockwell and Francis 'Cork' O'Keefe, band-bookers with whom both he and Armstrong had been associated in the past. And in the autumn of 1935, Glaser approached Jack Kapp of Decca and negotiated a record contract for Armstrong, who by October was cutting his first discs for the label.

Later that month the old Harlem club Connie's Inn was set to re-open downtown on 48th Street between Broadway and Seventh Avenue. Owner Connie Innerman wanted Josephine Baker to 'fill the starring role in the huge extravaganza ... of all-colored talent'[2] called *Stars Over Broadway*. But negotiations fell through with the Mills office, which was booking the acts for the revue, three weeks before opening night. With no headliner, the opening was delayed by two weeks, until 29 October. This enabled Glaser to sell Mills the idea of putting Armstrong into the top spot.

Armstrong was backed by the Luis Russell Orchestra, and among the other artists Mills lined up for the show were Ted Hale, Earl 'Snakehips' Tucker, Sonny Woods and Billie Holiday. They all featured in a Mills office press release announcing the review sent out a week before opening night.[3] For all the artists concerned it represented an important showcase at a prestige downtown venue. Five days after opening night, for example, a big photograph of Billie appeared in *New York Amsterdam News* headed 'Charming Billie Holiday'. Describing her as 'one of the better known torch singers', the *News* said she was called back onstage to take an extra curtain call on opening night.[4]

Yet by the end of November *Amsterdam News* was reporting 'B'way not raving over Billy (sic) Holiday's moanful blues yodelling at Connie's Inn'.[5] Her singing, quiet and undemonstrative, was not really suited to a musical revue, as her handling of her big feature number, 'You Let Me Down', recorded with Teddy Wilson on 3 December, showed. Broadway audiences were used to singers who socked it to them.

By the end of January 1936 Billie had been pulled from the show; a report filed in the 8 February edition of England's *Melody Maker* by Leonard Feather diplomatically says she was 'stricken with ptomaine poisoning' – what we would today call food poisoning – and was 'out of action'. Such reports, according to Feather in 1994,[6] were sent surface mail to England and typically appeared in the press two weeks later. Thus Feather's news round-up would have covered events up to 25 January. Yet by 30 January it was clear that Billie had recovered from the food poisoning, if indeed that was the reason for leaving the show, since she was in the recording studios with Teddy Wilson to record 'Life Begins When You Are in Love'.

Billie was replaced in the show by Bessie Smith at the behest of Nat Nazarro, a performer turned promoter. What the audiences at Connie's Inn heard was a new Smith; gone were the blues and in their place that powerful voice belted out popular songs of the day with a 'modern' swing beat. It was her most prestigious engagement in several years and she made the most of it. She scored a huge hit, attracting such publicity that it enabled the show to go into an extended run. With such interest in her 'comeback', prompted by a series of 'Where's Bessie Smith been all these years' articles in the press, Billie's role in the show was quickly forgotten.

But at least her recordings were beginning to attract interest: 'Billie Holiday, the torch singer ... with Teddy Wilson's band furnishing the music can be heard in the popular frequented "hot spots" [around Harlem]. You should hear the buxom lass go to town with two very fine recordings, namely "Miss Brown to You" and "Painting the Town Red",' said Ted Yates in *New York Amsterdam News*.[7] And when Brunswick released their best-selling singles listings in November and December, it was the Wilson–Holiday sides, along with those by Duke Ellington, that topped the list.[8]

Despite being unceremoniously bumped from 52nd Street's Famous Door the previous autumn, Billie was invited back by Eddie Condon to appear at the club's regular Sunday afternoon jam sessions that began during the February and March of 1936. Billie enjoyed Condon's company. He was a raconteur, *bon vivant* and wit, and his sessions brought a new meaning to the word bacchanalian, his guitar-playing less important than the good-time ambiance his personality projected. Musicians still spoke of the occasion a couple of years earlier when a musician turned up to play a one-night stand with Condon and returned to his wife six months later. He had got dead drunk after the gig, but unknown to him, the next day the band was booked to play a liner on a round trip to South America, and by the time he sobered up they had long left port. Billie loved the Condon gang and they loved and respected her, as much for her singing as her drinking.

For the Famous Door gig, Condon co-led a band with Red McKenzie. Included in the line-up was the trumpet player Bunny Berigan, who while at the Famous Door began featuring 'I Can't Get Started'. Berigan was also a regular at the Sunday jam sessions where Billie got to respect his great ability. 'It was absolutely unreal,' said Joe Bushkin, then Condon's pianist, 'Sunday afternoon jam sessions – Fats

Waller, Bessie Smith … people like Billie Holiday, Roy Eldridge. Imagine what went on!'[9]

At the beginning of March Billie auditioned, along with Teddy Wilson, for some engagements in Europe,[10] but declined an offer of £50 a week, claiming she was worried that British musicians could not swing.[11] However, if the real reason was that she was hoping to reclaim her spot in *Stars Over Broadway*, she was to be disappointed. At the end of the month the press announced, 'Bessie Smith has been held over again at Connie's.'[12]

To keep Billie working, the Mills office sent her out as 'an added attraction' with the Jimmie Lunceford Orchestra, another of the important black big bands with whom Irving Mills was involved, for short series of theatre dates.[13] While she was out of town she missed a recording session with Teddy Wilson on 17 March and was replaced by Ella Fitzgerald. It is interesting to note how Ella had been listening to Billie; she copies her characteristic vocal inflections on her entry to 'All My Life' and on the tenth bar of the second chorus of 'Melancholy Baby'.

When Armstrong abruptly pulled out of *Stars Over Broadway*, the show's days were numbered. His affair with an 'ofay corine' had ended in tragedy when she jumped out of a fifteenth-storey window.[14] With the girl's mother threatening adverse publicity, Glaser immediately sent his major client out on the road. When Billie returned to claim her spot in the show at the end of April it had just three weeks to run. During those last weeks she began dating dancer Chink Collins and hanging out at a new night-spot popular with the theatrical crowd called the Brown Derby which had opened in May at West 126th Street and Lenox Avenue. On Sunday, 14 June 1936 Billie and Collins held a joint party there to announce their intention to marry. But within weeks their affair had blown over.

Sadie, who for the greater part of Billie's formative years had abandoned her to the care of others, had now become intensely protective of her daughter. Embittered by her own experiences with men, she constantly presented herself to Billie as living proof of their fecklessness. She had come to rely on her daughter for friendship as much as financial support and was now scared to lose her to 'some no-good man'. Besides, she had come to live her life vicariously through her daughter; the excitement and romance of show-biz with all the personalities and stars with whom Billie rubbed shoulders could not have been in greater contrast to the bleakness of her own life.

Meanwhile, Joe Glaser had begun signing a number of black performers to exclusive management contracts and he approached Billie with a promise of work with the Fletcher Henderson Orchestra for $250 a week. This was big money, and Henderson was widely recognized as the top black bandleader of the day. Billie rashly turned her back on the Mills office and signed with Glaser. She joined Henderson at the end of June at the Grand Terrace Ballroom at 3955 South Parkway in Oakwood, Chicago: 'Billie Holiday, the plumpish songstress who has recorded with Benny Goodman . . . is a perfect fit for Fletcher Henderson's torrid tunes at the Grand Terrace Café. She can sing,' reported the Baltimore *Afro-American*.[15]

She was soon heard broadcasting with Henderson on Radio WJZ, relayed live nightly to New York at 12.30 a.m., 'Whee!! but does that Fletcher Henderson set a torrid pace? I'll say he does but you can't help but go for Billie Holiday's songs,' said *New York Age*.[16] However, Ed Fox, the Grand Terrace owner, did not share such enthusiasm for Billie's singing. An overbearing character, he dominated Fletcher Henderson to the extent of picking his tunes and dictating the way he should play them, and he even fired Henderson's male vocalist Teddy Lewis in an abusive tirade in front of a group of startled onlookers shortly before Billie joined. Needless to say, when Billie arrived from New York she was next in the firing line. 'They run me out of Chicago,' she said in the 1950s. 'Ed Fox . . . he say, "What the hell . . . you stink my goddam show up! Everybody says you sing too slow. Get out!"'[17]

Within days Billie found herself back on the train to New York. 'Babe Mathews is slated for the Grand Terrace . . . Billie Holiday must have been a fizzle?' inquired the *Pittsburgh Courier* somewhat wryly.[18] (In fact Mathews did not stay long with Henderson either, being replaced in November by Arthur Lee Simpkins.) Back in the Big Apple, Billie was called for a recording session on Tuesday 30 June with Teddy Wilson.

'I got the call for that session,' recalled guitarist Lawrence Lucie, '"These Foolish Things" and "Reaching for the Moon", I remember playing from the piano lead sheet; get the chords, go ahead and record it. That particular session was ad lib, no arrangements, there's a feeling on there that's spontaneous.'[19] The distinctive sound of Johnny Hodges on alto immediately imports a distinct Ellingtonian hue and suggests a pathos and emotional depth that are not really sustained during Billie's vocals on 'It's Like Reaching for the Moon' and 'These Foolish Things'.

Here her phrasing is rather broad, and she uses an uncharacteristic vibrato that is not entirely successful, suggesting she is having trouble 'customizing' the song within the parameters of her quite specific style. Typically, Billie used vibrato very sparingly, if at all, and then usually only for dramatic emphasis at the termination of a sustained note. Her style was still maturing in 1936 and the general use of vibrato here seems to have been just a flirtation. Brief rehearsal time might have been the reason for her uncomfortable handling of 'These Foolish Things' where she approaches, somewhat uneasily, the top of her range during the first eight bars. Thinking on her feet, she makes sure she avoids reaching that high again in the subsequent A sections of the song.

On 'Reaching for the Moon', Harry Carney's noodling clarinet obbligato is industrious to the point of distraction but 'I Cried for You' and 'Guess Who' emerge as distinctive performances where Billie peels the words away from the groundbeat with often outrageous syncopations. Her vocal on the former is preceded by a four-bar modulation by Teddy Wilson who takes the key down a minor third to suit her range. Her economical entry avoids the jump of a fifth between 'I' and 'Cried', but handles the octave jump from 'For' down to 'You' with great confidence and perfect intonation. It sets the scene for an important performance which helped establish her reputation in musicians' circles at the time; her handling of the middle eight is particularly impressive, a testament to her growing confidence and ability.

With her recordings for Teddy Wilson seldom dropping out of Brunswick's listing of best-sellers, Billie was offered a contract in her own right with Brunswick's subsidiary, Vocalion. Here, recordings by 'Billie Holiday and her Orchestra' came under the control of Bernie Hanighen, one of her early admirers, who at the beginning of 1936 had been appointed a recording supervisor by the American Record Corporation for their subsidiaries Brunswick, Columbia and Vocalion.

Hanighen was also a regular at the Sunday Famous Door jam sessions and, like Billie, was well aware of what a central figure Bunny Berigan was to their success. For their first session together on 10 July, he asked the trumpeter to line up a band to back Billie. Berigan's first call was to Artie Shaw, who played in his 18 Club Swing Gang; next, since, he had recently completed a session with guitarist Dick McDonough, he returned the favour, and along with Condon's regular pianist Joe Bushkin, Red Norvo's bassist Pete Peterson and drummer Cozy Cole, an inveterate sitter-in at the Condon sessions, the group was complete.

'It was hot and the Vocalion studio didn't have any air conditioning,' recalled Joe Bushkin. 'I remember being so intrigued by Billie. If I looked past her, I had a view of Cozy sitting there and sweat was just pouring off this man . . . It was that hot, but we got through those sides and they sure don't sound like we were suffering!'[20] Throughout Billie's vocals have great assurance, but Berigan's elegant lines are not quite matched by Shaw, whose playing was yet to enjoy the astonishing transformation it underwent by 1938–9. The trumpet and clarinet combination, not balanced by a saxophone, does have a tendency to sound shrill, particularly on 'Did I Remember?' and 'No Regrets', but their extraordinary rhythmic vitality more than compensates.

On 'Summertime' only Billie and Berigan truly seem to sense the song's great potential as a mood piece; both Cole and Shaw tend to be somewhat overbearing. But it is on 'Billie's Blues' that she creates one of her all-time classics. In the second chorus she leans into a crotchet–triplet feel that makes the number take flight. Her worldly-wise delivery has the effect of making Shaw sound naive, but Berigan matches her for intensity, *gravitas* and invention. Although the words are all but public domain blues lyrics, telling of her loving her man but being done wrong by him, Billie invests them with a powerful realism. Six months later Artie Shaw said it was one of his favourite recordings.[21]

The following day Billie was again in the studios, this time for her first appearance on the *Saturday Night Swing Club* broadcast on radio WABC from 8 to 8.30 p.m. It was a bold step by CBS to present an unsponsored half-hour of pure jazz and today the programmes are regarded as the most influential and venturesome jazz radio shows of all time. Berigan emerged as a key figure in these broadcasts, aired every Saturday night until 1939. But Billie was not destined to become the show's regular vocalist. Four weeks later Lee Wiley, Berigan's mistress, landed the job.

Billie returned downtown on 2 September where John Hammond had managed to book her into the Onyx at 72 52nd Street, a one-room club at street level, decorated in bands of colour from silvery grey to black that reached from ceiling to floor. The previous month owner Joe Helbock had extended violinist Stuff Smith's contract for six months because of the phenomenal business he was attracting, and Billie was booked to sing the intermissions. After her first week, Billie and Smith had a falling out. As a result, Smith refused to let her sing encores and told Helbock that he wanted her out.

Thirty years later in 1966[22] Helbock said that he had been so mad that he seriously thought of firing the violinist, but could not ignore the business he was bringing into the club. Billie had to go. He said he still got a thrill when he recalled her version of 'What You Gonna Do When There Ain't No Swing?' which she featured at his club. In the 1940s Billie would put in more than a year at the Onyx, but by then it was under different management and in a later era.[23]

Billie was still performing at the Famous Door's Sunday jam sessions, however, and for her second recording date under her own name in

September, she and Hanighen again went with the Famous Door crowd to provide her accompaniment. There were a couple of changes, though, most notably Irving Fazola in for Shaw, who was now in the midst of forming his own big band.

It is immediately noticeable that Fazola achieves a far better blend with Berigan than Shaw, simply by largely remaining in the deep chalumeau register of his instrument. Gone is the predominantly treble effect of the July date; here Berigan and Fazola unite to frame the singer, in contrast to Shaw's flaunting of his instrumental virility. Even their solos appear more as logical extensions of the ensembles rather than the somewhat autonomous quality that Shaw, and to be fair, many others, achieved.

Perhaps the most interesting song is 'One, Two, Button Your Shoe', which illustrates how powerfully Billie could swing a number when she was in the mood. From the jive introduction, both she and the band generate an infectious swing that is epitomized by Billie's out chorus, pared to the absolute minimum of notes and phrased in such a way that it seems to swing the band.

In October she was reunited with Teddy Wilson in the recording studios for three numbers. Wilson brought with him three Goodman sidemen, including tenorman Vido Musso, who played clarinet on the session and promptly botched the intro of 'The Way You Look Tonight'. However, the introduction on 'Easy to Love' is fielded by the secure playing of Jonah Jones, followed by Ben Webster on tenor. Although Billie employs uncharacteristic vibrato and returns to a 'broader' style of singing, Bessie Smith's note economies are immediately apparent as she changes the opening phrase from a C and an F to two Cs. However, her *allargando* style contrasts here with her tight, swinging approach on 'With Thee I Swing', which has just the slightest hint of terminal vibrato. As an aside, it is interesting to note the influence of Johnny Hodges on Ben Webster's playing which is most apparent on this number.

After her unsuccessful engagement at the Onyx, Billie returned uptown to join a new band being formed by trumpeter Louie Metcalf at the Renaissance Casino at West 138th Street and Seventh Avenue. Metcalf, just returned from a spell in Chicago, had put together a fascinating personnel: Oran 'Hot Lips' Page, trumpet; Lester Young, Rudy Powell, Happy Caldwell, reeds; Jonas Walker, trombone; an unknown pianist; Billy Taylor, bass; Clarence Holiday, guitar; and Alfred Taylor, drums. Along with Billie was vocalist Orlando Robeson and the dancer was Earl 'Snakehips' Tucker.[24]

Quite apart from being the only known occasion Clarence and Billie

Holiday actually worked together, the formation of the band was of particular interest for the appearance of Lester Young, who had just attended his father's funeral on the West Coast. Due to the insecure working conditions in Kansas City with the Count Basie band, who were preparing to go on the road, he put in a month with Metcalf in New York. Young was doubtless recommended by 'Hot Lips' Page, who would not have omitted to point out the presence of Billie Holiday; Young had an immensely high opinion of her after getting to know her in 1934, and she would have been the reason for his journeying to New York.

Young only played with Metcalf during October, since he had to leave for Chicago to rejoin Count Basie during the first week of November. According to the *New York Amsterdam News*, Metcalf's band was at the Renaissance from 4 October, but also played the 'Grand opening of the Bedford Ballroom, 1153 Atlantic Avenue, Brooklyn, NY' and appeared there on subsequent Sundays. Here, Billie was featured along with Valda Hatten, Orlando Robeson and Ethel Fray.[25]

Billie was fortunate to step into a job so quickly after being ousted from the Onyx. At the time the Harlem night-spots were being hit by a new low in attendances. Only the 101 Ranch, Small's Paradise, the Ubangi and Dicky Wells' seemed unaffected. Clubs had begun cutting back on entertainment. Even so, the money with Metcalf was not great, and in November Billie was spotted arguing over a fare with a cab driver at 144th Street and Seventh Avenue, a reflection of how hard times had become.[26] But at least the recording sessions continued; she was in the studios with Wilson on 28 October, albeit for just one number, with him again on 19 November, and under her own name on 12 January 1937.

Of the three dates, the 19 November session is perhaps the most memorable. 'Pennies from Heaven', with its rhythmic displacements and unexpected melodic shifts, has an excellent Goodman obbligato, while 'I Can't Give You Anything But Love' explains more plainly than any number Billie had recorded to date why Teddy Wilson thought she was an Armstrong imitator. Here she captures the essence of Armstrong's vocal on the March 1929 OKeh recording: his almost surreal entry, his complete rewrite of the melody, his mischievous humour and his huge rhythmic displacements.

When 'Billie Holiday and her Orchestra' assembled in the recording studios on 12 January 1937, it was to be the last date under Bernie Hanighen's supervision. He was about to move to the West Coast to take up an appointment within the musical division of Warner's where he would compose 'Bob White (Whatcha Gonna Do Tonight)', 'The

Week-end of a Private Secretary', and go on to contribute songs for the Fred Astaire motion picture, *Second Chorus*.[27]

Billie does not sound emotionally engaged by 'One Never Knows – Does One?', singing with an Ella Fitzgerald-like concern for melody and a rather uneasy handling of the words 'and then', but even so she reduces the middle eight to just five notes. 'I've Got My Love to Keep Me Warm' is negotiated far more securely, notwithstanding the high word-count, so relies more on direct expression than harmonic or rhythmic ingenuity, the warmth of her voice contrasting with the chill of the winter-inspired lyrics.

Unknown to Billie, however, just four days earlier in Chicago Mildred Bailey recorded the same number with Red Norvo's immaculate midband. In the event it is Bailey's version that impresses most; not only does she swing more convincingly, she sounds far more secure both rhythmically and harmonically, her exceptional execution syncopating some words with casual, almost disarming charm. Billie is far more convincing on 'If My Heart Could Only Talk' and 'Please Keep Me in Your Dreams' where she floats free of the undertow of the groundbeat and puts together two poised, intelligently phrased cameos of her art. After the session, Hanighen and the musicians went uptown to party. With Hanighen's departure, it would now be Morty Palitz who would produce the sides under Billie's name for the American Recording Company, or Columbia, as it would shortly become.[28]

On 7 November 1936 the Count Basie Orchestra, fresh out of Kansas City, opened at the Grand Terrace Ballroom in Chicago. They drew some cautious reviews; the *Pittsburgh Courier* liked the band better than Fletcher Henderson's, which it had just replaced, while the *Chicago Defender* claimed Basie was doing a 'great job' filling the 'hot seats of its predecessors'. Ed Fox wanted Basie out, but the band's booking agents, the Music Corporation of America (MCA), controlled the radio wire over which the band broadcast and insisted it stay. In New York, *Metronome*'s George T. Simon heard the broadcasts and was not impressed: 'The sax section is invariably out of tune, and if you think the sax section is out of tune, catch the brass!'[29]

At the beginning of December the job at the Grand Terrace ended and the band began a tour that wound its way into New York, where they arrived at the end of the month. On Christmas Eve 1936 they opened at the Roseland Ballroom at 1658 Broadway at 51st Street. John Hammond, who had been instrumental in plucking the band from the obscurity of Kansas City's Reno Club, had recommended Basie to Willard Alexander of MCA, the booking office that represented Benny

Goodman. But after a shaky Roseland debut night Hammond demanded Basie make a few changes to his personnel. 'We got screwed up on the ending of "King Porter Stomp" and the band sounded like a cat fight at the end of the number,' said Buck Clayton, Basie's star trumpet player. 'John Hammond was so upset that he almost pulled his crew-cut out.'[30]

Not surprisingly, the initial reaction to Basie's band was lukewarm; by the end of January he was described as 'practically buried at the Roseland Ballroom through lack of publicity'.[31] But it was not the star-studded outfit it would soon become. While certain key players like Lester Young, Buck Clayton, saxist Herschel Evans, bassist Walter Page and drummer Jo Jones were in place, the line-up also included several soon-to-be-replaced musicians such as Joe Keyes, Claude Williams, Caughey Roberts and George Hunt.

When the band arrived in Harlem, many of them, Young included, moved into the Theresa Hotel. Young quickly re-established contact with Billie and was soon invited back by her and her mother to their rooms at 9 West 99th Street, where Sadie was running a restaurant downstairs. At this time, Billie was working at Monroe's Uptown House. Run by Clark Monroe, it had no liquor licence so was forced to compete with other clubs by providing good food, service and entertainment. Besides Billie, who was backed by Charlie Drayton on bass and a Kansas City pianist, Vivian Smith, there was an energetic young MC with a very hip line of patter.

On 25 January 1937 Billie entered the studio again, this time with a Teddy Wilson group. With Basie's band fresh in town, Hammond was keen to use some of its key personnel and brought in Lester Young, tenor sax; Buck Clayton, trumpet; Walter Page, bass; and Jo Jones on drums. Benny Goodman, who along with Hammond was among the first to rave over Basie's broadcasts from the Reno Club on Radio W9XBY out of Kansas City, filled out the front line on clarinet.

As many have noted, there was electricity in the air that day as Billie and Lester Young, one of the greatest partnerships in the whole of jazz, made their debut together on wax. It was also the first meeting of guitarist Freddie Green with Walter Page and Jo Jones, destined to become three-quarters of the 'All American Rhythm Section'.

It was the most musically intimate of all Billie's sessions to date, the optimum environment for her great talent and those of the soloists who surrounded her. Gone was the rhetorical bombast of a Jonah Jones or the exuberance of a Roy Eldridge; now Billie was supported by musicians who were acutely aware of what she was trying to achieve and were uniquely qualified to help her realize it. Goodman, Young and Clayton, accustomed to the grander gestures required in big band solo work, would revel in the atmosphere of free exchange in Wilson's relaxed musical democracy.

The opening chorus of 'He Ain't Got Rhythm' is a perfect example of the wealth of counterpoint and elegance to be found throughout the session. After Wilson's introduction, Goodman states the melody against the pianist's suave counterpoint, reflecting their growing musical empathy, and when Lester Young floats in with one of his most cunningly wrought solos, the picture is framed.

'This Year's Kisses', with its unusual structure (the first phrase is elided from eight to six bars), is handled with great *élan* by Young, whose melody chorus is a masterpiece of symmetry. But it was not only with Billie that he shared such great affinity; Wilson's calm yet empassioned demeanour meshed well with Young's. On 'Why Was I Born?' Billie touches base with Helen Morgan's musical vulnerability, and although Young is next to inaudible here, Clayton contributes a solo that suggests he has never been given credit for the true original he was.

Of the four numbers that went down that day, perhaps the most memorable was 'I Must Have That Man'. Here Billie and her accompanists achieve a unity of emotional expression quite new in jazz up to that moment – even Armstrong, whose own free-wheeling ensembles had changed the course of jazz in the 1920s, had never recorded with a band of equals like this. Their whole performance was a model of cooperation rather than competition; Goodman, with technique and passion to spare, remained understated, careful not to disturb the emotional balance of the moment. It was highly appropriate he should be present; Billie had made her recording debut with him, he was there when she began her association on record with Teddy Wilson, and here he was again as her great talent finally bloomed, surrounded by the finest jazz musicians of the age.

It was not long after the 25 January session that Basie took up Hammond's suggestion and replaced Claude Williams with Freddie Green. Hammond also passed a few of Billie's recordings on to Basie, urging him to sign her as well. Basie remained ambivalent; he already had the powerful Jimmy Rushing handling vocals and was reluctant to increase his wage-roll with another singer. Hammond persisted throughout February and finally persuaded Basie to accompany him to Monroe's Uptown House to hear Billie. Basie was impressed, but still wanted time to think about it. The band were about to leave for a week in Philadelphia and he told Hammond he would audition her there.

Prior to her audition, Billie was again in the recording studios with Teddy Wilson on 18 February. Trumpeter Henry 'Red' Allen's no-nonsense approach to taking care of business seems to concentrate Billie's mind, providing an extravagant foil for her inherently subjective style. It is interesting that Billie got to record 'You Showed Me the Way', written by Ella Fitzgerald, Teddy McRae, Bud Green and Chick Webb, over a month before Ella got her version on to wax. In the event, Ella's version takes as many harmonic and rhythmic liberties with the song as Billie's – both latch on to the crotchet triplets that spell out the song's title with ease – and throughout Ella is bright, shining and musically beyond reproach. She seems to suggest she has just been shown the way to fix her make-up.

Billie's version is slower, with the timbre of her voice importing an additional subjective dimension; the song is transformed into the spiritual yearning of a young woman for someone who first revealed to her the subtleties and pleasure of sexual interaction. Yet in contrast, when she sang the final number of the session, '(This is) My Last Affair', she shows an Ella-like concern for the musical characteristics of the song rather than revealing the emotional possibilities of its libretto. Here the number begins near the top of her range and descends to almost the bottom in the release, which she handles with aplomb.

At 4.30 a.m. on 23 February 1937 Clarence Holiday died of 'influenzal pneumonia' at the St Paul Sanitarium in Dallas. He was touring with the Don Redman Orchestra. While he and Billie had not been close – he once complained that she used every guitar player in New York on her sessions except him – when word reached her of his death she was shocked. There were more shocks in store at the funeral: Clarence's mistress turned up with two illegitimate children and Sadie lost her way to the church, making a distraught appearance at the very end of the service.

Shortly afterwards, Billie travelled down to Philadelphia for her audition with Count Basie. By coincidence, trumpeter Ed Lewis had also been asked to audition, and he too made the trip to Philadelphia. Both travelled down the same day and on the same train to see Basie, whose engagement at the Chatterbox in the William Penn Hotel between 1 and 12 February was the first for a black band. It was only when Lewis saw Billie in Basie's hotel foyer and recognized her from the train that he introduced himself, guessing they were both there for the same purpose. They wished each other luck and each auditioned in turn in Basie's hotel room.[32] Both got the job and both joined the band on 13 March 1937 at Energetic Park, Scranton, Pennsylvania, about 125 miles from New York. 'Basie has two of the best vocalists extant,' wrote Stanley Dance, reviewing the date. 'Billie Holiday joined him on that memorable night at Scranton and he already has James Rushing. Basie is extremely fortunate.'[33]

It did not take long for most of the Basie band to feel that way about Billie too. But although she got on with most of them, she could never hit it off with tenor saxophonist Herschel Evans, who neither smoked nor drank. Instead, she was to be seen almost constantly in the company of Lester Young and Buck Clayton, the 'Unholy Three', as they liked to call themselves.

On 15 March the Basie band plus Billie appeared at the Apollo for a week. She was not advertised in advance, but she stole the show, 'Billie Halliday [sic] raised the roof at the Apollo Theater last week as did Count Basie's ork,' raved *New York Amsterdam News*.[34] Later, Basie recalled: 'Billie Holiday sure was a great help to us on that programme . . . [she was] the sensation of the show.'[35] Billie's choice of numbers was particularly interesting: 'I Cried for You', '(This Is) My Last Affair', 'One Never Knows – Does One?' and 'Them There Eyes' were all songs associated with her through her Brunswick and Vocalion recordings. This was most unusual; singers were usually required to project a specific identity that related to the band. Here Billie was projecting Billie Holiday.

It is clear that Billie was allowed a degree of autonomy with Basie far beyond that customarily associated with a big band vocalist; it was such that she was able to preserve her own identity as a singer within the Basie band set-up. Even though she sang 'Swing, Brother, Swing' and a Buck Clayton arrangement of 'I Can't Get Started', these numbers were at her discretion. Equally significantly, the theme of unrequited love, which had her labelled as a torch singer, predominated in her artistic choices – 'I Cried for You', '(This Is) My Last Affair', 'One Never Knows'. Even within a big band with a very specific musical personality, Billie refused to relinquish control of the character part she had created for herself.

On 11 May 1937 Billie again returned to the studio with a pick-up group including Lester Young. Their continuing association on record during Billie's Columbia period lasted until 21 March 1941 and left one of the most important recorded legacies in the history not only of jazz, but also of twentieth-century music. Taken together chronologically, as they are here, it is difficult to believe that one woman's voice could be so exciting and inventive and that a tenor saxophonist could reach such a level of sympathetic and sophisticated interaction with it.

Lester Young was one of the finest instrumentalists jazz has ever known. His playing on these sides shows why. At the time he was the most concise and smoothly swinging soloist around. Although his solos did not have the complexity of Coleman Hawkins, his melodic ideas were certainly the equal of Hawkins, indeed they were often more sophisticated. His playing implied new and additional chords that even in 1937 were pointing to the harmonic complexities of bop. It was no fluke that Charlie Parker, the prime mover in introducing the new music, modelled his style on Young's.

Listening to Young's solos with Billie, one is immediately struck by their restraint, one of the hallmarks of his style. He always sounded unhurried and there is never the crowded feeling of gratuitous virtuosity in his work. He seemed unhindered by cadence points, turnarounds and bridges within a sequence of chords; like the solution to a vast musical acrostic, the organization, logic and balance of his musical ideas always seemed to present the perfect answer to such problems. His solos always seemed conceived as a whole, minor architechtonic miracles where nothing could be added or subtracted without destroying the symmetry of the whole.

At the time of these recordings, Young was a member of the Count Basie band where he played big band arrangements based on less than half a dozen basic chord structures, mainly blues and 'I Got Rhythm' contrafacts, which were played in standard keys. Add to that the brevity of solo opportunity within a large ensemble and limitations for a player of Young's enormous talent are clearly apparent. However, performing with Billie, Young now had greater solo space and the opportunity to address challenging chord structures in a variety of keys and to develop variation within his solos to an extent that was impossible with Basie.

In addition, the emotional climate in Billie's little backing groups was quite different to Basie's big band, allowing Young to access far more facets of his style. Not least was the opportunity of spontaneous interaction with his fellow musicians in general and Billie in particular, who often ended up in some strange keys. Young took full advantage of this to look at songs in a new light, pursuing ideas in unexpected directions. 'Me, Myself and I' from the 15 June 1937 session, for example, is in the unwieldy key of D major, a key which, rather appropriately, classical composers associate with vigour and clarity of expression.

From the 11 May session came 'I'll Get By', perhaps the most economical of all Billie's vocals, essentially based on only six notes, with just two forays to the bottom of her range. At one point she sings no fewer than twenty-six repeated As, which depend for their impact on her remarkable rhythmic freedom within form. And it is worth noting that the form here is by no means straightforward. It is a twenty-eight-bar rather than thirty-two-bar song, with an ABAC structure where the B and C sections are six bars instead of the usual eight. But even within the A sections there is an attractive lack of symmetry in the melodic line which made this a difficult vehicle for improvisation.

Take 1 of 'Mean to Me' that followed is one of Young's great tributes to Louis Armstrong, who made at least as big an impact on him as the more commonly cited influences of Bix Beiderbecke and Frankie Trambauer. When Billie sings the lyrics 'I don't know why' at the end of her first eight bars, it is like a jolt of electricity, as is her phrasing of 'Can't you see?'. The way she subsequently sings these phrases on take 2 shows how both singer and saxophonist warmed up as the date progressed. Indeed, the first two numbers that went down that day, 'Sun Showers' and 'Yours and Mine', sound much like the 'Chatterbox' Young, the way he played on the Basie airchecks of 'Moten Swing', 'Tattersfield Stomp' and a few others. Here the tone is thicker, the articulation heavier and the virtuosity less masked, which may have been how he sounded in the Henderson band.

'Foolin' Myself' has Young really singing, again full of Armstrong, as Wilson is similarly playing off Hines. This is one of the great dates for Wilson, especially in his fills behind Billie and the front line. Her vocal on 'Easy Living' sounds as if she had been honing the song to perfection for years. 'I'll Never Be the Same' has an imperious opening chorus from Wilson and the first fully realized duet between singer and tenor saxophonist. Young's counterpoint points to Armstrong, in content as much as feeling; that 'beautiful feeling' Billie discovered as a teenager in Armstrong's records.

'Me, Myself and I' is one of the great classics of the Billie Holiday–Lester Young collaborations, a feeling sustained through both available takes. Part of the magic is in their duets, in that they go beyond mere accompaniment into the realms of pure counterpoint – who can say which of the two lines predominates? This was something that was perhaps born on Count Basie's bandstand with Young's treatment of the middle eight in 'I Can't Get Started'. Over the years there has been some confusion over the identification of the two takes of 'MM&I'; take 1 ends on the tonic; take 2 on the dominant.

'Sailboat in the Moonlight' picks right up where 'MM&I' left off. Billie and Lester Young drift further into their special musical universe during the first chorus, a universe where they effortlessly play off each other, as in Young's anticipation of Billie's melody phrasing just before she sings 'what a perfect setting'. Equally, Billie's reaction to Young's overtone high F-sharp, almost like a squeak of delight halfway through the last bridge, is to respond with such powerful swing, sitting right on top of the beat, that it seems to capture the very essence of 'jazz'.

'Sailboat in the Moonlight', 'Born to Love' (with, for Billie, a rare exposition of the verse) and both takes of 'Without Your Love' suggest the highpoint of their creativity together. The key element is their interplay; 'Without Your Love', for example, seems more a duet with Young underlined by a casual background phrase of his that actually flowers in the last chorus into a formal figure adopted by the whole ensemble.

Many of these sessions include the Basie rhythm team of Freddie Green, Walter Page and Jo Jones and much has been written about the 'even four' they came to personify within the context of the Count Basie big band. However, with Billie, even from their very first date together, Walter Page frequently played *alla breve*, or cut-time, behind her vocals, which seemed to give her a greater degree of improvisational freedom. Later in her career, when musical fashion dictated an even four from all members of the rhythm section, her use of syncopation is significantly less than it was against 2/4. In fact, most of her finest recordings of the Columbia period (1935–42) are a contrast of 2/4 and 4/4; 'Without Your Love', for example, is 2/4 behind Billie *and* Sherman's piano, with only Buck Clayton riding on an even four.

Billie's strong, assured singing coincides with her tenure as a vocalist in Count Basie's band, and there is no doubt that this helped her to become remarkably focused in her singing; her projection on 'Getting Some Fun Out of Life' must surely have been the result of singing night after night with a big band swinging behind her. 'Who Wants Love?' brings back a Young obbligato, though slightly more off-mike than usual. Claude Thornhill's piano is stunningly abstract for the time, but the highlight comes with Billie's re-entry where she and Young imitate each other's phrasing.

'Travellin' All Alone' was one of Ethel Waters's early records and a number that Billie had been using for some years by the time she recorded it here; perhaps it is the fact that the record is in an 'even four' throughout – a rarity – that makes its 2 minutes 12 seconds seem to pass so quickly. 'He's Funny That Way' is another melodic masterpiece, an AABAC form with Thornhill's 'chime' chords inspiring and propelling Young through the introduction; in a 1946 live performance of the song, there is a magical moment where both Billie and Young hook on to the scaler ascent in the bridge and 'climb the ladder' together.

'When You're Smiling' has a 'straight' reading of the melody from Benny Morton's trombone, which serves to highlight just how sophisticated were the rhythmic and harmonic alterations Billie introduces during her vocal. When Young steps forward to take his solo after Wilson's piano, he is at nothing less than the peak of his powers (on both takes). In fact, both he and Wilson loved Armstrong and Beiderbecke and both play with great cohesion, elaborating here on the amalgam of both influences.

However, on 'I Can't Believe You're in Love with Me' it is Wilson, not Young, who duets behind Billie, and suddenly the interplay between voice and saxophone is conspicuous by its absence. The jam-out chorus is quaint, but inappropriate here. It is a shame that the dramatic and arresting introduction to 'If Dreams Come True' could not have been developed further; however, this January 1938 session seems to be moving away from the high plateau achieved in the summer of 1937.

Since the matrix numbers between the 6 January 1938 session and the one that follows are only thirty apart, the next session is probably not 27 January, as given in some discographies, but the 12th. 'Now They Call It Swing' is a classic (both takes). The structure is unusual: A (8 bars), A (8 bars), B (8 bars) and A (8 bars plus 4 bars); what is particularly arresting is the unexpected modulation before the bridge (B section), moving up a major third, as in songs like 'Too Marvelous for Words' and 'Raincheck'. Billie's mispronunciation of 'modern' adds great charm in a laid-back, free-and-easy vocal, while Young contributes a perfectly structured, Bix-like solo that incorporates triad climbing to great effect.

Both takes of 'Back in Your Own Backyard' begin with a commanding fanfare from Buck Clayton; the faster take 1 seems far more focused than the second, which slows down noticeably after the introduction. However, Billie's out-and-out jazz phrasing is very 'instrumental' in both concept and execution, while Young's finely focused, almost zen-like solo on take 2 palls in comparison with his lucid ideas on the previous take.

It is hard to realize that when Billie and Lester Young met in the recording studios on 15 September 1938 it would be the last of the intimate sessions with the Basie-ites and the penultimate session where they shared musical confidences. 'The Very Thought of You' is a drastic recasting of Ray Noble's tune, with Clayton taking solo honours this time. Young's clarinet is almost ethereal; it is fascinating to compare his tone here with his playing on the Kansas City Six sides on the Commodore label. Surely the full, round sound that attracts the listener on his Columbia work cannot be too dissimilar to the effect a snake-charmer has on his charge.

Although 'I Can't Get Started' has an intriguingly abstract Young solo on take 1, the general direction of Billie's recording dates in 1938 was heading for less interaction between Young and Billie, although

'I've Got a Date with a Dream' has remnants of pre-1938 Billie and another of those brief, pungent, melody clarinet solos from Young. 'You Can't Be Mine' is very short and could have taken a thirty-two-bar solo from Young; both singer and saxophonist sound 'relaxed' on the tune, done at the end of a session.

The 31 October and 9 November dates have a larger ensemble sound, but Billie is not in the least intimidated. They are perhaps the most animated of the Columbia sessions, and come closest to Holiday-as-Swing-Era-chirp taking choruses with a 'big band', something we hear her do only five times during this period: three airchecks with Basie, one with Goodman and just one side with Artie Shaw. The arrangements are by Benny Carter and illustrate his ability to provide a vocalist with tasteful accompaniment which is unobtrusive without being bland. A good example of this is his reed figures behind Billie's vocal on 'They Say' which, while cushioning her, do not detract from the lyrics. Interestingly, this number was also recorded by Mildred Bailey and Ethel Waters in 1938. Carter also gets in some excellent solos, while Harry James on lead trumpet swings the ensemble with great authority.

In contrast, Billie's 13 December 1939 session sounds somewhat dreary. 'Night and Day' has a complicated form, its ABA^{1}BCB^1 spread over a somewhat tortuous sixty-four bars, and at the slower tempo Billie uses, it seems to unravel for ever. However, 'The Man I Love', with its modified AA^{1}BA^1, structure is the first recording of a song she returned to throughout her career, a song of yearning that would assume more and more subjective meaning as the years passed. Billie would have had no opportunity of hearing Louis Armstrong's Decca version of 'You're Just a No Account' before she cut her own, since he recorded his version five days later, but even so comparison of the two is interesting since she learnt so much from Satchmo.

Far better is her next date with Young on 7 June 1940, bolstered by the presence of Roy Eldridge, where her singing is more animated, as the construction of her line on 'Time on My Hands' reveals. 'Laughin' at Life' is reminiscent of her approach on 'When You're Smiling', while 'I'm Pulling Through' and 'Tell Me More' see her again disconnecting the lyrics from the rhythm and making them float along somewhere behind the beat.

On their final Columbia session together, Young is given only two brief solos on the sides selected for release. However, it was only the arbitrary limits of the ten-inch 78-rpm record that prevented the magical, longer, 3:58 take 3 of 'All of Me' from seeing the light of day. Here Billie Holiday and Lester Young are captured at the zenith of their abilities, with Young taking sixteen bars after Billie's vocal, Heywood eight bars and Young returning for eight to lead back into Billie's final chorus.

The way Billie and Lester Young phrased had now taken on a weight and deliberation of pure beauty that neither seemed ever to recapture. Pianist Eddie Heywood said afterwards that he was mesmerized by their performances on this number; indeed the listener is abruptly brought back to reality by an exchange between the control booth and Billie at the end of the take: 'It's a bit long.' 'Yeah, I know,' responds Billie, 'we'll bring it up a little bit.' 'It's a half a minute long,' the disembodied voice insists.

Although the master chosen for release had more Heywood than Young, take 3 stands as a fitting climax to a unique partnership in jazz; here it is Young and Billie who dominate, both achieving a level of creativity that at the time neither realized they would ever exceed. It was a poignant climax to an astonishing musical relationship.

Chapter Six

1937–38

As soon as she joined the Count Basie Orchestra, Billie was immersed in the day-to-day life of a road band. Her wages were low, in keeping with a band trying to make a breakthrough with the public at large, although not as low as some. Billie herself said it was $14 a day, other reports say $70 a week, either way it was certainly more than she would have got in the Chick Webb band, for example; trumpet player Mario Bauza said he left in 1938 because he was only getting $35 a week.[1] But whatever her pay, she found it difficult to make ends meet. She had to pay for her overnight accommodation, food and gowns, and at the end of the week there was very little – if anything – left over.

After Billie's first notable success at the Apollo, the band went out on a string of one-nighters that took in Baltimore, Cincinnati and Newark. 'In Baltimore,' recalled Jo Jones, 'we were leaving the Royal Theater . . . and Freddie Green was sitting with Billie. Some guys were having fun. They had been on Pennsylvania Avenue and they come in and they was using all kinds of language. I said, "Wait a minute. You guys can't do that. There's a lady present." So Lester Young . . . bursts out laughing and says, "What do you mean, lady?" I said, "There's a lady in here . . ." So right away he says, "Lady Day."'[2] Like so many of Lester Young's nicknames, Lady Day stuck. In return, Billie dubbed Young The President. 'She said that Lester was next to F.D.R. He *was* the President,' continued Jones.[3]

The band returned to New York to open at the Savoy Ballroom on 1 April 1937. As soon as she was back in town, Billie was in the recording studios on 31 March with Teddy Wilson, followed by a session under her own name the next day. The Wilson session included 'Moanin' Low', a number torch singer Libby Holman made popular in 1929, but here owing more to the Ellingtonian hues Billie's accompanists brought to the song than to her own relatively straight delivery for its success. Her own session the following day produced a similar mood piece, 'Where Is the Sun?' but this time it is the singer who controls the emotional destiny of the piece, her accompanists remain exactly that. However, neither structure nor lyric content of 'Let's Call the Whole Thing Off' seemed to sit well with Billie; the rather wordy A section contrasted with a less congested bridge: both contained 'cute' lyrics – her handling of the 'ooohs' sounds uncomfortable – and left no scope to reveal any emotional possibilities. Here love sounds like a happy-go-lucky flirtation around the soda fountain. Yet in contrast, her secure, behind-the-beat rewriting of 'They Can't Take That Away From Me' is so contagious that it lingers in the memory long after the record has stopped.

After the Savoy, the band played the Nixon Grand in Philadelphia and the Howard in Washington; but although Billie and Lester were close musically, she was now making a play for guitarist Freddie Green. Billie later confided her true feelings for Green to Helen Oakley-Dance, saying he was the only man she really loved. In 1977, Oakley-Dance put this to him: 'She really did love you. Now I always thought that was very sad; it was in the early part of her career and the way Billie spoke to me was . . . if she could have made it [with] you . . . this is what she wanted . . . she was really happy about you.' Green said he was married at the time and 'did not want to get into that'. But, as Oakley-Dance pointed out for the record, Green did not deny anything of what she had just said.[4]

Working night after night with some of the finest musicians in jazz was bringing a confidence and verve to Billie's singing that she would never match again in her career. She took chances with lyrics, she played with songs as a cat would with a mouse; her voice was in good shape and rhythmically and harmonically she was approaching what many consider were the most artistically rewarding years of her life. Yet never before had so much been demanded of her creativity; her talent was being extended and examined on a daily basis, and on occasions she was finding it a strain. Unlike the bar-and-grill circuit in Harlem, singing with Basie demanded a high degree of professionalism every night and sometimes she had to struggle to be at her best. Her schedule had become a whirl: a solo appearance at a midnight benefit concert for the Harlem Children's Centre at the Apollo on 30 May; a recording session with a Teddy Wilson group dominated by Basie-men on 1 June; a return to the Apollo for three shows daily from the week commencing 4 June 1937, back to the Savoy Ballroom from 25 June, followed by dates in Hartford and Boston.

But at least this frenetic activity was giving her a profile she had not enjoyed before. 'Have you noticed how Billie Holiday has improved?'

said the *New York Amsterdam News* after seeing her at the Apollo. 'My Gawd, we remember the gal when she first started out and the road wasn't any too easy; remember the nights over at the Hot-Cha, Billie? She really is almost as popular as Ella and she has learned the secret of make-up and dressing which every artist needs to know.'[5]

With Hollywood defining the conventions of physical beauty, appearance played a complementary role in contributing to a singer's image. Make-up, hairdo and dress may be a facade, but they were all part of the unacknowledged source of a singer's personality. Later, two or three gardenias worn in her hair became part of Billie's visual signature, a potent costume accessory that even today transcends the black and white imagery of old photographs to compel and attract us.

Two airchecks from Radio WOR-Mutual at the Savoy in June, together with one from a CBS wire later in the year at the Meadowbrook Lounge of the Cedar Grove in New Jersey, provide the only recordings of Billie with Basie's band. They confirm that Billie's role was not typical of the way band singers were used. She sang her songs with the minimum of instrumental intrusion. After a four-bar introduction, 'Swing It, Brother, Swing' is pure Billie; she takes two choruses, the second a repeat of the first, but the band remain discreetly improvising riffs in the background. 'They Can't Take That Away from Me' again has a four-bar intro and except for sixteen bars at the beginning of the second chorus, the song is once again all Billie. Even Buck Clayton's uncomplicated arrangement of 'I Can't Get Started' follows this simple scheme; an eight-bar introduction, with Billie taking a chorus, the band taking the next sixteen bars with Billie taking the song out – although her attempted rallentando for a big finish was not picked up by her accompanists. Lester Young is the only band member allowed to intrude on these performances, his part-solo-part-obbligato on the middle eights of 'I Can't Get Started' presaging his studio performances with Billie in the summer.

Basie himself confirms that she was quite uncompromising about preserving her identity within the band. 'When she rehearsed with the band, it was really just a matter of getting her tunes like she wanted them because she knew how she wanted to sound and you couldn't tell her what to do . . . she had her own style and it was to remain that way. Sometimes she would bring in new things and would dictate the way she'd like them done. That's how she got her book with us. She never left her own style.'[6]

While in New York, the band moved to the Woodside Hotel at 2424 Seventh Avenue at 142nd Street, a haunt extremely popular with musicians in the pre-war years and immortalized for generations of jazz fans by 'Jumpin' at the Woodside' recorded by Basie on 22 August 1938. Billie, however, returned to her rooms with Sadie on West 99th Street and hardly ever hung out with the band. 'She still had connections at Monroe's . . . she had her own little things going,' said Basie.[7]

Those little things included two recording sessions with Teddy Wilson and two sessions under her own name in May and June, both with a strong contingent of Basie-men. She also appeared on Radio WABC's *Swing Club* with Duke Ellington and members of his band on 3 July, ''Twas swell,' said *New York Amsterdam News*.[8] Basie, meanwhile, had also been busy in the studios, recording for Decca in March, July and August 1937, but without Billie who could not join them because of her contract with Vocalion.

While playing the Meadowbrook Lounge of the Cedar Grove in New Jersey, Billie returned to New York on 1 November for a recording session with Teddy Wilson. Her entry on 'My Man' seems to suggest she would have preferred a slower tempo, aware that a less optimistic approach – the band tear it up at the end – would suit the number better. In contrast, the deadpan irony of 'Things Are Looking Up' makes the song resonate in a way that would have been impossible at a brighter tempo suggested by the lyrics. Four days later they were back at the Apollo for a week on Friday, 5 November, where Basie and Billie were now a popular attraction: 'We liked Billie Halliday's vocalizing with Count Basie's ork at the Apollo,' affirmed *New York Age*.[9]

Their period around the New York area ended with a week in the Howard Theater in Washington, a string of one-nighters at the end of November and a week in Detroit's Fox Theater in December where 'Somebody out there had some pretty screwed-up notions about black-face minstrels,' as Basie recalled.[10] Billie's complexion was considered too 'white' for a singer with a black band, and she had to wear dark make-up.

On the road again heading for the Grand Theater in Philadelphia for the last two weeks in December, Young and many of the band members indulged in a little gambling to pass the time. It was purely for fun; Young, in particular, loved to play dice, despite the fact he usually lost. 'Billie was left-handed and she never shot dice in her life,' recalled Jo Jones, 'Lester Young had one dollar and he said, "Come on, Billie, shoot this dollar for me." She's in the back of the bus . . . [and] she broke up everybody. She just took everybody's money because they told her wrong and she shot the dice wrong and broke the whole band . . . This was a very cute thing . . . you're telling somebody wrong and she didn't know what she's doing but she's winning!'[11] In the end

Billie won so much that she had to lend Young and the others 'a little change' to get them through Christmas.

16 January 1938 was one of the most memorable dates of the Swing Era. Early in the evening the Benny Goodman Orchestra rocked the music world with a jazz concert at Carnegie Hall. Count Basie, Lester Young, Buck Clayton, Freddie Green and Walter Page were featured guests in front of the 2500-plus audience; the whole event was recorded and produced one of the highest-selling jazz albums of all time. Afterwards, the Goodman family, most of the Goodman band including Gene Krupa, Hymie Schertzer and Lionel Hampton, together with a group of notables including Duke Ellington, Mildred Bailey, Red Norvo, Teddy Hill, Jimmy Mundy, Eddie Duchin, Ivie Anderson and Willie Bryant, gathered uptown at the Savoy Ballroom to watch Basie and the resident band, led by the redoubtable Chick Webb, battle it out.

Not only was it a head-to-head for the bandleaders, it also thrust Billie into direct competition with the most popular vocalist of the day. 'Ella Fitzgerald, entering the microphonic arena in white fighting togs, held a "Bei Mir Bist Du Schön" advantage over the blue-clad Billie ... On the other hand Billie ... threw her notes at Queen Ella in grand fashion,' mused *New York Amsterdam News*.[12] When it came to the crunch on that cold January night, *Metronome* credited Webb with the spoils of victory, while *Downbeat* considered they were taken by Basie. It was that close. However, when the ballot was taken to decide the winning vocalist, Ella polled three times as many votes as Billie. But, as *New York Amsterdam News* shrewdly observed, 'The final vote of Judge Public will not necessarily show a superiority in ability, since the two types of singers vary so differently, but a preference for a singing style.'[13]

While Ella, the great swinging optimist, broke it up with a cover version of the current Maxine Sullivan hit, 'Loch Lomond', Billie responded with her version of 'My Man'. At once it separated the individual styles of both singers: Ella, who sang almost anything with great ability, swing and obvious delight, and Billie, whose central style continued to emerge through her specific choice of songs, mainly those which invoked emotional mini-dramas which more often than not dealt with the pain of love. Her frequent use of direct style, songs where the 'I' or 'my' addresses itself to 'you' or 'your', invited the listener to identify with the central character of the song, the singer. This identification was as much through a combination of lyric content and direct expression of feelings as, at a more discreet level, through intimacy, by exploiting the expressive potential of the electronic microphone.

Billie's ability to select songs with which she could become emotionally entangled, awakening listeners' memories of their own misfortunes and experiences in love, had led to her being dubbed a torch singer, but she was much more than that. She had open ears and her singing was a continuing dialogue with the jazz musicians around her; the deep, dark, rhythmic lift she generated in 'Swing, Brother, Swing' with Basie, her bold melodic departures and her behind-the-beat syncopations revealed that she was developing into a supreme jazz singer.

After the Savoy came a profile appearance in Loew's State on Broadway for the week of 20 January 1938 where Billie hit it big with the audience. It was followed by a road tour that took in a band battle with Lucky Millinder's on 2 February at the Armory, Baltimore. According to the *Pittsburgh Courier*[14] – under a photograph of Billie, Basie and his then fiancée, Baltimorean Alyce Dixon – the Count had the edge. With the press now saying Billie was keeping Basie on top,[15] her star seemed in the ascendant, looking set to duplicate Ella Fitzgerald's meteoric rise to fame with Chick Webb.

Then, at the end of February, *New York Amsterdam News* abruptly announced, 'Count Basie Eliminates Billie Holiday's Singing.' The official reason was, to say the least, opaque: 'Because he felt it would be "easier" to work without a girl singer, William (Count) Basie . . . has eliminated Billie Holiday . . . It was explained that with constant jumps facing the group, dropping the vocalist would facilitate movement.' It was the sort of statement that would have done credit to a politician. The gossip column, however, was more forthcoming: 'The split between Billie Holiday and the Count Basie Orchestra, they say, is merely a matter of shekels,' it reported. But as if to emphasize what an opportunity had now passed Billie by, the same page carried a story of Ella Fitzgerald's remarkable popularity with Chick Webb's band.[16]

For the next few weeks recriminations abounded. Billie complained of poor pay and after-hours rehearsals, Jimmy Rushing described her behaviour as unprofessional, band booker Willard Alexander said her work was inconsistent and Basie said it was all down to money. When the band opened at the Apollo on 25 February it was without Billie; but Basie's press pronouncements notwithstanding, he was soon in search of another girl vocalist. 'Knowing the need for feminine charm with the band,' reported *New York Amsterdam News* ten weeks later, 'the novel idea of allowing the public to select the fortunate young lady has been decided upon.' A talent contest would be held at the Apollo to decide Basie's next singer: 'There is no restriction as to amateur or professional standing and the decision of the audience must stand as final.'[17] The contest was held on 21 May; the winner was Erline Harper. She never got the job. Basie, at Hammond's behest, made an offer to Helen Humes, who had been singing with Vernon Andrade's band at the Renaissance since October 1937. She accepted.

Over the years, many fingers have pointed to John Hammond's role in Billie's departure, not least by Jo Jones, Dicky Wells and Dan Minor. But Billie posed several specific problems for Basie; she would only sing songs with which she could identify, refusing to sing current pops or even the blues; she wanted a say in how her accompaniment was framed in what she did sing, and, to cap it all, it was impossible for Basie to link her appeal to that of his band through recordings, as Chick Webb had done with Ella, because of her contract with Vocalion. In many ways, being a singer in the Basie band was good for Billie but not for Basie.

The impasse was brought to a head by John Hammond, the nearest thing Basie had to a personal manager. Norman Granz once said God created personal managers to do the tasks artists did not like to do themselves. Hammond tried, at Basie's request, to get Billie to sing some blues. She refused. 'I had a fight with John Hammond and got fired,' she explained in forthright mood in a 1947 interview.[18]

'I think that Billie was ruled by her feelings,' observed Helen Oakley-Dance. 'It was very hard for her to always have her feelings in check . . . I think that she felt she was right and she didn't like to be told . . . You couldn't persuade her . . . for Basie as a leader that [situation] wouldn't really work.'[19]

Billie was now between jobs or 'taking a holiday', as Leonard Feather diplomatically put it, after interviewing her in her apartment on 99th Street in March 1938. 'Possibly if she had not clung to her own style . . . she might be more famous today,' he said, '[she] prefers to sing the way she feels rather than the way audiences would like her to feel . . . The fact her star has not ascended with the rapidity that might have been expected does not perturb her . . . success and renown are easy come, easy go; music, friends and a good time are the things that matter.'[20]

Artie Shaw was born 23 May 1910. He began playing the saxophone professionally at fifteen and after stints with Johnny Cavallaro's band in New Haven, Connecticut and Austin Wyllie in Cleveland, came to New York with Irving Aaronson's band in 1929. By now Shaw had taken up the clarinet in earnest, and for a while came under the influence of Willie 'The Lion' Smith at Pod's and Jerry's, where he first heard Billie Holiday. Gradually he established himself as a successful studio musician and by the age of twenty was playing first saxophone for the

CBS staff orchestra and frequently recording as a freelance in a variety of ensembles, most notably those led by Roger Wolfe Kahn.

Shaw was tempted into forming a band following a jazz concert sponsored by Joe Helbock of the new Onyx Club on 24 May 1936 at the Imperial Theater. He assembled a group built around the novel concept of a string quartet to perform his composition 'Interlude in B Flat'. He was the hit of the show, which prompted him to form a dance orchestra using the unique 'strings' idea. A contract with Brunswick Records soon followed but after a season at the Silver Grill of New York's Hotel Lexington and a period on the road, Shaw reluctantly had to concede that the band, in his own words, was 'popular with everyone except the audience', and he was forced to disband in March 1937.

The following month he formed what he vowed would be the loudest band around and assembled a conventional big band with six brass and four saxes. Unable to afford top sidemen, Shaw became music teacher, coach and father confessor to a band of young unknowns whom he nursed into vibrant musical health. Only Tony Pastor on tenor sax, Jerry Gray, a former violinist and now arranger, and, for a while, vocalist Peg La Centra, came across from the strings band, and the new band was billed as Art Shaw and his New Music to differentiate it from the previous outfit. As Shaw defined his vision of what a swing band should be, he was also developing his band of unknowns into a tight, swinging unit. But the path was long and hard. A year later he had still not made a breakthrough with the public at large and had been forced to borrow money while working towards that elusive break into the big time. When Billie left Basie, Shaw was playing a ballroom circuit owned by Sy and Charlie Schribman in the Boston area.

When Shaw heard she was not working, he immediately offered her a job. 'She was a good singer,' he said, 'I wouldn't have hired her if she wasn't! She was out there looking for work and I could afford her; she wasn't that well known back then.'21 One of Billie's first jobs with Shaw was a try-out at Madison Square Garden, playing the Harvest Moon Ball on Friday, 9 March 1938. Afterwards she decided to throw in her lot with Shaw, travelling up to Boston where she took a tiny room for the season in a fleabag hotel in Warrenton Street.

Billie was paid what the rest of the band got, $60. This did not leave much to send back to Sadie, who was looking for work to make ends meet. 'So Mildred [Bailey] hired Sadie as a maid,' said Red Norvo, 'as a second maid. Billie had a chance to go with Artie Shaw in the Boston area, so we hired her mother Sadie as a maid to help them. But I fired her because we had guests coming one night. The regular maid was off and we had a turkey on but she found the liquor closet and was out on the kitchen floor, the turkey was the size of a squab. So I said, "Mildred, you take the guests out to dinner and I'll take Sadie home!" So I got her sobered up and drove her home, and then she must have told something to Billie, because she had to protect herself. Billie said, "My mother loves you but she doesn't like Mavis [Mildred]." That was bad rap for Mavis, I mean, that was never the case because Mavis had done more than anybody to help her get started, what with John Hammond and so forth.'[22]

Shaw saw out the summer playing two nights a week at Boston's Roseland State Ballroom and filling in with one-nighters around New England for a guarantee of $1000 a week. Of prime importance in building the band's popularity was a radio wire from the Roseland State. This was an era when young America listened to its favourite bands on nightly radio broadcasts. Bandleaders knew they could only become successful if they were heard regularly on coast-to-coast radio. By the end of March, Shaw and Billie could be heard broadcasting on Radio WABC a half-hour before the weekly *Swing Club* show. By April their exposure had increased to two weekly spots, midnight Tuesdays and Saturdays at 6.30 p.m. 'Whatever you do, don't miss Billie Holiday with Art Shaw's band . . . that gal has improved no little,' advised *New York Amsterdam News*.[23]

Almost next door to the State, the Chick Webb band with Ella Fitzgerald was playing an extended run at Levaggi's Restaurant. Webb often looked in on Shaw's rehearsals and, impressed with Shaw's ability and dedication, was convinced his band would become the best 'white band in the worl'.' His own band, he felt, would become the best black. By 1939 both bands were riding high in the popularity stakes; to all intents and purposes Webb's prediction had come true.

For the time being there was still a gulf between aspiration and achievement. But at least *Metronome* had noticed that 'the addition of Billie Holiday to Shaw's band has put this outfit in the top brackets'.[24] As with Basie, Billie steadfastly refused to sing pops, sticking with her own repertoire. As it happened, this was fine by Shaw who had an aversion to song pluggers in general, and their often forgettable plugs in particular. Indeed, even in the 1990s, he still regretted recording 'You're a Sweet Little Headache', one of the songs he considered a blemish on his discography. But as Billie became more established with the band it was becoming clear to the song pluggers who had begun to hang around Shaw that Billie – like Shaw – simply did not give a damn for what she considered run-of-the-mill Tin Pan Alley output. 'She is at her best when she's singing a song she feels deeply and not when she is mouthing inane words to please a song plugger,' declared *Down-*

beat.[25] The songs she sang with Shaw's band were much the same as those she had been singing with Basie, including 'I Must Have that Man', 'Summertime', 'Nobody Knows the Trouble I've Seen', 'Travelin'', a song she had been singing since her Hot-Cha days, and an arrangement Shaw wrote for her of 'I Was Doing Alright'.

Song pluggers, aware that with Billie in the band the chances of getting airtime for their plugs were slim, began a whispering campaign to induce Shaw to replace Billie with a run-of-the-mill 'fem chirper' who would have no compunction about singing their wares. 'The whole business stinks to high heaven, but one has to know pluggers to appreciate what limits they will go to accomplish their ends,' observed *Downbeat*.[26] Sy Schribman, whose office held a monopoly control of band business in New England plus a financial stake in Shaw's aggregation, also had his reasons for wanting Shaw to take on another girl. He too began to lean on the young bandleader. Auditions began in April.

'In order ... to do ballrooms, Sy Schribman had the idea that Billie should come on as a single and they should have a white vocalist on the bandstand that performed with the band,' said Cliff Leeman, Shaw's drummer at the time.[27] Shaw decided on a young girl who was singing at Boston's Hi-Hat club and had been hanging around with Leeman: 'Her name was Selma Cord and Artie hired her as the "white" singer,' continued Leeman. 'She was very young and had a good voice and [sang under] ... the name Nita Bradley.'[28]

Billie and Nita did not hit it off; Billie suspected racial prejudice, having to endure tension from without as well as within. In the 1930s an integrated band was always going to be difficult and Shaw was under no illusions as to the problems he would have to confront. 'One night, in New England of all places,' recalled Leeman, 'they didn't want to let us in the hotel because we were playing a college town, so Artie Shaw would not check in unless the whole band checked in.'[29]

In May, Shaw won two important band battles, one against Tommy Dorsey in Dartmouth and the other, on 16 May, against Red Norvo in Boston. Against Norvo, Shaw's star singer found herself in stiff competition with her early mentor Mildred Bailey. However, 'with Nita Bradley doing her bit between rounds',[30] the crowd's verdict went in Billie's favour.

Meanwhile, on 11 May she had taken a day off to travel down to New York for a recording session under her own name with a pick-up group intended to be a reasonable facsimile of the John Kirby band. In fact Billie's singing on 'If I Were You' even suggests Maxine Sullivan, then the Kirby vocalist, at certain points.[31] Outside of her debut with Teddy Wilson and the Billie–Lester Young sides, these sessions number among Billie's best. The lyric and melodic content engage her; only on 'You Go to My Head' does she sound a little wooden on the crotchet triplets. The tempos, predominantly slow-medium, and tightly written Kirby-sextet-like accompaniment by Shavers, give a strong intimation of how she would subsequently define her style.

On the medium-bounce numbers, 'I'm Gonna Lock My Heart (and Throw Away the Key)' – a contrafact based on 'I'm Gonna Sit Right Down and Write Myself a Letter' – and 'The Moon Looks Down and Laughs', she swings with a snap and purpose that suggest she did enjoy singing the occasional novelty song. As an interesting aside, it is worth noting that the today obscure 'I'm Gonna Lock My Heart' was listed sixth in a list of the fifty highest-played songs on the airwaves for September 1938, while Vocalion listed Billie's version as their fourth biggest seller that month.

At the end of May 'Art Shaw and his Orchestra featuring Billie Holiday' were playing a residency at downtown Broadway's Plantation Club. Meanwhile, Shaw had left Brunswick and signed with RCA Victor, recording for their cheaper-priced Bluebird label. At this point Art became Artie because, as Shaw put it, 'Art Shaw sounded like a sneeze.' His first recording session for Victor was on 24 July 1938, an event that would change his life for ever. One of the numbers he recorded that day, despite the protests of the recording manager, was an arrangement of a forgotten Cole Porter song called 'Begin the Beguine'. It was based on a sketch he had passed to Jerry Gray, his arranger, to work on. It was put out as the 'B' side of a bright, romping version of 'Indian Love Call'. Also among the tunes he recorded that day was an original he had written and arranged himself for Billie Holiday called 'Any Old Time', which still remains her only known recording with the Artie Shaw band. 'It came about when we were off on a couple of one-night stands,' said Shaw. 'We were in a town, Binghampton, New York and there's not a hell of a lot you can do of an evening in Binghampton.'[32]

Here Billie is presented in the role of a 'band singer', taking a vocal chorus in a predominantly instrumental number, in contrast to her features with Basie where her vocals assumed a central role. However, it is a significant performance in the context of the Big Band Era as it represents one of the few occasions a tune was composed and arranged for a big band with the specific characteristics of the style of its singer solely in mind. Examples of an arranger framing a singer to this extent were rare until Billy Strayhorn's arrangement of 'Flamingo' for Duke Ellington's vocalist Herb Jeffries in December 1940, and later, Helen Forrest's 1941 performances with Harry James, where James specifically instructed his arrangers to support and enhance Forrest's voice.

'Any Old Time' is a minor gem and, with its unusual binary construction, by no means a run-of-the-mill pop tune. It is a thirty-two-bar AB song where both A and B are sixteen bars each. Shaw has designed the song with Billie's specific vocal characteristics in mind in terms of lyric content, rhythmic phrasing and melody. Written in the major, the song is once more an 'I' song directed to 'you', this time depicting total infatuation in love, suggesting 'you' may not want me now, but 'I' will always be there for 'you'. It was a variation on the character part Billie was constructing for herself of a woman unlucky or frustrated in love.

The song begins with a four-bar introduction, followed by a chorus shared between ensemble and Shaw's clarinet before a two-bar modulation into Billie's vocal. Here she syncopates the melodic line, already a paraphrase of her 'behind the beat' style, even more than the melody as written. The whole performance presents her like a jewel in an elegant setting; the individual characteristics of her style are spelt out by the ensemble and expanded on by the singer. After her vocal, the band modulate, this time into Tony Pastor's eight-bar tenor solo, followed by eight bars of ensemble plus a four-bar tag where Shaw incorporates a clarinet-above-lead-sax passage some eighteen months or so before the device was called up for active service with Glenn Miller's band.

After the Plantation Club booking the band continued their summer in the Boston area. At the end of their stay they emerged with a book of over 200 arrangements and a modest national following because of the radio wire. Then followed a long road trip which took in the Southern states. 'I knew there was going to be trouble,' said Shaw, 'because Billie was a pretty hot-tempered woman . . . I could see trouble brewing when we went below the Mason-Dixon line and we took her down there, I don't want to repeat the language, but it was rough stuff.'[33]

To save money on expenses, the band travelled in individual cars with the band equipment in a truck. Billie often rode with bass player Sid Weiss, trombonist Harry Rogers and drummer Cliff Leeman, or she would travel with Shaw, who at the time was driving a second-hand Rolls-Royce. Frequently diners or restaurants would not serve her, or only if she sat out in the back kitchen, flanked by her travelling companions. Conditions were oppressive and offensive and, because she was the only black in a white band, the injustices were thrown into sharp relief.

In Louisville, Kentucky, she lost her temper when a redneck requested the 'nigger wench' sing another song. The place erupted

103

when Billie responded in kind and she had to be smuggled to safety. 'Some of the things we went through down South when Billie was in the band made me think of the title I gave to my theme song,' said Shaw. 'I might have been looking into the future. I wrote that thing in 1936. I called it "Nightmare".'[34]

As Billie bridled, Shaw was considering his own position as a band-leader. 'He was thinking of dissolving the band,' continued Leeman, 'but he had a commitment in a hotel in St Louis . . . in the middle of the engagement . . . he got a call from RCA Victor . . . He was already going to dissolve the band but "Begin the Beguine" was a sensation, sweeping the nation.'[35]

Shaw had opened at the Chase Hotel in St Louis on 4 October where Tommy Rockwell, Shaw's booking agent, offered him a choice between New York's Waldorf-Astoria or the Blue Room of the Hotel Lincoln on Eighth Avenue at 44th Street, which he described as a 'rat trap'. Rockwell's recommendation was to go for the Lincoln booking; anyone, he reasoned, could make a go of the posh Waldorf-Astoria. But if Shaw could put the Blue Room on the map, which also had the attraction of a national radio wire, then it would be the making of the band. Shaw took his advice.

On his return to New York, Shaw hired another girl singer who had been performing on CBS as Bonnie Blue. He had heard Helen Forrest the year before singing in a Washington, DC club and decided now was the time to return to his two-girl-singers policy since by now Billie had more or less decided the big band life was not for her. 'Billie told us she was leaving . . .' said Helen Forrest. 'Artie knew it when he hired me, which was one reason he hired me.'[36]

Forrest would become one of the great band singers of the Swing Era, but when she joined Shaw she was young and relatively inexperienced. 'I started out copying Mildred Bailey and Ella Fitzgerald and picked up a bit on Billie,' she said later.[37] One number she sang with Billie's influence plainly apparent was a version of 'I Have Eyes' from the movie short *Artie Shaw's Class in Swing* recorded in 1939.

Just as Forrest joined Shaw, the band was literally on the launchpad to stardom. With 'Begin the Beguine' taking off, Shaw opened at the Blue Room of the Hotel Lincoln on 26 October 1938. 'We were a sensation,' said Leeman, 'everything went crazy.'[38]

Like all the vocalists with the big bands, Billie and Helen Forrest had to sit on the bandstand when not singing. But simply sitting on the bandstand between numbers imposed its own kind of strain. The talented pianist and singer Daryll Sherman landed the job of singing with

Artie Shaw's orchestra when he came out of retirement in 1983. She found it a completely new experience: 'It's so different singing with a big band,' she said. 'I am used to handling a song in its entirety; present a song and try and tell a story, build it up towards the end for that big note and milk it! But a "big band singer", so-called, gets one chorus, sometimes not even that, to make their point.

'Then I discovered there's an art to just sitting on the chair, waiting your turn. You must look interested and animated and not look off into space; cross your legs the right way, while you wait for that one chorus that generally isn't at the beginning of the song. You've got to work out when to get out of your chair and make your way to the mike. Then the anticipation, sitting through all the instrumentals, there's a kind of tension waiting for your spot. Even though you've heard the modulation a hundred times, when you're standing up in front of all those people there's a little nervous edge there when you come in with your first note; is it going to be there after waiting so long?! And finally the awkward moment when you've finished your chorus and the band hasn't finished the number, and you have to find a way of getting back to the chair and sitting down but still look involved in the song! So it's a mini-drama in a way.'[39]

There is no doubt that Billie greatly respected Shaw, both as a musician and for his humanity in taking a stand on the race issue. But events were quickly moving beyond their control. After about two weeks tension began rising as she struggled to accept the house rules for black employees in the Lincoln; when she returned uptown one night she was on a short fuse: 'There was no rhyme or reason for Billie Halliday [sic] to perform the way she did the other night at the Turf Club. It was very unbecoming,' commented *New York Amsterdam News* in early November.[40] However, there was no sign of tension on 2 November when she accompanied Shaw to a farewell party given for Count Basie at the Famous Door in 52nd Street.

Meanwhile, Billie had been approached by John Hammond with an offer of playing a season in a new night-club he had become involved in, due to open in Greenwich Village in about eight weeks' time. She decided to accept, and to finish with Shaw at the end of the month; indeed Shaw offered her financial backing to get gowns and arrangements, but she declined. Then sometime between 3 November and 19 November, Maria Kramer, owner of the Lincoln Hotel, stipulated that Billie should use the service elevator because hotel guests, on encountering the singer in the passenger elevator, had complained about the Lincoln 'taking coloured'. It was the last straw; as Billie said a few weeks later, '[I] was never allowed to visit the bar or the dining room as did other members of the band ... [and] I was made to leave and enter through the kitchen.'[41]

In the end Billie simply tired of working with a big band; the constant hassle over racial issues, the discipline of being at a certain place at a certain time to sing a certain song, was too much. She wanted to be a free agent. Some evenings she got to sing just two songs, the rest of the time was spent sitting on the stand with Helen Forrest until the band finished their programme. By 19 November 1938 Billie Holiday had left Artie Shaw's band.

The circumstances of Billie's parting caused widespread comment; Walter Winchell, the popular columnist for the *Daily Mirror*, wrote: 'The jazz critic, John Hammond ... was sitting in the Lincoln Hotel supper room enjoying Artie Shaw's band ... not knowing Billie had given her notice two days before. The outside billboards, however, still stated she was among the Lincoln's attractions. The hotel manager tried to explain why they were forced to pass up her contract, "People," he said, "objected to a coloured girl singing here." Said Mr Hammond, "And this hotel is named the Lincoln!" '[42]

The black press also took up the issue; Billie was described as the 'last survivor' of coloured singers with 'ofay bands' and Shaw made the headlines by denying prejudice caused her dismissal. Even in the 1990s he remained stung by the furore: 'The press were on to me at that time; they said I fired her because she was black, conveniently overlooking that when I hired her she was black too! She didn't change colour when she was with me,' he asserted angrily, 'I've even been castigated for hiring her; I was told I was exploiting a black person. I was not exploiting her; I was doing the best I could to present her in an impartial light as a musician singing with my band. No matter what I do it seems I'm wrong!'[43]

Shaw's courageous stance in presenting Billie Holiday with his band has frequently been overlooked or downplayed over the years, over-shadowed perhaps by his own phenomenal success that was to come in the following months. His part in fighting for racial equality never received the recognition of his great rival Benny Goodman, but Shaw employed drummer Zutty Singleton in his first ensemble as early as 1936. He also featured, at various times, Hot Lips Page and Roy Eldridge and featured the work of composer William Grant Still. 'I was doing what I could,' said Shaw, 'but I wasn't in a position to change the attitude of the masses of people toward black–white relations.'[44]

With the band beginning to attract national attention and just embarking on a nightly series of coast-to-coast broadcasts on NBC, and with Billie due to return to a solo career in a matter of days rather than weeks, now was not the time for Shaw to make a noble, futile gesture by pulling his band out of the Lincoln. 'Artie was just starting to make it,' said Helen Forrest. 'He might have gone broke and the band might have vanished if he continued to buck the times.'[45]

In February 1938, as Artie Shaw and his Orchestra moved ever upwards, they were replaced at the Lincoln Hotel by Jan Savitt's orchestra, a white band with the black singer Bon Bon (George Tunnell). The engagement passed without incident, even though Bon Bon, articulate and intelligent, was fiercely proud of his Afro-American heritage. He simply pretended to be the band manager's valet.

Reflecting on Billie's time with his band, Shaw said, 'She was always shooting towards tragedy, it was just a question of how and when . . . I never heard her hit a bad note that was off by even a sixteenth of a tone. She had a remarkable ear . . . and a remarkable sense of time . . . She had her own thumb-print, when she sang it was unmistakably her . . . [when] she sang something it came alive, I mean, that's what jazz is about.'[46]

Chapter Seven

1938–42

On 7 December 1938, *New York Amsterdam News* announced that a brand-new downtown night-spot called Café Society was set to open in two weeks' time. Willie Bryant had been lined up to act as MC while Robert H. Gordon was already directing the floor-show rehearsals, described as 'a burlesque of café society and its foibles'. Among the featured artists booked to appear were pianist Albert Ammons, who had just been awarded *Life* magazine's prize for the 'best jazz recording of all time', and Billie Holiday.[1]

Although John Hammond was responsible for Billie getting the Café Society job, he had come to feel she was not making the most of the opportunities that had come her way. And certainly her contemporaries, such as Ella Fitzgerald, Maxine Sullivan and Lena Horne, who all made sure they took care of business, were now beginning to see their careers take off. In contrast, Hammond's tireless, unpaid efforts on Billie's behalf had not been matched by her dedication to work. She had fouled up several deals he had arranged for her, most notably a tie-up with the Irving Mills office, and she regularly provoked havoc by getting high on recording dates.

The fact that Ella Fitzgerald and Maxine Sullivan were now ahead of Billie in the popularity stakes was even the cause of a raised eyebrow in the pages of *New York Amsterdam News*. 'Somehow she just seems to miss receiving the build-up and public appreciation that would put her in the top niche where she really belongs,' it pronounced.[2] As far as Hammond was concerned, that 'somehow' was down to Billie's disposition, which, he later said, could be moody and was not helped by drinking and marijuana.[3]

On more than one occasion she had put her recording career in jeopardy when record company executives walked into her sessions and sniffed the air, leaving Hammond to carry the can. But try as he might to dissuade her, she persisted in having a joint when recording. Eddie Durham remembered an occasion[4] when he was asked at short notice to deputize on guitar for Freddie Green on the 'Back in Your Own Backyard' session in January 1938. Billie had just split with Freddie and, feeling bitter towards her former lover, did not want him on the date. Durham, brought in as a last-minute replacement, recalled how Billie, Jo Jones and Lester Young took a break mid-session. When they returned, in mellow mood, they left a dreamy, unused alternate of 'Back in Your Own Backyard' for posterity.

Signs of Hammond's growing disenchantment with Billie came when he mounted his now legendary *Spirituals to Swing* concert at Carnegie Hall on 23 December 1938. Although Albert Ammons and Meade Lux Lewis, whom he booked for the Café Society opening, were on the Carnegie bill, Billie was not. For her part, Billie's attitude towards Hammond had become strained since she had left Basie's band. A parting of the ways was in sight, particularly after she complained about the quality of material she was given to sing on her 28 November 1938 session with Teddy Wilson. The next time she went into the recording studios under Hammond's supervision, on 30 January 1939, it would mark the end of his involvement in her career.

The 28 November date Billie felt so badly about involved a simulated big band, and it is quite possible that it was the quality of the arrangements, rather than the songs, that caused the friction point. Certainly they were no more than functional and were without the cohesion and ingenuity of the Benny Carter charts from the two preceding sessions. The four songs chosen that day were in general word-heavy, not allowing the singer much elbow-room to assert her style. To cap a rather lacklustre session, 'Let's Dream in the Moonlight' was marred by trombonist Trummy Young's uncertain pitch during his eight-bar solo.

Not much better was the following date under Billie's name called for 20 January 1939. Although Sonny White on piano emerged as a convincing Wilson apostle, the singer, even at this early stage in her career, was in the invidious position of having to compete with her past. Already her best work recorded between 1935 and 1938 had become the yardstick by which she was judged. Of the two songs that went down that day, 'Dream of Life' was especially written for her by her young friend, admirer and, for a while, maid, Carmen McRae. While it conformed to the lyric content Billie preferred, it was so crammed with words it allowed her little rhythmic latitude.

Billie and John Hammond parted company as far as recordings were concerned on 30 January 1939. Even though a gulf of misunderstanding had grown between them, their association ended on a high note with some commanding playing by Teddy Wilson, Roy Eldridge on trumpet and Benny Carter on both alto and clarinet. Although Carter did not arrange the material, he plays a greater role as soloist than on his previous sessions with Billie in October and November 1938. His presentation of 'Sugar', for example, transforms the melody into a piece of exquisite art which has the effect of putting what follows into the shade, while his clarinet can be heard playing obbligatos on 'What Shall I Say?' and 'It's Easy to Blame the Weather'. But it is his alto solo on 'More Than You Know', together with Billie's engaging vocal, that makes this the most rewarding title of her last three sessions.

The Café Society was scheduled to open on Thursday night, 22 December 1938. However, delay in obtaining the liquor and cabaret licences meant the big opening had to be held over. Owned by Barney Josephson, a businessman from the Trenton, NJ area, the club was a milestcne along the long road towards racial integration in America. It presented a racially mixed band and encouraged a racially mixed audience. 'I always had strong feelings of social consciousness. I guess I just had a democratic upbringing,' said Josephson.[5]

Josephson was intellectually inclined and found life in the bohemian areas of New York preferable to his staid existence in southern New Jersey. In the late 1930s he moved to New York to live with his brother and sister-in-law and had a vague idea of opening a supper-club. There were many things he did not like about Manhattan's night-spots which was why he eventually decided to open a club, running it in the way *he* thought it should be run. In tongue-in-cheek fashion he was determined to make fun of the smart set, the playboys and their girl-friends in café society.

There were precedents for putting down customers; El Dumpo in Chicago was doing huge business as waiters spilled soup intentionally and were deliberately rude, but Josephson wanted to be subtle. He leased a former speakeasy in a basement in Sheridan Square where West 4th Street merged with Washington Square in Greenwich Village. His first step was to employ a group of artists and cartoonists to work on the wall murals. They worked on a motif spoofing the high-society night-time set.

But the most important factor in Josephson's club was his intention to feature jazz. The only problem was that he knew very little about either the music or the music business. He turned to John Hammond for advice. They hit it off immediately on a personal basis and Hammond became responsible for booking the musicians; subsequently Josephson was always adamant that Hammond be credited for the high standard of the Café Society's performers. He brought in Billie as featured attraction, backed by 'trumpet tootin'' Frankie Newton and his band with Newton's pianist, Sonny White, assigned to accompany Billie. The rest of the band was: Tab Smith and Stanley Payne, alto saxes; Billie's friend from 1930, Ken Hollon, tenor sax; Ken Kersey, piano; John Williams, bass; Ed Dougherty, drums. Willie Bryant, lined up to become MC, pulled out (he eventually took over in early 1941) and was replaced by Jack Gilford. Boogie-woogie pianists Albert Ammons and Meade Lux Lewis were joined later by Pete Johnson from Chicago and Kansas City blues shouter Joe Turner.

Publicist Ivan Black worked overtime to put the club on the map, claiming 'Jazz will be presented for the first time with dignity and respect.' Although opening night was delayed until Friday, 30 December 1938, things were still not ready. Food had to come from a hot-dog stand across the square and although the liquor licence had arrived, the cabaret licence had not. The club was packed to overflowing with some 600 patrons (the limit was 210) but it was not until 11.30 p.m. that the liquor licence was finally delivered. 'The opening of Café Society in the Village Friday night was definitely something for the books,' reported *New York Amsterdam News*. 'Billie Holiday, who packs them in, puts over tunes with Frankie Newton's band as only Billie can.'[6]

Celebrities, artists, show people, musicians and society people turned up. 'I met Roosevelt's son . . . in the Café Society,' said Billie, 'I had nerve enough to go up to him and say hello.'[7] Benny Goodman, who had a financial interest in the club along with Hammond, was so taken by Billie's performances that he booked her to appear on his *Camel Caravan* radio programme on 17 January.

The murals were a big hit with the clientele, while table cards and menus poked fun at the idiosyncrasies of cabaret patrons. The club's slogan, 'The Right Place for the Wrong People', was everywhere, and comedian Jack Gilford derided snobbishness as part of his act. The New York press greeted the new club enthusiastically, and although *Downbeat* noted that '[it] promises to be a new mecca for the music moochers and swingomaniacs',[8] jazz fans usually found the place crowded and a lot of time taken up by the floor-show. One-beer standees were not encouraged; author–poet Maxwell Bodenheim wrote that his circle could not afford the tariff. In the event it was the affluent midtown set that kept the club in business; Burgess Meredith, Paul Robeson, Carole Landis, Merle Oberon, Don Ameche, Gregory Ratoff and Lionel Stander.

Billie's residency at the Café Society gave her the opportunity to define her style in a prestige downtown location to an extent that had been impossible before. Although she had sung with Basie and Shaw, she was unable to record with either of them ('Any Old Time' was withdrawn soon after release because of her pre-existing contract with Vocalion) and the time she spent with each bandleader was before either became well known. Consequently she had failed to build her reputation to any significant extent while she was with them. And despite her recordings, which sold consistently, during the Swing Era it was broadcast time that built reputations. Prior to her Café Society debut, Billie was popular with audiences above 145th Street but virtually unknown below it. Josephson, Billie claimed, paid her $75 per week, about the same as she could command in a Harlem club.

Always careful in her selection of songs, she had Danny Mendelsohn prepare arrangements of numbers she had been working with for the past few years. 'Although Frankie was the bandleader, Billie had her own numbers arranged and *she* picked the numbers for her set; we did what *she* wanted,' said John Williams, Newton's bass player.[9] The aircheck of Billie singing from Café Society with Newton's band from this time, 'I'm Gonna Lock My Heart (and Throw Away the Key)', was originally recorded by her in June 1938 as a bright novelty number. But her Café Society version, with a neat, well-executed Newton solo that begins with a beautiful phrase that could have been played by Lester Young, plus tightly written saxophone counterpoint, is appreciably slower.[10] It transforms the song into a worldly-wise reflection of someone hurt in love – 'I'm wise to all those tricks you played on me' – and who, once bitten, will be twice shy about falling for someone – 'If I never fall in love again that's soon enough for me.'

It is a superb example of how Billie claimed a song for the character part she had created for herself as a singer, of someone unlucky in love. In this role she consumes the original meaning of the song and reveals another dimension that even the lyricist could surely not have envisioned. It fitted in well with the other songs in her repertoire: 'Yesterdays', 'More Than You Know', 'My Last Affair', 'This Year's Kisses', 'Some Other Spring', and 'Travelin' All Alone'. All had lyrics that drew on the romantic conventions of being let down or stood up, about loneliness and frustration in love.

It is small wonder, therefore, that when Billie was presented with a song by Abel Meeropol, who wrote under the name of Lewis Allen, about a lynching in the South, she demurred at first. 'Strange Fruit' is about 'black bodies swaying in the Southern breeze', and even today, remains a harrowing song. Lyrics that speak of 'the bulging eyes and twisted mouth' invoke a mental image of a hanging body more terrifying than any photograph or news clip. More a dramatic soliloquy than song, for the left-wing audiences of Café Society with *The New Masses* stuffed in their pockets it represented a powerful message delivered with a powerful punch. As Billie reached the searing, climactic line, 'Here is a strange and bitter crop', it was delivered with a power and emotion that chilled the blood, forcing her predominantly white, middle-class audience to stare unblinkingly into the face of racist violence.

The song's inherent drama was reinforced by waiters who, immediately prior to Billie's singing it, insisted on perfect silence. The scene was set; house lights went down and only a pin-spot picked out the singer's face. On the final chord the lights went out. When the house lights went back up she was gone. Josephson insisted on no encore to underline the stark imagery of both song and singer.

The reality of what she was dealing with was brought home to Billie when Columbia refused to record 'Strange Fruit', surprising and upsetting her. She turned to Milt Gabler of the Commodore Music Shop at 46 West 52nd Street. Gabler also ran Commodore Records, the first ever specialist jazz record label. 'Billie was very sad,' he recalled, 'she had this great number that was so important to her and they wouldn't let her record it. I told her that if she could get a one-session release from her contract I'd like to have her do it for Commodore.'[11] A deal was made with Columbia where she was loaned to Gabler for one session of four sides.

Billie cut 'Strange Fruit' on 20 April 1939 at Brunswick's World Broadcasting Studios with Frankie Newton's Café Society band. The uncommonly long introduction by Newton and pianist Sonny White owes much to the live presentation of the song. On one level it was functional, allowing the audience time to settle and focus on the singer, while on another level it heightened the dramatic impact of Billie's entrance.

Schematically simple, a modified AABB structure, its key of B flat minor was frequently used by classical composers for their more sombre pieces. Its slow, solemn beat[12] underlined the profundity of the song's message, which was subsequently banned from countless radio stations, including Britain's BBC. Billie's handling of the subject matter represented a new challenge quite unlike the rhythmic and harmonic liberties she had been taking with songs in the past. The lyric content was one of just a few she sang where she was not at the centre of the song's emotional drama; it was not an 'I' song addressing itself to 'you', but a song describing a disastrous social condition requiring from her a wholly new approach to vocal interpretation.

Ignoring the melody outlined by White in the introduction, she realizes that it is the words of 'Strange Fruit' that give it its impact, not any specific feature of the song's melodic or harmonic construction.

Consequently she relies on both the grain of her voice, hard and worldly-wise, and careful, dramatic enunciation that would have done credit to a classically trained actor, to exploit the unequivocal drama of the lyrics. Her note choices are simple and uncomplicated, yet she somehow makes it sound as if she was a witness of that awful lynching. The resultant performance, however, was by no means a true representation of her art, even though it would forever be associated with her. While there had been other protest songs before, such as 'Supper Time' from *As Thousands Cheer*, sung by Ethel Waters in 1933, which depicted a black woman who could not face dinner without her husband who had been lynched, 'Strange Fruit' was the first unmuted cry against racism in words and music.

'When we played "Strange Fruit" in the club the number really went over,' said John Williams, 'you didn't expect it to be as big as it was. It drew great attention to Billie. You could always tell when the audience was listening, it was a show stopper. We thought it was good, we knew the words and the meaning – what the number really meant, so when we recorded it we never thought it was going to be as big as it was. Naturally, playing it was a moving experience; the words were unheard of for a song, especially at that time. We made blues number on that particular date and that's what we thought was going to be the hit.'[13]

'Strange Fruit' was a landmark recording, but of a very different kind than was perceived at the time. It was one of the first examples of a popular song becoming impossible to disentangle from a single, specific recording of it. This would later become commonplace in pop and rock; songs such as 'Heartbreak Hotel' or 'What's Going On?' or 'Bohemian Rhapsody', for example, are impossible to separate from the performances of Elvis Presley, Marvin Gaye and Queen. Singers and songs are bonded in a performance that exhausts the song's meaning, achieving an autonomy that transcends simplistic chord progressions and mediocre lyrics by embracing musical as well as non-musical factors, among them style, fashion and sex appeal. These non-musical factors often have social significance to a given group which identifies meaning in them; for example, appalled at the prospect of America's youth being corrupted by the early Elvis Presley's swivelling hips, television executives panicked: by his tenth appearance they were shooting him from the waist up. The appeal of his music to his teenage audience was as much the attitude he struck when singing – his gestures, his clothes, his shoes, his hair-style and more particularly his sex appeal – as the songs he sang.

At the time 'Strange Fruit' was recorded, and for years after, popular

114

songs were covered by several artists as a matter of course; Broadway success for a Fanny Brice or an Ethel Merman, or a gold disc for Glenn Miller's 'In the Mood', for example, did not confer 'ownership' of a song in the way Queen 'possessed' 'Bohemian Rhapsody'. While audiences are happy to hear show tunes sung by a wide variety of singers, and a performance of 'In the Mood' by any big band is a safe bet for a round of applause, another artist recording 'Bohemian Rhapsody' is unthinkable – and, indeed, no one has even tried to 'cover' it.

Billie's performance of 'Strange Fruit' achieved a similar autonomy because it set in motion a whole battery of reactions and associations to which a given social group attributed significance. These 'signifiers' differed from the way modern pop addresses itself to a teen and pre-teen audience, through sex appeal, fashion and so on, but nevertheless had quite specific meaning to both New York's left-wing intelligentsia gathered in Josephson's club and succeeding generations of record buyers sensitive to the issue of racial inequality.

Later selected for the NARAS Hall of Fame, 'Strange Fruit' showed up on the record charts at sixteen on 22 July 1939. 'A record that's going to cause tremendous controversy,' predicted *Metronome*.[14] In contrast was the B side, 'Fine and Mellow', a blues number whose theme of unrequited love was borrowed in part from Ethel Waters. In the long run it turned out to be the bigger hit for Commodore; although Billie was not a blues singer *per se*, she nevertheless sang songs in a way that evoked the blues mood in general, leading to her frequently being incorrectly labelled a blues singer. Yet when she did sing the blues she had complete command of the idiom, as her handling of 'Fine and Mellow' showed.

Of the other two songs from the session, 'Yesterdays', with its unusual ABAB construction, became an unlikely vehicle of affirmation with its fast second chorus, something Billie would drop in subsequent performances to become a lament of yearning and one of the staples of her repertoire. Harold Arlen's 'I Gotta Right to Sing the Blues' had Billie singing a simplified version of the melody line, much like Armstrong did in his 1933 Victor version, but similarities do not end there. It is impossible not to believe she did not base her own version on Armstrong's vocal as much as his trumpet-playing.

'Strange Fruit' is usually portrayed as a key moment in Billie's career. The popularity the song brought her, including a mention in *Time* magazine, is said to have brought about a sea-change in the underlying aesthetic direction of her singing. John Hammond, for one, expressed the opinion that 'artistically it was the worst thing that ever happened to her', implying that because of the song's success she turned increasingly to slow, dirge-like torch songs, a sweeping generalization echoed by many commentators. However, Leonard Feather has pointed out that he and John Hammond shared enough evenings in Café Society in the 1940s to know that this was not the case,[15] and it is worth noting that it was not until two years later, in mid-1941, that Billie began recording slow tunes in earnest (see Appendix 3).

The effect of 'Strange Fruit' was perhaps more subtle in that it affected less Billie's choice of material and more the way she subsequently directed her talent in the recording studio. Instead of being one of several soloists lined up for a 'blow', her backing became gradually more and more neutral in terms of jazz improvisation, favouring instead arranged passages with perhaps just one solo interlude, exemplified by Lester Young's drastically changed role in 'The Man I Love', recorded on the second session following 'Strange Fruit' eight months later. And even then, this is perhaps not so much the effect of 'Strange Fruit' *per se* as of having a regular backing band at Café Society and arrangements that framed her singing for a night-club context which she wanted to emulate on record. But simply changing the back-drop behind Billie's voice, by removing a free-wheeling jazz ensemble in order to make her the centre of interest, did not in itself lessen her great talent as a singer. As her popularity increased it was inevitable that she would want to become the focus of her recordings.

The success of Billie's run at Café Society was certainly felt in her recording sessions of 21 March and 5 July. With what, to all intents and purposes, was her Café Society band, 'You're Too Lovely to Last' immediately impresses with its dark ensemble textures and the feel of a set working group through the degree of organization and cohesion in the ensemble passages. However, 'Under a Blue Jungle Moon' struggles on the shore-line between good and bad, as does 'Everything Happens for the Best', a song which includes Billie in the composer credits. Here, pianist Kenny Kersey's comping is weak, yet paradoxically he contributes a good, Wilson-influenced solo. 'Why Did I Depend on You?' is a contrafact based on the chords of 'I Cried for You'; like its predecessor, the metre of the lyrics is slower than the rhythm of the song, allowing Billie improvisational latitude to kick free of the groundbeat so that her vocal seems to assume an independent life of its own, parallel to rather than a part of the song itself.

'Long Gone Blues', later coupled with 'Am I Blue' from May 1941, was not released until mid-1947. 'Long Gone Blues', with Tab Smith's lead soprano sax, is an exciting, semi-jump band performance. The theme is the singer's active sexuality – 'I'm a good girl but my love is

116

all wrong, I'm a good girl but my love has gone.' Lips Page tops it off with a convincing and powerful plunger solo on trumpet.

Billie and Frankie Newton took a long break between sets at Café Society on 29 May 1939 when they appeared at the National Swing Club of America's big concert at the Hippodrome in New York. Newton was a part of an ad hoc group backing Billie, which also included Charlie Barnet on saxophone, Duke Ellington on piano, Sandy Block on bass and Henry Adler on drums. Even away from the intimacy of a small night-club, Billie was able to electrify the huge crowd, a testament to her growing talent which many thought reached its peak during the early 1940s.

Billie's next recording session, on 5 July, immediately yielded a gem, written by Teddy Wilson's wife Irene Kitchings, titled 'Some Other Spring'. Again, it is impossible not to believe that the song and arrangement were not part of her Café Society repertoire. 'Our Love is Different' is another song where Billie is listed among the composer credits and takes her to both the top and bottom of her range in what is a good performance both as singer and interpreter.

One of the highspots of this period, however, was her performance of 'Them There Eyes'. Perhaps more than any performance it brings to mind Teddy Wilson's observation that Billie was 'like a girl doing a take-off of Armstrong'.[16] Yet it is more than simply a vocal that pays homage to Armstrong; it is a celebration of Billie's talent, with her joy and sense of fun clear for all to hear in the way she makes one long, bumpy word out of the first twelve words: 'IfellinlovewithyouthefirsttimeIlookedinto – them there eyes.'

Billie had worked out her vocal line at least a year before she recorded the song; she was present when her then paramour Freddie Green sang the lyrics at the Kansas City Five session on 8 September 1938. She had taught Green her vocal line and as he sang it, she was standing in front of him mouthing the words to remind him of rhythmic inflections she had taught him. The overall architecture of Green's vocal is echoed strongly in Billie's subsequent vocal, in quite detailed nuance.[17]

A week at the Apollo from 11 August ended Billie's season at Café Society. 'Working with Billie all those months, it was a pleasure to come to work,' said John Williams. 'No one bothered you; you had to make time and be a gentleman, that's all. Billie was a lovely person to work for and Barney treated everyone the same.'[18] For his part, Josephson was as deeply moved by Billie's singing as he was fascinated by her unique personality. 'Billie Holiday was this kind of a girl,' he observed, 'she did what she liked. If a man she liked came up, she'd go with him; if a woman, the same thing. If she was handed a drink, she'd drink it. If you had a stick of pot, she'd take a cab ride on her break and smoke it. If you had something stronger, she'd use that. That was her way. She didn't apologize for it and she didn't feel ashamed. All she wanted was to have fun in whatever way it struck her. She was sensitive, she was proud. She could tell a good joke; she knew all the words to use if you rubbed her the wrong way. When she told you off, you were damn well told – white, black, rich, poor. She had a real zest for life. As a performer, she could make you fall in love, she could break your heart. A lot of what she did ended up breaking her heart. That was her life. There was no other person on the face of this earth who was like her. Billie Holiday was a single edition.'[19]

But for all her success at Café Society, it was the boogie-woogie pianists who grabbed the headlines. A boogie-woogie craze was sweeping the airwaves and dance-halls and at the Apollo they received top billing as 'Café Society's Sensation'; Billie had to settle for 'Queen of Song'. From there she returned to her adopted base, Clark Monroe's Uptown House, and on 11 September sat in along with Count Basie, of whom she was always fond, at a party for Valda, Harlem's popular snake-dancer.

Four days later she was booked into Chicago's Off Beat Club with Muggsy Spanier and his band, but returned briefly to Harlem on 24 September to give a benefit concert for the Women's Welfare Club at Westchester County Center. On her return, trumpeter Jimmy McPartland had taken over the bandstand. 'I was MC of the deal,' he recalled. 'Billie Holiday was our star singer and Art Tatum was playing intermission piano. She was a real musician; it was the first time I heard "Strange Fruit" and was really impressed with the lyrics . . . our rehearsal for Billie there, we finished playing "Strange Fruit" and she sang it and boy . . . I told her, "What you're doing, we can hear you!" . . . She was drinking a lot of brandy as I recall. But she could sing!'[20]

In November 1939 she was back for a new season at Café Society, along with a small group led by pianist Joe Sullivan and still riding high on the success of 'Strange Fruit'. Then, without warning, sometime in the week of 11 November, she was out: 'Hazel Scott Succeeds Billie Holiday at Café Society' read a large leader in *New York Amsterdam News*.[21]

'I got the job because Lady Day quit,' Scott recalled later.[22] Money was blamed for the row; because of her growing success Billie demanded a higher fee. Ernie's in the Village had come up with an offer which she wanted Josephson to match. He did not and she called his bluff.

Although Ernie's was a small club, she did standing-room only business every night.

For much of 1939 Billie had been involved in a serious affair with pianist Sonny White. 'He was a wonderful young man, he was madly in love with her,' recalled guitarist Al Casey, who had known White since childhood. 'She seemed to like him too, they were together for a while. Sonny was a hell of a pianist and got a lot of work; later went with Benny Carter.'[23] But by the end of the year the affair was over. 'Like me, he lives with his mother,' explained Billie, 'our plans for marriage didn't jell.'[24] At the time, she and Sadie lived together at Apartment 2E, 286 West 142nd Street, and within their complex mother–daughter relationship, it is impossible to guess what role Sadie played in coming between Billie and Sonny White. But it seems that Sadie's admonitions about men being no good, about how Clarence Holiday left her to fend for herself, were pushing Billie too far; within eighteen months it would provoke an equal and opposite reaction.

On 21 January 1940 Billie went to a birthday party for Inez Cavanaugh at the Golden Gate Ballroom at 46/8 West 135th Street. Again she was with Count Basie, also there was Clark Monroe, who ran the Uptown House. A few days later Billie's regular boyfriend, 'a well-known sports-man', was seen to hit her outside the 'Little Gray Shop on 7th Avenue'. Billie told her mother she was held up by thugs on 140th Street.[25] That 'well-known sportsman' was James Norman Monroe Jr, Clark Monroe's brother.

James Monroe was born in Georgia on 25 July 1911. While Clark was heavy and upright, James was described as 'frail'. Billie had briefly played around with Clark after her affair with Sonny White, but towards the end of 1939, with war clouds gathering, Jimmy had returned from a long sojourn in Europe. There his marriage had been annulled in England in 1937, where he was cited as the plaintiff, and for a while he ran a Paris club. One of the hipster elite in dress and attitude, when he made a play for Billie she fell for him, saying he was the most beautiful man she had ever seen. His occupation was variously described as that of a 'sportsman', 'impresario', 'marijuana dealer' and 'pimp'.[26] They were euphemisms for doing what he had to do to get by. And in Billie he saw a meal-ticket.

While Billie was at Ernie's in the Village, another record date was lined up for her on 29 February 1940. 'Well, Roy was the trumpet player on that one, it was going to be Frankie [Newton], with some Café Society guys,' recalled John Williams. 'I was with Louis at the time, I just came

119

into town and she called me to make the "Body and Soul" date.'[27] The session began with a dark, moody 'Ghost of Yesterday', a haunting theme provoking memories best forgotten: 'Ghost of yesterday, every night you're here, whispering away what might have been, might have been.' It was a song that sounded as if it might have been a part of her regular repertoire at Café Society.

'Body and Soul' follows the methodology Billie had applied to abstracting a song since her earliest recordings; she dramatically recasts the first sixteen bars, but remains closer to the melody in the bridge and final A section. In the last middle eight she sings the lesser-known alternate lyrics, 'What lies before me, a future that's stormy?' that suggests much more than a passing acquaintance with the song.

It is interesting to compare Billie's version of 'Falling in Love Again' with that of Marlene Dietrich. Here it is Billie who sounds the innocent who almost 'can't help it'; Dietrich's highly stylized version is one of deliberate innuendo.

On Sunday, 16 March 1940, Billie was the guest star at the NY Crisis Committee's cocktail party given at the Witoka Club in Harlem before opening the following day at the Howard Theater in Washington, DC for a week. Then followed a month at Chicago's swanky Hotel Sherman, where she broadcast each night before returning to New York's 52nd Street. When she opened at Kelly's Stables on 25 April with trumpet star Roy Eldridge, also handled by Joe Glaser, it marked a triumphant return to the Street, where just a couple of years earlier she had failed to make an impression. '[When] we worked together at Kelly's Stables,' recalled Eldridge, 'she seemed to have such rapport with people. Billie could get to them, I have seen her make people cry and make people happy. She was out of sight.'[28]

On 9 May Billie was asked to guest on John Kirby's radio show, *Flow Gently, Sweet Rhythm*, but failed to turn up when she heard Ella Fitzgerald was also appearing. She did however appear on WOR's *Sheep and Goats* at 8 p.m. on 1 May, backed by the Clarence Profit trio who were also her accompanists at Kelly's. Profit, a brilliant pianist, was set to replace Fletcher Henderson in the Benny Goodman Orchestra in 1939. He played the World Fair in New York on 1 and 2 October in a trial run with Goodman, but upstaged the clarinettist. Johnny Guarnieri got the job. Billie's run at Kelly's was an unprecedented success; yet when Teddy Wilson opened his season at Café Society on 9 July 1940, it is ironic that after all their superb recordings together, Billie was just a member of the audience.

In August she added another Lewis Allen song called 'Over Here' to her repertoire. Originally performed on 8 July that year by the Peace Troupe of the New Theater League at the New Theater at 110 West 47th Street, it was a parody of Irving Berlin's 'Over There', subtitled 'The Yanks Aren't Coming'. As much a propaganda song against American involvement in the European war against Hitler as 'Strange Fruit' was against lynching, the song was beginning to enjoy modest success when FBI agents leaned on club owner Ralph Watkins to stop Billie singing what was considered 'unpatriotic' material. Outraged, she was forced to accede. What she did not realize was that in Washington, DC, the Federal Bureau of Investigation had now opened a file numbered 4855389 in the name 'Billie Holiday: Singer'.

When the Billie Holiday–Roy Eldridge combination finished their extended run at Kelly's Stables, they were replaced by Una Mae Carlisle, surprising everyone by her reappearance after a mysterious three-month absence when she had been rumoured to be dead, blind or hospitalized. Meanwhile, Billie and Roy Eldridge went straight into the Apollo for the week commencing 27 September 1940. It was a profile appearance. The opening night was a gala premiere for a Ralph Cooper feature film, 'Am I Guilty?', one of the very few films of the time with a black leading man. Everyone who was anyone in Harlem turned out to see it. However, on Tuesday, 1 October Billie was set to open at downtown's Café Society, to precede the grand opening on 8 October of Barney Josephson's new venture, Café Society uptown at 128 East 58th Street.

Billie was stretched to alternate sets between uptown and downtown, but she made it. 'The opening night of Art Tatum and Billie Holiday with Joe Sullivan's all-negro band at Café Society was the week's gayest affair,' reported *New York Amsterdam News*.[29] But Josephson was unhappy about Billie's double booking; *Downbeat* reported he wanted to cancel her contract, saying he could manage without her very well.[30] In the event he and Billie reached a compromise; she would see the week out at the Apollo and rejoin Café Society on Friday, 4 October.

After about six weeks Sullivan left for the Famous Door on 52nd Street, so Art Tatum took over as Billie's accompanist. It was an unusual combination; a laid-back singer who dallied behind the beat, whose suave and economical style was a study in understatement, paired with a pianist who was her complete antithesis; a musician who frequently pushed the beat and whose multi-noted squalls were beyond the ken of almost any piano player alive. It was a partnership of opposites that never quite jelled. '[Art] couldn't accompany a singer,' said pianist Roger 'Ram' Ramirez, a mutual friend of them both, 'he couldn't subjugate himself to that ... he played for Billie Holiday and poor Billie, you know; she just had too much piano being played.'[31]

Billie left Café Society after Christmas and went into Kelly's Stables on 52nd Street. Meanwhile, Milt Gabler had instituted a series of jam sessions on Sunday afternoons at Jimmy Ryan's. 'I went over and did a deal at Ryan's, which was across from my 52nd Street store,' said Gabler, 'because they weren't doing any business at all. I ran them until 1946.'[32] Billie became a regular at those first sessions, just as she had done at the 'Friday Club' at the Park Lane Hotel on Park Avenue in late 1938 and early 1939. The common link was Eddie Condon, who booked the musicians. At Ryan's she could be heard with all her old friends from the Condon gang: Condon himself, Joe Sullivan, Hot Lips Page and Bobby Hackett.

On 1 May 1941, Billie emerged from the small, smoky environs of Kelly's Stables to perform in the open air. The occasion was the annual May Day celebrations in Union Square where she performed 'Strange Fruit' for the holiday crowds assembled there. A week at the Apollo from 13 June announced the end of her short season at Kelly's Stables. For the first time ever she was the headline artist there.

Due to open at the Famous Door on 52nd Street on 12 July, Billie spent three weeks hanging out with Jimmy Monroe at his brother's Uptown House, spending night after night there and regularly sitting in with the house-band led by Floyd 'Horsecollar' Williams. One night in June, jazz enthusiast Jerry Newman took a wire recorder up to the club and caught her in performance.

While she had been at Kelly's Stables, Billie's earning power had leapt to around $300 a week and all through the engagement she had been getting closer to Monroe. Something of a dandy, his days as an international playboy had taught him the importance of dress and deportment and in his new role as a self-styled impresario, he supervised Billie's wardrobe and insisted that if she wanted to be a star, then she should act like one. As an ever-growing group of hangers-on began to grow around her and Monroe, the faster she made money, the faster it was being spent for her by her good-time crowd.

Around this time Billie was introduced to the songwriter Jimmy Davis, who had recently completed three years' study at the Julliard School of Music. He was trying to get Billie interested in some of his songs, among them a number entitled 'Lover Man', which he co-wrote with Roger 'Ram' Ramirez, then pianist with Vernon Andrade, and Jimmy Sherman, the accompanist for a group called the Charioteers. 'Lover Man' had been introduced by Josephine Hall that summer at the Plantation Club to some success and he was trying to get someone to record it. For the time being, however, Billie had her mind on other things.

After she finished her run at the Door on Saturday, 15 August, Billie played a week at the Howard Theater in Washington, DC. She had Jimmy Monroe in tow; they hired a car and drove to Elkton, MD, the 'lovers' paradise', where they arrived late in the evening of the 23rd. At 10.55 p.m. they applied for a marriage licence and were married on Monday, 25 August 1941 by Rev. William F. Hopkins at the Circuit Court for Cecil County.

Coinciding with Billie's nuptials, Columbia re-released an album of eight Holiday–Wilson sides in a retrospective dating back to their very first session together. "This album is a gem,' commented *Downbeat*, adding, 'Somehow jazz of this caliber isn't being put on wax today.'[33]

On 29 August Billie was booked into Chicago for four weeks as a double attraction with Joe Glaser's recent signing, bandleader Lionel Hampton. 'Billie Holiday was a positive sensation in Windy City's Hotel Sherman,' reported *New York Amsterdam News*.[34]

From Chicago Billie headed for a much-publicized opening of a West Coast edition of New York's Café Society in Los Angeles on Wednesday, 1 October. Backed by a band of West Coast studio musicians, she stayed on the Coast for exactly three weeks, until the club unceremoniously closed down, leaving her out of pocket and without enough money for the fare home. She went alone. Jimmy did not demur, he had made some connections of his own. A small-time drugs dealer, he had linked up with a smuggling ring which brought marijuana over the border from Mexico.

When she returned to New York, Billie was reunited with the Hampton band on 28 November for a week at the Apollo. This was followed by a season at the Famous Door on 52nd Street from 11 December, backed by Benny Carter's band with Clark Monroe acting as MC. By now the musical landscape was beginning to change. Young musicians, gathering at places like Monroe's own Uptown House, Minton's and other afterhours joints, were experimenting with new ideas that would culminate in what would be dubbed be-bop.

To those in Harlem and the 52nd Street clubs, it was clear that something new was in the air. Musicians were experimenting with moving from the essentially diatonic conventions of the Swing Era to chromatic harmonies, so enlarging the number of possible note choices open to the improviser. They were also seeking to break up the smooth, rhythmic flow of swing with more agitated phrases that no longer respected bar lines. Be-bop musicians used more angular, often fragmented phrases that began and ended in unexpected places. In Benny

Carter's band at the time was one of the foremost rethinkers of this exciting new musical development, trumpeter Dizzy Gillespie. 'With Dizzy,' said Carter, 'something was popping all the time. His sense of humour was unorthodox, like his playing at the time.'[35]

Billie, however, remained impervious to the new direction. She had now defined her style, and even though the musical climate around her was changing, she gave no indication of going with the new music. 'In her slow, torchy manner, Billie Holiday, employing techniques that come only from a seasoned performer, has the audience in the palm of her hand as she sings "Jim" and "Them There Eyes" and several encores,' approved *New York Amsterdam News*. '"King" of the alto sax, Carter demonstrates his right to the latter title . . . Manager Irving Alexander said the show is set for a long run here.'[36] Then suddenly, while Dizzy Gillespie was temporarily out of the band playing with Charlie Barnet in early January, Billie abruptly cut out to take a job in Montreal. Benny Carter says he cannot remember why she took off,[37] but she was replaced at short notice by Maxine Johnson, who filled in until a permanent replacement could be found. That turned out to be Helen Humes, who had followed Billie into the Basie band in 1938.

Whatever the reason for her sudden departure, Billie was back in New York by 10 February 1942 for her last session for Columbia which had been preceded by a flurry of recording activity. On 12 September 1940 she had been backed by a nine-piece band including Roy Eldridge and Teddy Wilson. Here she produced four sides split between fulfilling her jazz sensibilities and developing her character part on record. 'I'm All for You' and 'Same Old Story', for example, seem to have been chosen for lyric content consistent with the role of a woman unlucky in love: 'I'm all for you, come what may, I'll be by your side', and 'Same old story of a boy and girl in love, same old story but it's new to me'.

'I Hear Music' is by Billie as out-and-out jazz singer and is a poised and elegant performance. Even though the thirty-two-bar ABAC construction is unusual, the lyric line a little congested and the tempo up, she clearly liked the song and had worked out how she wanted to handle it. Equally, 'Practise Makes Perfect' suggests the abandon of three or four years previously; the song in itself is less interesting than the way in which she sings it, and, as with any great artist, it is the performance rather than the material that compels our attention.

On 15 October 1940 Billie cut two W. C. Handy numbers with a band directed by Benny Carter which were less successful than they might have been. Billie remains at arm's length from her material and Carter's backing is far from engaging. After her final session with Lester Young on 21 March 1941, she was again in the studios with an Eddie

Billie Holiday in 1935 behind the Apollo Theatre on 125th Street near 9th Avenue. At the time she was dubbed 'the buxom torch singer' by *New York Age* and *New York Amsterdam News*. (*Ken Whitten Collection*)

On 4 June 1937, Billie Holiday appeared at the Apollo Theatre as vocalist with Count Basie and his Orchestra. 'Have you noticed how Billie Holiday has improved?' said *New York Amsterdam News*. (*Ken Whitten Collection*)

OPPOSITE: With the minimum of movement or gesture, Billie Holiday could freeze an audience in their seats. Here she transfixes onlookers at Café Society in early 1939. (*Ken Whitten Collection*)

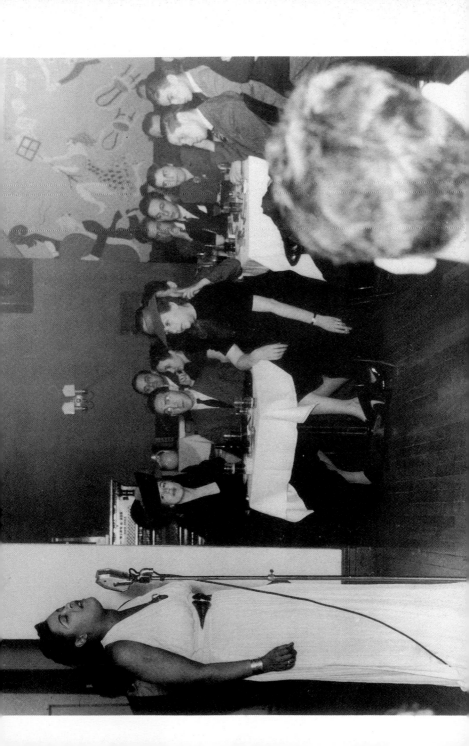

Billie Holiday at the Ken Club in Boston in 1944 with (left to right) Floyd 'Horse collar' Williams, trumpeter Frankie Newton and George Jenkins. (*Inst. of Jazz Studies, Rutgers Univ.*)

OPPOSITE: Signing autographs outside Café Society, 1939; 'I opened . . . as an unknown,' said Billie, 'and I left two years later as a star.' (*Inst. of Jazz Studies, Rutgers Univ.*)

Billie Holiday was fêted as a major star at the First Esquire All American Jazz Concert at the Metropolitan Opera House on 18 January 1944. This backstage shot shows her at the microphone accompanied by Art Tatum (p), with Barney Bigard (cl) just discernible on the right. (*Ken Whitten Collection*)

OPPOSITE: On 8 February 1947 Billie Holiday made a surprise appearance at Louis Armstrong's Carnegie Hall concert to publicize *New Orleans*, due for release later in the year. According to *Downbeat* magazine, Billie 'broke things up' as soon as she appeared on stage. (*Dave Bennett*)

The original 78rpm record labels from the 1930s and 1940s of six key Billie Holiday recordings. (*Stuart Nicholson*)

Heywood pick-up band on 9 May. Here she was joined by Roy Eldridge and a small contingent from the Savoy Sultans who helped create a swinging, tightly organized 'Café Society' sound. 'I'm in a Low Down Groove' is again a number that serves her character part: 'I'm in a low down groove, from carrying a torch for you.'

The remaining numbers, 'God Bless the Child', 'Am I Blue', and 'Solitude', together with 'Jim', 'I Cover the Waterfront' and 'Gloomy Sunday' – the latter nominated by Billie as one of her favourite recordings in 1952 – from the subsequent 7 August session, were songs that placed emotions within semi-narrative settings. They are 'story-telling' songs that situate emotion in a time or place and relate to the system's losers. They sentimentalize human nature, but achieve their realism by unsentimental performance. Such songs, where the formal conservatism of the music is contrasted with the emotional drama created by the singer, seem, to a lesser or greater degree, to need the reinforcement of live performance to enhance their meaning.

Nuance, gesture, facial expression, atmosphere can all assume a crucial role in the context of storyline, particularly with these mini-melodramas where a slow moving melody plays a subservient role to the words. The combination of image, words and music projected by the singer's performing personality and the public's desire to identify with it gave these 'storyline' songs a meaning far greater live than we can experience today when listening to the CD; the video performances of Billie singing 'God Bless the Child' from 1950 or 'Strange Fruit' from 1959, for example, reveal detail of facial nuance that exploits words and manipulates their significance – all part of her artistic elaboration to invite the listener to become a part of the song's fantasy. 'When she was in the spotlight she was absolutely regal,' recalled Milt Gabler, 'the way she held her head up high, the way she phrased each word and got to the heart of the story in each song.'[38]

With Billie's 10 February 1942 session, her last for Columbia, there is clearly a lack of animation in her work. Bassist John Williams recalls that several of the arrangements for this, and the previous 7 August session, were provided by former Chick Webb arranger Van Alexander.[39] The sides from this final session, however, were not released for years after they were recorded. 'Wherever You Are' is dedicated to the fighting forces overseas while 'Mandy is Two' returns to the theme of Billie's previous sessions: more storyline than song. And while 'It's a Sin to Tell a Lie' fails to overcome the memory of Fats Waller's memorable put-on, it does at least include the only rallentando ending of the Columbia series.

From August 1942, the American Federation of Musicians imposed a recording ban. They were claiming a fee for every record broadcast on radio. The strike dragged on for over a year; what no one knew at the time was that the days of the big bands were numbered. The optimism and excitement of Roosevelt's 'New Deal' had given way to the sombre realism of a country at war. Lovers were being parted and the mood was sentimental. Billie's 'All of Me' became a favourite of countless homesick GIs, and a re-release of Harry James's 'All or Nothing at All' became one of the first big hits for Frank Sinatra. His sensational opening at the Paramount Theater in New York in September 1942 ushered in a new era in popular music. Singers were set to dominate the music business, but no one seemed interested in picking-up Billie Holiday's recording contract. The finest singer of them all was seen as too 'difficult'.

In all, Billie had recorded 153 titles for Columbia since her debut with Benny Goodman in 1933. Together they comprise a remarkable body of work that virtually defines the jazz singer's art. Although accompanied by some of the finest musicians of her day, it is very often Billie's rhythmic ideas that now sound the most subtle. Her best recordings had an easy unselfconsciousness that conveyed sentimental memories with a tough-mindedness that realized love was not magic and a directness that acknowledged the facts of life. As she developed as an artist, her later sessions revealed an ability to exploit the emotional possibilities of sentiment while still remaining forthright and uncompromising.

What these recordings reveal is a singer of broad emotional range, able to narrow her focus at will, using detail, nuance and above all irony to profound effect. She sang a variety of material, at first taking her chorus in turn with the instrumentalists. At times her dramatic syncopations and daring note choices seized the pressure points of a song to reshape it so profoundly that once heard it went on to enjoy a second life, a life within the memory; indeed, many of her songs from this period are truly unforgettable.

As Billie's popularity increased, so too did the opportunity to bring to the fore the character part of someone unlucky in love. It was a role that was able to survive the conflicting demands of jazz singer and cabaret artist by careful choice of material, songs sung in a way that invoked the blues mood without being blues at all.

Despite no formal musical training she was capable of learning up to four completely new songs literally hours before a recording session, usually just the day before but often, no doubt, during the session itself. With just a minimum of preparation Billie made the songs completely her own. In so doing she left no doubt about the sophistication of her musical mind, without which it would have been impossible to produce such intelligent and coherent rhythmic and harmonic variations. To manoeuvre with such temporal freedom within form required an aural 'snapshot' of a song firmly planted in her mind that included such things as the tonality of the tune, where the individual chords of the progression modulate one to another (what musicians refer to as the 'changes') and the thematic construction of the song (for example, an AABA form).

However, quite often Billie was confronted with songs that did not fall into the standard thirty-two-bar ternary AABA format. But even its more sophisticated variations, such as ABCD or ABAC, for example, posed no problems for her and neither did a song that did not subscribe to the usual thirty-two-bar length, such as thirty, thirty-six or forty-eight bars. To place this in perspective, it is worth noting that even today, in an age of college- and conservatory-educated jazz musicians, straightforward song forms are much preferred as a basis of improvisation. Yet here, in the late 1930s, this young autodidact was negotiating with ease complex songs from the canons of a Cole Porter or a George Gershwin. Her grasp and understanding of form and structure were such that they also brought great symmetry to her vocal variations, and the best are minor miracles of organizing harmonic and rhythmic ideas to maximum effect.

Within just seven years, between 1935 and 1942, Billie Holiday had defined her art; what was to follow would offer no significant advance on these achievements. Today these recordings are not only remembered for the brilliance of her singing, but also for the remarkable empathy she generated with her accompanists on several key sessions. Her creativity could ignite inspiration as those around her raised the temperature with their own improvisational gifts. The results were imperishable.

127

Chapter Eight

1942–45

The problems that caused Billie Holiday to leave the Famous Door abruptly for Montreal seemed behind her in April 1942. She again joined forces with Benny Carter, this time for a theatre tour. Carter had just signed with Joe Glaser after forming a new big band which he broke in with a booking at Harlem's Golden Gate Ballroom in March. The Billie Holiday–Benny Carter package opened with a week at the Apollo on 10 April. 'Benny Carter and Billie Holiday are two of the great names in jazz. This show was a beautiful demonstration of just why they are,' enthused *Metronome*.[1]

Between tour dates with Billie, Carter put in a week at the Gaiety Theater on Broadway, a date he remembers with great clarity; Glaser took 10 per cent from the theatre and 10 per cent from Carter. Later in the year, when Carter again went out on the road, he turned to Tommy Rockwell's General Amusement Corporation for representation.

In May Billie headlined at the opening of the Boogie-Woogie, a new night-club in Cleveland, with the popular Cats and a Fiddle quartet comprising Austin Powell, guitar/vocals; Tiny Grimes, guitar; Ernie Price, ukelele and George Steinbeck, bass. Booked in for a month, they lasted two weeks; despite favourable notices, business was only fair and the club went to the wall. Billie immediately travelled out to the West Coast, where Jimmy Monroe's drug-smuggling activities had ended in his arrest by the authorities. With his arraignment set for the end of the month, Billie looked around for work to help pay for his defence. She quickly linked up with Lee and Lester Young, who led the house band at Billy Berg's Trouville Club. Between them they persuaded Berg to add her to a bill which included Leo Watson's Spirits of Rhythm, Joe Turner and Slim [Gaillard] and Slam [Stewart].

Berg formerly owned the Capri Club, but in April 1942 opened the much larger Trouville, which sat about 250 people. The club attracted a considerable following from the movie studios, including Betty Grable, and Howard Hughes, who used to turn up in tennis shoes, while in her autobiography Billie drops the names of several stars who frequented the club, among them Lana Turner and Bette Davis. The Lee and Lester Young band included 'Red' Morris Mack on trumpet, Bumps Meyers and Lester Young on tenor saxophones, Red Callender on bass and Lee Young on drums. Jimmy Rowles, the sole white member, was on piano; at first Billie was suspicious of him as the only 'ofay' until she was reassured by Lester that 'this cat can blow'.

Billie's stay at the Trouville is documented by an aircheck from June: 'Let's tell you right now we're broadcasting for the next twenty-five minutes from the Trouville on Beverly Boulevard, one block east of Fairfax, no cover, no minimum – right here in Hollywood!' They reveal a tightly arranged, cohesive ensemble, often with intricate arrangements from the likes of Nat 'King' Cole, Gerald Wilson and Dudley Brooks. The band was hot. The tempos were up and on some numbers they were frantic; as the announcer said, it was music for jitterbugging. There was no let-up for Billie's 'I Hear Music', where she delivers at probably the fastest tempo of her career, and certainly of her recorded performances.[2]

Only on her ballad feature 'Solitude' does the tempo relent before powering into an instrumental 'Broadway'. To all intents and purposes this was a jump band, albeit with a Basie-like rhythm section. It can only be a matter of speculation what influence a band like this, at a top Hollywood night-spot, with a nationally known soloist in Lester Young, had on the Central Avenue music scene. Echoes of the band seem to reverberate through West Coast jump bands; Jack McVea's sides for the Black and White label or Big Jay McNeely's for Exclusive, for example, capture those tightly arranged instrumental passages, frantic tempos and tenor saxophone solos exploding from the ensembles.

Billie says it was at the Trouville that she first met impresario Norman Granz; in fact Granz's recollection is hazy on this point, although he is certain they first met on the West Coast.[3] However, he does remember the Trouville well; it was here that he began his distinguished career in jazz by promoting a regular series of jam sessions on the club's 'off' nights in July 1942. As the Trouville Sunday sessions gradually became popular, he was able to develop a circuit of clubs, each with a different 'off' night, insisting on racially mixed audiences, tables on the dance-floor to create a listening-only policy, and proper payment for musicians, rather than tips, hitherto the norm for such sessions.

In 1944 Granz put the jam-session concept on to the concert stage at Los Angeles Philharmonic Auditorium, and Jazz at the Philharmonic was born. Live recordings leveraged the concerts and concerts leveraged the records; within ten years Granz owned Verve, the largest independent label in jazz, with a roster of artists that included Charlie Parker, Lester Young, Ben Webster, Bud Powell, Stan Getz, Ella Fitzgerald, Oscar Peterson and Count Basie.

When Jimmy Monroe came to trial, his defence was not accepted by the jury and he was sent down for twelve months. Lawyers' fees had taken almost everything Billie had earned at the Trouville and she was about to be evicted from her hotel room, along with trombonist Trummy Young, whom she was now seeing with Monroe out of the way. Young had written a number called 'Trav'lin' Light' and in a bid to raise some money fast, he approached Billie's old acquaintance Johnny Mercer, who had recently formed Capitol Records with record retailer Glenn Wallichs and songwriter Buddy DeSylva. Mercer supplied the lyrics and passed the song on to Jimmy Mundy to make an arrangement for the Paul Whiteman Orchestra, due to make one of the first Capitol recording sessions on 12 June 1942. Billie, still trying to persuade Columbia to renew her contract, sang under the pseudonym 'Lady Day'. The record was a minor hit, but there was no question of royalties. Billie sang for a flat session fee like the rest of the Whiteman orchestra, which quite possibly included Lester Young in the saxophone section. Her vocal, the last she made before the American Federation of Musicians called a recording strike at midnight on 31 July, provides an intriguing miniature of her art.

'Trav'lin' Light' is a standard thirty-two-bar AABA song, presented with three instrumental A sections preceding the vocal. The first A theme is played with excellent control by trombonist Skip Layton, the second by the band plus solo sax, and the third is another straight melody statement by Layton. The only time the middle eight is heard is during Billie's thirty-two-bar AABA vocal. During it the string section adopt a prominent role in accompaniment – they had been barely audible in the ensemble – thereby touching an Achilles heel. The next time Billie recorded for a big record label she wanted strings.

By comparing Layton's straight reading with Billie's interpretation, it is immediately clear that in order to alter the melody line in the way in which she did, she must have had exceptional rhythmic sureness, as can be seen by contrasting the first two bars of the first A section or the third A section with the lyrics 'Some lucky night he may come back again' with Layton's 'straight' version. By altering the melody she brings greater expressive weight to bear on the lyric content. Mercer's lyrics are once more an 'I'-addressing-'you' story of being unlucky in love; here Billie is travelling light because her man is gone, once again consistent with her character part in song. Johnny Mercer, as in her very first recording session, came up with the lyrics that conform to this persona.

When the money for the Capitol session came through, $75 each for Billie and Young, they paid their hotel bill, had some Chinese food and went out to celebrate. After the fun there was only $5 left, so Billie wired Sadie for the cost of a busride for two east. Her place at the Trouville was filled by Marie Bryant.

Billie opened at Joe Sherman's Garrick Stagebar in Chicago on 15 August with a band fronted by Henry Red Allen including Allen's long-time associate, trombonist and four-times *Metronome* poll winner J. C. Higginbotham. Their drawing-power was such that they opened to capacity crowds; Sherman immediately offered to hold them over until December.

While Billie was being driven to work one evening the car in which she was riding collided with an ambulance. Billie, with cut knees, required medical attention and asked to be taken to a hospital. Leaving the scene of the accident, her car was stopped by police and she was immediately taken into custody. Calls to Joe Sherman resulted in his thinking it was all a gag until Billie lost her cool and Sherman hastened to the police station to stand bail. First aid was obtained and she appeared that night as usual, but glared at Sherman all evening, muttering, 'Man, you just ain't nowhere' every time he was in earshot.[4] Perhaps this was also the night she discovered that when Sherman originally booked her, he thought Billie Holiday was a man.[5]

Although there were reports that Billie was about to walk out of the Garrick bar because she could not tolerate Sherman,[6] she was playing to such enthusiastic crowds that she saw out her contract to December. 'Billie has exceptional taste and she chooses only those songs which strike her as sincere and those in which she can really believe,' observed *Downbeat*, '. . . from a good blues like "Fine and Mellow" through "I Cried for You", "He's My Guy", "Them There Eyes", to . . . "Strange Fruit".'[7] It was a song-list that was becoming etched in stone; the same songs night after night was beginning to see artistic creativity blur into stylization.

At the end of December Billie was replaced by Louis Jordan, but stayed in Chicago to see in the New Year of 1943 with a midnight concert at the Regal Theater with the Lionel Hampton band. Then followed a theatre tour with Hampton, also a Glaser client, and by February she was back on 52nd Street.

She opened at Kelly's Stables with an impressive line-up; once again she was with Red Allen and J. C. Higginbotham plus added attractions

Coleman Hawkins and a late-night jam session led by ex-Goodman saxophonist Jerry Jerome. However, those same old songs sung in the same old way were now beginning to cause comment: 'Instead of improving her style through practice and new ideas it sounded very much as though she has been content to go along using the same old phrases over and over again as she did on "Embracable You" . . . "You Go To My Head" and "Them There Eyes",' remarked *Downbeat*.[8]

It was a charge with some foundation. Where alternate takes are available of her Columbia and Commodore sides, Billie's vocals, like identical templates one upon another, frequently showed only small variation. She seemed to conceptualize her approach in terms of sweeping gesture and significant detail, which remained essentially unaltered in subsequent performance.

At the end of March 1943 Billie returned to the West Coast, where Jimmy Monroe had got a job with the Douglas plant after serving time, less remission, in Los Angeles County Jail. Their marriage now existed in name only, both going their separate ways. Monroe, who from time to time was involved with the singer and entertainer Nina Mae McKinney, was not beyond putting the squeeze on Billie for money. Billie, who still remained irresistibly drawn to Monroe, also enjoyed casual sex with a variety of partners. However, for a woman to enact her sexuality is not the same as a man. Women on stage are viewed by men as sexual commodities, usually assumed to be publicly available; Billie, on stage and off, seemed to reinforce this stereotypical image. Yet while she wanted to be looked after by her men, she never seemed wholly controlled by them either; sexually, she was at once both dominated and dominating. Strong, sexually aggressive women, however, are perceived as a threat to a 'natural' or patriarchal sexual hierarchy; for example, in operas such as *Carmen*, *Lulu* or *Salome* the victimized male who has been aroused by the temptress must kill her to reinstate social order. Equally, this metaphor seems to have been enacted in Billie Holiday's sexual relationships; physically and sexually dominating, she seemed only to conform by the use of physical violence. But within the pain and pleasure of this desire-purge mechanism, which perhaps had its roots in her Catholic past, she wanted something in return; she expected her partner to exert equal control in the turbulent world she inhabited. She called her men 'Daddy' and looked to them as protectors; when they failed, or were not there for her, like Jimmy Monroe, she moved on.

In April Billie began a long residency with Roy Eldridge in the Onyx Club on 52nd Street. Except for the week of 15 July when she played

Loew's State with violinist Eddie South, she remained a mainstay at the club throughout 1943 and 1944.

Just as in her early days on the bar-and-grill circuit in Harlem, Billie's professional life merged seamlessly with her personal life, hanging out with musicians and patrons, socializing all the while. Eventually she would get to sing, her ability often blurred by Brandy Alexanders. 'Billie is not singing at her best in our opinion, nor does she sing often enough, but Eldridge more than makes up for her by putting on a show every night,' observed *Downbeat*.[9]

During her period at the Onyx, she had a variety of accompanists. Her most requested pianist was Nat Jaffe, who later died from a vascular ailment. He had a reputation as a superb accompanist and if he had a job elsewhere, Billie would try and get him to double in whatever club he was playing to back her. Jaffe emerged from the Teddy Wilson school with an original approach of his own, described by *Downbeat* as 'inventive and technically adroit'.[10]

With countless servicemen transiting through New York, the Street was enjoying a boom period. To musicians and the public alike, Billie was the Queen of 52nd Street. Her songs of love and longing exactly reflected the mood of the nation. Lovers were being parted; soldiers, sailors and airmen were going off to war, some never to return. Night after night Billie was playing to standing-room-only crowds, time after time the Onyx extended her contract. Accompanists came and went; when Nat Jaffe moved to Kelly's Stables he was replaced by a trio led by Cozy Cole. Then followed a trio led by pianist Johnny Guarnieri. 'When you heard her do "I Cover the Waterfront" you had to say that her draggy delivery was perfectly suited to the song,' recalled Guarnieri. 'She made a timeless tune out of "I Didn't Know What Time it Was". To me her greatest quality was not the one that everybody fixes on – the expression and feeling – but her innately and absolutely perfect sense of timing.'[11]

In September 1943 *Life* magazine sponsored a jam session in photographer Gjon Mili's studio. Among those present were Teddy Wilson, Eddie Condon and his band, a contingent of musicians from Don Redman's big band and blues folksinger Josh White. 'I remember the first time I played for Billie,' said White, 'Gjon Mili, the *Life* photographer, threw a party. I'd met her before, casually, but this was the first proper meeting . . . Following the *Life* party she started coming into the Café Society where I was working . . . then we would drive around the after-hours spots together.'[12] As men came and went in her life, Billie was beginning to get a reputation as an easy mark. Such a reputation meant she was also vulnerable and could be taken advantage of.

A photograph of Billie performing at the jam session appeared in a centre spread of *Life* magazine in October, along with several other Mili photographs of the event. Billie's was captioned 'She has the most distinctive style of any popular vocalist and is imitated by other vocalists'.[13] One of those imitators was a singer called Willie Dukes who was building a name for himself on 52nd Street singing the Jimmy Davis–Ram Ramirez number 'Lover Man'. 'Willie Dukes sang like her,' said Ramirez, 'only stronger than her. Imitation is a strong form of flattery ... But look, when you get a gay imitator ... the public began to accept "*Love*-er Man".'[14] Willie Dukes' modest success with the song encouraged Billie eventually to add 'Lover Man' to her repertoire. 'Naturally with her following, that gave it the carte blanche,' continued Ramirez, 'those were lurid and sexy lyrics for the time, "You'll make love to me", in those days it was a no-no.'[15]

Still at the Onyx, Billie's backing group again changed in October when guitarist Al Casey's trio took over from Guarneri. 'When she sang she put her whole self into it,' Casey recalled, 'she felt what she was doing. I used to watch her when we played for her. It was like she used to go out, she was like singing in another world. When it was her time to come on you could hear a pin drop, no matter how crowded the place was, and she would mesmerize people, seem to me, she was stood in one spot, no gyrations, nothing like that.

'There was a big-time night-club near the Street, and Frank Sinatra worked there, and he'd come by and see us, play a couple of songs with us, late at night, most of the crowds had gone by then, he just came to relax, I suppose.'[16] In later years Sinatra looked back on those years with affection. '[Billie] was a good friend of mine,' he said. 'She affected me in singing as many others, Louis, Crosby, Jack Leonard, Big T, Mercer, Astaire. Tricks they use, I didn't listen to copy. I used to watch Billie in New York night after night, as much as I could. A great contributor to my career in the sense of articulating a song. She didn't know it and I didn't know it until it came to me later.'[17]

During December Billie went out on the road, backed by a band led by saxophonist Teddy McRae, once straw-boss of Ella Fitzgerald's big band. But it was the Street that provided her with the ideal forum; it allowed her talent to blossom, freed from the rigid time-keeping of theatre shows. When *Esquire* magazine announced the results of a poll they conducted among jazz critics at the end of 1943, Billie was the clear winner of the vocal section.

All the poll winners were invited to perform at the 'First Esquire All-American Jazz Concert', held at the Metropolitan Opera House on 18 January 1944. And while Marion Anderson, the famous opera singer, has always been rightly cited for breaching the racist barriers there, it was Billie who was the first black artist ever to sing at the Met. It was also the first gala occasion where she was treated like a major artist. She appeared amongst an impressive roster of talent: Louis Armstrong, Roy Eldridge, Jack Teagarden, Barney Bigard, Coleman Hawkins, Art Tatum, Oscar Pettiford, Sid Catlett and Al Casey. ''43 Esquire Awards, another thing that unhinged me,' recalled Casey, 'all those names. Couldn't play properly for listening to that fabulous music; Art Tatum just about amazed everybody! And Billie, she sounded great. I had a thing for her then, but I got nowhere!'[18]

The show was recorded as part of the 'Coca Cola Parade of Spotlight Bands' series and the results found their way on to V-Disc. Billie performed 'Do Nothing Till You Hear From Me', the blues 'I Love My Man' and the standard 'I'll Get By', and if her performances sounded perfunctory it was because it was a live broadcast where she was whistled onstage twice, the second time just to perform 'I'll Get By', at an unusually brisk tempo.

From the end of 1943 Billie became involved with the bass player John Simmons, whom she first met when he was playing in Eddie Heywood's band in the Village Vanguard. 'She was a masochist. She was doing things to make me fight her,' recalled Simmons. 'There was a pet shop across the street and I went over and bought a cat-of-nine-tails . . . I caught her with this whip . . . I hit her everywhere but in her face and the bottom of her feet . . . I say, "She won't be to work tonight," before I left home I run a bathtub full of cold water with a box of table salt to close the welts. I just knew she wasn't going to be at work . . . I took an intermission. Went across the street. There she is under this pin light with this gardenia in her hair, singing her ass off. Never fazed her.'[19]

It is around this period, either the end of 1943 or the beginning of 1944, that Billie became involved with narcotic drugs. 'When Billie started, I say don't do it baby, I say you don't know what you're letting yourself in for,' said Simmons. 'Her being adventuresome, she went for it . . . So I left . . . Having had it and knowing what it involved, I just didn't want to be around it.'[20]

Since she was a teenager Billie had been getting her kicks from alcohol and marijuana. This had been part of the scene in the fast crowd she mixed with in the 1930s. But within the status gradations that existed among the 'hip' people opium smoking was considered the epitome of cool, the province of the big-timers. Small but elite circles considered it a luxurious vice and within the society in which Billie moved, it was associated with desirables: the big spenders, the flashy dressers and the big tippers.

Opium smoking, however, takes time. The hipster elite would gather for their smoking sessions like ritual drinking on a Saturday night, with a sense of occasion; first there was the preparation of the pipe with the *gee*-rag and bowl. When this was ready the pipe was passed around the assembled company before the hours spent languishing in the twilight world of opiate effect. Afterwards the bowl, or *yen hok*, would be scraped clean of opium with a *yen-she gow* and either resmoked or, if there was enough, recooked.

However, the danger of opium smoking was the distinct odour it gave off. To prevent discovery wet towels had to be put around doors and windows to stop the smell escaping. But even with this elaborate and time-consuming preparation, any kind of hipster who aspired to style and class, like a James Monroe, smoked opium, either on a casual or regular basis.[21]

Part of Jimmy Monroe's attraction for Billie was that he was a member of the fashionable elite in the world to which she belonged. Monroe's concern for how she dressed, how she projected herself both on and off stage, and the company she kept were all reflections of his concern that Billie should appear hip. It was inevitable that when she moved into his world she would be sucked into opium smoking.[22] However, around 1943–4 the illicit drugs market began to be radically restructured, as much through the effects of World War II as through federal narcotic control measures. One important result was an underworld shortage of opium, a void that was quickly filled by heroin. This was due in part to the Mafia, who preferred heroin to the more bulky opium.

Times were changing. People had less time for the leisurely rituals of opium smoking. The war had pushed up costs for all illicit drugs and users needed more time to hassle for money to indulge themselves. Consequently, from the mid-1940s to the end of the decade almost all opium smokers went over to heroin (and later cocaine) so that by the early 1950s opium smoking was extremely rare outside Chinese communities. But from having a fairly safe time in the world of opium, users took a hard fall to heroin. To begin with, the incidence of injecting the drug was rare. Most started by 'sniffing', but as supplies of the drug varied in quality, users gradually turned to injecting the drug to make sure they got high.

Billie was just one of many who got caught up in the changing fashion within what was then a restricted drug sub-culture. For while the war meant that supplies of opium had greatly diminished, heroin too was in short supply at the time. Only those with money and connections could get supplied, and one area where money and supply bisected was the music business. By the mid-1940s heroin had become fashionable, particularly with the young players in the burgeoning be-bop movement. Billie, however, was one of the few musicians from the previous generation, the so-called Swing Era, who became involved with the drug.

The stark statistics of be-bop musicians' involvement with heroin were appalling. Some 50–75 per cent of the bop players had experience of the drug, a quarter to a third were seriously addicted, and as many as 20 per cent were killed by their addiction. Yet jazz has never been without the taint of drugs. From the very beginning cocaine was sold freely in New Orleans' Storyville district, as was marijuana, widely thought to have been brought into the South by Mexican labourers at the turn of the century. And because jazz existed within an entertainment infrastructure, alcohol was widely available from the start. But while the effects of marijuana are relatively harmless and alcohol abuse takes time to work its effect, hard drugs, if the dosage is high, provokes dependence quickly.

Viewed in a broader context, of course, jazz was not alone in its secretive drug subculture. The arts and literature have long had a relationship with drugs; a dark yet intimate link that has lurked almost hidden from view beneath the veneer of culture for almost two centuries. Art and drugs both involve a flight of the imagination, and from George Byron to William Burroughs, artists and writers have taken drugs and used the experience as subject matter in their work.[23] Somehow the theme of drug-taking among the risk-takers in the arts, the people who are at the creative cutting edge, has always mystified and fascinated.

Drug use has become synonymous with a familiar theme, a theme beginning with a pleasure happily entered into, with only one ending, eventually surrendering to the tyranny of demand. It is a myth, however, to believe that drug use invariably ends in the chaos of addiction. People can live and work using heroin; there are incidental users, 'chippers', who do not become strung out or give up their lives for the procurement of the drug. There are those, for example, who shoot up on a weekend and do not do so again for a week or a month. Even among addicts, many stop using the drug; in the majority of cases the pattern of addiction ends after about ten years for a variety of reasons, not least because hustling for drugs becomes less attractive as middle age looms. Others run out of money, form a secure relationship or simply settle down to a stable lifestyle. Of those who stop, some might become involved again and still manage to stop. Yet addiction itself is seldom the cause of death;

rather, people die through the lifestyle associated with the drug culture. They die because they have no idea of the potency of the drug they are injecting and overdose, or they die through infection of needle sites or of diseases passed on through infected needles.

The attraction of drugs is escape or transformation. They invoke changes in perception, sometimes visual, sometimes auditory, and most invoke altered feelings of time and space. But the question of whether drugs help artists to make better art is debatable. Marijuana activates the mind, sometimes connecting ideas in unusual ways. It forms a focus on the here-and-now, 'the minute particulars' of life, as Blake called them, and distorts the passage of time on to a seemingly faster scale. Opium users who smoke just a small amount of the drug experience a kind of rêverie, a phantasmagoric world, while retaining their consciousness. In contrast, heroin is a very powerful drug. It produces a kind of oblivion and relaxation coupled with euphoria and feeling good; a dreamy-smooth world, but ultimately a disfunctional one.

One of the most consistent themes among drug users, especially addicts and ex-addicts, is their desire to confess and talk about their problem. Most tell dramatic and wonderful 'war' stories, which, in the instance of Billie Holiday at least, have contributed immeasurably to the mythic qualities of her legend.[24] But for musicians who were around her through 1944, a consistent theme emerges. Her use of drugs was very private and discreet to begin with, and many musicians were unaware of it. Any inconsistency of behaviour or performance during this period was initially put down to alcohol. However, it is entirely possible that Billie could have been an occasional user of heroin throughout 1944 since it was not until 1945 that it became more widely known that she had succumbed to addiction.

In September 1943 Decca reached an agreement with the American Federation of Musicians to lift the recording ban, and it was expected that the other majors would quickly follow. Gradually musicians were finding their way back into the recording studios again, and Billie decided that she too wanted to record. '[She] told me she was free and wanted me to try some new sessions with her,' said Milt Gabler. 'I was overjoyed. I went to Joe Glaser, her agent ... and I paid a very good price for Billie to do three sessions for Commodore ... we waxed eleven great standards and one more blues, "I Love My Man".'[25] Gabler had Eddie Heywood, working at the Café Society Downtown, do the arrangements and run through them with Billie before showtime at the club. 'The recording dates were a joy,' said Gabler. 'Billie was in great shape and artistically at the peak of her career.'[26]

She returned to the recording studios on 25 March 1944 with Heywood's little combo, followed by two further sessions, each a week apart. The pianist's arrangements are workmanlike but not much more, and leave the singer little space; on 'Embracable You', 'I Cover the Waterfront', 'How Am I to Know', 'As Time Goes By' and 'I'm Yours' (where Billie leaves out the second 'dear' of 'Couldn't tell you though I try, dear, just why, dear, I'm yours'), Heywood has written front-line organ chords. There is nothing wrong with that, but as a musical device they are best saved for the end, where they can give a little lift to the final chorus. Heywood, however, plays his hand early. In come the chords with the vocalist at the beginning of her chorus and they drone on and on throughout each song, creating a kind of musical treacle for the singer to wade through. In contrast, the uptempo 'I'll Get By' is all hustle and bustle, with irritating-to-the-point-of-distraction riffs suggesting that little thought has been given to instrumental light and shade on either the slow or brighter tempo numbers. In fact, it is the sides with Heywood's trio that today appear more engaging, but even so Billie herself seems to be going through the motions and here a preference for agonizingly slow tempos emerges. Equally, there are times when she seems to rely on overt stylistic devices: 'Only inveterate Billie fans will want these,' observed *Downbeat*.[27]

In contrast to the 1944 Commodores, many commentators who saw Billie perform live during 1943–4 say these were her peak years.[28] Commercially, her drawing-power continued to rise. In early 1944 she was at the Onyx on West 52nd Street with second headliner Dizzy Gillespie. Between their sets, Al Casey's trio played what *Downbeat* described as 'wonderful mood music'.[29]

Following her Onyx engagement, Billie went from 57 West 52nd Street to 56 West, where the Spotlite painted her name on the canopy in April. From there she left for a short theatre tour, taking in Loew's State in New York and the Regal in Chicago, where she had become a favourite. On her return to New York in May she was expected to return to the Onyx but instead opened at the Apollo for a week and then went into an upper-crust East Side club called the Ruban Bleu, supported by society deb Daphne Hellman who played boogie-woogie on the harp. Billie's first three nights were marred by the loss of her dog, which had become something of a trade-mark at her 52nd Street appearances. A few weeks later a boxer became her regular companion, which, at the end of the 1940s, was replaced by a succession of chihuahuas, all of which figured prominently wherever she appeared.

After a guest spot on *The New World A'Comin'* radio show on 25 June, with an all-star band including Roy Eldridge and Art Tatum, Billie travelled to Chicago in July for two weeks at the Grand Terrace. Her return to a venue where she had been bumped while trying to establish herself as a teenager was marked by 'house-full' signs every night. It was followed by a week in the Regal from 21 July, her second appearance there that year, and from there she made her way to the West Coast for a screen test with Warner Brothers: 'Successful cinema efforts by Lena Horne and Hazel Scott probably helped WB in making their minds about Lady Day,' reported *Downbeat*.[30] Somehow, however, Lady Day flunked the test.

On Friday, 18 August 1944 Billie opened at the Downbeat, headlining a bill that included the Red Norvo sextet and the Bascomb Brothers' big band. 'When I worked with her at the Downbeat it was three horns, xylophone and bass and piano,' said Red Norvo. 'Getting to work and things . . . She couldn't get started. But we got along pretty well, played for her. There were things, but I don't speak about those, she was a nice girl.'[31] By October, Coleman Hawkins had replaced the Bascomb Brothers and Red Norvo had moved on, leaving his pianist and bassist to accompany Billie.

While at the Downbeat, Milt Gabler called in one night to see Billie perform. By now 'Lover Man' had become a staple in her repertoire and as soon as he heard her perform it, he decided it had huge hit potential. 'I went to Glaser saying I wanted to sign her to Decca,' he said.[32] The contract was signed on 7 August 1944, calling for twelve numbers over a one-year period with an option for a further year. For the first time in her life she was to receive royalties. And in Decca she had a company who could afford to commission special arrangements and hire an orchestra to give the backing she wanted, which was strings.

At 1 p.m. on Wednesday, 4 October 1944, Billie walked into the Decca recording studios at 50 West 57th Street. 'She came into the studio, turned around and walked right out,' said Toots Camarata, the musical director and arranger for the session. 'I went after her and asked her what was wrong. She said, "Oh man! These strings hit me pretty hard!"'[33] The use of strings created a new and, it must be said, wholly appropriate backdrop for Billie's voice at this point in her career. The use of small instrumental combos had placed her for some while in the invidious position of having to compete with her past triumphs on Columbia. By deftly changing the context in which she sang, the listener is forced to consider Billie's singing on its own merits. 'Every time I had listened to Billie she was either with Teddy Wilson's band or one of the great bands that John [Hammond] put together with all-star musicians,' said Gabler. 'But I felt Billie a different way, as a pop singer. To me, when you went into a club she'd lovingly sing these slow ballads. She would sing for losers and really read a lyric. So I wanted torch songs for Billie.'[34]

'Lover Man' is perhaps the most enduring of all Billie's output on Decca. Just as Henri Cartier-Bresson referred to the 'decisive moment' that captured the perfect photographic image, here perhaps is a 'lyric moment' that defines the singer in the character role she had created for herself. Taken together with 'That Ole Devil Called Love' from the subsequent 8 November session, we have a quite different artistic approach to the free-wheeling Wilson Columbias. Here the instrumental backdrop frames the singer in quite a different way; the whole emotional climate is given over to the singer who takes centre stage. The jazz elements of her singing, such as syncopation, modifying and simplifying the melodic line, are less important than the almost perfect symmetry between words, rhythm and personality, the latter signified by the 'grain' of her voice. Here Billie seemed to be less concerned with jazz considerations than with offering her audience the chance to be in on the public construction of emotion. Once again she is singing about her love and her man; but love can also be an obsession, and it is from this standpoint that Billie sings.

'We did "Lover Man" and only got half of the date done because she was quite sick,' said drummer Johnny Blowers. 'She was very lovely and a very sweet girl but her health didn't hold up that well. She was quiet, very much of an introvert. So was Ella; Ella never came out and said I'd like it this way or I'd like it that way, it just seemed that these girls with their talent were capable of doing just about anything that was put up for them – they were naturals.'[35]

After her stay at the Downbeat, Billie moved a few doors down the Street to the Spotlite where she was backed by a small group led by guitarist Tiny Grimes. 'I started with my own group playing for Billie Holiday,' recalled Grimes, 'There were no problems about jobs at that time. When I was working with her in the Spotlite, Charlie Parker used to come around and jam.'[36] By now, however, the weekly listings of the *New Yorker* had taken to calling her 'moody Billie Holiday', because of her erratic time-keeping. Slowly but surely the effects of heroin were making themselves felt. The use of almost any opiate is accompanied by tolerance. To provoke the same effect within the short space of an hour actually needs fractionally more of the drug since the body adjusts very quickly and heroin provokes a high tolerance. But with each increased dosage, the threshold of addiction advances ever faster. Billie had a strong constitution; who knows how much and how often she was taking before she became addicted?

In the first week of December 1944, while playing the Apollo, she learned that Jimmy Monroe had again been arrested for smuggling marijuana from Mexico. Billie, who continued to regard Monroe with great affection, said later that the first time was 'okay', the second 'too much'.[37]

The news came at a time when she was drifting into a relationship with Joseph Luke Guy, a young trumpeter born Alabama in 1920, who was playing in Lucky Millinder's band. By then he was an experienced sideman with stints in big bands led by Teddy Hill, Coleman Hawkins and Cootie Williams and had also led the houseband for a period at Minton's at 210 West 188th Street. Billie had got to know him because he had drug connections. He began supplying her and, as the months passed, they began living together as man and wife. 'He was a personable cat, nice-looking,' recalled Al Casey. 'She was in love with him, I guess. She got around, though.'[38]

From the very beginning of their relationship, Guy charged Billie sums that were ridiculously over the top for drugs. Billie, who surely knew what the street price must have been, seemed able to turn a blind eye to this. She wanted him as 'her man' and besides, she had the money; once again it was easy come, easy go, with no thought for tomorrow. And to begin with perhaps it did not seem so much if she was a 'chipper', only using the drug occasionally, for kicks. For his part, Guy, an unassertive man, seemed content to allow Billie to make the running and to take from the situation what he could. 'He seemed to me an introvert,' said Norman Granz, 'didn't push himself forward.'[39]

On 17 January 1945 Billie appeared at the Second Annual Esquire Magazine Jazz Concert, this time at the Philharmonic Auditorium in Los Angeles, and performed to a sell-out crowd of 2800. Duke Ellington made his first West Coast appearance for three years with solo spots for the other Esquire winners, including Billie, Art Tatum, Al Casey, Sid Catlett, Willie Smith and Anita O'Day. The musicians received their awards, an 'Esky', from Lena Horne, Judy Garland, Lionel Barrymore, and Jerome Kern, who presented Billie with hers. Afterwards Danny Kaye moved onstage to effect a connection with a radio network that piped in Louis Armstrong in New Orleans and Benny Goodman in New York to jam with Ellington's band. Something went wrong and only forty-five seconds were hooked up. The concert, predominantly given over to Ellington's band, meant that Billie only had time to sing two numbers. No one, other than Ellington, had 'time to get into the right groove', observed *Downbeat*.[40]

Billie remained on the Coast after the concert, putting in an unpublicized stint at the New Plantation Club in Los Angeles. On 12 February Norman Granz, a long-time Billie fan, engaged her for a guest appearance on his monthly Jazz at the Philharmonic concert series. What immediately impresses is the huge ovation she received; her accompaniment for 'Body and Soul', however, is of a gathering but confused intensity, with an occasional wrong note from a trumpet player, while 'Strange Fruit' is sung with almost equal weight given to each word, lessening its inherent recitative drama.

Ten days after the JATP concert, the Decca coupling of 'Lover Man', 'That Ole Devil Called Love' was released: 'Where so many other singers have lost something by having strings in the background, Billie Holiday has gained ... [her] velvety, subtle inflections fit beautifully into this setting,' commented *Metronome*.[41]

In March Billie was interviewed, along with Duke Ellington and Ted Lewis, on Al Jarvis's *Which is Which* show on Radio KFWB. She was still on the West Coast in May 1945, when Columbia put out 'I Cover the Waterfront'. Again she picked up good reviews: 'Billie puts a world of feeling into this fine song and gives a performance that is dramatic but not melodramatic.'[42] With her rising public profile, the Downbeat Club back in New York moved to take advantage of the situation. Her name went up on the billboards outside the club in huge letters as 'Lover Man' went into the charts at sixteen at the beginning of May. In small print at the bottom could just be seen: 'Opens 22 May' – *caveat emptor*!

While on the Coast, Billie put out a story that she had secured a divorce from Monroe in Mexico and married Joe Guy. 'Friends were puzzled by Billie's announcement as no one seems to know when [she] visited Mexico to secure the divorce,' reported *Downbeat*.[43] In fact, there was no divorce and no remarriage. There were also stories that she had been 'sick' on her trip back to New York;[44] later, in her autobiography, she said this was the first time she experienced withdrawal symptoms. If this was the case, then it is worth noting the distinction between addiction and withdrawal symptoms. However unpleasant, withdrawal symptoms do not necessarily imply addiction. To become fully addicted, or 'hooked', users need to understand why they are sick, that their sudden, confusing illness – usually a violent stomach-ache accompanied by cold-like symptoms of a running nose and fever – are caused by absence of narcotics. Once they have made the connection and understood that they can solve (or 'fix') the problem with another injection, then the powerful association is established between the continued use of drugs and the prevention or relief of discomfort. To the original motive of pleasure is now added a second even more compelling incentive; keep using or get sick.[45] From now on, if Billie's account is correct, she was well and truly hooked, and she knew it.

Following her Downbeat opening, Billie was a guest at an afternoon jazz concert promoted by Timme Rosenkrantz at Town Hall on Saturday, 9 June featuring Red Norvo and Teddy Wilson, then members of the Benny Goodman sextet. It was MC'd by Art Ford, who at the time was presenter of WNEW's late night *Milkman's Matinee*. Meanwhile, her appearances at the Downbeat had once again become erratic; the July edition of *Downbeat* magazine carried a report that she was 'worrying her associates again',[46] and in August it reported: 'Attractions at the Downbeat seem as much a mystery to the management as the musicians. Billie Holiday was under contract but not appearing regularly.'[47]

Around this time, trombonist Eddie Bert, called up the previous year, returned to New York on furlough. 'I had been with pianist Jimmy Rowles in this Band Training Unit at Camp Lee, Virginia,' he recalled. 'We hung out quite a bit and I got to know Jimmy pretty good. When I went up on a furlough to New York, he said, "Why don't you stop by and give her my regards." Well, that's a chance to see her, so I stopped by and knocked on her door and she came out with some pretty strong language shall we say! And I said – I was like about eighteen or something – I said, "Jimmy Rowles sent me up, he wanted me to say hello." She opened the door. She had that big dog with her. She was rolling this joint, it looked like a cigar, it was so thick. I didn't indulge in that sort of stuff and I didn't know what to say! Then she said, "Here, why don't you get high!" I didn't know what to do! So I said, "I'm so high right now, do you mind if I save it?" So she gave it to me. We talked a little bit and I split. Meanwhile, Nick Travis the trumpet player, he got drafted the same day as me out of Woody Herman's band and we were buddies, he was hanging around waiting for me. He used to indulge, so I said, "Billie Holiday wants you to have this!" So he said, "Oh man! Billie Holiday, a joint from Billie Holiday!" He couldn't understand why I thought it so funny!'[48]

Meanwhile, Joe Guy was working with Coleman Hawkins at the Spotlite. But his addiction was making him unreliable and on the nights he failed to show his spot was eagerly filled by a young trumpet player who had moved to New York to study at Julliard. Miles Davis got no pay, but valuable experience instead. When Hawkins moved on, Davis got a job in the house band with tenorist Eddie 'Lockjaw' Davis for a month; it was his first professional job in New York.

With his job with Hawkins at the Spotlite at an end, Guy came up with the extraordinary idea of venturing into the big band business. Billie had the money, Guy the ambition. In wages alone, a big band requires a large outlay of capital. But by the time arrangements, uniforms, music stands, public address and transport are paid for, the investment is huge. However, the time was not right to sink huge sums in such a venture. Wartime travel restrictions were still in force and the draft continued to claim young musicians who were willing to put up with the inconvenience of life on the road.

To cap it all, however, the certainties of the Big Band Era were being replaced by a fragmenting music scene. On the one hand jump-bands were replacing big bands in popularity in the black communities, bands whose music would soon be dubbed Rhythm and Blues, while on a broader musical front bop was creating a new musical agenda of its own, quite different to anything that had gone before. But even so, Billie and Joe Guy might have made it; after all, others did. What doomed it from the beginning was the temperamental unsuitability of Billie and Joe Guy as leaders. Heroin, not music, was now the most important thing in their lives.

After headlining at the new McKinley Theater in New York on 17 August for a week, backed by Don Redman's orchestra, Billie went out on the road with Guy's big band, which was managed by Monte Kay. They opened in Richmond, Virginia, on 11 September and were booked for a series of one-nighters through the South and Midwest, including dates in Chicago and Detroit. While playing the Royal Theater in Baltimore, Billie learned of her mother's death. Sadie had been ill for several months but after suffering a stroke on 23 September had been admitted to Wadsworth Hospital, New York, and it was there that she died on 6 October 1945.

Billie immediately asked Joe Glaser to put funeral arrangements in hand and returned to New York. June Richmond took her place at the Royal over the weekend, with Beverley 'Baby' White taking over on the Monday and Tuesday.[49] Billie was distraught; her relationship with her mother had been confused and tempestuous, but despite Sadie's maternal shortcomings during Billie's childhood, their shared struggle for survival when they moved to New York had brought them close. 'She got on with her mother as well as anybody does with a "stage" mother,' said Artie Shaw. 'Her mother was essentially a "stage" mother, she lived a large part of her life through Billie. And she was a nice little lady. She was cute and I liked her; she was funny and humorous.'[50] At the time of her death, Sadie had been living at Billie's home at 1293 Union Avenue in the Bronx. For the rest of her life, particularly when drinking, Billie would choke back tears, saying, 'Duchess is gone.'

Chapter Nine

1945–48

There were only a few close friends at the funeral mass given for Sadie Gough. It was given by Father Owen Scanlon at the St Charles Boromeo Church at 211 West 141st Street at 9 a.m. on Tuesday, 9 October 1945. Afterwards, she was interred at St Raymond's Cemetery in the Bronx. It was a day in Billie Holiday's life that she would never forget. Throughout she was traumatized with grief. Her childhood fear of being abandoned rose up to engulf her. Alone and desperately insecure, she believed she had no one else to turn to other than Joe Guy and she told him so.

Sadie's death was a blow Norman Granz believes she never recovered from.[1] Certainly it seems that from a relatively happy-go-lucky attitude to casual sex and her relationships with men, she quickly changed to being dependent on her partners to an abnormal degree. For the rest of her life she would be haunted by a fear of loneliness so great that she would endure almost anything rather than confront it. As soon as her men sensed this, it left her open to exploitation and abuse.

During the period following Sadie's death, she sank into acute depression, turning to drink and drugs with a vengeance. Two years later, while undergoing treatment for heroin addiction at the Federal Reformatory for Women at Alderston, West Virginia, she told the doctor handling her case that she had been depressed for some time and that her work demanded more strength than she appeared to have. She spoke of the deep grief her mother's passing caused her; 'It was then she began using narcotics because of emotional tension . . . Her manager, Mr Joe Glaser confirms Billie's statement,' said her case notes.[2] However, it seems clear from contemporary accounts that she had started using much earlier; perhaps this explanation was a way of justifying her habit to the prison medical authorities or, more likely, a period she associated with using heroin excessively.

Billie returned to the Royal in Baltimore to complete her engagement on Wednesday, 10 October, returning to New York the following

Saturday. Her emotional state was such that she no longer had any interest in her big band venture and had Joe Guy play a few dates before winding up the ill-advised project once and for all. In the end, when broken contracts and expenses were taken into account, the venture left her with a $35,000 price tag.

Life on the road did not suit Billie. All she wanted to do was to return to what she liked best and where she felt secure, singing in a small club. She opened at the Club Downbeat at 66 West 52nd Street on 30 October 1945. For the first time in her career, she hired a regular pianist. Joe Springer, who had worked with musicians as diverse as Wingy Manone and Oscar Pettiford, replaced Sam Clanton in Al Casey's trio during Billie's sets to form her backing trio. 'We had changed pianists by then,' recalled Al Casey, 'we had a boy by the name of Sam Clanton, he was a beautiful pianist, but he couldn't read. That's why Billie changed, Sam couldn't read. That's no good behind a person like her.'[3]

During most of 1946 Billie remained at the Downbeat, where in good voice or bad she was always a draw. Occasionally she would make a guest appearance, such as the *Amsterdam News* annual benefit on 2 February 1946 at the Brooklyn Academy of Music. Here she was one of a remarkable line-up of singers who had donated their services for charity, including Ella Fitzgerald, Dinah Washington, Billy Eckstine, the Ink Spots and Savannah Churchill. By now, Billie was reputed to be the highest-paid star on 52nd Street, commanding as much as $1000 per week and enjoying the greatest popularity of her lifetime.

However, her drug habit came as a shock to Ralph Watkins, who had run Kelly's Stables in the early 1940s. Called up for military service in 1943, he returned in 1945 to find a very different Billie Holiday. 'When I came back from overseas she was a changed girl,' he said. 'Before that the worst thing she ever did was to smoke pot. But everyone did . . . when I saw her after the war she was on a very expensive habit. By then she never had enough money, no matter how much she made. She was borrowing all the time. She was making over a thousand a week.'[4]

Although during her first year with Decca, Billie had cut only five numbers, in August 1946 the option to renew was picked up, plus a further twelve-month option. During the second year of her contract she produced just eight titles which Decca could use, a total of four 78s. By now there were hints of problems in getting her to learn new songs, songs that in some instances had been specially written for her at the behest of Milt Gabler, such as 'Ole Devil Called Love' and 'Good Morning, Heartache'. 'She was becoming a little more difficult to work

with,' confirmed Gabler. 'She would arrive late for the sessions ...
After a few run-downs, her voice would open up, sometimes with the
help of some old brandy, and we would be ready to record. Billie was
generally a one-take artist. Her rendition would never vary much from
one take to another.'[5]

Her 14 August 1945 session produced 'You Better Go Now' which
was coupled with 'No More' from her 'Lover Man' date and released
in February 1946. Critics at the time were by no means dismayed by
the continued use of strings. 'Billie has never been in better voice or
better accompanied than on these sides,' declared *Metronome*, 'we're
enthusiastic about the continued use of strings as a setting for her
voice.'[6]

'Don't Explain', from the same August '45 session, with its 'story-
telling' lyric based on 'lipstick lies' set against a haunting *film noir* backdrop, is inescapably music of its time, yet still able to communicate
across the decades. Released with 'What Is This Thing Called Love?'
from the same date, featuring capable solos from Joe Guy and Tiny
Grimes, *Metronome* pronounced: 'This kind of Holiday doing this kind
of material will earn admirers for Lady Day among the thousands of
unconverted.'[7]

The 22 January 1946 date produced 'Good Morning, Heartache',
one of her classic Deccas; even the popular bandleader and alto saxophonist Louis Jordan featured the song in his 1946 film, *Beware*. Along
with 'Lover Man', 'That Ole Devil Called Love' and 'Don't Explain',
it seems to encapsulate the essence of her best work for the label in
terms of performance, lyric content and evocative 'period' backing. Both
'Good Morning, Heartache' and 'No Good Man', cut the same day,
were written by Teddy Wilson's ex-wife Irene Higginbotham, who knew
Billie well; once again, there can be no mistaking how lyric content can
be confused with the singer's real life history. However, when the
numbers were released, *Metronome* sounded a note of caution: 'There's
a danger that Billie's present formula will wear thin, but up to now it's
wearing well.'[8]

For Gabler, the 22 January date was a three-hour session fraught
with problems which produced only two usable sides. The next time he
was in the studios with Billie on 13 March it was worse, taking three
and a half hours to produce one take of 'Big Stuff', the number heard
on the jukebox in the opening scenes of Leonard Bernstein's ballet,
Fancy Free. Billie had tried at each of the preceding three sessions for
something usable, although the failure of her first attempt was not her
fault. The lyrics were unsuitable for a female singer. The number,
intended for release as part of an album of music from *Fancy Free*, was

slightly more complicated than usual, but today stands among her better Decca sides.

The success of Decca's widely distributed 'Lover Man' connected Billie to a wider, non-jazz following. 'I made Billie a real pop singer,' said Gabler. 'That was right in her. Billie loved those songs.'[9] Her popularity was growing to such an extent that it was increasingly taking her out of the night-club and on to the concert stage. On 13 February she was part of a three-hour recital given at Philadelphia's Academy of Music and presented by Nat Segall, owner of Philadelphia's Downbeat Club.

'She took my trio to Philadelphia to play that concert,' recalled Al Casey. 'It was a big thing for me to play behind, come out of the Downbeat where we were backing her, play a huge hall, but we did very well behind her. Joe Springer was the pianist. She went down well and we had a big ovation. I played then with my regular trio.'[10] Both Casey and Billie received high praise from *Metronome*, Casey's trio producing 'Extremely subtle music embodying unique arrangements and fine technique', while Billie got the vote as 'Tops in her field'.[11] In the event, the Philadelphia concert turned out to be a curtain-raiser for what *Downbeat* announced as Billie's 'solo concert debut'[12] at New York's Town Hall three days later. Her programme notes described it as 'a major event in the jazz world'. Indeed, a solo concert for a *jazz* singer was almost unheard of in 1946.

On the afternoon of Saturday, 16 February the Town Hall was filled to capacity, with seating erected on the stage for the overspill. Backed by a quintet headed by Joe Guy on trumpet, Billie enjoyed a rapturous reception and excellent reviews. 'A startling success in every respect', said *Downbeat*, 'should establish Miss Holiday in the top bracket and win for her the fame due to her long before this.'[13] The enthusiasm was not confined to the music press; most dailies covered the event, including the *New York Times*: 'The glamorous Miss Holiday's singing was pure enchantment,' it reported.[14]

Billie was nervous at first, but the reception she got for the first few numbers helped calm her. 'Gone was the moodiness she has sometimes shown in her night-club work,' said another review, 'the hostility to 52nd Street crowds, the reluctance to perform that have often made her seem a singer with no real love of her work . . . she was glad to be singing, perhaps no less than her audience was to be hearing her.'[15]

With the sole exception of 'Strange Fruit', the songs which Billie chose were all consistent with the character part she played as a singer of a woman unlucky in love: 'Trav'lin' Light' (her hit with Paul

Whiteman), 'I Cover the Waterfront', 'The Man I Love', 'Lover Man', 'You Better Go Now', 'Body and Soul', 'Summertime', 'Embracable You', 'My Old Flame', 'I Can't Get Started' (one of the most applauded numbers of the evening) and four numbers where she was named as composer: 'Fine and Mellow', 'God Bless the Child', 'Don't Explain', and 'Billie's Blues'. During the whole afternoon there were only three up-tunes: 'All of Me', 'Miss Brown to You' and 'Billie's Blues'.

While the concert was a personal triumph at one level, on another it presented little contrast in what was essentially an emotionally one-dimensional concert. Artistically, placing songs of similar lyric content and tempo end-to-end can have an ultimately limiting effect overall. If art is a reflection of life, then creating one mood and sustaining it means by definition that it excludes more than it includes. Life, after all, is a contrast of emotions, but if the metaphor and parable of Billie's songs appeared to reflect the extent of her emotional horizons on the one hand, on the other the public construction of one central emotion had become an identifying characteristic of her vocal style. It was a conscious musical thumbprint that claimed the music she sang as her own, as distinctive as Johnny Hodges' alto or Lester Young's tenor. 'There is one small objection,' put in the *New York Herald Tribune*, 'cumulatively her variations on the given melodic line of a song are . . . too homogeneous. The tendency is to smooth away all the differences between songs, to create a kind of ideal Holiday type song . . . even the tempo was kept the same from song to song.'[16]

The success of the Town Hall concert encouraged Billie to emerge from the Downbeat more often. On 4 April, with Joe Springer and two-thirds of Al Casey's trio, she appeared at Carnegie Hall in a concert of American folk music for the Russian Relief Programme on a bill that included the Hall Johnson Choir, Josh White, Woody Guthrie and Pete Seeger. It is quite possible, however, that this was not Billie's Carnegie debut; Phil Schaap points out that photographic evidence suggests this may have been at a memorial concert for Fats Waller in 1944. Eleven days later, on her birthday, Billie appeared at McKinley Gardens in Brooklyn, where she gave 'a large crowd of dancers a musical treat'.[17]

After a week at the Apollo at the end of April with Coleman Hawkins, she took Casey's group plus Springer to Eaton Hall on 29 April for another joint concert, again to an enthusiastic reception. When Al Casey finally moved on to the Onyx in May, Springer was retained and her backing group at the Downbeat was expanded to include Joe Guy on trumpet, Tiny Grimes on guitar, Lloyd Trotman on bass (who had been playing the club opposite her in Stuff Smith's group) and Eddie Nicholson on drums.

Meanwhile, Billie had been called for a Decca session on 9 April 1946, which produced just two sides. In essence this was a return to the intimacy of the Wilson sessions, a feeling heightened by Billy Kyle's Wilson-inspired piano. 'Baby, I Don't Cry Over You', with its reference to boyfriend Joe Guy on trumpet – 'I went out to a show with a swell guy named Joe' – was coupled with 'I'll Look Around' from the same session and released in July 1947. However, listening to these sides alongside her Wilson Columbias, there is no freshness, no feeling of spontaneity. Instead they suggest her art was no longer moving forward but relying on stylization for effect.

In May 1946, Jazz at the Philharmonic arrived in New York, and Norman Granz took the opportunity to present Billie as a 'special guest' to climax his New York concerts. Never a regular touring member of the group, her appearance at Carnegie Hall on 3 June was none the less greeted with a roar of delight, an enthusiasm which is not reciprocated by the singer. Her tempo sags on 'Fine and Mellow' in a particularly dreary performance. On 2 June at the Apollo and at Carnegie Hall on 27 May and 3 June, Joe Guy appeared with her, and also in a band featuring Lester Young and Coleman Hawkins. On the Young–Hawkins recordings of the Apollo concert, Guy appears as a competent, lyrical swing-into-bop trumpeter who balances the opposing styles of Young and Hawkins well; he had clearly done his swing-era homework, winding up his solo on 'I Can't Get Started' by copiously quoting Bunny Berigan. 'He was a good player,' said Norman Granz, 'I liked his playing.'[18]

With Billie's career reaching ever higher, United Artists offered her a role in the feature film, *New Orleans*. In early September she flew out to Hollywood to begin work on the soundtrack, which began on 11 September at Studio & Artists Recorders. The movie was originally conceived as a drama set against the closing of the Storyville area of New Orleans in 1917, and hope was running high that jazz would be properly represented on screen when a second unit crew was dispatched to New Orleans to film an authentic funeral and street parade by George Lewis with Kid Howard's Brass Band. When it was announced that Billie Holiday, Louis Armstrong, Meade Lux Lewis and Woody Herman and his First Herd were signed, it seemed as if a definitive jazz film was in the offing.

What emerged was anything but. Instead of the film doing justice to the array of musicians, the emphasis throughout was on whether or not the young white opera singer portrayed by actress Dorothy Patrick would

152

give up her career to run off with the gambler and restaurateur played by Arturo de Cordova. Billie's part was that of maid to Dorothy Patrick, a role she carried off with some aplomb. 'She dealt with it gracefully, given the circumstances,' said bass player Red Callender, who appeared in the film as a member of Armstrong's band. 'That's the way the script was written . . . Hollywood had certain hiring tactics. There was a general consensus that black people should only be given subservient roles.'[19]

Although *New Orleans* started out with the best intentions when shooting started, to celebrate 'the music that rocked the world', its intentions were quickly subverted by the then rising tide of McCarthyism. Defining black people as creators of anything, let alone jazz, meant producer Jules Levey and writer Herbert Biberman came under increasing pressure because of their 'liberal' views to revert to the stereotypical way black people were treated by Hollywood. 'It was gradual the way McCarthyism seeped in,' said Red Callender. 'Eventually things became more and more uptight. The picture was brought to a hasty finish. Our part was cut short. In the original script Louis's band was slated to appear on the same bill as Woody Herman's at the big stage concert. We had our tuxedos and everything, filmed it, but thanks to McCarthyism it was never shown. Later, in 1947, Biberman was one of the "Hollywood Ten" . . . and was sent to jail.'[20]

Had the music occupied a more central role, it would have gone some way towards compensating for many of the film's shortcomings. Sadly, much of the music is relegated to the background, although studio pre-recordings exist of the original music before sound effects and dialogue were dubbed over them.[21] Billie sings 'Farewell to Storyville', 'The Blues Are Brewin'' and a pop song which runs through the film, 'Do You Know What It Means to Miss New Orleans?'.

While Billie was in California, Guy travelled from New York to supply her with heroin. When he was discovered on set, Joe Glaser had him banned from the studios and had him returned to New York, although it was Billie who paid for his plane ticket.[22] However, Glaser could not keep Billie's problems under wraps. Her timekeeping was poor. She simply could not surrender to the discipline required by the studios and often caused the filming to run into overtime. A big opportunity had come her way, which, because of the problems associated with her addiction, was never going to be repeated.

During the filming Billie took time out to appear at the Shrine Auditorium in Los Angeles at a jazz concert promoted by Norman Granz on 7 October, and the effects of her addiction are all too plain. With Trummy Young in her backing band she had him play the trombone introduction of his composition 'Trav'lin' Light', but debilitated the song by a slow tempo and her struggle to stay in tune. 'He's Funny That Way' that followed was marked by a significant audience response, reflecting just how popular Billie was, but sadly she reciprocated with a lack-lustre vocal. Later that month she returned to New York, opening at the Downbeat Club on 16 November, on a bill that included Eddie Heywood and Lawrence '88' Keyes. She was now billed as 'America's No.1 Song Stylist', a statement which says much about how she now viewed her art.

Billie's return to 52nd Street was to a scene much changed since the wartime years. There were no more soldiers, sailors and airmen on furlough, and business had dropped off dramatically. In an attempt to attract crowds back, Swing Street was gradually but inexorably changing into Strip Street. An era was drawing to a close.

Because of falling receipts the Downbeat management was forced to drop the Lawrence Keyes trio who backed Billie and asked Heywood to play behind her. This meant Heywood doubling as featured star and back-up pianist, which initially he refused to do. The situation was further confused by Billie complaining that Heywood had equal billing to her. Heywood stuck a week of this, then abruptly left to play the Brown Derby in Washington, leaving Billie without an accompanist.

'One night in October 1946 I just happened to be going past the Downbeat on 52nd Street,' said pianist Bobby Tucker. 'Billie Holiday was supposed to open and she had no one to play for her. Eddie Heywood had been playing for her but they had a little beef and they had removed his billing. So someone called me to come and play for her. That was how I started playing for her.'[23]

Tucker quickly found Billie a complex yet beguiling personality. After reserving judgement for a short while, she offered him the job. 'I did not realize it for a while,' he observed, 'but she was always nervous about performing. I guess her nervousness was shown up as arrogance, but she wasn't arrogant at all. So often she was not sure what she was doing, but she did it in such a way that everybody thought she knew.'[24]

Tucker appears on her 27 December recording session, which was another frustrating affair for Milt Gabler. Although called for 2 p.m., Billie turned up half an hour late and produced only one usable side, 'The Blues Are Brewin'', intended to capitalize on her film part in *New Orleans*, scheduled for release in April the following year. 'She'd take time out between records to go in the ladies room, the powder room to get herself together,' said John Simmons, the bass player on the date. 'She'd be in there an hour, an hour and a half. People were pulling out their hair, it was like money running out of their pockets.'[25]

After three attempts at 'Guilty', the session was abandoned after running an hour and ten minutes into overtime. 'The publishers were going to work on "Guilty" again,' said Gabler, 'which is why we did it. It was a revival. I tried it with Billie, it didn't work, we gave up on it, so I had Ella Fitzgerald do it in the end.'[26] Billie's version of 'Guilty' eventually appeared in 1958 as a part of the Decca LP, *The Blues Are Brewin'*. 'She seems less deeply involved,' commented the *New York Times*[27] when the record was released.

Billie's popularity was reflected in the annual *Downbeat* popularity poll announced in January 1947 where she had held on to the number two spot from the previous year. It was the highest ranking she would achieve in a poll open to the public at large. Yet in their very next issue, *Downbeat* announced the gloomy news that 'Jazz blows final breath on 52nd Street', and, with just four clubs surviving, 'Billie Holiday and Art Tatum may find contract problems forcing one of them out shortly.'[28]

In January 1947 Billie took some time out of the Downbeat; on Saturday the 18th she appeared at Brooklyn's 13th Regiment Armory with the Jimmie Lunceford and Luis Russell bands and then got in some radio work. On the 13th she appeared on *Arthur Godfrey Time* with Bobby Tucker and on the 25th she inaugurated *Saturday Night Surprise Party*, a new radio show on WNEW, along with Red Norvo and Charlie Shavers. It was MC'd by Art Ford, a Holiday fan, who would subsequently feature her as often as he could on his radio and, later, television shows. But celebrity or no, the Downbeat told Billie they could only retain her if she took a 20 per cent drop in her earnings. She had no option but to accept.

If the ignominy of a paycut hurt her pride, then she certainly did not show it at Carnegie Hall on 8 February where she was a surprise guest at Louis Armstrong's big concert intended to give some advance publicity to *New Orleans*. Armstrong played most of the show with clarinettist Ed Hall's group, blowing hot and cold, and for the final section brought on his big band which, remarked *Metronome*, was 'a distinct let down until the inclusion of a couple of songs by surprise starter Billie Holiday broke things up'.[29] They appeared together again at a big premiere for the film, held in the Saenger Theater in Crescent City on 26 April. They sang 'Do You Know What It Means to Miss New Orleans?' together, with Billie doing 'Don't Explain', accompanied by Bobby Tucker.

Even with Billie's cut in pay, the Downbeat could only manage to limp by until the beginning of March, when Rudy Breadbar decided to cut his losses and close its doors until the summer. Now that Billie was 'between' engagements, Glaser made her confront her drug problem. He was well aware that she was spending everything she earned on her habit and had become a meal-ticket for Joe Guy, who during the previous eighteen months had worked only intermittently, acting out the part of a pimp with his woman bringing home the money. Glaser was insistent she should try to kick the habit once and for all. The pressure he put her under was unequivocal. Either she take the 'cure' or he would end their professional relationship.

Billie admitted herself to a private hospital in Westchester in mid-March in an attempt to rid herself of her addiction. By now her tolerance to heroin had increased to such an extent that she was 'fixing', shooting to stop the pain of withdrawal. She had reached the point where if she stopped using she would have had a very uncomfortable withdrawal. She was now using fifteen to twenty grains a day,[30] which although not as high a dose as some addicts use, is nevertheless considerable; a quarter grain is the equivalent of 15 milligrams. To put this into the context of a legitimate medical situation, a pain-relieving dose of morphine for, say, a broken leg, would be 10–12 milligrams.

At the levels Billie was taking heroin, any feeling of joy would be replaced by numbness. But despite the magnitude of her problem and her questionable commitment to undergo a detoxification programme – most addicts do not want to confront a 'cure' – there is really no treatment *per se* for heroin addiction. While much work has been done to medicalize the problem, treatment remains, in essence, exhortation. The only real cure to heroin addiction is to stop using the drug; the routes to achieving this end can be facilitated by lowering the tolerance levels or by switching to methodone, but at some point the pain of ultimate withdrawal has to be confronted.[31]

But whatever the success of her treatment after some six weeks in a private sanatorium, the problem Billie had to confront on discharge was that nothing in her life had changed. There was no reason for her not to continue in her previous lifestyle. Joe Guy was still an addict and the temptation to continue using was omnipresent. Glaser was aware of this, and hired Ella 'Tommy' Thompson as Billie's assistant in the hope of keeping pushers at bay. The ploy was unsuccessful. On 28 April Billie was booked into Club 18, formerly the Onyx Club, on 52nd Street. She had a release to play a long-standing engagement at the Earle Theater in Philadelphia from Monday, 12 May until Friday, 16 May and left with Joe Guy, Jimmy Ascendio, who acted as her road manager and fetcher and carrier (usually of drugs), and a chauffeur.

Billie, Guy, Tucker and Ascendio checked into the Attucks Hotel at 801 South 15th Street, Philadelphia for the duration of their engagement. On her last night, the Friday, Billie's chauffeur picked her up as usual after the show, together with Tucker and Ascendio – Guy had already left for New York – and returned them to the Attucks at about 11.45 p.m. However, the hotel was under surveillance by agents Roter, Sorel and Regan of the Federal Bureau of Narcotics and two police officers.

'I saw James Ascendio and the man known as Robert Tucker enter the hotel; the lady, Billie Holiday, remained seated in the car and drove away,' Agent Roter later stated under oath. The agents entered the hotel and asked for Billie Holiday's room number. 'In the company of the lady who was seated at the desk I proceeded to Room 7,' continued Roter. 'The door of the room was open and I saw James Ascendio and Robert Tucker in the act of packing suitcases ... Mr Ascendio and Mr Tucker gave me permission to search the room ... I looked under the bed and found a package; this package was wrapped in a lady's stocking.'[32] Inside was a spoon, two hypodermic needles, one eye-dropper, sixteen capsules of narcotics and nine half-empty capsules. Later, chemical examination proved the capsules contained heroin hydrochloride.

Billie told her chauffeur to get her back to New York; legend has it that either the police or narcotics agents discharged shots at the departing car, but no mention is made of this in either Billie's or Guy's trial transcript. It was left to Agent Ryan, of the Federal Bureau of Narcotics in New York, to arrest Billie and Joe Guy on behalf of their Philadelphia office. At 5 a.m. on the morning of 19 May he, with five other officers, arrested Billie at 142 West 44th Street, and took her, on her say so, to Room 32 of the Grampion Hotel on St Nicholas Avenue to arrest Joe Guy. The room at the Grampion was kept by Billie to do her drugs.

'When we attempted to gain entrance, Joseph Guy opened the door slightly, but before we could enter shut the door again,' said Ryan under oath. 'When we entered the room a window was open about six inches. Outside that room we found a capsule and a half, approximately 1½ grains of heroin.'[33] At his trial Guy testified under oath that he used 1½ grains of heroin a day. However, the testimony offered by Agent Ryan was put aside as it did not relate to the Philadelphia case.

Billie and Joe Guy were taken to the Federal Bureau of Narcotics at 90 Church Street, New York City where they were questioned at 10 a.m. the same day. Billie, without legal representation, admitted that the capsules found in Philadelphia were hers, and was charged for possession.

*   *   *

157

Billie was back performing at Club 18 the evening she was arrested. On 24 May, during her intermission, Billie and Bobby Tucker had a car laid on by Norman Granz to make an appearance at Carnegie Hall for a Jazz at the Philharmonic concert. Despite her personal circumstances and the bad press she had attracted, the crowd went crazy when she walked on stage and her version of 'You're Driving Me Crazy' sounded positively joyful. But then she reverted to slow tempos and a mood of unrelieved introspection for 'There Is No Greater Love' and 'I Cover the Waterfront'.

Three days after her Carnegie Hall appearance Billie Holiday appeared in the District Court of the Eastern District of Pennsylvania charged with receiving and concealing a narcotic drug. Crucially, at Glaser's behest, she waived the right to legal representation. It was the biggest mistake she made in her whole career. When asked how she wanted to plead she said, 'I would like to plead guilty and be sent to a hospital.' The court had earlier spoken to Billie's lawyers who confirmed they did not want to represent her.

The extent of the evidence for the prosecution case was that the drugs and hypodermics found in the Attucks bedroom belonged to Billie and Joe Guy. The evidence, however, did not in any way whatsoever link either Billie or Joe Guy to the scene of the crime: indeed, Billie was in a car outside and Guy was in New York. However, when the identical evidence was subsequently offered by the prosecution on 17 September 1947 at Joe Guy's short trial for receiving and concealing narcotic drugs, he was found not guilty. This verdict was arrived at despite Guy's admission in open court that he was a drug user and had in the past procured drugs for Billie Holiday. Quite simply there was nothing that linked him – or indeed Billie Holiday – to the evidence.

Because she admitted the drugs were hers and because she pleaded guilty to the charges brought before her, Billie was sentenced to one year and a day at the Federal Reformatory for Women, Alderston, Virginia. 'I want you to know you are being committed as a criminal defendant,' said Judge Cullen Ganey Jr. 'You are not being sent to a hospital primarily for treatment. You will get treatment, but I want you to know you stand convicted as a wrongdoer.'[34]

The conduct of Billie Holiday's case was by any standards extraordinary. At best the prosecution evidence was tenuous, as the Joe Guy trial reveals, yet the most striking aspect remains the absence of any legal representation whatsoever for Billie, either on her arrest or at her arraignment. The only person she would have turned to in such adversity was her manager Joe Glaser, yet rather than making sure his client had access to proper legal channels, he did the complete opposite.

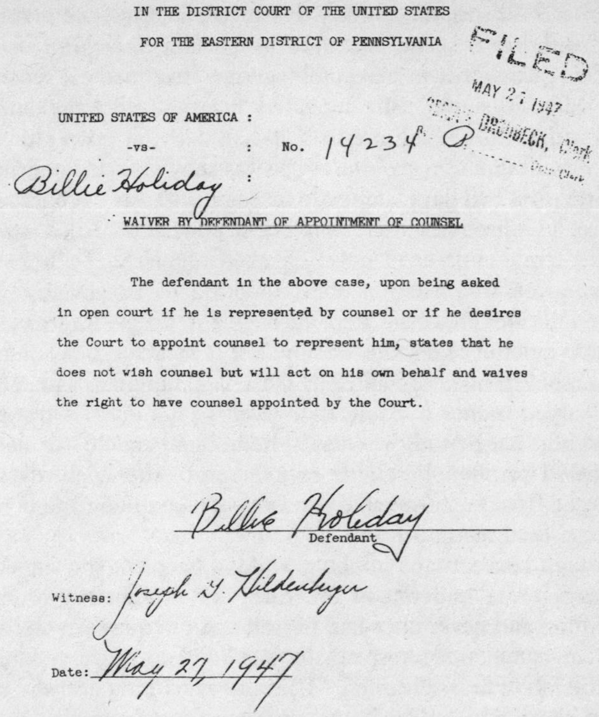

IN THE DISTRICT COURT OF THE UNITED STATES

FOR THE EASTERN DISTRICT OF PENNSYLVANIA

FILED
MAY 27 1947
DROBECK, Clerk
Dep. Clerk

UNITED STATES OF AMERICA :

-vs- : No. 14234

Billie Holiday :

WAIVER BY DEFENDANT OF APPOINTMENT OF COUNSEL

The defendant in the above case, upon being asked in open court if he is represented by counsel or if he desires the Court to appoint counsel to represent him, states that he does not wish counsel but will act on his own behalf and waives the right to have counsel appointed by the Court.

Billie Holiday
Defendant

Witness: Joseph G. Hildenberger

Date: May 27, 1947

Figure 6: The signature that changed Billie Holiday's life. Her trial on 27 May 1947 became a travesty of justice when she waived the right to legal representation. Her sentence of one year and one day had disastrous consequences for her career.

When Billie reached Alderston, Margaret Jones, the Acting Warden, wrote to the United States District Court Probation System in New York, requesting their cooperation in compiling a profile and social history of Billie Holiday to aid in her treatment. In answer to her request E. Fred Sweet, Chief Probation Officer, and Violet A. Jersawit, Probation Officer, held an extensive interview with Joe Glaser. In a letter under their joint signatures they replied: 'Mr Glaser states that he cooperated with the Federal Narcotic Agents as he had no recourse except to have her "forced" to take proper treatment [for drug addiction].'[35]

Billie was given a 15-milligram injection of morphine for her train journey to Alderston. She was admitted to Room 117 of the prison hospital at 9.30 a.m. on 28 May. However, far from the dramatic 'cold turkey' withdrawal scene portrayed in the film *Lady Sings the Blues*, or in Billie's own words in her autobiography, her medical records reveal a very different story.[36] She appeared 'nervous and weak' and was put to bed with a little nembutol to help her sleep; at noon she was given another small shot of morphine as she was showing signs of drug hunger.

For the first two days she felt 'nauseous' and was encouraged to take fluid freely. Throughout she was under constant medical supervision, with her temperature and pulse checked regularly. To help her relax she was given frequent hot baths followed by an analgesic massage; her file indicates that 'she went through the drug withdrawal with the minimum amount of discomfort' and her clinical records confirm this.[37] Withdrawal was no doubt aided by her recent period as a private patient, which helped reduce her tolerance levels to the drug. Throughout her brief withdrawal period, whenever she became agitated or nervous she was treated by phenobarbitone or nembutol. After eight days she was discharged from the hospital in good physical condition and in no further need of special medical care.

Although once caught smoking while in hospital, she signed a statement saying she understood the rules and 'voluntarily promised her cooperation and never once laid herself open to question on that score'. When she came out of hospital she was limited to light assignment and given the job of brass cleaning. 'This and everything else she attempted she did thoroughly and without assistance, preferring to work alone. Except for one reprimand for the use of profanity she was quiet, well-mannered and appreciative of suggestion ... [she] never asked for aspirin, stating that she wished to get away from anything associated with narcotics ... she was neat and clean personally ... and very interested in her appearance ...

'When she went into the clinic she was surrounded quickly by fans both colored and white and it was interesting to see how she changed in deportment, brightened and acknowledged their welcome. When speaking to officers she often spoke of the importance of being cured so that she could return quickly to her "public" before she was forgotten ... she made no reference to her singing before the group, never asked for selections to be played on the phonograph, so that one would never know of her musical interest. She played cards and sewed during most of her leisure hours.'[38]

During her period at Alderston, Billie became very friendly with the Warden, Helen Hironimus. In her autobiography Billie suggested Hironimus had private means, but in fact she was a career civil servant. She had begun work in 1918 at the age of twenty as a clerk in the War

Department, Washington, DC and worked through various grades of Government service until she was transferred to Alderston as a stenographer in 1922. Except for two years as a Warden in Dallas, Texas, she remained at Alderston until she retired in 1949. It would be difficult to imagine a more sympathetic, helpful and understanding mentor to enter Billie's life at this time.

Helen Hironimus virtually took over Billie's affairs while she was in prison. Not only did she respond to fans, magazines and radio stations inquiring after her welfare, she became deeply concerned with Billie's professional affairs and did her best to help her get her life in order. She wrote to the Internal Revenue explaining that Billie was not in a position to file a tax return, and wrote frequently to Joe Glaser for current statements of accounts of her earnings.

Glaser responded with promises to visit Billie, to send an accounting and to get a copy of *New Orleans* sent to the prison for the benefit of the inmates. He did none of these things and Billie expressed her concern in a letter to Leonard Feather on 19 July 1947:

> How is Jane [Feather's wife] I am so glad she liked the picture *New Orleans* Joe Glaser was supose to have it sent here but I haven't even heard from him lately. Oh yes I know he is a busy man but he has my money and I wrote these letters asking for some, I can only spend ten dollars a month but I can use that green stuff even here . . . Please call Joe Glaser and ask him what he intends to do for some good publicity . . . I do think he should do something so that people won't forget me.[39]

In August Glaser sent Billie $50 plus a further $10 a month until January 1948 but continued to remain at arm's length on every other matter. As each month passed, Billie and Helen Hironimus became increasingly concerned at Glaser's lack of cooperation. Helen Hironimus finally interceded on Billie's behalf, explaining that 'Billie was not too articulate' and insisting that as her manager he send her a statement of accounting.

Glaser's only response was to write to Helen Hironimus in August saying that Billie was indebted to his office in the sum of $715.29, asserting, 'It is a pity what she did with about $100,000 she made in two and a half years but that is exactly what happened during her association with Joe Guy.'[40] Norman Granz, aware of her financial plight, arranged a benefit concert at Carnegie Hall on 29 November 1947 with his Jazz at the Philharmonic stars; Glaser made Billie disown it, so Granz donated the proceeds to charity. 'Billie was broke, but Glaser didn't want people to think that that was the case,' he said.[41]

By the year-end nothing further had been heard from Glaser and Billie decided to change to Ed Fishman's booking agency on the West Coast. In December Helen Hironimus wrote to Fishman expressing her concern about Glaser, 'Billie . . . mailed the request to Mr Glaser asking him for an accounting, but she had no reply. We doubt that one will be received for she has written previously and so have I.'[42]

When Glaser heard that Billie had signed with Fishman, he refused to release her wardrobe. 'He will no doubt attempt to intimidate her again and by coercive tactics get her to sign with him again,' Fishman confided to Helen Hironimus.[43] He was under no illusions as to the lengths Glaser would go to to hold on to his client, and tried to reassure Billie. 'I know very well the tactics he resorts to,' he wrote. 'My advice to you is that you do not go to Joe Glaser's office and leave yourself open to his threats and intimidations and abuse . . . He has no right to withhold your clothes from you and if he is attempting pressure of that type it only bears out my contention [that he is unscrupulous].'[44]

Meanwhile, Billie was called as a prosecution witness at Joe Guy's trial on 17 September 1947. Although *Downbeat* announced 'Billie's Testimony Saves Guy',[45] following the failure of the prosecution case, in fact she simply stated she was not sure who got her drugs for her, that she believed Jimmy Ascendio got them for Joe Guy who in turn gave them to her: 'I know that between him and Jimmy, that one of them had it [the drugs],' she said.

'You don't know as a matter of fact which one did have it, do you?' she was asked in cross-examination.

'One of them had it,' she replied.[46]

On 7 January 1948 Billie was called as a witness for the prosecution in Jimmy Ascendio's trial. She cooperated with the authorities, resulting in his conviction for possession and a sentence of a year and a day: 'The information given by Billie Holiday was found to be absolutely correct and had not been revealed previously throughout the investigation . . . Billie can be assured that the information was handled most carefully and confidentially by the Judge,' said the Chief US Probation Officer in a letter to Helen Hironimus.[47]

Billie became due for release on parole in December 1947, one press account even going so far as to say she would be released for Christmas,[48] but under Helen Hironimus's advice and counselling, she consented to remain in custody until 16 March 1948 in the hope of effecting a complete cure. With no word from Glaser, however, Hironimus was growing increasingly frustrated by his complete lack of cooperation, particularly in the matter of accounting. On the day Billie was released from Alderston, she could suppress her anger no longer. She had recently learnt that Billie was to give a Carnegie Hall concert on 27 March 1948 and wrote a prophetic letter to Glaser telling him exactly what she thought:

> [Billie] seems sincere in her desire to refrain from further use of narcotics. But you are placing her in a position where she will be filling engagements when she is not ready and there will be a vicious circle as in others who are forced beyond their strength – benzedrine to bolster failing nerves, sleeping powders to overcome the benzedrine and an easy drifting into the use of narcotics . . .
>
> How would you feel if you were being released from prison without funds and clothing that did not fit you? Suppose you had a manager who withheld your cheques and gave you no reason for doing so? What would you think if he ignored your requests for an accounting? What would you think if he made an important engagement for you to perform eight days after release when you needed an operation and needed two teeth replacing before you could perform in public? And how would you feel if a third person informed you of the engagement but the manager did not do so? You would object vociferously and so would I.[49]

The 'operation' referred to was a slight tumour on Billie's cheek which had developed a week before she was due for release, leaving no time for surgery at the prison hospital, but which would nevertheless necessitate a minor operation for its removal. But that would seem as nothing in comparison to what was waiting for her on her release.

Billie was to remain on parole until 27 May 1948 and one of its conditions was that she should stay with Bobby Tucker and his mother at 17 Cleveland Avenue, Morristown, New Jersey during this period. However, when she arrived at Newark at 9 a.m. on 17 March, Glaser was already frantically manoeuvring behind the scenes to retain Billie as a client. Finally, in April, Ed Fishman wrote to Helen Hironimus, whose counselling had encouraged Billie to engage him:

> My Dear Miss Hironimus
>
> I regret exceedingly to advise you that my predictions in connection with Billie Holiday have come to a head. Since her husband, Jimmie Monroe, appeared on the scene he was somehow able to persuade or induce Billie to withdraw her discharge against Glazer [sic] and his ABC company and have Billie serve me with a discharge which now puts me in the same position that Glaser was in . . . There is no question in my mind that there was some terrible pressure brought on her . . . after Billie repeatedly advising me that she would not sing for Glazer [sic] if it meant she had to give up singing and then have her do the reverse of what she

did with me, you can imagine my feeling. I want you to know I did everything in my power. I fought Mr Glazer and everybody right down the line and victory was positively assured . . .[50]

Immediately prior to her imprisonment, Billie had given a long interview to Michael Levin of *Downbeat* magazine. In it she concluded: 'Remember, nobody else in show business has made as many mistakes as me.'[51] Now her career was about to take off again, and with it the tantalizing trail of 'what if's' that seemed to flow in her wake.

Chapter Ten

1948–50

When the press announced that Billie Holiday would be appearing at Carnegie Hall on 27 March 1948 there was an immediate scramble at the box-office. Promoter Ernie Anderson was amazed to discover demand outstripping his recent Stan Kenton concert at Carnegie, a remarkable feat since Kenton was the biggest draw in jazz during 1948. However, Anderson was somewhat bemused to find himself dealing with two managers who claimed to represent Billie, Ed Fishman and Joe Glaser. In the end he signed a contract for a fee of $2500 with each to protect himself. When Billie arrived in Manhattan the day before the concert, Anderson met her and booked her into a mid-town hotel on 47th Street. 'I got the distinct impression that she was clean and was going to stay off drugs,' he said. 'She was trying to stay downtown and keep away from Harlem drug pushers.'[1]

When Anderson told her that both Glaser and Fishman claimed to be her manager she laughed and asked for Glaser's phone number. In the discussion that followed it became clear to Anderson that she was sticking with Glaser. As he prepared to leave, she asked for some comic books. 'I went out to Times Square and found a big news-stand and bought a huge stack,' Anderson continued. 'She was terribly grateful but it made me very sad. Here was this great contemporary artist and the only education she ever got was on the Harlem streets.'[2]

Billie's concert gross set a house record at Carnegie Hall with 2700 seats sold in advance. On the night of the concert, hundreds milled about on the streets outside vainly trying to buy tickets, while several hundred luckier ones obtained seats and standing-room on stage. When Billie appeared she was glowing and radiant. '[She] was cold sober but was excited by the crowd and their emotional and loving reaction,' recalled Anderson. 'I'm convinced there were no drugs that night. So again I booked the hall for a second concert three weeks later and that sold out on announcement.'[3]

Backed by a quartet headed by Bobby Tucker on piano, Billie had little time for preparation. 'We went up to the studio one day to run through some things and they were so natural feeling that we didn't rehearse,' said Tucker. 'Everything just came out with no problems, so on the date of the Carnegie thing we just picked the keys and the tunes and lined them up and went through the programme.'[4]

It was a spectacular return, dissolving once and for all the fears Billie had harboured in Alderston about losing her public. She seemed to have the world at her feet; Carl Van Vetchen, in the audience that night, described the concert in a letter written the following day to his friend Karl Priebe:

> Well Billie is a really gone girl. She weighs considerably more. Prison fare must be good ... They not only sat, they stood, hundreds of 'em ... Then Fred Robbins introduced her, all in black, a little black lace here and there, the skirt slit at the front showed her legs when she moved. White gloves long with no fingers, just caught around the thumbs. Her hair in a twisted and unbraided coronet on top her head. White gardenias ... She was nervous and perspiring freely, but her first tones were reassuring and rewarded with a whoop. There was no set programme. She turned to the pianist and announced her numbers sotto voce ... Some Other Spring, All of Me, Billie's Blues, No Greater Love, Travellin' Light, No More, You're Driving Me Crazy, She's Funny That Way: you know, you're hep. All with that seesaw motion of the arms, fingers always turned in, that swanlike twitching of the thighs, that tortured posture of the head, those inquiring wondering eyes, a little frightened at first and then as the applause increased they became grateful. The voice the same, in and out between tones, unbearably poignant, that blue voice.[5]

However, the following day Van Vetchen reflected on the concert from the artistic rather than emotional standpoint. In an aside to himself he wrote:

> This was quite an exciting evening of course, but my own reservations concerning it are as follows. There is exceedingly little variation in her manner of singing songs and they all sound perilously alike, especially as she seldom sings the actual notes and seldom sings them on the beat. Further practically everything is sung in the same key. Her arm movements are unvaried and so is her stance. A little of this goes a long way and a whole evening is too much.[6]

Billie appeared again at Carnegie Hall on 17 April. This time she broke her own Carnegie box-office record, although she was limping badly from a sprained ankle. 'I don't honestly know whether Billie was back on the stuff for this second show,' reflected Anderson afterwards, 'I rather think she was. But it was not too long afterwards that she was certainly back on it.'[7] Yet the paradox of Billie's sell-out concerts on the nation's foremost stage was that with a prison record, she was denied a Cabaret Card and could no longer work in premises that served alcohol, which effectively barred her from working in New York clubs.

The Cabaret Card system had been common practice since 1940, when the police began to fingerprint every person who worked on licensed premises and to issue identification cards, denying them to people who they thought were 'not of good character'. It became unlawful for a club to hire a person who did not have a card, which was renewable every two years.

The scheme arose out of a Presidential directive in 1939 to the FBI instructing them to list everyone whose presence might be considered a threat to the security of the United States. It was thought that many of the unions, particularly the waiters' union, were dominated by Communists. Later, when the police became involved in an attempt to break one of their strikes, they passed on details of potential Communists among staff to restaurants and took the opportunity of barring anyone with a previous criminal offence from work.

In fact, there was actually a provision in the Alcoholic Beverage Control Law, enacted after Prohibition, that expressly forbade the employment where alcohol was served of anyone convicted of a felony or certain other offences, including narcotics crimes. But if the intention of the Cabaret Card system was to protect patrons from undesirable influences, the regulations were clearly hypocritical since artists denied a card could perform in theatres, Central Park and, as Billie had demonstrated, the nation's foremost stage, Carnegie Hall. In practice, the system was degrading and conducted in an atmosphere of petty graft, corruption and personal influence. Musicians, for example, were often sent to a photo studio next door, even if they had brought a suitable photo with them. More particularly, many who were denied a card found that by hiring a lawyer and getting a hearing they were eventually granted one.

Significantly, musicians such as Sonny Stitt and Bud Powell, both with drugs offences on their police records, were able to get a card through this route. 'Hearings were usually before an inspector who was usually sympathetic,' said lawyer Maxwell Cohen. 'They were simple hearings. I would produce the applicant and he would testify that he was married and had not committed an offense for a number of years. In other words he was rehabilitated.'[8] However, there remained some musicians who were unable to get a card at all, perhaps because they did not know their way around the system or did not have the money to do so.

Certainly, when Billie was released from Alderston she could claim to be rehabilitated and to have paid her debt to society. Yet it seems odd that Glaser, whose cooperation with the Narcotics Agents culminated in Billie's imprisonment, did not foresee the problem. Despite this, her drawing-power could not be ignored. Consequently, promoter Al Wilde got the idea of presenting Billie in a Broadway theatre, with a revue built around the theme 'Holiday on Broadway'. Backed by the Bobby Tucker quintet and supported by Cozy Cole, the Slam Stewart trio, and the organ duo of Wyatt and Taylor, Billie was set to open at the Mansfield Theater on 27 April.

The reviews were mixed. 'It is time Billie Holiday be recognized, not as a jazz singer which she will never be, but a singing actress of great potentialities,' declared the Broadway critic of *New York Herald Tribune*.[9] In contrast *New York Amsterdam News* enthused: 'Never before in a Broadway playhouse had critics and first-nighters listened to a torch singer and jazz instrumentalists present their different talents in a legitimate theater . . . Most of them had never heard the peculiar mood songs she made famous but at the end of the evening they too stood up and cheered for five minutes. It took four curtain calls and a speech to quiet them.'[10]

The short run was booked for six nights. 'I played for Billie on that show,' said guitarist Mundell Lowe. 'The critics didn't know what to make of it. They came in expecting a Broadway show and got a jazz revue which they didn't understand at all.'[11] Business was good, if not spectacular, but tailed off on the last two nights. However, in an interview she gave *PM* that week, Billie confirmed she was now reunited with her husband Jimmy Monroe. *New York Amsterdam News* was also on to it: 'A famous singer prominent in the news has all her friends worried because she's gone back to her old love.'[12]

During her week at the Mansfield, Billie made her split with Ed Fishman official at a hearing at the offices of AGVA, and signed again with Glaser. Any chance of getting away from the circle of people that had brought about her downfall was now as far away as ever. Back with a convicted drugs pusher, she found the temptation to return to her old ways was as strong as it had ever been. When her run at the Mansfield ended on 2 May, Billie opened at the Club Ebony at 1678 Broadway near Times Square on 7 May for a four-week run. Significantly, she got her Cabaret Card through John Levy, a co-owner of the club along with Dicky Wells and Al Martin: 'Levy was the one who got her a cabaret card,' confirmed Bobby Tucker. 'He was doing business with both sides of the law. He was an unscrupulous person.'[13]

On 21 May Billie made her first uptown appearance since her release, headlining a benefit concert for Sydenham Hospital at the Renaissance Casino. By now she had a new Cadillac with which she was clearly delighted. After finishing at the Ebony one evening at the end of May she emerged with Jimmy Monroe to drive back to New Jersey. At the 52nd Street intersection some college kids crashed into her, removing a fender. 'La Holiday climbed out,' reported *New York Amsterdam News*, 'and in the traditional motorists' squabble one of the grey kids got nasty. Billie conked him with a big silver-plated trophy she won in a recent *Courier* band poll, bending it in half. The youngster's manners immediately improved. Walter Winchell's car passed as the crowd gathered. Somebody coming out of Lindy's remarked, "You don't get sassy with Billie Holiday, young man, she's Miss Broadway now!"'[14]

Billie's run at the Ebony, or Club Agony as the chorus girls called it because of John Levy's strictness, was the biggest attraction of any major New York club that season. In the band backing Billie was bassist Ted Sturgis. 'Club Ebony was a big place,' he recalled, 'not like those 52nd Street clubs. They had chorus girls and comedians and everything; Joe Louis, Adam Clayton-Powell and Nat King Cole all got married there. Billie was big business there. I had heard about her problems, but I didn't pay it no mind. I didn't see that side of her. She was always to work on time, she did her work, she was a real popular person.'[15] Night after night Billie had to beg to get off the stage and was held over until the club closed for the summer on 24 June.

Billie's tidal wave of popularity was all the more remarkable without a current hit record. 'The gal with the gardenias in her hair has proven to be as strong a box-office attraction as there is among gal vocalists right now,' observed *Downbeat*.[16] There were radio spots; on 7 June she appeared on WHN as Leonard Feather's guest on *Jazz at Its Best*. Then, in the midsummer heat, she broadcast every night for the week of 7 July with Lionel Hampton in Geneva, New York, before opening at the Strand Theater in New York on the 16th for six weeks, playing to the largest audiences seen there in years.

The movie *Key Largo* certainly was an attraction, as was the Count Basie band with whom she headlined, but Basie had appeared at New York theatres before. It was Billie the crowds had come to see. Despite this, however, she was plagued by self-doubt when interviewed by Barry Ulanov for *Metronome* magazine: 'They come to see me get all fouled up,' she told him, 'just waiting for that moment. But they're not going to get it.'[17]

Gradually, Billie's character part was beginning to assume far greater meaning than ever she could have dreamt. Clearly she was attracting the curious as well as her fans. But her image was undergoing transformation; no longer was she seen as simply unlucky in love, the original character part she had created for herself. Now she was seen as unlucky in life. This new slant was reinforced by a series of articles in the press; an article by Larry Newman entitled 'Lady Day's Comeback', for example, appeared in *American Weekly* and *Negro Digest*. It told of her fall from grace, her addiction, and her cure culminating in her Carnegie concerts. In interviews for *PM* and *Metronome*, Billie spoke freely of her past addiction: 'When I was on it, I was *on* it!' she asserted.[18] It all contributed towards her notorious history, which in turn gave her a new base for singing about life.

Now, metaphorical turns of phrase and the way she unfolded a song's text assumed greater subjective meaning. Here was a tragic singer whose personal problems presented an image of someone only in control of herself on stage when moulding language in service of a song. This interrelationship between the singer's personal life and what she sang was defined as much through her choice of songs as the way she sang them. The irony of the 1930s was giving way to pathos, enhanced by her quite specific vocal mannerisms. Paradoxically, the style which made her unique in the 1930s and early 1940s and which attests to her greatness as a twentieth-century artist receded in importance, ultimately having no bearing at all on her contemporary image as a singer. Now it was *what* she sang, the *authenticity* of her voice and the way her audience attributed special significance to it, that mattered. Billie's real-life story had become the source of meaningfulness in her voice.

Despite the spectacular success of her comeback concerts, Billie's life again began to collapse around her. Her problems mounted slowly at first but then with ever-increasing velocity, and error followed error, as if to suggest that the current truth was incomplete. She was back on drugs and her life was once more a scramble for a fix. Following her Strand Theater appearance with Basie, she appeared at the Club Bali in Washington, DC before returning to headline at the Ebony Club when it re-opened its doors at the end of September after a summer break. Also on the bill was Buster Harding's bop band, with whom, incidentally, Billie never once held a rehearsal.

While Billie was at Club Ebony, Decca called a recording session for 22 October. With the musicians assembled, parts rehearsed and sound engineer ready to go, Billie failed to show up. Isabelle Marks, on behalf of Decca, wrote to her, with a copy to Joe Glaser, on 26 October:

Due to your having failed to appear for the recording session scheduled for you and at which you agreed to perform on Friday, October 22, 1948 at 2 p.m. we will find it necessary to charge the cost of all expenses involved to your royalty account.[19]

The costs of a three-hour session bit into Billie's earnings hard. Later in life she would claim that she never earned much in royalties, but the musicians' costs, studio costs and recording staff costs for this date alone would run into thousands of dollars. And more importantly, it was not a way of endearing oneself to a major recording company.

After a month at the Ebony, where Sarah Vaughan substituted for her on a couple of nights because she was too sick to perform, Billie travelled to Chicago to co-feature with Jimmy McPartland at the Silhouette Club until 16 November. She opened with a cold, and although this soon passed, she hardly seemed interested in singing. She appeared late night after night for each of her three sets, then only singing three or four songs, to the obvious disappointment of her fans.

Jimmy McPartland was left having to placate the crowds by playing long and hard. With five days to go, owner Joe Saletta tried to fire Billie, citing habitual tardiness as the reason. After much ill-tempered wrangling, Billie was given just half an hour leeway. 'Fans might have tolerated the waiting,' reported *Downbeat*, 'if there had been some musical reward in the end . . . Her presentation was so mechanically stylized as to seem a mimic's mockery of what she had done before.'[20]

While Billie was sandwiched between a week at Ciro's in Philadelphia, where Helen Hironimus, who had never heard Billie sing, was in the audience, and her opening at Billy Berg's in Hollywood, Decca again tried to get her into their New York studios on 10 December. Called for 2 p.m., Billie eventually arrived an hour late, forcing the date into overtime when it finished at 7.15 p.m. 'We got there *very* late,' confirmed Bobby Tucker. 'She was indisposed most of that date. Those were one-take things; the orchestra had been thoroughly rehearsed ready for her.'[21] The first two numbers, 'Weep No More' and 'Girls Were Made to Take Care of Boys', included a choral accompaniment: 'The Stardusters are little help on both,' *Metronome* observed gloomily.[22]

However, 'Porgy' and 'My Man' were decided on at the session, as there was not enough time to get Billie to learn the other new material that had been planned. Mercifully it made the Stardusters, with no music, redundant. 'We had never done those before,' continued Tucker, 'there was no rehearsal for them, no preparation, they were something she wanted to do.'[23]

'My Man' is a far more satisfactory version than Billie's November

171

1937 version; here she imposes herself on her material in a way she was unable to do on the Brunswick version because of somewhat ribald accompaniment; with just piano, bass and drums she achieves a degree of intimacy that is wholly absorbing. The long verse marks a return on record to the 'story-telling' performances of 'Strange Fruit' or 'Gloomy Sunday' which had become so much part of her live performances. There is just time for one chorus. It is enough, and, as with 'Porgy', is another controlled, affecting performance, where lyric content can be confused with the singer's performing personality and her much-publicized personal life. Again these songs represented a careful choice by the singer, songs she felt suited her and with which she could become emotionally entangled; when she sings 'he beats me too' in 'My Man', for example, the social truth about the singer stood revealed.

Despite Billie's reunion with Jimmy Monroe when she was released from Alderton, buried in Dan Burley's gossip column in *New York Amsterdam News* at the end of May 1948 was a little item that suggested things were about to change: 'Yep. Billie Holiday has sung her way into the heart of that co-bossman at Club Ebony.'[24] John Levy was a balding, overweight, middle-aged businessman who had drifted into show business from retailing. He had a penchant for good-looking women and was once married to the dancer Tondaleyo, which had ended in violence and acrimony. When Billie began working at Club Ebony he went after her in a big way. He bought her the Cadillac and started showering her with gifts, telling her he wanted to manage her. 'He just took her over,' said Bobby Tucker. 'He was a pimp, an awful person; he became her current boyfriend and a sort of pseudo-manager.'[25]

Soon Levy was controlling Billie's finances. Her now abnormally dependent character, coupled with the diminished sense of self that Bobby Tucker and others spoke of, allowed Levy to take full advantage of her vulnerability, 'He makes me wait on him, not him on me,' she said later. 'I never do anything without John telling me.'[26] In the end he took her for every penny he could. Once in a relationship, Billie would do anything to sustain it, including enduring physical and mental abuse, such was the extent of her dependency. Levy used her craving for drugs to his own advantage, to exercise power and control her. It was a sordid relationship, one that had friends and bystanders looking on in helpless disbelief. 'To suit me a man has got to be dominating at all times,' she explained.[27]

Billie's slow descent down the slippery slope continued at Billy Berg's plush night-club in Los Angeles. 'I got her a band at Billy Berg's,' recalled Red Norvo. 'It was a good band; Jimmy Rowles, Herbie Harper, Iggy Shevak, a couple of others. Then New Year, they had trouble there, a big scene.'[28] Just after midnight Billie once again exploded into the national headlines. According to bystanders and police reports, some of her followers were gathered in the kitchen. When Billie finished her set, she joined them, and suddenly complained to Levy that one of them had been fresh. Action followed words and according to the police, Levy grabbed a butcher's knife and lunged at Billie's so-called molester. Instead, the knife was deflected into the shoulder of a bystander, who stumbled on stage with the knife still sticking out of him. By then the argument had degenerated into a free-for-all, with Billie throwing plates and kitchenware at all and sundry.

By the time the dust had settled, three people, Robert Donovan, Marion Epstein and Henry Martin, were in hospital and Levy had been arrested, although he was subsequently released on a $2500 bond. Four days later Billie too was arrested, following a warrant alleging she had injured Marion Epstein in the mêlée. She was later released on bond, giving a radio interview on 8 January 1949 on Radio KQW. On 15 January, now a centre of media attention, she moved on to San Francisco's Café Society Uptown on Fillimore Street, which was immediately booked solid with curiosity-seekers. Following what she considered adverse publicity, Billie fired her press agent Jerome Lee, replacing him with Floyd Snelson. As events turned out, it was something of a futile gesture. On 23 January 1949 she was back again on the front pages of the national press. She had been arrested for possession by Federal narcotic agents.

From the start, Billie, now older and wiser, maintained she had been framed. A Police Special Service Detail of three men assisted by Colonel George White of the Federal Bureau of Narcotics entered Room 602 of the Mark Twain Hotel at 345 Taylor in San Francisco during the afternoon of 22 January. There they claimed to have discovered a small quantity of opium and an improvised pipe. Both Levy and Billie were charged and released on bail.

Levy emphatically denied the charges to the waiting pressmen, claiming that Billie had not even slept in the hotel room that night but had allowed an acquaintance she knew only as 'Mandy' to do so. The same evening Billie was back performing at Café Society Uptown to what one report described as 'sympathetic' crowds. Amazingly, Colonel White himself was in a ringside seat, making requests for his favourite tunes.

Billie's FBI file says the Narcotics Bureau possessed 'no definite information of any narcotics', but 'presumed that since they were together they probably possessed some narcotics'. Since the laws governing searches and seizures were more liberal for the State Police than Federal law enforcement agencies, the assistance of the San Francisco Police Department was enlisted for the raid.[29]

In effect, the raid was no more than a fishing trip. It was prompted by Colonel White's interest in demonstrating that the law applied to celebrities as much as to the junkies on Central Avenue. However, the matter went as high as Edgar Hoover himself, who wrote to White offering what assistance he could. On the face of it, Billie and Levy had been caught red-handed.

Billie appointed J. W. Ehrlich as her counsel, who immediately suggested that whatever substances she may or may not have been taking, with her previous record the only way to beat the rap was to 'take the test'. To give her time for detoxification he set about postponing the trial after her hearing on 11 February, where she pleaded not guilty to 'Violation of Section 11500 of the Health and Safety Code'. A trial date of 14 March was set and adjourned, with subsequent adjournments on 15 April, 12 May and 19 May when a date was finally set for 31 May. Meanwhile, Levy had been let off at his hearing, prompting Ehrlich to suggest (incorrectly) at Billie's trial that he had framed her.

With the impending trial and the problems of weaning herself away from drugs, Billie went into acute depression. 'The hounding and the pressure drove me . . . to think of trying the last solution, death,' she said in July 1949. 'I brooded and fretted . . . I didn't end it all. Instead I went to sleep, rose early and went to see my dearest friend in California who suggested I see her psychiatrist. I had several interviews with the psychiatrist and felt a whole lot better.'[30]

Her 'dearest friend' was Tallulah Bankhead, whom Billie dubbed Lula. During the 1952 trial of Bankhead's secretary, who stood accused of tampering with cheques, unsubstantiated accusations were exchanged in court about Bankhead's involvement with narcotics. Certainly both Billie and Bankhead enjoyed living it up and both enjoyed hanging out together. Indeed, several musicians claim that Billie made no secret about her lesbian relationship with 'Lula' and, more sensationally, a brief, explosive affair with Marlene Dietrich.

With Billie terrified at the prospect of being returned to prison, this time for a long stretch as a second-time offender, Bankhead was moved to phone Edgar Hoover, the Director of the FBI, to intercede on her friend's behalf. Using what influence she could – her father was a congressman – she clearly believed Hoover subsequently helped in some way, although quite how is not clear, and she wrote to thank him on 9 February 1949 (see Appendix 6). However, Billie's relationship with Bankhead ended in acrimony at the end of 1954 with the publication of *Lady Sings the Blues* looming. Lula threatened legal action, afraid of what dirty washing might be aired in public. 'There's nothing in it to hurt you,' Billie reassured her in a terse letter. 'Straighten up and fly right, Banky. Nobody's trying to drag you.'[31]

When Billie Holiday finally appeared in court on 31 May 1949, there was no mistaking her large black eye. The trial records say the day was given over to the selection of the jury or 'drawing and examination of talesmen' as it was called, which continued into 1 June when they were finally 'drawn and sworn'. On 2 June, 'the test was taken' by Billie, with a continuance into the following day. On 3 June, Ehrlich's strategy paid off: 'Test taken: "Not Guilty"' was marked on her trial papers.[32]

'A jury of six women and six men acquitted Billie Holiday last night on a charge of possessing opium,' reported the *New York Times*. 'The torch singer testified that her manager handed her a paper-wrapped parcel and told her to get rid of it. Before she could dispose of the packet, she said, somebody grabbed her.'[33] As a postscript to the affair, Ehrlich's fee for defending Billie never got paid, while in April 1974, Will Rogers, the then owner of the Mark Twain Hotel, 'dedicated' Rooms 203–4 as the 'Billie Holiday Suite'. He claimed the rooms were 'tastefully decorated with relics of the era including headlines of her arrest and subsequent acquittal'.[34]

Some weeks before the trial, Billie had entered a private hospital for five days under the supervision of Dr Herbert Henderson to help in the detoxification process. Here she apparently turned increasingly towards alcohol to subdue her drug hunger. However, although she appeared at Shrine Auditorium, Los Angeles with Duke Ellington on 11 March, a forthcoming engagement for April at Chicago's Music Bowl in Chicago fell through. Forced to take a few one-nighters in small clubs to fill in, she picked up her schedule on 22 April for a week at Detroit's Paramount. But an even bigger blow came when she was abruptly forced to cancel two weeks at the Royal Roost in New York, reputedly at a loss of $3000 a week, when again denied a Cabaret Card. As a result she was badly advised to sue the Police Department, who simply pointed to an outstanding narcotics trial as good reason for withholding it; at her appeal, Justice Aaron J. Levy said the Police Department 'deserved commendation' for their action.

With her trial at last behind her, Billie played to standing-room-only crowds at Fox's Million Dollar Theater in Los Angeles from 15 to 22 June. It was followed by a series of one-nighters with Red Norvo's septet, promoted by Van Tonkins, and began with an appearance on Gene Norman's *Just Jazz* show, broadcast out of Los Angeles. 'We went up and down the coast,' recalled Norvo. 'We played Seattle, Tacoma and some other inland towns.'[35] However, when she unexpectedly drew a tiny crowd at Bakersfield, Billie pulled out in disgust; two months later she was facing another legal battle when Tonkins sued for breach of contract.

Meanwhile her regular trio, left high and dry with little or no work from their boss for the best part of 1949, were forced to break up. Bassist John Levy (no relation of Billie's current paramour) and drummer Denzil Best accepted an offer from George Shearing who was in the process of forming his now famous quintet, while in June Bobby Tucker joined Billy Eckstine, beginning an enduring relationship that would last into the 1980s.

After six tumultuous months, Billie returned to New York at the beginning of July and began her search for a new accompanist. She chose one of the great, unsung musicians of the Swing Era, pianist and arranger Horace Henderson. 'She came down to hear my group where we were playing,' he recalled. 'We were playing a theatre. What knocked Billie out is the fact that she had some music, it was for a big band, and it hadn't been condensed to where six pieces could play, so what I would do . . . was make it full, and that knocked her out. She turned around to her husband John Levy and says, "See, John, this is it," she liked that.'[36]

Almost as soon as he joined Billie, Henderson was involved in a recording session directed by Buster Harding on 17 August. Once again Billie was reunited on record with Lester Young, who remains tucked away in the saxophone section. Although only two sides were recorded that day, they are the only Decca sides where the instrumental work is of value in itself. Harding's arrangements are very well crafted and are played with great cohesion for a large pick-up band. The band is brassy, but Billie manages to manoeuvre around its energetic blasts with grace; 'Baby Get Lost' is a blues which despite the hip lyrics represents a superb performance by the singer, while ' 'Tain't Nobody's Business if I Do' is more personal statement than enduring performance. ' "Business" will of course be interpreted by everyone in light of recent events in Billie's private life,' observed *Downbeat*.[37]

Then followed three sessions under the musical directorship of Sy Oliver, and three times Billie failed to get the usual four sides in the can. 'Them There Eyes' serves to show how her art had become less important to her than her lifestyle. Her vocal traces the same route as her Columbia version, turning precious few new turnings on the way, the arrangement even institutionalizing some of her pet phrases. 'Gimme a Pigfoot and a Bottle of Beer' is an update of Bessie Smith's November 1933 version for Columbia, but substituting 'Oo-Bop-a-Dop' for 'Shim Sham Shimmy' and dropping the line about reefers. However, it is robbed of its rough-and-ready intimacy by the context in which it is sung.

Billie's duets with Armstrong, her teenage idol, on the second Sy Oliver session, fail to capture the sort of magic Ella Fitzgerald did when she went into the Decca studios with Satchmo. By now Billie's voice was typecast into the service of songs with deeper emotional purpose, but even so, her entry after Armstrong's opening chorus on 'You Can't Lose a Broken Heart' is a special moment, something she seemed unable to sustain throughout the session.

Armstrong hams it up, but there is a strained bonhomie summed up by his unmistakable use of the 'F' word in the final chorus of 'My Sweet Hunk o' Trash'; shades of Patricia Norman on Eddy Duchin's 'Old Man Mose'. 'Here it is not only in bad taste, it doesn't make much sense in the lyric line,' said *Downbeat*. 'And since when does Louis have to use obscenity to sell records?'[38]

For Billie, it was another black mark among many when Decca came to consider renewing her contract; a missed record date, poor time-keeping, inability to produce the industry norm of four sides a session, dates running into overtime and now, the last straw, having to recall 'My Sweet Hunk o' Trash'.

Henderson went out on the road with Billie on a series of one-nighters in the Boston area, where he was alarmed to see Levy cynically manipulating her. 'Her husband always tried to work a psychological on her,' he recalled. 'I never approved of it, but there was nothing I could do. He always made it a habit of making her mad five minutes before she got ready to perform . . . she would go on stage with tears in her eyes and give one of the greatest performances . . . and mad with John Levy her husband, but nobody knew it.'[39]

With the rise of television in 1949, Billie appeared on NBC's Eddie Condon Floor Show produced by Esme Sarnoff and Art Ford's Television Show. She made several appearances on Condon's show, frequently accompanied by Henderson, beginning with an appearance on 27 August when she sang 'Billie's Blues', 'Lover Man' and the Bessie Smith number, 'Keeps on a Rainin' ', which she would record two days later for Decca. The Condon version, slightly slower,[40] is far superior, the brassy power of the Decca big band keeping the listener at arm's length from Billie's one-to-one confessions.

Having recorded four Bessie Smith numbers for Decca – although not, says Gabler, for a Bessie tribute album – it seemed only natural one Condon programme paid tribute to the influence the Empress of the Blues had on her style, particularly since Condon had known Smith well. 'We did a programme a week,' recalled Jack Lesberg, Condon's bassist at the time. 'One was a dramatization of her playing the part of Bessie Smith, where she came into a night-club where Eddie Condon was playing. It was just a dramatization, Bobby Hackett was supposed to be Bix Beiderbecke, that sort of thing; the bit where she came in that was it! She did some blues and boy, did she sing!'[41]

Several musicians in Condon's orbit appeared on Billie's 19 October 1949 Decca date, including Hackett, old friend Bernie Leighton and bassist Jack Lesberg. 'Gordon Jenkins just adored her,' recalled Lesberg. 'He wrote these wonderful arrangements for the "Crazy He Calls Me" session, it was a string ensemble, a small orchestra, Milt Gabler wanted to do them like that. Gordon was just beautiful; we'd go in for a recording session with him and we'd have four songs to do and we'd get it done in half the time, that's because he was so exact. He was the arranger and he made sure before they started spinning the orchestra was OK. "Crazy" was one take, she might have rehearsed it, run it down in the studio once or twice, but with Milt in the control room as well you couldn't go wrong.'[42]

Plans to play at New York's Café Society in October fell through because of the Cabaret Card problem, so Billie had no alternative but to go out on the road, playing Detroit's new Flame Show bar backed by the Snookie Young band. 'It was a beautiful night-club,' recalled Horace Henderson, who had discovered that being accompanist to Billie Holiday was a full-time job. 'She was quite a girl. She had no conception of the time of day. If she had four shows, she would do her first and take her little dog, a chihuahua which was given to her by Xavier Cugat, and she'd walk up the street and at the first convenient bar she would sit up there and be friendly with people and forget in another hour she had a show to do. So you just had to stay with her. She was so friendly and nice yet once she got on stage, Lady Day did her thing.

'She drank and she did some other things but she had her faculties. It didn't seem to bother her. It seemed like she really needed this. It got so she depended on it. But it didn't affect her singing; I've seen it affect some people and it was pitiful, but you were afraid to deny her these things because you don't know what it might have done. So long as she performed and did a good performance you just couldn't disturb her.'[43]

While Billie was at the Flame Show bar, Chuck Peterson, who had played trumpet in Artie Shaw's band while she had been a member, looked her up. They agreed to meet at the upper-crust Old Colony bar when Peterson finished work in the pit band of the nearby Fox Theater. Peterson, with Billie and two white girlfriends, went to the bar but were denied service. After a woman sitting nearby got up and walked out, announcing that she was going somewhere where 'niggers are not served', the bartender asked to see Peterson in the lobby. Levy, who was just arriving, said the bartender asked Peterson if he thought he was in Russia and set about him.

Once again Billie was in the news, making the front page of *New York Amsterdam News*. 'Slug Billie Holiday's Escort in Bar' ran the headline, 'Musician beaten by Dixie Thug'.[44] Peterson's mother filed a law suit, while the bar's owner John Generious claimed his bar did not discriminate. But although Billie appeared strong in the face of racism, such incidents profoundly upset her and served to highlight that being denied club work in New York was like being doomed to roam the high seas for ever, like the Flying Dutchman.

The dignified Henderson soon decided that this was not the life for him. He was replaced by Carl Mark who saw the year out with Billie in the Blue Note in Chicago. It was an important date; club owners over the country were watching for signs of unreliability. She passed the test. 'Looking sleek, relaxed and comfortable, Billie sang ... "'Tain't Nobody's Business if I Do", "Where Are You?" and "Now, Baby or Never" ... Despite being nobody's business, numbers on this order are embarrassingly pertinent in their associations, which may be one reason for Billie's singing them,' observed *Downbeat*.[45] Her character part was beginning to consolidate; singer and image were now being consciously intertwined.

From Chicago she travelled to the West Coast, opening at the Bal Tabarin in Hollywood on 6 January 1950 for a week with Red Norvo. 'Every time she came to the West Coast she asked for my band to back her,' said Norvo. 'It got to be that if I wasn't available she refused to come.'[46]

Glaser kept Billie busy throughout early 1950; after the West Coast came a small tour with Charlie Ventura's band beginning with a week at Chicago's Regal Theater from 13 January, then a week at the Riviera in St Louis followed by a series of one-nighters through the Midwest. Then she was back on the West Coast with pianist Carl Mark to open at San Francisco's New Orleans Swing Club for two weeks on 11 February, where she was held over.

While Billie was on the West Coast, Decca set up a session for her on 8 March at their Hollywood studio at 5505 Melrose Avenue.

Although she did not know it at the time, it was to be her last session for the company. Gabler had been moved to head Decca's subsidiary, Coral, and when Billie's contract came up for renewal in August, there was no one to fight her corner. Consequently, she was unceremoniously dropped from the label, although it was not without some irony that she would see her work for the label recycled on to LP during her lifetime. Billie's replacement on the label was a West Coast singer called Kitty White, whom Decca announced they were 'building for stardom'.

Billie cut just two numbers during the three-hour session, another version of 'God Bless the Child', and 'This Is Heaven to Me', arranged by Gordon Jenkins, in which she was cocooned in a heavenly-host choir that, far from smothering her, showed her frayed-at-the-edges voice up in stark relief. These Eisenhower Era-meets-the-ghetto numbers have a curious but undeniable period charm today; Billie's voice, from time to time sounding as if it would slide out of tune, somehow makes it to the end. Clearly the choir was an attempt to connect with middle America, and, like the strings on her first session, the idea might have come from Billie or indeed Levy.

Significantly, on 28 May 1950, after a week at the Apollo, Billie mounted a concert at Brooklyn Academy of Music with the Edward Boatner A Cappella Choir, so the concept of working with voices was not just a record producer's foible. She sang 'God Bless the Child' and 'Strange Fruit' with voices while for her jazz repertoire she used her regular pianist Carl Mark plus a fascinating line-up of Miles Davis, Art Blakey, Percy Heath, Bennie Green and Mundell Lowe.

However, by the end of April some of Billie's sins of omission and commission came home to roost. Ed Fishman's suit for breach of contract in the sum of $75,000 was finally settled for $2145 by the California Superior Court and Marian Epstein was awarded $1540 by the court for injuries sustained in Billie's plate-throwing contribution to the Billy Berg débâcle. And when in August a brief series of one-nighters with a band fronted by West Coast trumpeter Gerald Wilson ended in disaster in South Carolina, Billie was left without a dime and had to beg John Levy for money to get home. When the money came through she pulled out with a promise to send for her stranded band when she got back to LA. The band waited in vain and the whole sordid affair was left for the Musicians' Union to unravel. It was then that Billie decided this was the beginning of the end for Mr Levy.

However, she was tied up for weeks in advance with contracts Levy had signed on her behalf. Gradually she untangled herself by working through the backlog of bookings and ran out on him one night when she was playing Washington, DC. After over eighteen months of degradation, she was finally free of his domination. 'Continual fights, bickering, life was hell,' she said. 'He had a terrible temper and tried to take it out on me.'[47] He had cost her thousands of dollars in gambling plus a house in Morristown, New Jersey, which he had bought with her money in his name, but even so she was overwhelmed by the pain of loneliness when the parting came. For a while she returned to Jimmy Monroe and then moved into a small apartment in the Hotel Henry on 44th Street. For help with her bookings and administration, she turned to Maely Bartholomew, who was something of a jazz groupie and had worked briefly in a similar capacity for Charlie Parker.

While on the West Coast during the summer of 1950, Billie appeared in a movie short featuring Count Basie, filmed at Universal Studios in Hollywood, produced and directed by Will Cowan. In a simulated night-club setting, far more elaborate than the subsequent series of Basie Snader Teletranscriptions that followed, it was one of twelve Cowan shorts that presented some of the better acts and orchestras of the time.

It is probably the most valuable document of Billie on film, showing how she used a kind of minimalistic choreography to underline a word here or suggest a nuance there. 'God Bless the Child' is performed under a pin-spot, something that had been a feature of her performances since 'Strange Fruit' in Café Society, focusing attention on her face while the set, or 'club', is in darkness.

With just a few exceptions[48] Billie's voice, so familiar, nevertheless remains a disembodied sound on recordings. But here, when it unites with her physical image on screen, it is not the voice for its own sake as much as the expressive power of the singer, using both tonal *and* visual nuance, that intrigues and commands our attention. Visual nuance goes beyond purely musical factors. Seeing a saxophonist, a trumpeter, a trombonist or pianist play 'Body and Soul', for example, adds little to our understanding or appreciation of the music *per se*. Yet, as in day-to-day conversation, expression and gesture heighten our understanding of narrative and equally, seeing a singer interpret a song adds greatly to our appreciation of its lyrics.

Opening with the 'storytelling' line of 'God Bless the Child', the workaday melody is brought alive by gesture and expression, albeit minimalistic in comparison to singers from the Broadway stage. At the faster tempo of 'Now Baby, or Never', a revamping of 'Gotta Be This or That', Billie's face becomes alive with animation, visually underlining a word here or casting a doubting glance at a word there as the lyrics become a pleasure shared between singer and audience. And Billie swings. In this over-the-shoulder glance at the out-and-out jazz singer of the 1930s rather than the 'song stylist' of the 1940s, she pares the melodic line down to the bone and syncopates her line so that at some points she almost appears to cross-accent Basie's swinging four. Only clumsy editing mars this superb snapshot of her outswinging Basie's tight little septet of the period.

'It was a nice session, it didn't start off too well,' said Jimmy Lewis, Basie's bass player that day. 'She was a little nervous or something was wrong, so she had a little rest. It went nice because we didn't have any rehearsals, they just called the tunes and we found out what key she was in and got it down. It seemed like she couldn't get together with the tunes too much at first, so she took a little rest, she went out the back, I don't know what happened, and she came back about ten minutes later and ran everything down, seemed like everything worked for her after that.'[49]

Billie was just thirty-five years old and should have been approaching the peak of her career, both artistically and financially. Instead, it was the child pianist 'Sugar Chile' Robinson who took the main feature spot with Basie's septet. Her unreliability meant, simply, that she was failing to command the sort of work that would have come her way had she been known to be clean and prepared to take responsibility for her career. Her contracts were a maze of sub-clauses protecting club owners against tardy time-keeping, excessive drinking, short sets and much else besides. Artistically her horizons had shrunk since the halcyon days of the 1930s when her talent was being extended almost daily. Now her habit stood between her and her art.

Chapter Eleven

1950–55

In August 1950, Columbia released an album of four Billie Holiday 78s, dating from 1937 through to 1941. If she had time to pause and reflect during her hectic and sometimes chaotic schedule, then those recordings must surely have acted as a reminder of happier times. After spending most of September 1950 at the Oasis in Los Angeles, Billie was due to open at Louis Landry's New Orleans Swing Club in San Francisco at the end of the month. But on 28 September Landry was convicted on a narcotics charge, so Billie accepted an engagement at Shirley Corlett's Longbar Club and once again headed for trouble.

Out on bail pending an appeal, Landry threatened to enforce Billie's contract in the courts if she appeared at the rival club. In the legal confusion that followed it was by no means certain at which club she was going to appear, if at all. The result was an unpublicized opening at the Longbar. Within three days, however, she stormed out after a dispute with Shirley Corlett over a missed show, leaving behind over $1000 that was due to her, representing her share of the door money.

To add to her problems, Attorney Jack Ehrlich was still pursuing her for his unpaid trial bill from the year before and her chauffeur, Cotrell Amos, was picked up with two packages of heroin in his possession. As a result her new blue Lincoln, which Amos had been driving at the time of the seizure, was impounded by the police. And, as if all this was not enough, her bad-girl image made the front cover of *Downbeat* magazine: 'Billie in Trouble Again.'[1]

Leaving a trail of confusion in her wake, Billie left town for an engagement in Chicago with Martha Raye's pianist Jack Russin in tow. She was booked into the Hi-Note Club at Clark and Illinois Streets, backed by a band led by Miles Davis. Davis too had been in the news; in September he had been picked up for heroin possession in Los Angeles with Art Blakey while touring with Billy Eckstine. For Davis, whose reputation was as yet nothing like it would be in years to come, this meant disaster. Club jobs simply dried up; owners were very much aware of how drugs and unreliability seemed to go hand-in-hand, but more especially, of the very real problems caused by increased police vigilance when a known user was in town.

Davis's bust meant that during the whole of 1951 he was barely able to string together more than five or six weeks of club work, a fact that serves to illustrate Billie's powerful box-office appeal, which was such that many club owners were prepared to put up with her 'notorious' reputation. In such circumstances it was remarkable that Hi-Note owner Mart Denenburg was willing to gamble on both Billie *and* Davis during the busy Christmas season.

Billie was filling a slot normally filled by Anita O'Day, a regular attraction at the club, who had accepted a booking in Milwaukee. She was still in Chicago when Billie and Davis were due to open, and was sitting in the bar humming a tune to herself while waiting to introduce herself to the musicians when they arrived. 'After a bit this good-looking black man got off one of the stools and came over to ask, "Where'd you get that tune?"' recalled O'Day. '"Oh, I don't know," I said. "It's in the air. Kind of a favourite of mine." "I wrote it," he said.'[2]

Davis and O'Day quickly developed a rapport, but Billie and O'Day did not. Although the younger singer idolized Billie, it was not reciprocated. For her part Billie seems to have derided O'Day as a second-rate white imitator who was getting the bookings she deserved.

Billie and Miles Davis played to capacity houses throughout the Christmas season. With Davis scheduled to play well into the New Year, Billie left on 7 January 1951 for the Rendevous in Philadelphia. Refuting the rumours of the day, club owner Denenberg confirmed there were no problems with Billie during her stay. 'Gets on stand in time,' he said, 'I couldn't ask for more.'[3] Although Davis's professional association with Holiday had been just one concert in Brooklyn and a season at the Hi-Note, he retained an indelible impression of her as a victim of unnamed exploiters. 'She was the nicest woman in the world,' he said more than a quarter of a century later. 'All she wanted to do is sing. They picked on her ... to get money out of her.'[4]

By March 1951, it had been twelve months since Billie had last cut a commercial disc. With no major label showing any interest, she signed with Aladdin Records. Interestingly, Louis Jordan, also once a best-selling artist for Decca, signed with Aladdin when he too was dropped by the label in 1953.

Aladdin was a West Coast R&B label run by Edward and Leo Menser out of 4918 Santa Monica Boulevard, Los Angeles. Its mainstays were artists such as Amos Milburn, Charles Brown and Lightin' Hopkins, but from time to time they had also signed jazz artists to the label, such as Lester Young and Jay McShann. When Helen Humes went with them and had a hit with 'Be-Baba-Luba', the number was covered by Lionel Hampton who had an even bigger hit with 'Hey! Ba-Ba-Re-Bop'. The result was that Humes, who had replaced Billie in Basie's band in 1938, turned increasingly towards R&B during her tenure with the label. Hits for Aladdin during 1951 were Peppermint Harris's 'I Got Loaded' and The Five Keys' 'Glory of Love', so quite what the label had in store for Billie was something of a mystery when she went into the recording studios in April with a Tiny Grimes unit.

During her entire career, Billie recorded at most a dozen or so blues, and here she cut two in one session. Both made plenty of concessions to public domain blues riffs in the accompaniment, but at least there is a degree of animation in Billie's singing that touches base with her thirties work. On the ballad 'Detour Ahead', a number she had been singing since 1949 and recorded by artists as diverse as Jeri Southern and Woody Herman's Second Herd, she returns to the lyric content and tempo that defined her character part. Here her performance sounds fresh and engaging, but more particularly it is free from an unknown saxophonist's excesses of enthusiasm (it was not Haywood Henry, who has confirmed he was not on the session) that had crippled the blues performances – albeit above the waterline. 'The Lady wails on "Detour", sounding convincing indeed,' observed *Downbeat*.[5]

Billie's life was now a round of club work and a daily struggle to score. In March she again featured at the Rendevous in Philadelphia, where the *Philadelphia Inquirer* found her in great form: '[Billie] is splendid as always with her fascinating combination of the sultry and the sad, her rich and feverish intonations and her warm clear phrasing.'[6] But the bad nights were beginning to crowd out the good; she might be late, she might fail to show or she might perform while high. Her remarkable constitution was somehow holding out, though. As she went from club to club, with occasional appearances at black theatres, such as an August run at the Regal in Chicago, her personal life was a mess, whirling faster and faster out of control. 'I was like a ship without a rudder,' she recalled in 1953. 'Then, just as I was sinking with nothing to grab to save myself, I got my reprieve [when] a tall, brown-skinned, serious-minded fellow (the first I had ever been that close to) came along.'[7]

Louis McKay was born in 1909 in New Orleans. He moved to New York in the 1930s where he befriended both Billie and Sadie and even dated Billie as a sixteen-year-old. 'When [Billie's] mother was worried about her she would send me to bring Billie home or see about her,' he said later.[8] While Billie was playing the Club Juano in Detroit during the spring of 1951 she sought out McKay, who had a regular job in a car plant there. 'Billie Holiday came to me for help, threatening suicide if I didn't help her,' he said. 'I told her I wouldn't leave my job in Detroit and abandon my obligations there until she was ready to kick her drug habit. I refused to go on the road with her until this was done.'[9]

By the time Billie made a profile appearance at Boston's popular Storyville Club in October 1951, she seemed to have done just that: 'A new Lady Day calmly conquered the jazz-oriented citizenry of Boston in the course of a rewardingly successful week,' reported *Downbeat*. 'Billie Holiday, singing better than anyone here had heard her in the last few years, demonstrated a new sense of responsibility and co-operativeness. As a result she made every set on time and even volunteered an extra set some nights for the WMEX wire from the club.'[10] Clearly she was revitalized and left Nat Hentoff, who wrote the feature and was also the radio compere, under no illusions as to what had brought about the change; her new sense of security and ease, he reported, was due to Louis McKay.

Billie's singing was extensively documented on a series of airchecks from Radio WMEX during her stay at the club. Her pianist was now Buster Harding, a highly regarded arranger–composer who had regularly contributed charts to the top bands during the Swing Era, including Count Basie, Benny Goodman, Woody Herman and Cab Calloway. Several of his originals were given prominence by Artie Shaw's 1945 Victor band, including the now classic feature for trumpeter Roy Eldridge, 'Little Jazz'.

As a member of Billie's backing group, Harding's comping was top-drawer. However, the harsh quality of Billie's voice comes as a shock after listening to her Universal short or the Aladdin sides which precede these performances. Billie was a very heavy smoker, and despite her heavy drinking and drug-taking, only smoking can have such a detrimental affect on the voice. On 'All of Me', for example, her voice rumbles and growls like Armstrong's. Equally, on some tracks the effects of alcohol are apparent on both her pronunciation, with slurred words, and, unusually for her at this stage of her career, on her intonation.

Although her rhythm section is good, it swings in an even four, reflecting contemporary taste, with no contrast, as with her Columbia or Decca sides, with a cut-time or *alla breve* feel, which would have been considered old hat. This has a profound effect on Billie's rhythmic approach. It propels her forward, rather than giving her space to use some of the outrageous syncopations of her Columbia period, typically done against a 2/4 time-feel. This is best illustrated by her performance of 'Lover Man'. Here the rhythm section plays an even four behind her, instead of the very specific cut-time feel of her Decca version, forcing her to give equal dramatic weight to the lyrics by smoothing out the lyric line to flow with the regular, even pulse.

Billie was back in Detroit to play Club Juano in December 1951 where this time she met McKay's family. 'His mother, she's eighty years old,' said Billie, 'and she had this dog and she loved this dog so much, and . . . the dog died, and they buried the dog and he preached . . . we were walking down the street and somebody says "Hey Preach . . ."' That's when I found out the story [he was once a Preacher].'[11] Billie was quite taken by the thought of McKay's lay work, writing the tune 'Preacher Boy', which she even got published by E. B. Marks & Co., in his honour, although the number was never recorded.

By now Billie had temporarily relocated on the West Coast, where she was not troubled by Cabaret Card considerations. During the early part of 1952 she played the Tiffany Club in Hollywood, backed by tenor saxophonist Wardell Gray's group that included drummer Chico Hamilton and pianist Hampton Hawes. She had met Hawes a couple of years earlier; when they were reunited he was on drugs. Taking one look at the young pianist, she said, 'You too, baby?'

In March she moved up the coast to play San Francisco's Say When on Bush Street and was greeted by capacity crowds night after night, with queues out into the street waiting to see her. 'Singer sported a black eye for a time, but she's still a "new" Billie,' commented *Downbeat*.[12]

Taking care of business to an extent she had not done during the past few years, Billie was very conscious of not having a recording contract. Although eight sides still remained outstanding for Aladdin, neither party appeared keen to pursue their obligations. For Billie's part, Aladdin's distributorship network was poor in comparison to a major label's and she was worried about losing her audience, concerns she voiced to Joe Glaser, who had Bobby Phillips, his West Coast representative, contact Norman Granz.

Granz, a long-time fan of Billie Holiday, was interested in recording her and set up a deal. He had national distribution through Mercury Records and a series of best-selling recordings of his Jazz at the Philharmonic concerts were in great demand with jazz fans across the country. As a spin-off he had begun recording individual artists, most of whom were associated with JATP, and was fast attracting some of the greatest names in jazz to his roster. When Billie signed with Granz she had found a recording producer who was wholly sympathetic to her needs as an artist.

In the late spring of 1952, she went into Radio Recorders studio in Los Angeles. 'My feeling about Billie was that she was best without the imposition of arrangements,' said Granz. 'I got some of the best musicians who were in town and had them back her. I always thought that she sounded best on those things she did with Teddy Wilson in the thirties, and I wanted to encourage that same spontaneous feel.'[13] Lined up to accompany Billie were Charlie Shavers, Flip Phillips, Oscar Peterson, Barney Kessel, Ray Brown and Alvin Stoller.

However, the most immediate problem Granz had to confront was Billie's repertoire. In live performance she stuck to a song-list that had hardly changed in years. To stretch her beyond her comfort zone, Granz collected a whole pile of lead sheets of songs he thought were appropriate and brought them to the session. 'Billie liked to do songs she had grown up with,' said guitarist Barney Kessel. 'She wanted . . . bluesy tunes. She also liked certain standards such as "Who's Sorry Now?" and "All of Me" . . . Norman brought her some more difficult songs to sing, at times he was very insistent about her making an effort to learn them . . . Sometimes Norman would persist, and sometimes he'd back off. But I think most of the time he got his way because she felt that, when the effort was made, she was very happy with the results. I thought Norman was responsible for reaching out and visualizing what Billie was capable of, and what would be good for her. In the thirties, John Hammond functioned in the same way, visualizing a little higher concept of artists than the idea they had of themselves.'[14]

Billie Holiday Sings, recorded for the Clef label but leased to Mercury, appeared in time for the 1952 Christmas season and was awarded a five-star rating in *Downbeat*. All eight tracks that went down on the session were used, and if four songs had been previously recorded by Billie, at least they were not too closely associated with her. The recording quality was good, and revealed her now thickening tone and diminished range. But in jazz and popular music, having a narrow range or even a harsh, rasping or cracked voice has never stopped anyone from becoming a singer. The key is that the voice should convey authenticity, which is perceived to be revealing of a singer's personality.

The *Billie Holiday Sings* session was followed a few days later by a further eight sides with the same musicians. Together with several sides from the subsequent 27 July session recorded in New York with a slightly changed personnel, the sessions were released on two Clef albums in 1954: 'Who can make familiar phrases of love requited, torches carried bravely and put down sadly, of passions so touching as the Lady does?' asked *Metronome*, reviewing both the albums.[15]

Perhaps the most memorable of these sides was Billie's duet with

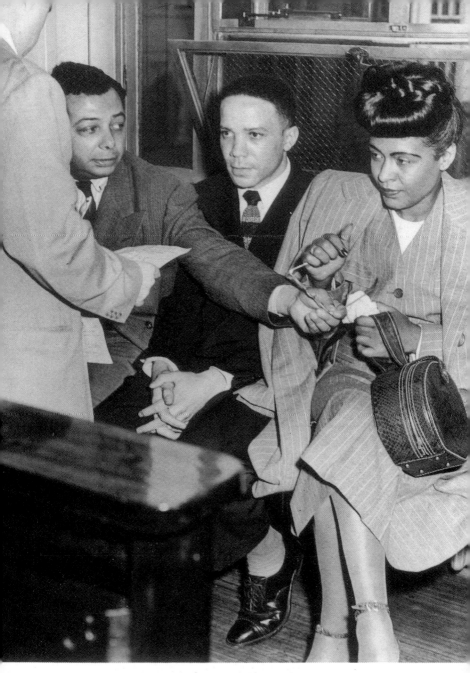

27 May 1947: the United States *v.* Billie Holiday. The charge of 'receiving and concealing a narcotic drug' is read out to Billie in the District Court in Philadelphia. (Left to right) Jimmy Ascendio, pianist Bobby Tucker and Billie. (*Urban Archives, Temple Univ., Philadelphia*)

ABOVE: Billie Holiday leaves the San Francisco Courthouse on 24 January 1949 with her current boyfriend/manager, John Levy. They had just been given bail after being arrested on 22 January for possession of opium. Jake Ehrlich, Billie's attorney, is on the right. (*Urban Archives, Temple Univ.*)

OPPOSITE: Billie Holiday and childhood friend Freddie Green at the Club Astoria, Baltimore, September 1948. (*US Drug Enforcement Agency/courtesy Prof. David Courtwright*)

OVERLEAF, TOP: In January 1954 Billie Holiday embarked on her first European tour as star of Leonard Feather's 'Jazz Club USA'. On 31 January, seven days before Ella Fitzgerald and Norman Granz's 'Jazz at the Philharmonic', Billie appeared in the Hague. With her are (left to right) Elaine Leighton (d), Carl Drinkard (p), Red Mitchell (b). The photo suggests the concert might have been recorded. (*Stichting Nat. Jazz Archief, Amsterdam*)

BELOW: The climax of the 'Jazz Club USA' concerts was the jam session at the end of the show. Again at the Hague, Billie is at the microphone with (left to right) Leonard Feather (mc), Beryl Booker (p), Bob White (d), Red Mitchell (b), Buddy De Franco (cl), Red Norvo (vib). (*Stichting Nat. Jazz Archief*)

To her surprise and delight, Billie was lionized by her fans during the 'Jazz Club USA' tour. Here she is surrounded by well-wishers as she gives a radio interview to Dutch station Wereld Omroep during her intermission. (*Stichting Nat. Jazz Archief*)

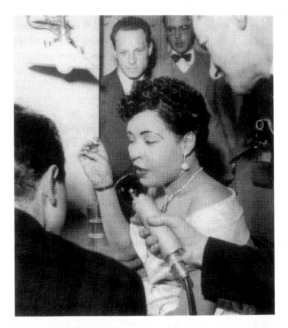

BELOW: Billie in trouble again. On 23 February 1956 she was brought before the court in Philadelphia with her then boyfriend/manager Louis McKay, whom she would marry the following year. They were charged with 'use and possession of drugs'. (*Urban Archives, Temple Univ.*)

Earle Warren Zaidins, Billie Holiday's attorney during the last years of her life. (*Raymond Ross Photography, NY*)

BELOW: After her estrangement from her husband Louis McKay, Billie became more and more isolated in her apartment at 26 West 87th Street. The photo says it all: a suitcase ready for another out-of-town gig and a box of dog treats for her only companion, a chihuahua. (*Inst. of Jazz Studies, Rutgers Univ.*)

OVERLEAF: Between 19 and 21 July, Billie Holiday's body was laid out at the Universal Funeral Chapel at Lexington Avenue and 51st Street for fans to pay their last respects. (*Raymond Ross Photography*)

Oscar Peterson on 'Love for Sale'. At the time the song was banned from radio and TV, its lyrics thought to be too vulgar for middle America. Billie stares the lyric content full in the face, singing from the standpoint of an experienced woman coyly suggesting her love is 'only slightly soiled'. It is a masterpiece of lyrical realism, of asserting a direct relationship between the lyrics and the social or emotional condition they describe.

Through her half-sung, half-spoken *rubato* exposition, she succeeds in transforming an uptempo swinger into a 'storytelling' song like 'Strange Fruit', 'Gloomy Sunday' or 'God Bless the Child'. It was her first return to the genre with new material since the 1940s. Yet while a 'Strange Fruit' or a 'Gloomy Sunday' relied on the inherent drama they described, here the assessment of realism is an assessment of the *conventions* of realism; Billie's voice appearing to assert a direct correlation with her lifestyle that authenticates lyric content.

'She was in complete control as far as the music went,' said Oscar Peterson. 'The rest of us just wanted to be there for her ... Norman came up with the idea of having us record "Love for Sale" as a voice-and-piano duet. He wanted to display the complete interplay between us, and he wanted her to have total freedom to express the song any way she felt ... It was all very spontaneous. She didn't like a lot of preparation; she just wanted to make music.'[16]

Billie is in far better voice than the October 1951 Storyville airchecks, but there are times when her pitch sounds uncertain. While this creates an inherent tension in her performances of the 'will she won't she stay in tune' kind on 'Everything I Have Is Yours' or even 'Love for Sale', she also uses vibrato to a greater degree than any of her previous recordings to help camouflage her shortcomings in pitch. On numbers she is familiar with, such as 'If the Moon Turns Green' which she had been singing since a teenager, her pitch, in contrast, is secure and her use of vibrato is minimal.

Getting Billie to learn new material was not always easy, however; 'I Can't Face the Music' was the only new song from the New York session. 'There are so many great tunes she *hasn't* recorded she should stop inviting comparisons,' cautioned *Downbeat* when the sides were released.[17]

During the summer of 1952, negotiations opened for an ABC television show featuring Billie called *Holiday with Strings* with David Rose pencilled in as musical director. A large string ensemble plus a jazz combo was proposed but the project never progressed beyond the planning stage when sponsors baulked at Billie's bad-girl image. More disappointment followed when plans for Billie's first European tour, due to begin on 12 October with thirty British concerts booked by Maurice Kinn, fell through. Instead she headed for Chicago and a headline appearance at the Civic Opera House on 19 October. From there she travelled to Boston for a four-week stay at George Wein's Storyville Club. This time, however, her opening was not the success it had been the previous year. 'Another index of imperfect performer–audience relations was Billie Holiday's opening night at Storyville,' reported *Downbeat*. 'Billie was less than perfect musically, besides being hampered by a rather disorganized rhythm section.'[18]

But a measure of just how variable her performances had become was promptly illustrated by her appearance at Carnegie Hall on 14 November. The night's two concerts (8.15 and 11.45 p.m.), co-sponsored by Birdland, the Broadway jazz spot, were a tribute to Duke Ellington by many greats from the jazz world. Ellington's band was framed by performances by Billie and several modern groups, including Stan Getz's, the Ahmad Jamal trio, Charlie Parker with a string group and a Dizzy Gillespie combo. But of them all it was Billie whom *Variety* cited as 'by far the most impressive performer on the night'.[19]

But despite being able to perform at prestige locations in New York such as Carnegie Hall, and Harlem's Apollo, where she appeared in December, Billie continued to be denied her Cabaret Card. By now it was drastically affecting her earning power; not only did New York clubs pay top money, but she also lost out on the prestige value of such appearances, which would have had the knock-on effect of putting her out-of-town asking-price up.

Even so, she continued to play the big clubs outside New York, such as San Francisco's Say When where she spent several weeks in early 1953 or Boston's Hi-Hat Club in the spring. 'The Hi-Hat was the first time I saw Billie in person,' said Dan Morgenstern. 'She was playing opposite Flip Phillips. There were three sets and we stayed for all three. Billie noticed us after the second set and came over to join us. She was very sweet and in terrific form in 1953. I think it is nonsense to suggest she was in steep decline throughout the fifties; there were some performances that maybe were not so hot, but here she was in wonderful form and no other problems as far as I could see.'[20]

By July Billie was in Chicago's Blue Note, but returned to New York to open at the Apollo on 14 August where she was second headliner to Duke Ellington. On the day before she was due to open, however, a deep-seated dental problem came to a head. Always reluctant to see the dentist, she had bluntly refused treatment in Alderston in 1947 (even signing a disclaimer refusing treatment). Neglect had caused an abscessed tooth to develop, causing one side of her face to swell to epic proportions.

'I got a call early that morning from Joe Glaser,' recalled Annie Ross. 'I had just signed with him and he said I was to stand in for Billie Holiday. I was scared out of my wits; number one it was the Apollo and number two, I was replacing my idol Billie Holiday. Duke Ellington took me by the hand to meet her. She asked if I needed a gown, a piano player and so on. She was truly lovely to me. The time came for me to sing; it's a tough audience at the Apollo. There were lots of hollers and hoots when I walked out but I was singing advanced stuff like "Twisted" and "Farmer's Market" and that saved my bacon. When I came off she gave me a big hug and we both started to cry; Duke said, "C'mon, you two lovely ladies, come out and take a bow," and that's how I first got to know Billie Holiday.'[21]

By the end of the week the swelling had subsided and Billie decided to perform the final few days herself. But she had continued to refuse dental treatment, so it was hardly surprising that one reviewer noted she did not impress in the final spot of the show as much as Ellington had done earlier. Soon afterwards, on 26 September, Billie appeared again at Carnegie Hall on a bill that featured Stan Kenton and his orchestra, Dizzy Gillespie and Bud Powell: 'Billie was in good voice and very charmingly gowned,' complimented *Downbeat.*[22]

The abscess flared up again in October while Billie was at Boston's Storyville, but despite the evident discomfort she was suffering, the *Boston Guardian* said she 'had the house rocking despite that abscessed jaw'.[23] The airchecks that exist of one set with Carl Drinkard on piano, who had replaced Buster Harding in mid-1953, reveal her repertoire revolving around the same axis as ever, but on 'Too Marvelous For Words' there is a return to *alla breve* in the first chorus and a far more fluid rhythmic feel from the singer. But while her voice had sounded in imminent danger of collapse on her airchecks from the same venue in 1951, here, in relative terms at least, it sounds far more secure.

Billie finally consented to a dental operation on Monday, 13 October, but health problems aside, she was now feeling confident about the future. Louis McKay had brought a degree of order to her life, and his imposing physical presence ensured she was not prey to every drug pusher in every club. Billie clearly felt she was back on the right track after the terrible lows she experienced with John Levy. After seeing a television script sent to her while at the Storyville, she consented to appear as the featured guest on George Jessel's TV show, *Comeback*.

Screened on Friday, 16 October, Billie's life story was told warts and all. With all the negative publicity she had received over the past few years, it represented an opportunity for her to have her say in front of an audience numbered in millions, even though the tooth extraction had done little for her facial swelling. She spoke about her drug addiction, her term in prison and about segregation, which must have been something of a shock for television audiences in the Eisenhower era. 'Tonight's comeback story is a little different from others we have presented,' said Jessel, setting the tone of the whole programme, 'for this artist's real comeback was made five years ago after she had paid the penalty for falling victim to one of society's most dread diseases – the use of narcotics. And in a sense she has been coming back with every song she sings.'

There were contributions from Mae Barnes, Pods Hollingsworth, Count Basie, Leonard Feather, Arthur Herzog and Artie Shaw, who, in a moving ad lib speech, said, 'The first time I met Billie I was almost as broke as she was. But I told her, "Some day I'm going to have a band of my own and when I do you're going to sing in it."' The narrations and interviews were alternated with extracts from Billie's recordings, including 'I Gotta Right to Sing the Blues', 'Good Morning, Heartache' and 'Lover Man'. Billie herself sang 'God Bless the Child' with accompanist Carl Drinkard's trio, but maybe because her jaw was still giving her trouble, she was not at her best.

Even during her lifetime, the mythic qualities of legend were being erected around Billie Holiday. Even though she was not in good shape on the programme it mattered little; if she looked or sounded as if she had been victimized by her lifestyle it merely reinforced her authenticity. It would become, in a way, similar to a musical gimmick but would also signify her right to sound the way she did as her voice slowly but inevitably deteriorated.

As if to celebrate the success of the programme, Louis McKay, who was making something of a name for himself in golfing circles, came third in the City Tournament at the Clearview course on Long Island. Three weeks later he undertook the long drive to the West Coast with Billie and accompanist Carl Drinkard, set to open at Hollywood's Tiffany Club on 24 December for the Christmas season. He allowed himself three days for the journey: 'I'll drive twenty hours a day and sleep for four hours,' McKay told Leonard Feather, 'I hope to make a thousand miles a day.'[24] He made it, but only just.

Meanwhile, on 2 December Joe Glaser had signed contracts with Swedish promoter Nils Hellstrom that would take Billie to Europe for the first time, heading an all-star jazz show, set to leave on 7 January

1954. Called *Jazz Club USA*, after the eponymously titled radio show hosted by Leonard Feather on Voice of America, Feather was also set to act as compere.

At the last moment, Billie realized she had no passport. Nor did she have a birth certificate. After a frantic journey back to Baltimore and the House of Good Shepherd for an extract from her baptismal certificate, she had Fannie Holiday, Clarence's widow, verify the details of her application as 'stepmother' before filing it the day before she left for the West Coast.

Billie's European tour, so long postponed, was the fulfilment of a long-held ambition. She joined the other members, Red Norvo's trio, the Buddy DeFranco quartet and the Beryl Booker trio, just as they were boarding at Idlewild airport on 10 January 1954. They arrived at Copenhagen airport the following morning. 'We had a rough trip going over,' recalled Red Norvo, 'we flew to Scotland and from there to Denmark and we got waylaid in Copenhagen by snow. We couldn't fly; planes were grounded, so we took a boat to Malmo and from Malmo we took a train to Stockholm so none of us had any sleep.'[25]

The opening concert in Stockholm on 12 January was given a poor reception, the audience unaware of how exhausted the musicians were, or of the problems they had faced on arrival. Guitarist Jimmy Raney, who hated flying, had travelled over the week before on the *Ile de France* but had fallen ill in London. Norvo therefore had to play with a local musician who knew none of his arrangements, while his bass player and drummer had to perform on borrowed instruments – their own had failed to catch up with them. Meanwhile, problems had developed over who should assist Carl Drinkard in accompanying Billie. Voices were raised backstage as Feather desperately tried to settle the argument. Meanwhile Billie, looking like anything but the star of the show, sat ignored in the corner making little whimpering noises. When asked by an anxious onlooker if she needed anything, she looked up tearfully and replied, 'I just wish those motherfuckers would make up their minds about me.'[26]

In the end Red Mitchell, Norvo's bassist and Elaine Leighton, Beryl Booker's drummer, agreed to back her, but there was no time for a rehearsal. In the circumstances Billie did not sing well and afterwards a hypodermic syringe was found in her dressing-room.

'We were beat up and everything after all that travel,' continued Norvo, 'so that night when Billie didn't sing very well, they thought she was "on" because they found a syringe backstage. They were going to send her back to the States. I pleaded and hollered and carried on like mad; I said, "My God you people, what's wrong with you? We haven't had any sleep, do you know how that affects a voice compared to a musician?" And that was the first night, and the second night she was singing like a bird, she got sleep and everything was fine. She was straight, she wasn't on anything.'[27]

Billie found the reaction of the European crowds beyond her expectations. She was genuinely uplifted; bouquets were presented to her onstage, autograph hunters crowded her dressing-room and the press and radio demanded interviews. It was in sharp contrast to the round of often second-rate clubs, drug pushers and racism at home. The itinerary was exhausting.[28] 'I thought she did very well,' said Norvo. 'She got caught once in some town in Germany, the weather was bad, she couldn't make it on the train so she had to fly, but she made it just in time to go onstage.'[29]

On one occasion, wearied by travel, Billie threatened to pull out of the tour after a particularly hard day's travel, but Louis McKay assured Feather she was 'just talking'. Throughout, Billie battled to keep her drinking under control. 'I will never forget the sight of [her] as she balanced herself on a bar stool,' said writer Chris Albertson, 'her facial muscles slightly out of control, almost begging for the drink no one thought she should have.'[30] Only once, when she drank before going onstage, was her performance less than impeccable.

The concerts were opened by Beryl Booker's trio who usually performed three numbers, and were followed in turn by Buddy DeFranco's quartet and Red Norvo's trio who performed six numbers each. But there was no question of who was the star; Billie followed at the climax of the show, nominally allocated ten numbers, which might be increased by encores. Then she would be joined onstage by the respective leaders of each group, Booker, Norvo and DeFranco, plus Jimmy Raney, for a jam session finale. The recordings that have been commercially released reveal the tonal quality of Billie's voice, now a variable commodity, in good shape. There are hints of uncertain pitching on 'My Man', where she hits one or two notes en route to the one she wants in a melismatic slide, but in contrast, her version of 'I Cover the Waterfront' was confident and secure, and surprisingly for Billie, *grandioso*.

When the tour party travelled back to the States, Billie, McKay and Carl Drinkard made their way to the United Kingdom. When they arrived on 8 February 1954, the music press were almost sobbing with joy at the prospect of seeing a jazz legend at first hand.

While musicians from the USA had been touring Continental Europe for years, the appearance of American jazz musicians in the UK was a rare occasion because of a Musicians' Union and Ministry of Labour

ruling which prevented them appearing unless reciprocity of employ-
ment had been arranged for British musicians in the USA. Consequently
Billie's arrival made front-page headlines in *Melody Maker* and *New
Musical Express*; 'Billie Holiday Is Here!' they proclaimed. It said it all.
'She took a sort of child-like pleasure in this open admiration she found
in England,' said critic Max Jones.[31]

Her tour began with an appearance at Manchester's Free Trade Hall
followed by a sell-out concert before an audience of 6000 at the Royal
Albert Hall on 14 February. Later Billie told Max Jones it was one of
the greatest receptions of her life. Her reviews were nothing short of
idolatry: '[She] took the place by storm. It was wonderful! She is lovely
to look at and even lovelier to listen to. To see her – and hear her sing
those songs which we have all played on our gramophones was something not to be forgotten,' enthused *Jazz Journal*, speaking for a jazz-
starved nation.[32]

'When I walked into the rehearsals,' recalled Jack Parnell, who with
his orchestra accompanied Billie, 'she really looked like a sack of old
clothes sitting on a chair. But by the end of the concert in the evening
she looked like a girl of eighteen, it was quite uncanny! But I'm afraid
there was an awful lot of junk pushed in there. She was very friendly,
down to earth, but tremendous swings and changes of mood. The only
trouble was that her and her pianist got so out of it we found it very
difficult to do what we had rehearsed; certainly she was quite a different
person to the one earlier in the day. But terrific, there's no doubt about
that!'[33]

However heartening the European interlude, when Billie returned to
the States the usual crowd of drug pushers and hangers-on soon caught
up with her. Booked into the Club Trinidad in Washington, DC until
4 April, her unrelenting haul around the night-spots outside New York
City was set to begin again, the inequity highlighted by a Carnegie Hall
appearance on 9 April for a charity concert in aid of the New York
Association of the Blind.

Four days later she entered New York's Fine Sound recording
studios, but was out again after three tracks because Norman Granz
was forced to close the session. 'I can't remember what Billie was drinking that day,' said Oscar Peterson, 'but she was in bad shape.'[34] This
is not immediately obvious listening to the recordings. However, 'What
a Little Moonlight Can Do' and 'I Cried for You' were numbers that
Billie had been singing almost every night of her life in live performance
since the 1930s. They were numbers that were indelibly printed on her
brain, numbers she could negotiate with confidence irrespective of her

sobriety. This also provides a clue as to why she broadly stuck to the same unvarying repertoire throughout the 1950s.

Billie's relationship with Lester Young had remained at arm's length for some time. It seems that some sort of falling out between them both occurred during a week they played together in Philadelphia in February 1951. Billie appeared to take exception to something Young said and while some trifle probably precipitated the actual rift, the main issue was said to be Young's admonishment of her heroin habit.[35] Even so, Young had remained very fond of her, despite the fact that they had not performed together since. 'Lady Day? Many moons no see. Still nice,' was his cryptic reply to a question about her in 1953.[36]

One of the most important jazz events in 1954 was the first Newport Jazz Festival, held at Rhode Island. Organized by George Wein, owner of the Storyville Club in Boston, the occasion was a huge success with some 13,000 fans attending over the weekend of 17 and 18 July. After a huge downpour of the sort specially reserved for outdoor events in summer, the first set began at 8.35 p.m. with fans wrapped in everything from shower curtains to blankets. The first group was to play a tribute to Count Basie; led by Oscar Peterson with Ray Brown on bass, the remaining members were all Basie alumni and included Lester Young, whose playing was described as an 'exhilarating experience' by photographer Burt Goldblatt.[37]

Then followed sets by Peterson's trio, Dizzy Gillespie, George Shearing, a Teddy Wilson group and the Lennie Tristano quartet. For the penultimate set of the night the rhythm grew muted as a vocalist stepped in front of the microphone. Billie Holiday began her set with 'Billie's Blues' to a huge roar of recognition from the crowd. She responded by singing at close to her best, boosted by her European success, the audience response and her accompanists, which included Buck Clayton, Vic Dickenson, Teddy Wilson, Milt Hinton and Jo Jones, all of whom had appeared on her classic recordings of the 1930s and 1940s. They were soon joined on stage by the one musician in all of jazz most identified with Billie, Lester Young. Later in the programme, baritone saxophonist Gerry Mulligan sat in with the group. At the finish, the audience and the press gallery burst into a sustained ovation.

It was a powerful set full of strong imagery, inspiring a rather romantic rewriting of history. 'Mulligan lugged his baritone on to the stage . . . this was enough for Lester. He shuffled onstage and once again was a part of a Billie Holiday presentation.'[38] The important thing, however, was that the so-called 'feud' was over.

Lester Young and Billie were again reunited in September, although

196

this time they did not play together, at two big concerts produced by Patricia Music Publishers at Carnegie Hall on 25 September and the following night at the Boston Arena. Dubbed *Birdland All-Stars*, it also included Count Basie, Charlie Parker, Sarah Vaughan and the Modern Jazz Quartet. The irony for Billie, of course, was that Cabaret Card problems had prevented her being booked by Birdland, the famous jazz club on Broadway at 52nd Street, although she had sat in on an informal basis many times.

Performing with the Count Basie Orchestra, with Carl Drinkard taking Basie's place at the piano, she went through what was now her standard multi-purpose set. Her voice was not in good shape when she opened at Carnegie Hall with 'All of Me', although her hoarseness added poignancy to "Tain't Nobody's Business If I Do'. However, signs that all was not well came when she missed her entry after the four-bar introduction of 'Lover', the band grinding to a standstill in confusion before being restarted. She follows it with a hesitant 'My Man' – 'Where are we?' she says to her accompanists at the beginning – but retrieves all with a moving performance; the crowd erupts. However, she had nothing of interest to add to her performances of 'Them There Eyes' and 'Lover Man' which seem to pass by on autopilot. 'For Miss Holiday it seemed something of an off night,' was *Downbeat*'s verdict.[39]

Meanwhile, while she was playing the Oasis in Los Angeles earlier in the month, Billie's talents had been recognized by *Downbeat* magazine with an award devised especially for her. Never having topped one of *Downbeat*'s famous popularity polls – the best she had managed was second position – they honoured her with a special award as 'one of the great all-time vocalists in jazz'.

In September 1954 and February 1955 Norman Granz called two more recording dates. On the September session she was reunited with her former accompanist Bobby Tucker plus an all-star group. Tight little charts had been written for the September date, which stood at either end of her vocals like book-ends. There were no instrumental solos, only obbligati, but she swings crisply on the first number up, 'Love Me or Leave Me'; no question of her singing the octave leap on the opening minor chord, instead she rides the tonic whenever she can throughout the first chorus, something widely imitated by vocalists who subsequently sang the song, contrasting with her more expansive phrasing in the second. Although her enjoyment on 'Too Marvelous For Words' is plain for all to hear, the session was notable for her heartfelt performances on 'P.S. I Love You', 'Softly', 'I Thought about You' and 'Willow, Weep for Me'.

On the February 1955 date Granz returns to the free and easy exchanges with the instrumentalists and again Billie's ability to swing powerfully is a feature of the session, exemplified by the final cut of the day, 'Ain't Misbehavin''. Shavers puts in a perfectly sculpted solo and just before Billie's second vocal chorus Budd Johnson steals the show with a jumping, barnstorming effort which is somewhat at odds with what had gone before, but is memorable nevertheless.

Of particular interest was how Billie fell back on her Baltimorean accent for expressive effect on 'I've Got My Love to Keep Me Warm'. It shows up clearly on the vowel 'o', formed at the back of the mouth, in 'The snow is *snowing*, the wind is *blowing*' and is one of the few times on record her home-town accent surfaces. It highlights the dramatic relocation of emphasis in Billie's singing style as the Verve sessions progress. As her range, her intonation and her breath control became progressively more limited, she began to rely more and more on non-verbal devices to make her point; sighs, hesitations, rasps, changes of tone and musical devices that were uniquely associated with her style, such as abruptly dropping a syllable down a minor third. She was now using such devices in far greater proportion than before.

These tonal inflections, combined with the increased graininess of her deteriorating voice, were used as direct signs of emotion, often taking a song beyond the semantic meaning of its lyrics. More and more over the ensuing years her voice would be described as 'having a whole world of meaning captured in it' or 'having a lived-in feel', but speaking of the singer's inner self being 'contained in the voice' means nothing unless, at a conscious or unconscious level, we relate to her real-life history that made her what she was. It is this mediation between the social truth of the singer and her audience's desire to identify with it that allows both flaws and her tonal inflections to assume the redeeming virtue as the source of 'meaning' in her voice.

Louis McKay was by now using Billie's money to dabble in property, all of which he placed in his own name. Billie Holiday was totally trusting; as with Joe Guy's fruitless big band venture, she had implicit, blind faith in 'her man'. One of McKay's first purchases had been a new home for them both at 160 76th Avenue in Flushing, New York. Yet it was significant that on Billie's death, any interest in real estate was conspicuously absent from her list of assets.

McKay liked any idea that had the prospect of making money and it was at Billie's now annual appearance at the Storyville Club in Boston over Thanksgiving, this time backed by a band led by Buck Clayton, that she revealed to *Downbeat* reviewer Bob Martin that her autobiography was a real possibility. It had been mooted several times before, particularly after Louis Armstrong's *Satchmo* and Ethel Waters's *His Eye Is on the Sparrow* had sold well on the bookstands. But Billie had always countered journalists' questions by claiming that what she had to say could never be printed. In reality, having left school at fifth grade she knew it was a task she could never undertake herself.

But over the last two years she had got to know a reporter on the *New York Post* called William Dufty. He had married Billie's long-time acquaintance Maely Bartholomew in 1953. Since Billie's parting from John Levy, Maely Dufty had continued to act as her unpaid secretary and assistant from time to time. When the idea of an autobiography was mooted, Maely suggested her new husband ghost-write it, since he got on well with Billie. Louis McKay liked the idea. And although Billie herself was not particularly interested, saying she had told her story several times over to magazines, Bill Dufty had an angle and was a more than competent writer. He promised McKay that he could come up with something that would sell and, more particularly, sell to Hollywood.

Chapter Twelve

1955–58

The death of the alto saxophonist Charlie Parker on 12 March 1955 was a crack of doom that reverberated throughout the world of jazz. Within days graffiti appeared in the New York underground proclaiming 'Bird Lives'. Parker quickly became portrayed as victim, martyr to the art he created, yet in reality he played it fast and loose, challenging death with excess, accomplishing his rite of self-destruction with drugs and alcohol.

It was a death that fascinated; a jarring protocol that established the hero of excess whose life achieved unexpected definition when cut prematurely loose from its mortal coil. Parker codified excess as a romantic convention in contemporary music, signifying the psychological and emotional vulnerability of people who are forced to reach inside themselves to create an identity.

Parker became the personification of a new romantic hero, someone whose death need not be noble; now the catalyst of transformation could just as easily be a needle in the vein. The contradiction was that while audiences did not approve, there was nevertheless a powerful draw in the collision of art and excess. In an attempt to understand what drives prodigious talent to such extremes of behaviour, audiences try to get a purchase on the value-system of the artist. And the most transparent way of achieving this appears to be through knowledge of the artist's real-life history.

Parker's life, probed to find a point of access to his music, exerted fascination beyond his recorded legacy. In the end more people knew about his lifestyle than were familiar with his music. He underpinned a new reading in popular culture, the fashionable music icon more famous in death than life, a template of excess that fitted subsequent heroes of popular music and later rock. But while portents in Parker's life were being echoed in Billie Holiday's own real-life drama, regular tabloid sensations and revelations were putting in place a tangible image *during* her lifetime whose momentum would carry it with increasing definition beyond the grave.

It would be wrong, however, to assume that Billie's tragic image implied she did not enjoy her excesses, despite the privations they involved. The real tragedy was that she did not see her life as such until too late, while her audience sensed it early on, witnesses to metaphor collapsing into reality, which would provide the continuing source of her posthumous authenticity.

Parker's death rather unromantically left a wife and two sons, Baird and Laird, to be cared for. To create a trust fund for them, a concert was held in Carnegie Hall on 2 April 1955. A stunning line-up of talent assembled, netting around $8000 for the fund. Billie was among several vocalists who performed that night; others included Pearl Bailey, Sammy Davis Jr, Herb Jeffries and Dinah Washington. A high spot was Lester Young's opening set, a prelude to a series of successful performances that could well have been preserved for posterity; Norman Granz had volunteered to record the concert and have the proceeds of album sales turned over to the trust fund, but pianist Lennie Tristano complained to the Musicians' Union and, as a result, all recording was banned.

A month later Billie was back at Carnegie Hall, this time singing in a Basie combo that included Lester Young, Buck Clayton and Buddy Rich at a *Jazz and Variety* concert on 6 May for Lighthouse, the New York Association for the Blind. She sang only one number, 'Stormy Weather', despite cries for an encore from the audience. By now she was considering a further appeal on her Cabaret Card ruling, but was still resigned to earning her living outside New York; on 1 June she appeared at Miami's Vanity Fair for three nights and then preceded Ella Fitzgerald into Boston's Hi-Hat Club at the end of the month. Negotiations for a tour of England opened with Joe Glaser in the summer, but fell by the wayside over money.

Once again, the West Coast became the centre of Billie's activities, beginning with two weeks at the Crescendo on Hollywood's famed Sunset Strip where she was photographed with Walter Winchell and Julie London. In between sets she would call in at the Garden of Allah, a favourite of the movie crowds, where Jess Stacy was pianist. 'Her voice was beginning to show the wear and tear by then, but it was still a beautiful instrument,' he said. 'She would go over to the bar and ask for two cognacs . . . she whispered something to the bartender who poured the stuff almost to the brim of two beer glasses . . . She listened, opening her eyes only to reach her glass which she slowly emptied. The liquor had no visible or audible effect on her, and afterwards she held herself very straight while walking out into Sunset Boulevard and back to her own job. I knew, of course, she was abusing herself to a point where it was bound to prove fatal.'[1]

While at the Crescendo, Billie appeared at a major jazz concert mounted at Hollywood Bowl on Friday, 19 August. Among a distinguished cast of West Coast jazz stars was Dave Brubeck, Buddy DeFranco, Andre Previn, Pete Kelly, Shelly Manne and Shorty Rogers and his Giants.

Four days later she was in Radio Recorders Studios in Los Angeles for the first of two double sessions for Norman Granz. Here the sidemen who included Benny Carter, Jimmy Rowles, Barney Kessel and Harry 'Sweets' Edison (whose playing credits since his Basie days now included Fred Astaire, Frank Sinatra, the Ronettes and Sonny Rollins), combined to provide one of the most satisfying ensembles of Billie's Verve period. Benny Carter in particular, with solos that were a model of construction and unity, proved an inspiration. He duets, rather than plays an obbligato, on Billie's second chorus of an upbeat 'A Fine Romance', shades of Lester Young with Billie in 1937. However, perhaps his finest solo on these sessions is on 'I Get a Kick Out of You'. Here he seems to leap beyond the mechanical and soar into the inspirational.

More importantly, however, these two songs show how Norman Granz sought to extend Billie and bring her out from under the shade of numbers like 'What a Little Moonlight', 'All of Me' and about a dozen others around which she steadfastly orbited in live performance. Here she had to think on her feet rather than rely on the tried and tested, accessing far more areas of her creativity. For example, although she recorded 'A Fine Romance' in 1936, she never returned to it again, and to all intents and purposes it was a 'new' song for this session. Here it is delivered at a tempo quicker than customarily associated with Billie during the 1950s, while its unusual ABAB construction meant it was by no means a run-of-the-mill pop song, but demanded her concentration throughout. Equally, 'I Get a Kick Out of You' has the rhythm section playing a latin beat, exactly like Benny Carter's treatment of the tune on his 1952 Clef album, *Cosmopolite*. The effect immediately takes Billie out of her comfort zone. She makes full use of rhythmic latitude offered her by the minim triplets in the melody line, playing with time just as she did as a twenty-year-old. Afterwards, bassist John Simmons, who split with Billie in the 1940s over drugs, looked up to say, 'Lady, how come you get no kick from cocaine anymore?'

However, with each succeeding record date, shortcomings in Billie's voice were gradually surfacing. Breath control is vital to a singer, but during the false starts on 'When Your Lover Has Gone', from the 23 August session, she displays a deep smoker's cough and a hoarseness that troubles her from time to time on voiced consonants. And, as she suggested in her February 1955 session, there were also moments when she showed difficulty in sustaining pitch, a problem certainly not helped by poor breath control, which she tried to compensate for by using a wide vibrato. Once again, this insecurity of pitch is especially evident when she sings new material, a 'wobbly' feel as she hunts out a note by gliding up or down to meet it.

Yet these sides number among the best she did on the Verve label. Problems with her voice, as one writer put it, 'scarcely diminish the enchantment of these haunting tracks. In fact they impart a special poignancy to her heartfelt performances.'[2] This is the dichotomy, of course; how this frayed-at-the-edges voice becomes transformed by the subjective weight of Billie's fallen-star quality arising from the nebulous interaction between image (her real-life story) and product (her voice). Her music, with its tics, faults and sometimes indigestible imperfections, assumes a soiled realism that signifies meaning. What would be unforgivable lapses and stylized mannerisms in another singer assume virtuous, even redeeming qualities, when the singer is Billie Holiday.

Although at this time she was only forty years of age, *Downbeat* was already referring to 'the old Billie Holiday, who owns dozens of ballads', at her annual autumn appearance at Storyville in Boston, and mentioning how she held an audience that 'included a healthy proportion of middle-aged couples with vocal excursions from the past'.[3] Intended as a laudatory review, it nevertheless served to reflect how Billie was being perceived in the changing musical landscape of jazz and popular music in 1955, and just how inflexible her repertoire had become; 'Willow, Weep for Me', 'Easy Living', 'I Only Have Eyes for You' and 'God Bless the Child' had been staples in her repertoire for over two decades. Once they defined her art. Now they were defining her.

Although Billie's dependence on narcotics had reduced during her association with Louis McKay, she still craved drugs. For a while she had become an incidental user of heroin, a 'chipper'. Quite simply, life on the road was full of temptation; when she returned to her home in Flushing, New York, she turned to alcohol to subdue her drug hunger. And certainly guest spots on radio and television around this time reveal unmistakably slurred speech patterns, as in her appearance for the second year running on Steve Allen's *Tonite* television show on 10 February 1956 or in her interview five days later with Willis Conover on Voice of America.

She was fast sliding back into her old ways. While others tried to protect her, Billie, just like Charlie Parker, sought both the sanctuary and euphoria of a fix. However, her hunger for drugs abruptly caught up with her on 23 February during a two-week run at the Showboat in Philadelphia. She was arrested for possession and use of narcotic drugs, along with Louis McKay, in a 3 a.m. raid on her hotel room by Captain Clarence Ferguson, four patrolmen and patrolwoman Ruby Mapp. McKay was also charged with possession and carrying a concealed deadly weapon. The police found five hypodermic needles, syringes, an eye-dropper and a spoon together with an ounce and a half of heroin and half an ounce of cocaine. Billie and McKay where taking 'speedballs', a cocaine and heroin cocktail.

The sedation of heroin and the cardiac excitement of cocaine when mixed together magnifies the rush that drug users crave. As one drug works with the other, a speedball moderates the jumpiness associated with cocaine and lessens the sedative effect of heroin, both combining to affect the brain with a feeling of euphoria. Examination by police physician Dr Thomas revealed that both Billie and McKay were under the influence of narcotics. Later, McKay told the *Pittsburgh Courier* that the police harassed them both and tried to plant the evidence, 'But they found us completely clean after all sorts of searches. I think that should prove something.'[4]

They were both released on bail of $7500 pending a possible grand jury trial and Billie completed her engagement to large crowds. The experience was a profound shock and she immediately went into a sanitarium in an attempt to detoxify. On 21 March, however, she was back on the night-club circuit, appearing for a week at the Orchid Room in Kansas City, following it with a week at Chicago's Birdland from 28 March. But her 'bad-girl' reputation on the club circuit was catching up with her; to keep working she was being forced to take downmarket as well as upmarket jobs. And worse, her lifestyle and the constant travel were beginning to take their toll as her formidable constitution began to crack. Again using her money in his name, McKay bought a share of the 204 Club at 204 East 58th Street in Chicago, opening a bistro within it called 'The Holiday Room'; he told Billie he intended her to play there several months a year. It never happened; instead, Billie went out to Las Vegas, where she used Corky Hale as an accompanist, who was then pianist with the resident band led by Jerry Gray.

With a summer publication date for Billie's autobiography *Lady Sings the Blues* scheduled, an album of songs strongly identified with her was recorded in June, while Norman Granz was in the Orient with Jazz at the Philharmonic. With clarinettist Tony Scott directing her accompaniment, Billie appears as the old trouper offering anecdotes polished by time on familiar routines like 'Strange Fruit', 'Travelin' Light', 'I Must Have That Man', 'Good Morning, Heartache' and 'God Bless the Child'. Pianist Wynton Kelly was an exceptional accompanist but was crowded out since the arrangements were structured with obbligatos instead of solo space mostly allocated to the front line. All too often Scott, Charlie Shavers and Paul Quinichette sound as if they are in the next room warming-up.

'Tony Scott was always nervous,' said bassist Aaron Bell, who played the session. 'He had written the charts and there wasn't anything difficult in them, but she was in very bad voice. The session went smoothly except for her; we had to give her breaks and let her get herself together.'[5] When the sides were issued at the end of the year they were combined with a couple of numbers from the September 1954 session on the album *Lady Sings the Blues*. Nat Hentoff, awarding the album four stars in *Downbeat*, said, 'I understand this was a rather stormy session, but to the listener who was not there it comes through as a . . . troubling, indelible Billie monologue.'[6]

However, Billie's next two record dates on the West Coast in August 1956 saw the return of Norman Granz, and they take their place alongside the Benny Carter sessions as her most satisfying for the Verve label. Here the presence of a major soloist, this time Ben Webster, draws a more animated performance from her than the date with Scott. She is more expressive, which is achieved through often conspicuous ornamentation: vibrato, melisma, a slur, a mordant, an appoggiatura, plus her inimitable 'growl', again underline how the emphasis of her style changed as the 1950s progressed.

As her range closed, she had increasingly come to inhabit the lower register of her voice, often manoeuvring her limited vocal options to telling and canny effect. Her delivery, already steeped in conversational intimacy, had become limited by poor breath control and was inexorably moving to a point within a stone's throw from *sprechgesang*. Indeed, the first sixteen bars of 'All Or Nothing at All' seem a harbinger of this, invoking the memory of a television interview Billie gave to Tex McCreary in November 1956 when he asked her to *recite* the lyrics, 'like poetry', of three of her favourite songs.

The August dates were closely rivalled for their cohesion and focus by a marathon run in January 1957 of five recording sessions with an almost identical personnel. On the first date, however, Billie does not sound in good voice at all; indeed, when she went beyond the comfortable core of notes which she shuffled and reshuffled to such telling effect in those years, the effect, as in the middle eight of 'Moonlight in Vermont', could be painful. Yet the contrast in her voice on the subsequent four dates is remarkable. Here, the spirit of the Hammond sessions of the 1930s seems to hover over the proceedings.

The choice of material frequently takes the singer to sunnier climes; songs such as 'Day In, Day Out', 'Let's Call the Whole Thing Off' or 'Comes Love' even allow a little humour to surface in Billie's delivery, something seldom glimpsed since her Columbia days. Yet on 'Embraceable You', with its complicated ABAC construction, she could be moving without being maudlin.

Just as with her best sessions in the 1930s under John Hammond, her accompanists brought the best out of her with good, wholesome, well-executed mainstream jazz. Solos from Ben Webster and Harry 'Sweets' Edison hit a balance between cooperation and competition to spur the singer on. But while Billie took no chances and pulled no surprises, the powerful interaction of 'image' and singer creates a compelling yet subjective afterglow that lingers after the recordings have finished.

Billie returned to New York on 23 August 1956 in time to appear at a huge jazz concert at Randall's Island in New York's East River on Saturday the 25th. From there she returned to Chicago and McKay's bistro where she was backed by Eddie Baker on piano. He also accompanied her at Hollywood's Jazz City for a week, where she drew the biggest opening night crowd the venue had seen, before moving on to Honolulu's New Continental for a month. On her return Billie headed for the Patio Lounge in Washington, DC for the last week in October, where she was rejoined by Carl Drinkard.

Meanwhile, August had seen the publication of *Lady Sings the Blues*. It was an autobiography that sought to make an impact, its opening lines bringing to mind the apocryphal story of a famous thirties movie actress who planned to begin her memoirs by saying, 'People say I am an alcoholic, a dope addict, a nympho and kleptomaniac. Well, it's all true.' Bill Dufty went for a similar effect, using what material he had to hand. Billie, however, who had been using memory-impairing drugs (most notably marijuana and alcohol) since puberty, discovered gaps and vagaries in her reminiscences. Consequently she wrote to Evelyn Conway, with whom she had spent long periods in Martha Miller's home, and her cousins Charles and Dorothy, with whom she had spent similar periods in Robert and Eva Miller's household, for any shared childhood experiences they might recall. They never replied and she never followed up her inquiry.[7]

Dufty filled in the blanks in the best jazz tradition; he improvised. On the one hand this ensured that *Lady Sings the Blues* would become the bane of jazz writers and magazine columnists for decades, condemning them to the uncertainties of what was fact and what fiction, and on the other it gave potent significance to Billie's character part of someone unlucky in love and in life. Ultimately, however, it is a book that lacks humanity, although this is not always evident thanks to the clever tabloidesque momentum of the writing. 'I cannot question Miss Holiday's sincerity,' said the *New York Times* reviewer, 'I for one am filled with compassion for Miss Holiday. She is beautifully gifted and has a touching admirable integrity. But I experience this in spite of the book.'[8]

In November *Lady Sings the Blues* appeared in condensed form, published by Coronet Books, and to coincide Don Friedman mounted a Carnegie concert for Billie on 10 November. The music was attuned entirely to her character part, reinforced by readings from her book by Gilbert Millstein. The lyric content of the songs she sang were essentially passive, sorrowful, bitter or fatalistic and dealt with a narrow emotional range, a world in which everything was painted, if not black, then certainly dark blue. As was usual with her repertoire, she used 'I' songs but changed the 'I' from positive to negative. She sang from the standpoint of an experienced woman who realizes the consequences of blind love; persona and person were now interchangeable, and now, more than ever, she had become dominated by her own legend.

The concert was recorded and was in many ways another way of presenting her now unvaried musical diet centred around a hard core of tunes. The songs were a familiar mix: 'Billie's Blues', 'Travelin' Light', 'Don't Explain', 'Yesterdays', 'My Man', and so on. Singing the same songs night after night depended for success on the quality of Billie's voice, the degree of animation she could summon, the quality of her accompanists and a nuance here or an inflection there that could often have the effect of a fresh lick of paint on a weathered facade. At Carnegie she was in good enough voice and she did, for the most part, sing well. 'Her rough, throaty croon and her expressive dips, lifts and dolorously twisted notes are the essential ingredients of a highly personal style. In the course of her career her control of these mannerisms has often been erratic but at Carnegie Hall . . . she sang with assurance,' observed the *New York Times*.[9]

In December 1956, John Levy, Billie's former lover-cum-manager, died of a brain haemorrhage.[10] He had continued to live on the fringes of the law until the end. Billie, however, did not get to hear the news until the end of the month; she was in Miami's Ball and Chain sharing the bill with the Australian Jazz Quartet for the first two weeks of December before playing Hollywood's Jazz City from 21 December until 3 January

207

1957. Across the street from Jazz City her long-time friend Carmen McRae was a counter-attraction at Peacock Alley.

After her recording sessions in January 1957 at the Capitol Studios in Los Angeles with Norman Granz, Billie saw the month out playing weekends only at the Harbour Bar in Santa Monica with Jimmy Rowles on piano. At the beginning of February, her three-day stand at the Blackhawk Restaurant in San Francisco represented the biggest draw in the night-spot's history, and was followed by a St Valentine's night opening across town at Fack's II, where she remained for the rest of the month.

Meanwhile, the narcotics charges against her and McKay had been continued on 6 February and 20 March, with a date now set for hearing on 21 October. Both Billie and McKay had become seriously concerned with the outcome, which clearly could not be postponed indefinitely. As a practical measure to prevent each being called to testify against the other, and to consolidate their relationship, they decided to marry as soon as Billie's attorney Andrew Weinberger confirmed that her divorce with James Monroe was absolute.

On 11 March Billie had opened at Mr Kelly's in Chicago for two weeks, with Carl Drinkard back on piano. When she finished her run she went shopping for a bridal gown, and the following day she and McKay headed for Juarez, in Chihuahua, Mexico. At 11.30 a.m. on Wednesday, 28 March 1957, Billie, who gave her name as Eleanora Fagan, and Louis McKay were married before the Civil Registrar. The marriage certificate copy reveals the large, generous loop forming the letter 'l' in Eleanora's signature to have been signed by a very shaky hand.

On her return from Mexico, Billie was due to open at Pep's, the mangiest of two Philadelphia night-spots, on 2 May. 'She found herself needing a pianist at short notice when she fell out with Carl Drinkard,' said Mal Waldron. 'Maely Dufty, who was sort of managing her, asked Julian Euell, the bass player, if he knew a piano player. He recommended me and I played a week at Pep's Musical Bar with her and ended up staying with her two and a half years. I had known Billie through her records, of course; the young Billie had more energy, but the old Billie had more experience. Sure, the voice was going, but the emotion and her *spirit* were as strong as ever. It was really equal in the end.'[11]

To keep her name in front of New York audiences, Billie appeared at Loew's Sheridan on Seventh Avenue at 12th Street on 11 June. Then followed a week in Detroit's Flame Bar and a return to Philadelphia for two weeks at the Bandstand. 'Drugs were a part of the scene in those clubs,' recalled Mal Waldron. 'You would go in and guys would come up to you and say, "You want a one-on-one?"[12] The police would search you when you came out of a club. They would be waiting outside for all the jazz musicians, embarrass you in the street. That's why for so many guys it became, "If you got the name, you might as well have the game." That was the attitude of most of the musicians. If you are treated like a common criminal, after a while you start acting like one.'[13]

By now pressures in Billie's life were such that incidental use of narcotics had once again given way to a pattern of addiction. Her personal problems surfaced at the Newport Jazz Festival on Saturday, 6 July where her performance was recorded and released with that of Ella Fitzgerald's Thursday evening set on *Ella Fitzgerald and Billie Holiday at Newport* in late 1957: 'Her thin, cracking voice quivered through the set in semi-recitative style,' commented *Downbeat*.[14] It represented her final album for Verve. 'I think we did all we could together,' said Norman Granz. 'In the end she destroyed her own strength through junk and drinking. She was very independent, very outspoken but it helped to be a fan.'[15]

The Norman Granz era was one of considerable significance in Billie Holiday's recorded legacy, which would otherwise have been remembered for a recording career that ended in 1951. Since she was dropped by Decca in 1950, no record company was interested in her, and other than four poorly distributed sides for the small, West Coast Aladdin label in 1951, there seemed to be no takers for her great talent. When Norman Granz signed Billie Holiday in 1952, her best Decca recordings were eight years behind her and she had failed to move her art forward; in live performance she was using the same twenty or so numbers she had been singing for years, prompting one *Downbeat* reviewer to dub her 'Lady Yester-Day'.

Granz moved her beyond the tried and tested, persuading her to apply her creativity to many fresh songs, and within the physical limitations of a gradually deteriorating voice she once again revealed her great gift for personalizing and stylizing a song in her own unique manner. What emerged was a series of performances that at their best were moving, uniquely personal and fascinating cameos of the 'less is more' ethic.

One of the most important factors in these recordings was the quality of accompanists Billie was given. Norman Granz was well aware of how significant her accompanists were to the success of her Columbia period, and sought to provide similarly copacetic company for her on Verve. Here she was reunited with musicians of her own generation, including Harry 'Sweets' Edison, Charlie Shavers, Ben Webster and Benny Carter with whom she had recorded in the 1930s and 1940s, plus some of the finest musicians from the succeeding generation of jazz musicians, such as Oscar Peterson, Ray Brown, Jimmy Rowles and Barney Kessel. 'In the end those records pleased both of us and I think that is all that matters,' said Granz.[16]

One of the great ironies of Billie's career was enacted at the Five Spot at Cooper Square in New York in late July 1957. She was in the audience with Mal Waldron, enjoying a few late-night drinks when she was invited to sit in and sing. Had she been employed by the club, it would have been illegal. As she was not, she was perfectly free to sing. Even so, because a police captain was present, she refused at first. Finally club owner Joe Termini said, 'He'd love to hear you.' She sang until 4 a.m.

Billie played out the summer of 1957 at a series of jazz festivals and even made an appearance in Central Park where, as Leonard Feather noted, 'There was a reasonably kind response for Billie Holiday, even though this was definitely one of Lady Day's off nights.'[17] During the autumn she was centred around the West Coast playing club dates, but again there was evidence that her constitution was becoming weaker. During an engagement at the Avant Garde steak-house in Hollywood during October she fell ill and was forced to return to New York.[18]

In December, however, she seemed in excellent health when she appeared on a unique telecast in the *Seven Lively Arts* series. Called 'The Sound of Jazz', it not only provides the most indelible and poignant footage available of Billie Holiday in performance, but is also a representation of jazz musicians and their art that has not been surpassed to this day. Billie seemed happy and at home with musicians, many of whom she had known since her teens. Its most memorable moment came when Billie sang 'Fine and Mellow' with the big band and Lester Young contributed his only solo of the whole programme. Billie watched with an expression that was halfway between laughter and tears.

'I was fresh out of the Cleveland Institute of Music when I played "The Sound of Jazz",' said guitarist Jim Hall. 'Here were all my idols; my reaction was that of any fan who had grown up with the music of Basie, Lester Young, Ben Webster and Billie. Lester Young was supposed to have played with Basie's big band but he was on his way out through alcoholism, so Ben Webster took his place. I remember he was really upset because Lester was in such bad shape.

'To me the climax of the whole show was when Billie sang those blues; Lester was sitting down because he was so weak and when he stood up he was just about able to play. That Lester was actually able to stand up and play his solo was electrifying. I was standing behind him off camera, it was quite a moment. I was watching Billie Holiday watching him too. I'm not sure what her feeling was, it seemed kind of loving. I'm sure she had some kind of wisdom that she didn't quite understand herself.'[19]

Towards the end of 1956, the lawyer Earle Warren Zaidins entered the life of Billie Holiday and Louis McKay. The meeting began casually enough; Billie and Zaidins were exercising their dogs and struck up a conversation. 'When we met Mr Zaidins,' said Louis McKay, 'he was living in a little room with a big dog in a West 47th Street hotel. I had never seen a lawyer in such circumstances, and for a long time I didn't believe he was a lawyer. Later he had a sign put up in the lobby and I realized he must be a lawyer after all, even though he had no office or no secretary.'[20] Zaidins had not been in New York long after moving from Wisconsin after a marital break-up. McKay found him nervous and upset, and although he talked a great deal he seemed unfamiliar with New York law, or any legal matters in show business. 'We didn't take him very seriously,' he said.[21]

Gradually, by sheer persistence, Zaidins gained both Billie's and Louis McKay's confidence. 'He said he was a jazz fan and was always following us around offering to help us,' continued McKay. 'At the beginning we thought he was just clumsy, like an overgrown friendly puppy ... He hung around our place sometimes when he wasn't wanted.'[22]

McKay warned Zaidins from the very beginning that he and his wife had no money to pay a lawyer. Yet Zaidins was not to be deterred. He told Billie over and over again that tens of thousands of dollars were due to her from record company royalty accounts and she would only have to pay if and when he collected any of the money he believed was outstanding. Gradually he gained Billie's confidence and she and McKay began to use him as their lawyer.

When in May 1957 Norman Granz indicated he would not be renewing his option on Billie's recording contract, Zaidins and McKay began looking around for another record deal. One of the recording companies they contacted was Riverside Records, run by Orrin Keepnews. A meeting was set up and McKay and Zaidins arrived on time. 'Neither impressed me,' recalled Keepnews. 'Zaidins in particular did not seem to know the music business.'[23] Billie finally turned up an hour and a half later, very drunk. Zaidins then announced he wanted an advance of $4000 on signature for his client. This was a lot of money for a fledgling company like Riverside, then just establishing itself. 'We could scrape it together but it represented a significant investment in Billie as an artist,' said Keepnews. 'If we thought it would be matched by her commitment and her ability to fulfil the contract, we would have gone with it. But it was just too much of a risk. We had to turn them down.'[24]

Zaidins was a frequent visitor to Billie's apartment and after about nine months he began to get familiar with her when McKay was not around, '[Billie] would laughingly report that Zaidins was making passes at her,' said McKay. 'She would say, "Would you believe that fat faggot, Earle Zaidins, tried to talk sex with me? What's his story?"'[25] At the time, it did not seem unusual to McKay. Billie was frequently the object of attention of amorous fans – it turned her on, she used to say. So at this stage McKay was not overly concerned. 'She always told me about people like Earle Zaidins, unpleasant though it was,' he said. 'I didn't take it very seriously because many jazz fans confused their admiration of Billie Holiday with their own romantic desires or problems. I realized Zaidins was very nervous, he bit his fingers deeply.'[26]

By mid-1957 Billie's use of drugs had become incidental; instead, she relied on brandy to subdue her hunger for narcotics. 'Zaidins knew,' explained McKay, 'as did anyone who was familiar with her background, that she waged a continual battle against her addiction to narcotics as a result of which she was consistently and usually under the influence of alcohol.'[27]

In case Billie became nervous or jittery, McKay seldom left her alone for any great length of time, arranging for someone to be with her in his absence. On one particular occasion he left her in the care of Zaidins for an afternoon. 'When I returned,' said McKay, 'a number of my papers were gone. Earle was gone and Billie was obviously under the influence of drugs.

'I knew she didn't have any cash because with her consent I handled all the money. To her, money meant drugs. The doctor had told me the last time she had been through withdrawal from drugs that her health would not permit her to "kick the habit" again. Earle Zaidins knew very well that he should not give Billie Holiday sizeable sums of money. When he went behind my back he co-signed her death warrant.'[28]

Earle Zaidins was also aware that McKay had always told Billie he would leave her if she went back on drugs. This was a source of great torment for her. She loved McKay, but she loved to hate him for it. Her yearning for a fix was so strong it created an ambivalence that exasperated her and baffled those who knew her; one minute McKay was her 'Daddy' who could do no wrong, the next he was cursed-out as 'that Motherfucker'.

McKay discovered his wife was hooked again on the weekend of

2–3 June 1957, just after Memorial Day. His rage spiralled out of control and ended in violence. 'The reason was that she confessed that this was not the first time she had been supplied with money for drugs by Zaidins,' explained McKay. 'Moreover, she confessed that Zaidins had attempted to perform an act of sodomy upon her.

'She explained that some money I had been asked to pay Zaidins was to repay him for money he had lent to her under cover for drugs, and not for legal services at all. To top it off, she admitted that there had been improprieties of a sexual nature between her and Zaidins, in addition to . . . [that other] attempt.

'I blew my top . . . I don't know which hurt the most . . . I was almost crying. I grabbed the phone from her and threw it. I would guess I didn't care whether it hit her or not . . . all that I could think of was that for weeks she had been using again and she was so hooked by now that I could never go through what was necessary to get her off alive . . . I started to question her and she admitted she had been using drugs for weeks. She admitted that on two other occasions Zaidins had given her twenty dollars and that he knew she was hooked again because he was at the house when the drugs were delivered.

'Everyone, including her agent, made a practice of notifying me whenever money was to be put directly into her hands. The same practice prevailed when agreements were discussed or signed. Our previous attorney, Mr Weinberger, usually required my presence or signature . . . This was one of the other reasons it was necessary to keep her off drugs. It was impossible to manage money unless she was clean . . .

'Zaidins . . . made secret deals with a woman who was not herself much of the time. I had over and over again explained how dangerous it was to make arrangements without consulting me. I was right there, Zaidins knew that if she was secretly asking him for money it had to be for drugs . . . Anyway I was responsible for Billie's wound since I threw the phone and started after her besides.

'Those who would judge me must have lived through what I had gone through with Billie Holiday. One would have to have learned her tricks for getting drugs and how she had to be outfoxed . . . I brought Billie to his apartment . . . and I marched her in. I confronted Zaidins and demanded to know why he had helped her back on drugs, why he had stolen my papers and why he made sexual advances to a woman who could not resist because of her condition. He did not deny one thing.

'I started after him and he ran out of the house and I ran after him. It's a good thing I couldn't catch him. Later, Billie told me Earle called the police and that she told him she didn't want any police, that I was her husband and it was all her fault.'[29]

213

A few days later McKay packed his car and headed for the West Coast. En route, after driving for hours, he became very ill. He was admitted into hospital in Chicago, where he nearly died from internal bleeding of ulcers which had perforated. He refused to allow surgery recommended by the doctors and remained in hospital for several weeks. When he was discharged he remained determined not to go back to New York until Billie Holiday was off drugs and had finished with Earle Zaidins.

'I was without the physical strength to do anything with her until she made her mind up to help,' he continued. 'I could never keep the pushers away from her. This was the first time there was anything like this and I knew I couldn't win . . . Except for a bitter telegram, which I sent, we were never estranged. Nearly every day or so we spoke. She phoned me nearly every week and I phoned her usually twice or more a week. I was trying to get well . . . I can't be sure whether Billie was on or off drugs. There are some signs that she might have had a rough time. But she told me that "Zaidins was keeping her happy". I stayed on the West Coast. Zaidins was in charge.'[30]

The break-up with Louis McKay was a body blow for Billie; just four weeks after they split up, her distress was all too apparent when she appeared at the Newport Jazz Festival on 6 July.

McKay was gruff, big and hard, and while, paradoxically, he had aspirations of going into the Church in his youth, he always remained a difficult man. He became the first black booking agent on the West Coast in the late 1960s, but never lost his hard-man image. In 1973 he was indicted by Nassau County Police in Mineola for shooting a man in the chest, but his plea of self-defence was accepted. He was outraged when, in August 1980, the singer Carmen McRae alleged he 'caused Billie to become involved in drugs' on the Mike Douglas TV show. He filed a $2.5 million lawsuit. The action fell with his death in March 1981.

With McKay gone, Zaidins did his best to ingratiate himself further with Billie. He decorated her living-room himself, free of charge (although he would later claim for it against the Billie Holiday Estate) and was soon acting as her manager and confidant. However, his inexperience in handling music business matters appeared to cost Billie dearly at a time in her career when she was badly in need of every penny and every opportunity that came her way. When she played the Apollo Theater in Harlem in January 1958, for example, the stage manager allegedly accused her of not liking to perform for black audiences since she had become a star. Her reaction was to phone Zaidins and tell him to sue. But instead of expensive litigation, it might have served

Billie's interests if he had counselled caution to his volatile client. The Apollo was one of the few places in New York where she could work without a Cabaret Card. Instead, charge and counter-charge were exchanged before the matter was resolved with an apology from Frank Schiffman, the Apollo's owner. Billie never appeared at the Apollo again.

The catalogue of Zaidins's errors and omissions appears horrendous. He failed to recover any money for Billie when her European tour collapsed in the autumn of 1958, even though it was bonded for the full amount with AGVA. But even worse, when he came to register Billie's compositions with BMI, he only forwarded two songs, which resulted in lost foreign and domestic royalties on more than a dozen numbers Billie had either written or co-composed. And, even though he claimed to have audited her royalty payments, he failed to notice that Billie was receiving only a fraction of her royalties for her most popular composition, 'Fine and Mellow', to which she was entitled 100 per cent.

During the production of Billie's appearance on *The Sound of Jazz*, the artists concerned cut an album of the same title for Columbia on 5 December 1957. It was at this session that producer Irv Townsend suggested to Zaidins that Billie might be interested in doing an album of her own for Columbia. A contract was signed and the first of three recording sessions scheduled for successive nights beginning 18 February 1958. The musical director and arranger was Ray Ellis, whom Billie wanted for the date because she liked his *Alice in Wonderland* album with strings. 'We started to pick the songs and I didn't realize that the titles she was picking at the time were really the story of her life,' said Ellis.[31]

Lady in Satin was released in autumn 1958 to instant controversy. 'I think that this . . . was a mistake,' said Martin Williams in *Downbeat*.[32] 'This is Holiday-fare of fine quality,'[33] asserted *Metronome*'s Bill Coss. Even today *Lady in Satin* remains an album about which people have strong and contradictory feelings. Certainly it is necessary to know Billie's real-life history to interpret the album properly. As one half of the mind struggles and reacts to the boozy huskiness in her voice and her shaky intonation, the other half listens, searching for meaning in both voice and lyrics. This disjunction produces an extremely uncomfortable listening experience. When the singer's history and her art are joined they become unified as a single self that is infinite and total, a subconscious bonding that enables *Lady in Satin* to realize its full meaning. Here the creative moment is distinguished by an immediate lyricism stripped of artifice and as close to the expression of pure feeling as words will allow. 'She would sing a phrase and she couldn't hold the note out,' said Ellis later. 'Yet every time I listen to it I get depressed.'[34]

After several continuances, Billie finally came to trial for her narcotics bust on 12 March 1958. She had Zaidins accompany her to Philadelphia even though she had engaged Philadelphia lawyers to handle matters; she simply wanted someone to lean on. Both Billie and McKay were put on twelve months' probation after a long lecture from Judge Bok who told Billie he had no desire to prevent her from earning a living. The singer had testified that she had helped with a crackdown on pushers and was now cured of her habit. Both were required to report to the police every time they visited Philadelphia; it was in stark contrast to Billie's previous appearance in front of a Philadelphia court in 1947 when she was left without proper legal representation.

When it was clear that McKay was not going to return, Billie moved to Apartment 1B, 26 West 87th Street. 'It was very sad,' said Annie Ross, 'this one-bedroom apartment in the West Side. It was so *temporary*.'[35] It was all Billie could afford. A measure of just how perilous her financial situation had become came with her television appearance on Art Ford's Jazz Party on 10 July 1958. She was contracted for $300, but she was so much in debt that as soon as she signed the contract she was forced to borrow $235 against it from Joe Glaser on 2 June. Well aware of her habit, Glaser made her spell out exactly what she needed the money for, which was in turn typed on a receipt she was required to sign: 'This will acknowledge the fact that I have received from you the following amount of money – $50 cash; $135 for my rent; $50 cash for my current necessities amounting to $235 in addition to other monies owed to you per signed receipts.'[36] The receipt was signed Billie Holiday. She made two appearances in July on Ford's show, filmed in studios in Newark, New Jersey; once a stunning beauty, she was now reduced to a shrunken, stooped hag. When she appeared as a guest on an *All Star Jazz Show* at New York's Town Hall on 13 September, the *New York Times* said: 'Billie Holiday walked out on stage somewhat hesitantly and dragged her way through a slow, slow ballad . . . The magic has been hard to come by for Miss Holiday in recent years.'[37] Later in the month, she appeared in a Leonard Feather production, *The Seven Ages of Jazz*, in the Oakdale Musical Theater in Wallingford, Connecticut. While waiting to sing her two numbers, she turned to Feather's wife over a drink backstage and said, 'I'm so goddam lonely. Since Louis and I broke up I got nobody – nothing.'[38] After a lifetime pursuing the good times, the hard times had arrived with a vengeance.

Chapter Thirteen

1958–59

Billie Holiday's alcoholism had made severe inroads into her health by autumn 1958, the gravity of the problem and its consequences overshadowed by her much-publicized addiction to narcotic drugs. On 30 September she opened at the Blackhawk Restaurant in San Francisco for a week. 'As far as being stoned, it's hard to explain,' said Dick Berk. 'She was physically very weak but her soul was strong. I remember one night at the Blackhawk, Max Roach had to help her on the stand, she was so unsteady through drink and yet the mood she created was incredible. Being a drummer I had to play brushes behind her very quietly, yet the emotion was so strong it made me want to yell. Then she asked me to play the Monterey Jazz Festival right after. I was nineteen years old and it was scary, but she was wonderful; put me at my ease.'[1]

Billie played Monterey on 5 October 1958 before 6000 people. On an outdoor stage in a horse-show arena adapted especially for the festival, hers was the final act on the last evening before the big jam session that ended the three-day event. 'She had no idea of where she was or where she was going,' said festival organizer Jimmy Lyons. 'I knew her condition, so I announced Gerry Mulligan and Buddy DeFranco. I told them to stand very close to her . . . She was swaying from side to side. Buddy would push her back and she would lean one way. And Gerry Mulligan would gently push her back the other way. The two of them kept her upright.'[2]

She once said that she could never sing the same way twice: 'I can't even copy me,' she told Jimmy Rowles.[3] However, the evidence of her live recording tells a different story. Here she again follows the same tried and trusted melodic contours through the same tried and trusted songs, simply because her condition allowed her to do little else. 'Billie Holiday has a songalong routine to which she adheres with almost pathetic tenacity,' was how *Downbeat* put it.[4]

The following morning she was sitting alone in the lobby of the San

Carlos Hotel, used by all the festival artists. 'The jazz musicians tried to ignore her,' said critic Ralph Gleason. 'Finally . . . she asked, "Where you boys goin'?" And when no one answered, she answered herself. "They got *me* openin' in Vegas tonight." '[5]

Almost as soon as Earle Warren Zaidins took Billie on as a client, he began using her name to ingratiate himself with other figures in the entertainment business. 'Whenever he had a chance, Zaidins used information about my . . . wife's affairs to help his other clients, even if it hurt [Billie],' recalled McKay. '[She] used to call it "putting my business in the street".'[6] One of the figures he came in contact with was Sarah Vaughan's ex-husband and manager, George Treadwell. Zaidins's ploy appears to have been to get Billie to sign a management contract with Treadwell so that he could have a shot at taking him on as a client. With Glaser remaining her booking agent, Billie signed with Treadwell on 15 October 1958 at Zaidins's instigation. Although Treadwell had recently separated from his former wife, at that point in his career he was still representing her. Although a parting of the ways was to come shortly, he nevertheless went on to an extremely successful career before his early death at forty-eight in 1967.

In November Billie set out on a brief European tour, arranged before Treadwell assumed management duties. She was booed and hissed at the Smeraldo Theatre in Milan and pulled off the bill after only two performances, although a private concert was arranged by the Milan Hot Club. When she arrived in Paris, she wrote to Leonard Feather saying, 'This Italy is something eles [sic], I was glad to get away.'[7] But the Olympia audiences were equally unsympathetic, and her performances were met with cat-calls. It prompted promoter Bruno Coquatrix to cut his losses and pull out. To get home, Billie and Mal Waldron were forced to perform for a percentage of the door money at the Mars Club on the West Bank.

During her enforced stop-over, the author James Jones, who had moved to Paris with his wife in 1958, met Billie at Le Blue Note, the famous Paris jazz club, where she occasionally used to hang out. 'She had been giving some concerts in Paris theatres,' said Jones, 'but we had been warned off going to them because she wasn't up to her best, so we only saw her at the Blue Note. She wasn't holding her liquor well by this time, and only a little of it was enough to put her over the line . . . [The club owner] Ben Benjamin had given his bartenders strict orders not to serve her any booze and while all of us knew this, nobody had the guts to tell her . . . Anyway, after asking politely two or three times, the Lady Day leaned her body languidly over the bar on an elbow and bawled at the top of her considerable lungs, "Hey, asshole! Gimme a drink!" She got the drink.[8] But the truth was that Billie had become a sad bar-fly.

Despite her mismanaged tour, Billie was full of bounce when she returned to New York. She had been cheered by the response of her audiences in the Mars Club and had discovered a new generation of admirers in the African Nationalist movement in Paris; tough cosmopolitans with whom she shared many bitter experiences of racism. Then, out of the blue, the US Customs Service contacted her on 14 January 1959. An Inspector McVeigh asked her to appear at Customs House in Manhattan the following afternoon for questioning.

Billie Holiday was mortified. At the suggestion of Bill Dufty she contacted Florence Kennedy, a brilliant young lawyer practising at 8 East 48th Street, to represent her. It became apparent that she had transgressed the Narcotics Control Act of 1956 (18 U.S.O. 1407): 'No citizen of the US shall depart from the US if he is addicted to or uses narcotics as defined in the Internal Revenue Code of 1954 unless such person registers with the Customs prior to departure and upon return to this country. Penalty for failure to register will subject offender to fine and imprisonment.'

The act also covered retrospectively anyone 'convicted of violation of the narcotic or marijuana laws of the US or any state, the penalty for which is imprisonment for more than one year'. Billie's conviction in 1947 was for one year and one day. That extra day meant she infringed the 1956 Act and could be liable for a prison sentence. It was a prospect that filled her with dread.

When Billie duly appeared before Agents Martin McVeigh and Mario Cozzi at the Customs House, she was asked if she had ever been convicted of narcotics offences. As she started to reply, McVeigh broke in saying, 'We have a copy of your record from the FBI which indicates that on May 27th 1947, you received a sentence of a year and one day at the Federal Reformatory for Women at Alderston, West Virginia, is that true?'[9] Of course there could only be one answer.

The agents wound up the meeting saying that the matter would be referred to the US Attorney for the Eastern District of New York. Then began a long wait for the singer, who was terrified by the prospect of prison. She drank even more heavily than usual, stopped eating completely and began losing weight so fast that her doctor was called in. He implored her to stop drinking. When he left, Billie told Dufty, 'If he had the Government breathing down on him, he'd be drinking too.'

Finally, on 12 February 1959 she was summoned before three US

Attorneys to decide her fate. After an hour and a half of wrangling they declined to prosecute. Billie's relief was deep and heartfelt; she headed for the nearest bar. She had been racked with extreme anxiety for a month and it showed.

At the end of February, Billie flew into London for a television appearance on the *Chelsea and Nine*. Well before leaving, she filled out Customs Form 3231, listing herself as a 'Violator', as required by law. When she returned in early March, after newspaper speculation about moving to Europe, she went into the recording studios for the MGM label to cut what was to be her valedictory statement as an artist. Treadwell, whose involvement with Ray Ellis a year before had resulted in Sarah Vaughan's first million-seller, 'Broken-Hearted Melody', once again secured Ellis's services as musical director.

The contract included a proviso that Zaidins was responsible for getting Billie to the dates on time. This duty usually fell to Alice Vrbsky, who had befriended Billie during the final two years of her life. She became her companion, shopping, taking clothes to the cleaners and often taking care of Billie while she nodded off watching cartoons on television. 'She was in the charge of a nurse,' said baritone saxophonist Danny Bank, who played the dates. 'She worked on a high stool, like a bar stool, and the nurse had to hold her for fear she would fall off. They worked hard, brought her coffee and led her to the ladies' room from time to time. Very feeble, but considering her condition she sang well.'[10]

Billie told arranger and conductor Ray Ellis she wanted to 'sound like Sinatra'. She had been very taken with Gordon Jenkins's scoring for strings on *Only the Lonely* and wanted to go for something similar; in the event she included Sinatra's hit with Tommy Dorsey, 'I'll Never Smile Again'. Even though her voice was half gone, she could still make 'Don't Worry About Me' a profoundly moving experience. Yet this performance, and the rest that make up the album *Billie Holiday*, remain one of the saddest things that ever happened to any great artist as she sang of her fate at the moment it was overwhelming her.

In her close, platonic love affair with the saxophonist Lester Young Billie could see a mirror-image of her own physical decline, as acute alcoholism took its toll of Young. 'I remember running across them in a place across the street from Birdland,' said the guitarist Mundell Lowe, who had worked with both Holiday and Young, 'and also at a place called Charlie's. Pres and Billie were sitting talking at the bar, not in a booth. She had her heels hung over the brass rail. Their relationship was very private, they had grown up musically together and loved to hang out together, they enjoyed each other's company.

'At the time my feeling was that they had decided their world was getting small, "Where do we go from here?", that kind of thing. I'm pretty sure that was the size of the situation. What I was seeing was both fires going out. It's as simple as that, the will for living diminishing, other people coming up, it was an era when musical styles were changing. You can't do your thing if your fire goes out. Shortly after that Pres died.'[11]

Young's death on 15 March 1959 was a great blow to Billie Holiday. When she turned up for his funeral at Universal Chapel at the corner of 52nd Street and Lexington on 19 March she was distressed but dignified. 'That was a very emotional thing,' said Dan Morgenstern, 'because she was there and she wanted to sing, of course. Lester's widow and the family were there, the kids were very young then, and they were a little classy and had no use for Lester's jazz affiliations. The service was square, I remember, Tyree Glenn played "Holy City" or something and there was a preacher who obviously didn't know anything about Lester. And of course, Billie was there, and she wanted to sing.

'She was about to and she was told they wouldn't let her; some musician friends who were there – the place was loaded with everyone from Zutty Singleton to the latest be-boppers – and Bud Johnson and Paul Quinichette, who were tight with Billie in those later years, led her away. I helped take her outside and she kept saying, "Those motherfuckers won't let me sing for Pres," she kept repeating it, she was really devastated. We took her outside in the front of the place and calmed her down, then went off to the nearest bar and had a couple of drinks and she was still saying, "They wouldn't let me sing." I think it would have been something if they had.'[12]

On 7 April Billie Holiday decided to celebrate her birthday. She asked a few friends around to her apartment, among them Annie Ross, Bill and Maely Dufty, Elaine Lorillard, Tony Scott, Jo Jones, Ed Lewis and Leonard Feather. She had cooked, something she enjoyed doing, and the party ended up in Birdland. Billie toasted herself non-stop as bottles disappeared at an alarming speed. 'Billie never stopped celebrating,' said Leonard Feather. 'Many of us, certainly including Billie herself, wondered if there would be any more birthdays to celebrate.'[13]

She was lonely and weary of life. 'I would go by her place,' said Annie Ross, 'not many people did, very, very few. She would cook and I would play records and I used to look after her when she went to bed. She'd watch cartoons all the time and I would stay awake so that she wouldn't burn the bed or anything like that, sitting in a chair watching over her.

'She didn't have a lot of people, especially towards the end. She was on her way down and people, for whatever reason, don't like to be associated with people who aren't doing it or making it. "Nobody loves you when you're down and out," all those clichés, but they are very, very true.'[14]

Few people were surprised when they heard of Billie Holiday's condition during those last months. Her addiction had made her unpredictable and her performances variable. Clifton Sherrard, a Holiday fan who attended one of her last Baltimore performances, remembered the show vividly: 'I swear I wanted to cry. She had on an evening gown that looked like she dragged the floor with it. The dress was filthy and she could hardly sing a note.'[15]

In April 1959 she had an important booking at George Wein's Storyville Club in Boston and considering her depressed state of mind, she performed well. Her vibrato was now difficult to control and she manoeuvred the melody line into something almost resembling a monotone, but her spirit was all too apparent, even though they were the same tunes sung in much the same way as ever. Ill as she was in Boston, she made every show. 'I've got no understudy,' she said. 'Every time I do a show I'm up against everything that's ever been written about me. I have to fight the whole scene to get people to listen to their own ears and believe in me again.'[16]

On 7 May she began a week-long engagement at the Flamingo in Lowell, Mass., which again went well. 'It was a very big, successful week for Billie,' said her pianist Mal Waldron later. 'She was weak, but always sang well.'[17] But he, like all Holiday's close friends, were disturbed at her sudden weight loss of some fifty pounds during the previous few weeks. By the end of May her condition had deteriorated rapidly but although she was seeing her doctor regularly, she refused to consider entering hospital. 'She continued to argue that she had cut down on her drinking and was taking care of herself,' said Leonard Feather.[18]

On 25 May she was booked as one of the headliners for *Jazz at the Phoenix* at the Phoenix Theater in Greenwich Village. She arrived in good time and was sitting in her dressing-room waiting for her call. Her long-time friend Leonard Feather, one of the two MCs, called in to see her. He was deeply shocked by her condition to the extent that he barely recognized her. She had wasted away to barely ninety-five pounds, her head was lolling and spittle was running down her chin. She had to be helped onstage by fellow MC Steve Allen, who had also previously expressed deep concern to newsmen backstage, saying, 'When I went to greet Billie in her dressing-room I didn't recognize her at first.'[19]

Yet despite her frail condition, Billie was able to transform herself into the creature of dignity that was her stage persona. While she sang only two of her planned seven numbers, ''Tain't Nobody's Business if I Do' and 'When Your Lover Has Gone', in a faltering voice, it was as if she was calling on every reserve of spirit to carry her through, but this time it failed her. 'She seemed finally worn down by her burdens,' said pianist Dick Hyman, who played the concert that night with Tony Scott's band.[20]

The following day a small deputation made up of Joe Glaser, Leonard Feather and Allan Morrison, the editor of *Ebony*, tried to persuade Billie to check herself into hospital. Glaser, aware of her financial situation, assured her he would foot the bill. However, she was determined to make an engagement in Montreal that began on 1 June. On 30 May she collapsed while her friend, sometime singer and drugs runner Frankie Freedom, was serving her a bowl of custard and oatmeal. 'She was fighting with me and wouldn't let me take her to a hospital in a cab,' he reported a few days later. 'She was holding out and she went into a coma.'[21]

Freedom called Billie's doctor, Dr Caminer, who immediately called for an ambulance and arranged for her admittance to Knickerbocker Hospital. The hospital records show that she arrived at 3.40 p.m. Then began a wait for over an hour before there was any sign of medical staff. When Billie was attended, track-marks on her arm and the smell of drink on her breath led to a diagnosis of drug addiction and alcoholism. Sadly, many private hospitals in New York closed their doors to anyone showing superficial signs of drug addiction. Billie was transferred to the Metropolitan Hospital, whose policy allowed them to take drug-related cases on 'life and death' basis only, and was admitted at 5.30 p.m. When Dr Caminer arrived, having had to track Billie down from one hospital to another, he found her still unattended on a stretcher in the corridor. He created a scene, demanding attention for his patient, and finally, three hours after an ambulance had originally been called, Billie Holiday was admitted into Room 6A on the twelfth floor and put into an oxygen tent.

As Louis McKay flew in from the West Coast, Joe Glaser was telling the press he would take care of all the bills. 'We've been together since she was fifteen,' he said, 'I'm taking care of everything.' Throughout, Billie remained on the critical list, with access restricted to just a few close friends and associates. But she was still being supplied with drugs.

Meanwhile, Zaidins had taken on the self-appointed role of Billie's spokesman to the media, giving television and radio interviews pontificating about Billie's health and generally increasing his profile before the public. Meanwhile, behind the scenes, he appears to have been using his privileged position to persuade Billie to move from Joe Glaser's Associated Booking Corporation to Shaw Artists Inc., one of the new clients he had taken on by boasting about his association with Billie. Now the time had come for him to deliver, since he had promised Milt Shaw that Billie would sign with him. In a clear case of conflict of interest, he got Billie to sign with Shaw's agency while in her hospital bed. He did it while Billie was high and had no knowledge of what she was signing.

On Thursday, 11 June Nurse Figueroa found white powder in a Kleenex box beside Billie's bed. She reported it to Dr Piazza, the Medical Superintendent, and the following morning the police arrived and sealed off Billie's room. They fingerprinted her and took mug shots and they took away her comic books, her record-player and records. Their petition threatened to take her to the Women's House of Detention regardless of any consequences to her health, unless she cooperated by admitting possession and disclosing her supplier. Access was denied unless visitors held a written permit from 23rd Precinct allowing entry to 'Eleanora McKay: Arrest No: 1660'.

The following day attorneys Don Wilkes and Flo Kennedy had a conference at the offices of Joe Glaser. They were asked to represent Billie once again. However, they pointed out that their bill for representing her earlier in the year for the Customs violation had not been paid. 'Because of her desperate financial situation a bill of $250 was sent to Miss Holiday,' explained Flo Kennedy, '[even though] the value of services rendered in the hearings regarding Miss Holiday's failure to register was $1000 to $1500.'[22] Joe Glaser promised to defray all their legal expenses.

A writ of habeas corpus was prepared and after some difficulty locating a Superior Court Judge on a hot Saturday afternoon, the writ was signed with a hearing scheduled for Tuesday, 14 June. This should have meant the end of the police guard. The matter was still not at an end, however. After a series of complaints about the continued presence of the police who were still holding the singer in virtual incommunicado, Wilkes and Kennedy were summoned again. After threatening the Police Department with another habeas corpus writ requiring them to comply with an order of the Supreme Court, access to Billie was granted at 10 p.m. that Saturday.

However, Don Wilkes had learnt that the District Attorney's office was now going after a High Court indictment. To prevent Billie's transfer to Bellevue Prison Ward, which they were warned would follow, Don Wilkes and Flo Kennedy requested that Billie appear before a Grand Jury. A date was set for 26 June 1959. As the date approached there was a flurry of correspondence and it was agreed that the case would be held in abeyance until Billie was well enough to appear.

Zaidins, one of the very few people able to secure access to Billie throughout the period the police had stood guard, continued to work for his own ends. He pressed Billie time after time to sign a contract with Valor Productions Inc. for the film rights of *Lady Sings the Blues*, which had come close to shooting in 1957 and 1958, with Dorothy Dandridge rumoured to be considering the leading role. Clause 11 of his contract stated:

> All notices, communications and/or reports hereunder from the producer shall be given in writing and shall be addressed as follows: Earle Warren Zaidins Esq., c/o Shaw Artists Corp., 565 5th Avenue, New York, NY.[23]

Billie, in command of her faculties, refused to sign. However, on 8 July she did sign a contract drawn up by Flo Kennedy with Vinod International Films, Inc. for a projected appearance in the picture *No Honor Among Thieves* for $750.

It was with a kind of despair that Joe Glaser learned Billie had signed with Shaw Artists Inc. As she gradually gathered a little strength and weight, Glaser visited her, taking with him his associate Frances Church. When the situation was explained to her, Billie was distraught; she had been unaware of what she had done. In desperation she tried to contact Milt Shaw the following day without success, sending a pathetic note to him on 8 July:

> Dear Milt
> I had a friend of mine call you and ask that you come to the hospital and see me. Your secretary said you were out of town. A message was left but I have not seen or heard from you. I am in no position to come and see ou [sic]. All I can do is write.
> I want you to return the so-called 'contract' I apparently signed with you. I was sick when it happened. I was in no position to judge what I was doing. If you were, it was wrong for you to get my signature that way, and you must know it.
> I want you to bring that piece of paper to the hospital to me. If you cannot do that I want an affadavit [sic] from you swearing that no valid contract with me is held by you.
> I want this done in twenty-four hours, Milt. Otherwise I will have no

225

recourse but to take legal and other steps which might be unpleasant and unnecessary for both of us.

The letter was signed 'Eleanora Fagan McKay (Billie Holiday)'.[24] Shaw never replied.

On 10 July the doctors allowed Billie to receive gifts of 'candy and ice cream, & fruit – not salty foods'. But just as she appeared to be rallying, she went into relapse. Throughout Wednesday and well into Thursday night, Louis McKay remained at her bedside. He left at 2.40 a.m. to phone his mother. Half an hour later Billie Holiday died.

Her illness was originally diagnosed as a liver ailment brought on through excessive alcohol consumption which had been complicated by cardiac failure. After her liver responded to treatment, a dangerous kidney infection developed. Before this could be controlled she developed congestion in her lungs. 'It's a result of a concoction of everything she's done in the last twenty years,' said Joe Glaser. 'She began drinking heavily to try and beat the narcotics habit and neglected her health.'[25] In the end, Billie Holiday's medical records mirrored the story of her life; a series of complications beset by further complications.

She died virtually penniless. Her worldly fortune amounted to just $848.54 in cash. She had overdrawn a total of $25,808.63 against future sales on four record company royalty accounts, the Internal Revenue Service was chasing her for $1424.69 in back-taxes, and she owed Joe Glaser's Associated Booking Corporation $1880.20 for loans against future earnings.[26] According to Louis McKay, she never had any savings accounts and had closed her small 'checking account' shortly before her death.[27]

During her last years McKay said she was forced to sell all of her 'valuable personalty' to secure money for her habit.[28] In January 1959 she had hocked her beloved minks. She got a few hundred dollars for them and her first stop was the grocery store; food for her Mexican chihuahua, some sweet potatoes, a chicken and a bottle of gin. When the time came to assess her assets, the value of her personal property was valued at $0 and her total net estate came to just $1345.36. It was so small it did not even qualify for estate tax.[29]

As soon as Zaidins learned of Billie's death, he rushed around to the hospital to tell McKay that Billie had run up some $12,000 in fees. Aware of Billie's precarious financial situation, he said he would waive them for a slice of her estate. There and then, in the hospital waiting-room just a few hours after Billie's death, he drew up a contract in longhand which he got McKay to sign:

[I] acknowledge that Earle Warren Zaidins . . . has not been paid for any of his services. That in consideration thereof I agree that as the surviving spouse of the decedent and as logical administrator of decedent's estate, when appointed, to pay to Mr Zaidins ten [10 per cent] of all gross monies received.[30]

When McKay later had a chance to consider his position he appointed Flo Kennedy to represent him. After lengthy litigation, Zaidins was forced to relinquish his claim and she took over handling Billie Holiday's estate for several years on McKay's behalf. Later, Flo Kennedy, whom Billie called the 'hip-kitty from Kansas City', went on to a distinguished career as a crusading lawyer; in 1994 the *New York Times* said she had been 'at the forefront of civil rights and feminist movements for more than thirty years'.[31] 'I guess Lou was a kind of hustler,' she reflected, 'a gambler and a lot of people said he had a string of whores. But this was not unusual; people in the black community did not have much money, this sort of thing happened. He lived off her earnings but he was kind of compassionate and caring towards her, a "take charge" type. I think he made her feel he cared for her. He was knowledgeable in many ways, streetwise and a pimp. But it was a struggle with Billie Holiday and I don't doubt he hit her but she depended on him. When I dealt with her I found her a difficult person. I did not admire her.'[32]

A solemn requiem mass for Billie Holiday was held at 11 a.m. on 22 July at St Paul's Roman Catholic Church on Columbus Circle. Over 3000 attended, 2400 crammed into a church built for 2100 with the rest outside. To the very end of her life Billie never knew who were her true friends and who were trying to make money out of her. 'The thing about Billie Holiday was that a lot of people clung to her because she was a celebrity,' continued Flo Kennedy. 'She was exploitative and exploited. Zaidins was slimy. He was typical of the kind of sleazy people she seemed to surround herself with. He pretended to be a big fan, but in her case she was so rude and gross it was not easy to be admiring of her. I had a low opinion of him; I didn't feel he knew what he was doing and he certainly didn't understand the royalties scene. Maely Dufty was again typical of the fairly unattractive people who latched on to Billie Holiday. She was overweight and smelly and not particularly appealing; Billie Holiday used to call her "a fat funky bitch", that was the way she talked. I think she depended on them as much as they seemed to depend on her; in other words Maely Dufty would be the only person she could depend on to get dope.'[33]

*   *   *

227

Billie Holiday was finally laid to rest in St Raymond's Cemetery, New York in the grave of her mother Sadie. The round of sleazy second-rate theatres with unpainted dressing-rooms and half-empty minor-league night-clubs outside New York that had been her life in those final years had now ended. But the complications continued. Within a year, *Downbeat* discovered that Louis McKay had not even bothered to erect a headstone on his wife's grave and invited contributions for a suitable monument. McKay protested, saying the matter was in hand, demanding *Downbeat* return all contributions. As in life, there seemed no peace for Billie Holiday. In 1960 her coffin was exhumed and she was reburied in a plot of her own at a cost of $717, which McKay claimed against the Holiday estate.[34] The inscription on the headstone read: 'Beloved wife Billie Holiday known as Lady Day, Born April 7 1915, Died July 15 1959'.

Epilogue

Today it is impossible to estimate the value of the estate of the late Billie Holiday, administered by the attorneys J. Mifflin Hayes in New Jersey. Since her death her recordings, prolifically re-issued into the age of compact disc, and her autobiography, finally the subject of a major Hollywood picture in 1972, have generated royalties on a scale unimaginable during her lifetime. When she died, hardly any of her recordings were in print and she was seldom heard on the radio. Yet within months Billie Holiday albums began finding their way back on to the record racks. It was in sharp contrast to 1958, when one record company royalty statement amounted to just $11.58. Now double albums at $10.40 were selling out as quickly as they got into the stores. What began as a stream gradually turned into a flood. In 1991, a spokesman for CBS/Sony confirmed that Holiday reissues were among the 'top-selling artists' of the Columbia Jazz Masterpiece series.[1]

Few careers in the performing arts have ended so ignominiously yet begun so promisingly as that of Billie Holiday. By the time she was twenty-three she had performed and recorded with some of the biggest names in jazz, including Duke Ellington, Count Basie, Benny Goodman, Fletcher Henderson, Jimmie Lunceford, Benny Carter, Bunny Berigan, Lester Young, Artie Shaw and Teddy Wilson. Her vocals go beyond conventional explanation that here was a great talent; so inspired and conscientious seemed the application of her musical gift that her work appeared touched by genius. During those years she created a body of recorded music that is amongst the most critically acclaimed of the Swing Era. Even today this work ranks with the finest of all recorded jazz.

Billie Holiday's triumph was to take the American popular song and find her place in the world. In so doing she stripped it of its innocence, transforming simple love songs into narratives of sexual desire through economic irony rather than the innuendo of a Mae West or Helen Kane. 'To me the things Billie Holiday sang came from the depths of the groin of life,' observed singer Sylvia Syms, a personal friend.[2]

229

The sound of her voice has people reaching for metaphor to explain its effect; it engages our deepest emotions because that was what she strove to reach within herself. 'You just feel it, and when you sing it other people feel it too,' she tried to explain.[3] She never used scat, remaining libretto-oriented, unlike an Ella Fitzgerald or a Sarah Vaughan, who often harnessed the device to reveal and explore the purely musical characteristics of a song.

Scat is vocal improvisation using phonetic sounds traditionally (but not always) similar to the instrumental sounds of jazz. Considering Billie's debt to Louis Armstrong in every other aspect of her singing, it may appear surprising she never attempted scat, particularly since this was what initially attracted her to jazz. '[On Armstrong's] "West End Blues" he doesn't say any words,' she said in 1957, 'and I thought this was wonderful, I liked the feeling he got from it.'[4]

Instead she steered clear of impressionistic, onomatopoeic gesture to develop melodic, rhythmic and emotional ideas based on lyrics. This specific artistic decision presents an insight into her aesthetic; scat is incapable of conveying anything but the most primitive emotions, so was something which did not interest her. She was only concerned with trying to express the often complex emotions she had felt within herself. Yet the great paradox of Billie Holiday was that the very singer who could freeze an audience into their seats with the emotional power of her singing struggled throughout her life with deep emotional problems of her own that she could not begin to understand.

It is impossible to view Billie Holiday from any perspective simple enough to understand her interior contradictions. Certainly many of her problems could well have had their roots in her traumatic childhood. Being constantly abandoned to friends and relations and the emotional havoc wrought by her rape as an eleven-year-old could well have contributed to the diminished sense of self, or crippling insecurity, that those close to her spoke of. This feeling of rejection would also go some way to explaining her abnormally dependent personality, her desire to attach herself to someone who would love her and care for her, and then, once in a relationship, to do anything and accept anything to maintain it. Equally, the absence of parental supervision might have had a bearing on her lack of moral discipline, expressed at an early age through truancy and lack of interest in academic activities.

Yet such calm rationalization can never fully explain with hindsight a life overtaken by the dark and destructive forces that inhabit human nature. Perhaps it is not what happens to us so much as how we handle what happens to us that decides our future. Ella Fitzgerald had to endure a family background and social conditions not greatly different from

Billie's; two years younger, Ella was almost certainly sexually abused as a child and she too hung around a whorehouse in early adolescence. Each was the product of a broken home, each suffered years of poverty and each stared racism square in the face in the musical milieu of the 1930s, 1940s and 1950s. Yet Ella worked her way to Beverly Hills luxury and was still singing in the early 1990s, while Billie Holiday was never able to come to terms with her personal demons. Much of her private life was spent running away from them, retreating into the pursuit of pleasure, something that was in conspicuously short supply during her childhood.

From her early teens Billie Holiday associated marijuana and alcohol with good times. As a young woman she lived it up with a vengeance, with alcohol, marijuana and sex at the centre of her social life. She was unconcerned if her indulgences affected her career, which progressively left John Hammond, her influential patron, more and more disenchanted. Initially, Hammond's admiration of her talent inspired him to work untiringly to create career opportunities for her. Just like Bill Daniels, responsible for lighting the sets of Greta Garbo's greatest films, Hammond as record producer illuminated Billie Holiday's gifts as a singer in a variety of interesting and challenging ways. But her attitude to the one man who might have guided her to the kind of success Ella Fitzgerald enjoyed was such that he eventually gave up on her. For Hammond it was all or nothing, as essayist Otis Ferguson observed in 1938: 'He hasn't established for himself the intervening marks on the scale of achievement between "it's terrific" and "it stinks".'[5] What Hammond wanted was for his commitment to her career to be matched by hers. When it became clear that Billie's temperament stood in the way of this, Hammond had nothing more to do with her.

In 1939 she was introduced to Buddy Tate, who had just taken Herschel Evans's chair in the Count Basie Orchestra, and the tall, elegant saxophonist and the beautiful jazz singer became an item for a while. Tate gradually became aware of the role alcohol and marijuana played in her life. 'Lady,' he told her, 'you can't get high all the time, not every day.'[6] By 1941, her affair with Tate behind her, she married small-time drugs dealer Jimmy Monroe and subsequently gravitated to opium for her highs. That all changed around 1943–4 when heroin began to fill a void caused by a wartime shortage of opium. Billie Holiday was one of many who began experimenting with the more potent drug.

For a while she used intermittently, but then succumbed to addiction, spending vast sums of money indulging herself and her former drugs runner Joe Guy – they were now living as husband and wife – in monumental highs. In an attempt to save her from herself, her manager Joe Glaser cooperated with the law enforcement agencies in 1947 to have her busted for possession. But by the time she was released from prison in 1948 she was no longer a leading creative force in jazz, a position she had surrendered incrementally as narcotics rather than music became central to her life. Subsequently, the joy and hope of her earlier recordings were progressively replaced by a world-weary fatalism as she suffered the increasing effects of nicotine, alcohol and drug addiction. But as she manoeuvred her steadily shrinking vocal resources around a song, her ability to make words sound profound never deserted her.

Audiences now read Billie Holiday's real-life history into her performances, as if each word might reveal some deep, dark secret about her private life. She was quick to capitalize on this, and songs such as 'Ain't Nobody's Business If I Do' reinforced her 'notoriety' while defiantly justifying her indulgence of the self. This simple step reinforced her stature as an artist. Before, she sang from the standpoint of young love being far more interesting or profound than the routine passion of marriage. Now, as an older woman never far from the clamour of the headlines, her life's experiences gave her a different perspective from which to sing as the reckless vitality of her youth gave way to a melancholy spirit trapped within the infinite loops of alcohol and drug addiction.

In 1952 her public confessional was interrupted by Norman Granz, who persuaded her to move beyond the numbers to which she had laid claim in live performance, and record songs that did not slot into the autobiographical subtext of her repertoire. He teamed her with two fine leading men in Benny Carter and Ben Webster and she responded by marshalling her resources and imagination to lift each song, sometimes painfully, into a new dimension where she considered it afresh.

Despite a clearly variable and deteriorating voice, there was nevertheless great wisdom and imagination in the way she used shorter phrase lengths to conceal poor breath control and vibrato to conceal her insecurities of pitch, and the way she used melismata, slides and swoops to claim a song as her own. But although there were times in those later years when soiled realism blurred into stylized realism, the raw nerve endings exposed in her voice served only to reinforce her authenticity as a jazz singer.

By 1957 Granz felt he had done all he could with her. Her Parthian shot was two albums recorded for other labels that defy conventional critique; here the emotional destiny of her work is ultimately commanded by knowledge of her real-life story in order to realize their

232

powerful emotional impact. They are harsh, even terrifying statements that make you afraid to listen because her voice contains a glimpse of death.

However, the white gardenia fidelity Billie Holiday brought to her earlier work has gradually been replaced by a tragic legend of unrelieved exploitation and persecution. That legend was codified by William F. Dufty when he began work on a book he provisionally titled *Bitter Crop*, Billie Holiday's autobiography which he had agreed to ghost-write for her. Dufty was well aware that Holiday's had been a story for sale whenever she was short of money. He combined her public utterances with her long, over-the-shoulder glance at the dues she paid, the wrong associations she made and the collapse of her promising career. Seasoned pro that he was, he latched on to the downs of her life rather than the ups of her music because he knew that this was what sold books. Besides, he had a 35 per cent share of the royalties.[7]

His rakish, side-of-the-mouth delivery set the tone for the book; his opening lines, the most famous in all jazz literature, 'Mom and Pop were just a couple of kids when they got married. He was eighteen, she was sixteen and I was three', were first used in a March 1953 *Our World* magazine article. Dufty was neither musicologist nor historian, something musicologists and historians have never forgiven him for. He was a good tabloid journalist who knew his craft, and like all tabloid journalists, he was not beyond taking an improvised chorus within the overall orchestration. When these imperfect truths later stood revealed, they served to undermine the credibility of the rest of his text. In the end no one was quite sure what to believe.

Yet, as now seems clear, the basic facts were all there, even though their tabloidesque treatment made them appear more as Dufty inventions. Tantalizingly, he made the truth appear to lurk behind a simmering portrait of a life engaged to disaster, and this only added to the mystique of the Holiday legend. But the singer herself was concerned with only two things, money and publicity. Norman Granz said she showed him galleys of the first edition and was only interested in whether he thought the book would sell. He strongly doubted whether Holiday read anything at all of what she showed him.[8]

When the book was finished, the publishers, Doubleday & Co, insisted on changing the title to *Lady Sings the Blues*. Since publication it has remained almost constantly in print, providing royalties for Billie Holiday's estate and a source of clichés for succeeding generations of 'hip' music writers. The narrative, intended as much to give Holiday's career a filip as to attract Hollywood producers, was kicked around by

233

several studios until 1972, when Sidney J. Furie directed a dramatically rewritten script for Motown-Weston-Furie Productions that had Dufty up in arms. 'I had nothing, but absolutely nothing to do with the screenplay,' he protested. '*Lady Sings the Blues* is a fantasy of Berry Gordy, Supreme Commander of Motown Records, the guy who put up the money.'[9]

Holiday, in her prime both stunning and statuesque, was played on screen by Diana Ross, a petite, pinched beauty and Motown super-star. She was moulded into a script that while doing justice to her powerful acting ability was no more than a lie told well. It shamelessly exploited the Holiday legend: drugs, racism, violence, jail and self-destruction, a story that has since become immortal.

Its victim-pays-the-price-of-fame routine failed to portray Holiday's achievements and instead substituted the zingy romanticism of failure. Yet as Ross was being nominated for an Oscar and her *Lady Sings the Blues* soundtrack album was reaching number 1 in the charts, original-issue Billie Holiday albums had begun changing hands for up to $60.

The stark imagery conjured up by the film created a momentum of its own, providing a launching-pad for fantasy and imagination. Lanie Robertson's off-Broadway show, *Lady Day at Emerson's Bar and Grill*, created a Holiday of simmering anger that wove fifteen songs into a biographical meditation; Reenie Upchurch's *Yesterdays* created a Holiday of bitter, self-lacerating humour, while Millicent Sparks created a one-woman cabaret with her own *Billie Holiday: The Lady Behind the Gardenia*. Aishah Rahman's musical tragedy, *Lucky Day*, focused on her relationship with Lester Young; Stephen Stahl's *Lady Day* was set, somewhat incongruously, in a London theatre; but perhaps the most bizarre portrayal of all was Archie Shepp's *Lady Day – A Musical Tragedy*, a musical revue with a man in drag imitating Holiday's singing style.

As these productions found their way into fringe theatres, actors' workshops and alternative festivals the world over, the real Billie Holiday receded further and further into history. With each new script something new was conjured out of the mythic qualities of legend. An image of Billie Holiday-as-all-purpose-victim began to fill the view-finder. Today she is part romantic martyr, claimed by feminists and civil rights campaigners, and part heroine of excess whose details of self-extinction threaten to obscure her genuine achievements in jazz.

Her 'tragedy' has assumed a fashionable universality that has inspired poems – 'Don't Explain' by Alexis DeVeaux, 'The Day Lady Day Died' by Frank O'Hara and 'For Billie Holiday' by Langston Hughes – and novels – *Listening to Billie* by Alice Adams, *The Heart of a Woman* by Maya Angelou and *Sleepless Nights* by Elizabeth Hardwick.

There have been posters and postcards of her clutching a drink and in 1994 the US Post Office issued a Billie Holiday commemorative stamp. She was given a walk-on part in the pages of *The Autobiography of Malcolm X*, and in Spike Lee's film, the young Malcolm's initiation to heroin is to the accompaniment of a Billie Holiday record. Her disembodied voice pops up again to provide period authenticity in the Whoopie Goldberg film, *Corrina, Corrina*, and was subverted to inspire executive consumerism in a TV ad for German production cars. There have been television documentaries, radio programmes and countless magazine features, while her face has appeared on everything from beer-mats to T-shirts.

The way legend has consumed artist has been as gradual as it has been inexorable. Billie Holiday has become someone it is good to feel bad about, a valentine to the depressed who see life's lessons refracted in the flaws of her latter-day voice. When in November 1956 she performed a concert in Carnegie Hall alternating readings from *Lady Sings the Blues* by Gilbert Millstein with songs that had become associated with her, she was consciously erecting the legend into which she would finally step, closing the doors firmly behind her. 'The jazz singer who over-drank, over-drugged, had a terrible time with men, with being a black person in white society; she's become the personification of all that,' observed Annie Ross. 'Lady and the legend. Sure, she had a voracious appetite, had her hangups too, but she would hate to be seen today as a tragic figure.'[10]

Billie Holiday was probably the most complete, unadulterated jazz singer of all time, something that has been overshadowed by that quirk of the human condition which sees fascination in those who gamble with life and lose. 'To live longer than forty years is indecent, banal, immoral!' said Dostoievsky's Underground Man, and Billie Holiday offended by only four years. Just like Charlie Parker, James Dean, Janis Joplin, Marilyn Monroe, Jim Morrison, Sid Vicious, Kurt Cobain and a host of others, her life found unexpected definition by taking a premature route to eternity. All share one thing in common – a sainted, metaphorical afterlife where the myth has grown larger than the truth. But the one great truth about Billie Holiday is that above all else she was a great artist, not because of her tragic childhood and the suffering her hedonistic lifestyle brought her, but in spite of it. Today she has been so consumed by her image that it has rendered her a victim at the expense of her music, the one thing that made her unique.

References

Preface

1. Francis Davis, *Outcasts,* Oxford University Press, New York, 1990, p. 131.

Prologue

1. *Ebony,* unprovenanced cutting, courtesy Free Library of Philadelphia.

Chapter One

1. 1900 US Census, taken 7 June 1900; however, details of the Harris family and their relationship one to another were confused by enumerator Owen Reed. For example, Sussie is given as twenty-three years old, married for fifteen years and the mother of nine children. Evelyn Conway (née Miller, 1906–1994) and Mathew Conway (b. 1901) confirm that the household of James and Sussie Harris was the one in which Eva (shown as Mary E., fourteen years) and Sadie (shown as Sarah J., five years) were raised, and were able to correct the census taker's errors. Thanks also to Evelyn's daughter, Janice Eleanora Blackwell (b. 1929) for talking through several of my queries with her frail parents. Janice was given her middle name through her mother's childhood association with Eleanora Harris. Interviews

on 21 May 1994, 31 May 1994, 6 July 1994 and 11 July 1994, and with Janice on 26 and 27 July 1994 following the death of her mother Evelyn on 19 July 1994.

2. Birth certificate of Eleanora Harris: certified copy, courtesy City of Philadelphia, Department of Records, City Archives.

3. It is interesting that while Baltimore has always been given as Billie Holiday's birthplace, as early as 1938, in a *Melody Maker* interview published on 16 April (p. 2), both Billie Holiday and Sadie Gough give Billie's place of birth as Philadelphia. Also US Passport No. 1047225: Eleanora Gough McKay aka Billie Holiday shows place of birth Philadelphia. So Billie was well aware she was a Philadelphian.

4. For example, in the case of Schmidt *v.* DeBoer in the Michigan High Court in 1993, it transpired that Mrs Schmidt falsely named another man, her boyfriend at the time, as the father of her daughter. The complex adoption wrangle that ensued illustrated only too well that the registered father is usually, but not exceptionally, the true father.

5. 1900 US Census for the household of Nelson Holliday, taken 11 June 1900 by Samuel D. Benton, enumerator.

6. Details from Draft Registration

Card 2396: Clarence E. Holiday, completed 5 June 1917.

7. Clarence Holiday's military record is taken from *Maryland in the World War: Military and Naval Service Records, vol. 1*, Maryland War Records Commission, Baltimore, 1933, p. 968.

8. Address from birth certificate of Charles Miller, b. 6 October 1916.

9. 1920 US Census for the household of Frank DeVeazy, taken 12 January 1920 by Harriett M. Simpson, enumerator, shows DeVeazy, now a driver, living with his wife Jennie, age twenty-four, at 817 North Burns Street, City of Philadelphia. Clearly between 1915 and 1920 there is time for Sadie, unable at any time in her life to form a lasting relationship with any of her partners, to have had a relationship with DeVeazy and subsequently for DeVeazy to have developed his relationship with Jennie.

10. Author interviews with Evelyn Conway (née Miller) and Janice Blackwell.

11. Ibid.

12. Ibid.

13. 1920 US Census for the household of Robert Miller, taken 6 January 1920 by Amalia J. Krebs, enumerator.

14. Television interview of Billie Holiday by Mike Wallace, November 1956. *Giants of Jazz* LP 1001.

15. Several photos from 1930s and 1940s show Billie Holiday wearing a necklace with a crucifix, not least the famous shot from the late 1930s, reproduced in *Metronome*, February 1957.

16. Admission summary. Federal Reformatory for Women, Alderston, West Virginia. Billie Holiday – Register Number: 8407-2, p. 2.

17. 1920 US Census for the household of Frank Cornish (Clarence Holiday, lodger), taken 14 January 1920 by Thomas W. C. Scott, enumerator.

18. 1922 *Baltimore City Directory*.

19. Details provided by Baltimore City Schools Records Retrieval Unit.

20. *Baltimore City Directory*, 1926–1930: Mrs Viola Green, shown as housewife, 609 Bond Street. No further entries checked beyond 1930.

21. *News American*, 28 March 1971, interview with Freddie Green, 'The Day Lady Day Died'.

22. When Leonard Feather was interviewing Billie Holiday in 1938, Sadie interrupted to recount the story; *Melody Maker*, 16 April 1938, p. 2. Also 'Billie Tells Her Story', *New York Amsterdam News*, 21 January 1939.

23. Billie Holiday with William Dufty, *Lady Sings the Blues*, Penguin Books, London, 1984, p. 15. Philip Gough is shown in the 1929 *Baltimore City Directory* at 614 Collett Street.

24. Charles Fagan's nephew, Charles Brooks (b. 1924), interview with Marsha Sharon Dennis, January 1994.

25. 1880 US Census for the household of Rebecca Fagan, 42 Little McElderly Street, Baltimore. Census taken 3 June 1880 by Charles J. Sebring, enumerator.

26. Charles Brooks interview with Marsha Sharon Dennis, January 1994.

27. Author interviews with Evelyn Conway (née Miller) and Janice Blackwell.

28. Ibid.

29. Commitment Papers: Eleanora Gough to House of Good Shepherd for Colored Girls. Signed 5 January 1925 by Magistrate T. J. Williams. Courtesy Good Shepherd Center Archives.

30. The Good Shepherd Center still exists today at 4100 Maple Avenue, Baltimore, with

programmes for adolescent girls with emotional and behavioural problems. Sister Mary Rosaria Baxter points out that time and again the Center is confronted with the complex problems that centre around mother–daughter relationships: 'We have hundreds of Billie Holidays today,' she points out. 'Rejection, neglect or abandonment, and in Billie's case it was abandonment, all too often produce feelings of inadequacy and disfunctional behaviour. Sadly it is a common problem, the Center even has a special unit with intensive programmes to help girls adjust.' Interview, 17 August 1994.

31. Author interviews with Sister Mary Rosaria Baxter of the Good Shepherd Center, 2 August, 12 August, 15 August and 17 August 1994.

32. Ibid.

33. Carl Schoettler Research, published in *Baltimore Evening Sun*, 6 November 1991, and author interviews, September and October 1993. Subsequently corroborated by Sister Mary Rosaria Baxter, Good Shepherd Center. Author interviews, 2 August, 12 August, 15 August and 17 August 1994.

34. Ibid.

35. Commitment Papers: Eleanora Gough to House of Good Shepherd for Colored Girls, 5 January 1925. Final page: 'Madge paroled October 3, 1925.' Courtesy Good Shepherd Center Archives.

36. Author interviews with Evelyn Conway (née Miller) and Janice Blackwell.

37. The *Baltimore City Directory* for 1926 shows Sadie Gough 'cook' resident at 1325 Argyle Street, Baltimore.

38. *Our World*, March 1953, p. 33.

39. Ibid.

40. File No. 4205: State of Maryland

v. Wilbert Rich, courtesy Maryland State Archives.

41. Ibid.

42. Commitment Papers: Eleanora Gough to House of Good Shepherd for Colored Girls, 24 December 1926. Courtesy Good Shepherd Center Archives.

43. Author interviews with Sister Mary Rosaria Baxter.

44. File No. 4205: State of Maryland *v.* Wilbert Rich.

45. Ibid.

46. Carl Schoettler research, corroborated by Sister Mary Rosaria Baxter.

47. Commitment Papers: Eleanora Gough to House of Good Shepherd for Colored Girls, 24 December 1926. Final page: 'Summoned by Habeas Corpus February 2, 1927. Did not return.' Courtesy Good Shepherd Center Archives.

48. Interview with Billie Holiday by Mike Wallace.

49. The *Baltimore City Directory* for 1927 shows no entry for Sadie Gough but in 1928 she is back at 1325 Argyle Street and her occupation is once again shown as 'cook'. The *Directory* also shows William Hill, labourer, at 609 Bond Street in 1929 and 109 Bond Street in 1930; one or other is surely correct for both years.

50. Not least the November 1956 TV interview with Mike Wallace and a radio interview with Willis Conover, published in *Metronome*, February 1957, and, of course, *Lady Sings the Blues*.

51. *Metronome*, February 1957, p. 24.

52. Ibid.

53. Interview with author, April 1993.

Chapter Two

1. The 1928 *Baltimore City Directory* shows Sadie Harris, 'cook', still resident at 1325 Argyle Street, Baltimore, but there are no

entries for her in subsequent years.

2. While it is hardly surprising that an appropriate 'Alice Dean', the Baltimore bordello owner cited in *Lady Sings the Blues*, does not appear in the *Baltimore City Directory* or in any relevant census, it is worth noting that Harlem bordello owner Florence Williams and 'Gladys', also cited in *LSTB*, did appear in the 1925 US Census at 261 West 131st Street. Florence Williams also appears in the 1925 New York Telephone Directory at this address; *LSTB* makes much of a telephone at her subsequent emporium at 151 West 140th Street.

3. *News American*, 28 March 1971.

4. All details from the records of Magistrates Court, 9th District of Manhattan for the year of 1929, pp. 218–19.

5. *New York Times*, 26 June 1931.

6. Ibid.

7. *Coda*, May 1974, pp. 4–5.

8. *Melody Maker*, 16 April 1938, p. 2; *New York Amsterdam News*, 21 January 1939, p. 16.

9. Interview with author, November 1993.

10. Spike Hughes, *Second Movement*, Museum Press, London, 1971.

11. Marge Johnson may have been the singer who recorded with Louis Armstrong and Sidney Bechet; courtesy Phil Schaap archives.

12. *Variety*, 17 February 1926.

13. *The Complete Billie Holiday on Verve*, 517658–2. Disc 4, track 32.

14. Interview with author, November 1993.

15. Hal Austin interview with Loren Schoenberg, May 1991.

16. Interview with author, October 1993.

17. Interview with author, November 1993.

18. Interview with author, April 1993.

19. Ibid.

20. Ibid.

21. Ram Ramirez interview with Stanley Dance. Jazz Oral History Project, Institute of Jazz Studies, Rutgers, NJ.

22. *Jazz Journal*, April 1963, p. 9.

23. Ram Ramirez interview with Stanley Dance.

24. Monette Moore recorded frequently as a blues singer in the 1920s, mostly in Chicago. When she moved to New York she worked extensively with Charlie Johnson at Small's Paradise and in shows and revues at the Apollo and Lafayette Theaters. In 1932 she went into Covan's, where she worked for most of the year accompanied by Garland Wilson on piano. Gunther Schuller has suggested in *The Swing Era* (Oxford University Press, New York, 1989, p. 529) that Moore's absence was to understudy Ethel Waters in the Irving Berlin revue, *As Thousands Cheer*, at Berlin's own tiny Music Box Theater on West 45th Street. It was in fact to play *Flying Colours*. When she finished the engagement she never returned to Covan's, going instead into the New Brittwood Café and Grill at 594 Lenox Avenue for the winter of 1934 where *New York Age* described her as 'one of the highspots' of the entertainment in December. From the Brittwood she went straight into a revue at the Lafayette Theater. There she was approached by Eddie Mallory, Ethel Waters's husband, to understudy his wife for *As Thousands Cheer*, which she accepted, a job that lasted for the next three years. There is no mention of her having her own club in the April 1963 *Jazz Journal* interview, something her quite detailed recollections would surely not have overlooked. For Hammond to have seen Billie substituting for Monette Moore in a Harlem club at this time, it could only have been Covan's; Moore did not have a club of her own –

'Monette Moore's place on 133rd Street' – as claimed by John Hammond in his autobiography, *John Hammond on the Record*, Penguin Books, London, 1977, pp. 91–2.

25. Linda Kuel and Ellie Schocket, assisted by Dan Morgenstern, *Billie Holiday Remembered*, New York Jazz Museum, 1972.
26. Interview with author, April 1993.
27. John Hammond and Irving Townsend, *John Hammond on Record*, Penguin Books, London, 1981, p. 93.
28. *Storyville*, issue 153, p. 96.
29. Louis Sobol, *The Longest Street*, Crown, New York, 1968.
30. Hammond, *John Hammond on Record*, p. 119.
31. Billie Holiday interview with Mike Wallace, November 1956. *Giants of Jazz* LP 1001.
32. Willie 'The Lion' Smith, *Music on My Mind*, Jazz Book Club, London 1966, p. 167.
33. *New York Age*, 29 December 1934, p. 6.
34. Interview with author, April 1993.
35. *Ebony*, July 1949.
36. Burt Goldblatt, *Newport Jazz Festival*, Dial Press, New York, 1977, p. 323.
37. Hammond, *John Hammond on Record*.
38. *Storyville*, Issue 153, p. 96.
39. Danny Barker, *A Life in Jazz*, Macmillan, London, 1986, pp. 135–7.
40. *New York Age*, 30 November 1935.
41. Artie Shaw interview, John Jeremy Archive, courtesy National Sound Archive, British Library.

Chapter Three

1. Clay's presence has often been incorrectly claimed as Goodman's first interracial recording session. That was on 21 May 1930 with Hoagy Carmichael and his orchestra which included Bubber Miley on trumpet.
2. Loren Schoenberg, Goodman's personal manager and archivist from 1980–1985, confirms that Goodman told him he dated Billie Holiday for a while in 1933. Conversation with author, November 1993.
3. Billie would later say it was pianist Buck Washington who was at the session; there is no doubt, however, that the pianist on the session was Joe Sullivan. It is possible that Buck Washington was the pianist on the audition session for Bernie Hanighen or that Washington was there simply to provide moral support. It has also been claimed that Frank Froeba was the pianist. However, *Benny Goodman: Listen to his Legacy*, the definitive bio-discography of Benny Goodman by D. Russell Connor, Scarecrow Press Inc and the Institute of Jazz Studies, Metuchen, NJ, 1988, p. 41, confirms that Sullivan is the pianist.
4. *Metronome*, February 1957, p. 24.
5. Ibid.
6. Try his 'I'm Just a Lucky So and So' from *What Because*, Gramavision GV 79453–2 for an example of the human voice singing several notes at once. Holiday's rasp is a simplified version that from time to time suggests one overtone (two notes).
7. Interview with author, November 1993.
8. Arnold Shaw, *52nd Street*, Da Capo Press, New York, 1977, p. 80.
9. Loren Schoenberg Archives. Also Russ Firestone, *Swing, Swing, Swing*, Hodder & Stoughton, London, 1983, p. 83.
10. Berger, Berger and Patrick, *Benny Carter: A Life In American Music*, Scarecrow Press and Institute of Jazz Studies, Metuchen, NJ, 1983, p. 313.

11. Lester Young interview with Chris Albertson, 1958, published in *A Lester Young Reader*, ed. Lewis Porter, Smithsonian Institution Press, Washington, DC and London, 1991, p. 167.
12. *Chicago Defender*, 14 April 1934, p. 8.
13. *Melody Maker*, 2 June 1934, p. 11.
14. Phil Schaap Archives. From an interview with Russell Procope, *c.* 1975.
15. *New York Age*, 29 September 1934.
16. From the 'Talk of the Town' entertainment columns of *New York Age*, January through December 1934.
17. For example, a 1940 appearance of trumpeter Roy Eldridge was advertised as 'Roy Eldredge' and a 1935 Chick Webb appearance had his singer Charles Linton billed as Charlie Lintin, and Bardu Ali as Bardoc Ali. *New York Age*, 27 September 1940 and 20 July 1935.
18. Billie and Bobbie Henderson's Apollo appearances were advertised in *New York Age* and *New York Amsterdam News* in their 24 November 1934 editions and are also included in their previews of forthcoming acts. The reviews of the week's presentations appeared in the 1 December 1934 editions.
19. *New York Age*, 1 December 1934.
20. Billie Holiday interview with Mike Wallace, November 1956, *Giants of Jazz* LP1001.
21. John Hammond interview, John Jeremy Archive, courtesy National Sound Archive, British Library.
22. *New York Age*, 1 December 1934.
23. *New York Amsterdam News*, 23 February 1946. Although Billie got to record 'Painting the Town Red' in July 1935, it was not until spring 1952 that she recorded 'If the Moon Turns Green'.
24. *New York Age*, 29 December 1934, p. 6.

25. Ibid., 20 November 1937.
26. Contrary to Schuller (*The Swing Era*, Oxford University Press, New York 1989, p. 72), *Symphony in Black* did not win an Academy award of any sort.
27. *New York Amsterdam News*, unprovenanced cutting, probably late 1935, courtesy Schomberg Institute of Black Studies, Harlem.
28. *Pittsburgh Courier*, 26 January 1935.
29. Brunswick 7310 mx BI 3078-A.
30. Schuller in *Swing Era*, p. 69, incorrectly hears 'told on man and beast'.
31. Schuller in ibid., p. 531, incorrectly hears 'I feel alone'.
32. *Duke Ellington Reader*, ed. Mark Tucker, Oxford University Press, New York, 1993, p. 459.
33. Metronome marking $\quarternote = 96$.

Chapter Four

1. *New York Amsterdam News*, 1 September 1933.
2. *New York Age*, 27 April 1935.
3. Ralph Cooper and Steve Dougherty, *Amateur Night at the Apollo*, HarperCollins, New York, 1990, p. 94.
4. Ibid.
5. *New York Age*, 20 April 1935.
6. Ibid., 27 April 1935.
7. Ibid., 20 April 1935.
8. *New York Amsterdam News*, 15 June 1935.
9. Interview with author, May 1991.
10. Ibid.
11. Ibid.
12. Hal Austin interview with Loren Schoenberg, May 1991.
13. *Hot News*, August 1935.
14. Fred Hall, *More Dialogues in Swing*, Pathfinder, California, 1991, p. 73.
15. Ibid.
16. Stanley Dance, *The World of Earl Hines*, Charles Scribner's Sons, New York, 1977, p. 181.

17. *Melody Maker*, 21 September 1935, p. 5.
18. Teddy Wilson interview with Milt Hinton. Jazz Oral History Project, Institute of Jazz Studies, Rutgers, NJ.
19. *Benny Goodman: On the Air 1937–8*, Columbia/Legacy C2K 48836. Originally released on vynil as *Jazz Concert No. 2*, but here with the addition of fourteen previously unreleased tracks.
20. *The Gramophone*, October 1935, p. 203.
21. Teddy Wilson interview with Milt Hinton.
22. *New York Age*, 10 April 1935.
23. *The Complete Billie Holiday on Verve*, 517658–2. Disc 4, track 8.
24. Teddy Wilson interview with Milt Hinton.
25. Hall, *More Dialogues in Swing*, p. 72.
26. Interview with author, April 1993.
27. Not least by Michael Brooks in his liner notes for the extensive reissue series of Billie Holiday's 'Columbia' output for CBS/Sony in the early 1990s.
28. Greil Marcus, *Mystery Train*, Omnibus Press, London, 1987.
29. Teddy Wilson interview with Milt Hinton.
30. Hall, *More Dialogues in Swing*, p. 73.
31. Ibid., p. 70.
32. *New York Amsterdam News*, 15 September 1935.
33. Max Kaminsky, *My Life in Jazz*, Jazz Book Club, London, 1965, p. 87.
34. Unprovenanced *Downbeat* clipping, Courtesy Institute of Jazz Studies, Rutgers, NJ.
35. *New York Amsterdam News*, 12 October 1935.
36. *New York Age*, 19 October 1935.

Chapter Five

1. Stanley Dance, *The World of Earl Hines*, Charles Scribner's Sons, New York, 1977, p. 50. Hines, among others, suggests that Glaser became involved in 'running the club'.
2. *New York Amsterdam News*, 9 September 1935.
3. Ibid., 2 November 1935.
4. Ibid.
5. Ibid., 23 November 1935.
6. Interview with author, Jan 1994.
7. *New York Amsterdam News*, 7 December 1935.
8. Ibid., 28 December 1935.
9. Robert Dupuis, *Bunny Berigan*, Louisiana State University Press, 1993, p. 122.
10. *Melody Maker*, 21 March 1936.
11. Ibid., 16 April 1938; also *New York Amsterdam News*, 21 January 1939. However, in a letter to British fan Jack Surridge, Billie said the reason was money (copy in author's possession).
12. *New York Amsterdam News*, 28 March 1936.
13. *Melody Maker*, 11 April 1936, p. 9.
14. *New York Age*, 1 February 1936.
15. *Baltimore Afro-American*, 27 June 1936; an identical quote appeared in *New York Amsterdam News* of the same date.
16. *New York Age*, 27 June 1936.
17. *The Complete Billie Holiday on Verve*, 517658–2. Disc 4, track 8.
18. *Pittsburgh Courier*, 4 July 1936.
19. Interview with author, April 1993.
20. Dupuis, *Bunny Berigan*.
21. *Melody Maker*, 23 Jan 1937, p. 2.
22. *Downbeat Yearbook '66*, p. 107.
23. The 5 December 1936 *Melody Maker* says that Billie returned to the Onyx that month. However, Holbeck does not refer to this in his reminiscences and is specific in saying she never played there again under his tenure (until 1938). Neither is a second appearance by Billie at the Onyx reported in Arnold Shaw's *52nd Street* (Da Capo, New York, 1977). More importantly, the event was reported in neither *New York Amsterdam News* nor *New York Age*, which would certainly have

mentioned a downtown booking for a black artist. It is thus safe to assume that the oft-repeated story of a December 1936 Onyx booking never happened.

24. *Record Research*, October 1962, p. 9. 'The Story of Louis Metcalf.'
25. *New York Amsterdam News*, 3 October 1936, p. 10; 24 October 1936, p. 12; 21 November 1936, p. 14.
26. Ibid., 21 November 1936.
27. From Hanighen's own typed *curriculum vitae*, with his handwritten annotations. Courtesy Institute of Jazz Studies, Rutgers, NJ.
28. In August 1934, the American Recording Company acquired Columbia and Okeh, but relinquished the latter shortly afterwards. Brunswick and Vocalion continued to trade under their own labels within ARC to February 1938 when they were purchased by Columbia. Vocalion was sold to Okeh at this time. Consequently Billie's 1935–41 period is generally referred to as her 'Columbia' period, for expediency.
29. George T. Simon, *Big Bands*, Macmillan, New York, 1967, p. 81.
30. Buck Clayton, *The World of Buck Clayton*, Bayou Press, Oxford, 1989, p. 98.
31. *Melody Maker*, 13 February 1937.
32. Phil Schaap Archives. Phil Schaap interview with Ed Lewis, 1978.
33. *Jazz Hot*, May–June 1937, pp. 5–6.
34. *New York Amsterdam News*, 27 March 1937.
35. Count Basie with Albert Murray, *Good Morning Blues*, Heinemann, London, 1986, p. 190.

Chapter Six

1. Interview with author, May 1991.
2. Jo Jones interview with Milt Hinton, Jazz Oral History Project, Institute of Jazz Studies, Rutgers, NJ.
3. Ibid.
4. Freddie Green interview with Helen Oakley-Dance, Jazz Oral History Project, Institute of Jazz Studies, Rutgers, NJ.
5. *New York Amsterdam News*, 26 June 1937.
6. Count Basie with Albert Murray, *Good Morning Blues*, Heinemann, London, 1986.
7. Ibid.
8. *New York Amsterdam News*, 10 July 1937.
9. *New York Age*, 20 November 1937.
10. Basie and Murray, *Good Morning Blues*.
11. Jo Jones interview with Milt Hinton.
12. *New York Amsterdam News*, 22 January 1938.
13. Ibid.
14. Unprovenanced news clipping, courtesy Institute of Jazz Studies, Rutgers, NJ.
15. *New York Amsterdam News*, 22 January 1938.
16. 'Count Basie eliminates Billie', etc. from ibid., 28 February 1938.
17. Ibid., 14 May 1938.
18. *Downbeat*, 4 June 1947, p. 2.
19. Freddie Green interview with Helen Oakley-Dance.
20. *Melody Maker*, 16 April 1938.
21. Interview with author, April 1993.
22. Ibid.
23. *New York Amsterdam News*, 2 April 1938.
24. *Metronome*, May 1938.
25. *Downbeat*, May 1938.
26. Ibid.
27. Cliff Leeman interview with Milt Hinton. Jazz Oral History Project, Institute of Jazz Studies, Rutgers, NJ.
28. Ibid.
29. Ibid.
30. *Metronome*, June 1938.
31. The personnel on this session and the one that follows it, on 23 June,

seem incorrect. Those involved on the first date are probably Charlie Shavers, trumpet; Buster Bailey, clarinet; Babe Russin, tenor sax; Clyde Hart, piano; John Kirby, bass; Cozy Cole, drums; with Ben Webster, tenor sax, replacing Russin on 23 June. Shavers, Russin and Webster can be distinguished aurally, but the piano is more problematical. It seems certain it is the same pianist on both sessions, but he sounds less technically endowed than either Claude Thornhill or Billy Kyle. Chances are it is the almost-there-but-not-quite-Teddy Wilson style of Clyde Hart. Courtesy of Loren Schoenberg.

32. Fred Hall, *Dialogues in Swing*, Pathfinder, California, 1989, p. 133.
33. Ibid., p. 134.
34. Artie Shaw interview: John Jeremy Archive courtesy National Sound Archive, British Library.
35. Cliff Leeman interview with Milt Hinton.
36. Helen Forrest, *I Had the Craziest Dream*, Coward, McCann & Geoghegan Inc., New York, 1982, p. 59.
37. Ibid.
38. Cliff Leeman interview with Milt Hinton.
39. Interview with author.
40. *New York Amsterdam News*, 5 November 1938.
41. Ibid., 21 January 1939, p. 16.
42. US *Daily Mirror*, 13 December 1938, p. 10.
43. Interview with author, April 1993.
44. Hall, *Dialogues in Swing*, p. 133.
45. Forrest, *I Had the Craziest Dream*.
46. Artie Shaw interview: John Jeremy Archive.

Chapter Seven

1. *New York Amsterdam News*, 7 December 1938.
2. Ibid., 21 January 1939, p. 16.

3. John Hammond with Irving Townsend, *John Hammond on Record*, Penguin Books, London, 1981.
4. Phil Schaap Archives. From an interview with Eddie Durham 1976, subsequently confirmed by Buck Clayton.
5. *Ebony*, unprovenanced clipping, courtesy Free Library of Philadelphia.
6. *New York Amsterdam News*, 7 January 1939.
7. Billie Holiday interview with Mike Wallace, November 1956, Giants of Jazz LP 1001.
8. *Downbeat*, February 1939.
9. Interview with author, April 1993.
10. From $\bullet = 160$ to $\bullet = 126$.
11. Liner notes, Commodore CCD 7001.
12. The tempo varies, but around $\bullet = 56 - 63$.
13. Interview with author, April 1993.
14. *Metronome*, July 1939.
15. Leonard Feather, *From Satchmo to Miles*, Quartet Books, London, 1974, p. 73.
16. Teddy Wilson interview with Milt Hinton. Jazz Oral History Project, Institute of Jazz Studies, Rutgers, NJ.
17. Loren Schoenberg Archives. Interview with Eddie Durham, 1976.
18. Interview with author, April 1994.
19. Barney Josephson interview with Stanley Crouch, 1979. Thanks to Stanley Crouch who points out that what Josephson told him was without any hint of sensationalism.
20. Interview with Jimmy McPartland. Jazz Oral History Project, Institute of Jazz Studies, Rutgers, NJ.
21. *New York Amsterdam News*, 18 November 1939.
22. *Encore*, October 1972, p. 47.
23. Interview with author, November 1993.
24. *Downbeat*, 1 November 1939.

25. *New York Amsterdam News*, 10 February 1940.
26. Several references in *New York Amsterdam News* and *New York Age* refer to Monroe as a 'sportsman'; 'impresario' appears on his marriage certificate to Billie; 'marijuana dealer' and 'pimp' appear on Billie's prison records at Alderston, Va.
27. Interview with author, April 1993.
28. Linda Kuehl and Ellie Schoket, assisted by Dan Morgenstern, *Billie Holiday Remembered*, New York Jazz Museum, 1972, p. 8.
29. *New York Amsterdam News*, 5 October 1940.
30. *Downbeat*, November 1940.
31. Ram Ramirez interview with Stanley Dance. Jazz Oral History Project, Institute of Jazz Studies, Rutgers, NJ.
32. Liner notes, *Commodore Years: Vol. 2*, Mosaic Records MR23–128.
33. *Downbeat*, 1 August 1941, p. 14.
34. *New York Amsterdam News*, 11 October 1941.
35. Berger, Berger and Patrick, *Benny Carter: A Life in American Music*, Scarecrow Press and Institute of Jazz Studies, Metuchen, NJ, 1982.
36. *New York Amsterdam News*, 20 December 1940.
37. Interview with author, November 1993.
38. *Downbeat*, 29 March 1973.
39. Interview with author, April 1993.

Chapter Eight

1. *Metronome*, May 1942, p. 20.
2. ♩ = 192.
3. Conversation with author, 25 April 1994.
4. *Downbeat*, 15 October 1942.
5. Ibid., 15 November 1942.
6. Ibid., 1 November 1942.
7. Ibid., 1 December 1942.
8. Ibid., 1 March 1943.
9. Ibid., 15 August 1943.
10. Ibid.

11. Arnold Shaw, *52nd Street*, Da Capo Press, New York, 1977, p. 304.
12. *Melody Maker*, 8 August 1959, p. 5.
13. *Life* magazine, 11 October 1943.
14. Ram Ramirez interview with Stanley Dance. Jazz Oral History Project, Institute of Jazz Studies, Rutgers, NJ.
15. Ibid.
16. Interview with author, November 1993.
17. Frank Sinatra interview with Sid Mark, BBC Radio 2.
18. Interview with author, November 1993.
19. John Simmons interview with Patricia Willard, Smithsonian Institution, Jazz Oral History Project, courtesy Institute of Jazz Studies, Rutgers, NJ.
20. Ibid.
21. I am grateful to David Courtwright, Professor of History at the University of North Florida, for his time guiding me through the social history of addiction in Harlem and the evolution from opium smoking through to heroin use in the 1930s and 1940s. Also for his permission to quote freely from the invaluable book he co-authored with Herman Joseph and Don Des Jarlais, *Addicts Who Survived (An Oral History of Narcotics' Use in America 1923–1965)*, University of Tennessee Press, Knoxville, Tennessee, 1989.
22. File No. 14234: District Court of the United States for Eastern District of Pennsylvannia: USA *v.* Billie Holiday, p. 15. Court makes it clear they knew she began her path to heroin addiction by smoking opium.
23. Examples of this interrelationship abound. A partial list to illustrate this theme must surely begin with Thomas De Quincey's (1785–1859) *Confessions of an English Opium Eater*, an autobiography of

romantic imagination close to Wordsworth's 'Prelude', yet reaching into more dark and secretive places. De Quincy, who took industrial doses of opium, claimed the drug 'stimulated his capacity for enjoyment'. Wordsworth, his friend, was more circumspect, yet it is widely thought that some of his work contained drug-induced visions. His contemporary Samuel Taylor Coleridge supposedly wrote 'Kubla Khan' under opium's influence, and work by Roget, Byron, Shelley and Robert Graves was equally inspired by the use of opium, as was the stark and terrifying imagery of Edgar Allan Poe. In Continental Europe, Charles Baudelaire's (1821–67) *Les Paradis artificiels* is the standard text for Romantic pharmacology. Theophile Gautier (1778–1850) and Amedeo Modigliani (1884–1920) used opium and Jean Cocteau always claimed Picasso told him he took drugs in 1904 to 'flavour his work'. Cocteau himself maintained that drugs gave him a 'euphoria superior to health'. In fifties France, students, intellectuals and artists had a high regard for amphetamine, claiming it made the mind sharper, more lucid and agile. Jean-Paul Sartre confessed to using amphetamine as a tool for 'intensifying work rate', although he never used drugs in his works of drama or non-fiction. In American literature of the 1950s the 'Beat Generation' of the San Francisco literary renaissance, Jack Kerouac, Alan Ginsberg, Lawrence Ferlingetti and William Burroughs, all had an interest in drugs and their effects on heightening and modifying reality. Kerouac's *On the Road* was an odyssey in search of experiences beyond the normal range of experience and invoked a whole range of drugs; *The Subterraneans* was coloured by his experiences with benzedrine and amphetamine, while *Dr Sax* drew on his experiences with marijuana. Other authors whose writing was coloured by marijuana include Gary Schneider, Frank O'Hara and Peter Bowles, while amphetamine users include Ayn Rand, Shirley Jackson and Margaret Mead. The powerful effects of heroin provided the backdrop for the work of Anna Kavan, *The Naked Lunch* by William Burroughs and *Last Exit to Brooklyn* by Hubert Selby Jr. In contrast, Ken Kesey turned to LSD after the success of *One Flew Over the Cuckoo's Nest*, while amphetamines were used extensively by science fiction writer Phillip K. Dick. Cocaine, a drug that achieved notoriety among the *nouveaux-riches* of Reagan's America and Thatcher's Britain, played a part in the construction of Robert Stone's *Dog Soldiers*.

24. Grateful thanks to Professor John Morgan MD, Department of Pharmacology, City University of New York Medical School, who kindly acted as a consultant and helped me with the preparation of the text on drugs, as well as checking for accuracy the text that relates to drug addiction.
25. *Downbeat*, 29 March 1973.
26. Ibid.
27. Ibid., 15 March 1944.
28. Not least Milt Gabler and Leonard Feather.
29. *Downbeat*, 5 May 1948.
30. Ibid., 5 May 1944, p. 2.
31. Interview with author, April 1993.
32. Liner notes, GRP 26012.
33. Ibid.
34. Ibid.
35. Interview with author, April 1993.
36. Stanley Dance, *World of Swing*, Charles Scribner's Sons, New York, 1974, p. 364.

37. Admission summary: Billie Holiday 8407–W, Federal Reformatory for Women, Alderston, Va.
38. Interview with author, November 1993.
39. Conversation with author, 15 April 1994.
40. *Downbeat*, 1 February 1945.
41. *Metronome*, April 1945.
42. Ibid., June 1945.
43. *Downbeat*, 1 June 1945.
44. Ibid., 15 June 1945.
45. David Courtwright, Herman Joseph and Don Des Jarlais, *Addicts Who Survived (An Oral History of Narcotic Use in America 1923–1965)*, University of Tennessee Press, Knoxville, Tennessee, 1989.
46. *Downbeat*, 15 July 1945.
47. Ibid., 1 August 1945.
48. Interview with author, April 1993.
49. All from *New York Amsterdam News*, 13 October 1945. *Lady Sings the Blues* incorrectly states that Billie Holiday was singing in Washington at the time of her mother's death.
50. Interview with Artie Shaw: John Jeremy Archive. Courtesy National Sound Archive, British Library.

Chapter Nine

1. Interview with Norman Granz, February 1994.
2. File No. 8407–2: Social history Billie Holiday. Federal Reformatory for Women, Alderston, Va.
3. Interview with author, Nov 1993.
4. Arnold Shaw, *52nd Street*, Da Capo Press, New York, 1977, p. 214.
5. *Downbeat*, 29 March 1973, p. 28.
6. *Metronome*, May 1946.
7. Ibid., August 1946.
8. Ibid., January 1947.
9. Milt Gabler interview with Loren Schoenberg, 1992.
10. Interview with author, Nov 1993.
11. *Metronome*, March 1946.
12. *Downbeat*, 11 March 1946.
13. Ibid.
14. *New York Times*, 17 February 1946.
15. Review by Seymour Peck, unprovenanced news clipping, courtesy Institute of Jazz Studies, Rutgers, NJ.
16. *New York Herald Tribune*, 17 February 1946.
17. *New York Amsterdam News*, 13 April 1946.
18. Conversation with author, 15 April 1994. 'I Can't Get Started' appears on Jazz Anthology 30 JA 5110.
19. Red Callender, *Unfinished Dream*, Quartet Books, London, 1985, p. 62.
20. Ibid.
21. *Giants of Jazz*, CD 1025.
22. File No. 14234: District Court of the United States for Eastern District of Pennsylvania: USA *v.* Billie Holiday, 27 May 1947.
23. Interview with author, April 1993.
24. Ibid.
25. John Simmons interview with Patricia Willard, Jazz Oral History Project, Smithsonian Institution, courtesy Institute of Jazz Studies, Rutgers, NJ.
26. Milt Gabler interview with Loren Schoenberg, 1992.
27. *New York Times*, 6 July 1958.
28. *Downbeat*, 15 January 1947, p. 3.
29. *Metronome*, March 1947.
30. File No. 14234: USA *v.* Billie Holiday, 27 May 1947.
31. Thanks to Professor John Morgan MD, Department of Pharmacology, City University of New York Medical School, for his help in preparing this text.
32. File No. 14281: District Court of the United States for the Eastern District of Pennsylvania: USA *v.* Joe Guy, 17 September 1947.
33. Ibid.
34. File No. 14234: USA *v.* Billie Holiday, 27 May 1947.
35. Letter to Margaret Jones, Acting Warden, Federal Reformatory for

Women, Alderston, Va., from E. Fred Sweet, Chief Probation Officer and Violet A. Jersawit, Probation Officer, dated 23 June 1947.

36. Billie Holiday's prison medical records indicate that she was menstruating when admitted, the first time in three to four months. This is a significant sign that she was by no means heavily addicted on admission. The majority of women who inject heroin do not menstruate.

37. Thanks to Professor John Morgan MD for interpreting Billie Holiday's prison medical records for her stay at Alderston.

38. File No. 8407-W: Billie Holiday, Federal Reformatory for Women, Alderston, Va.

39. Letter to Leonard Feather from Billie Holiday dated 19 July 1947, courtesy Institute of Jazz Studies, Rutgers, NJ.

40. Letter to Helen Hironimus from Joe Glaser, 1 August 1947.

41. Interview with author, 21 February 1994.

42. Letter to Ed Fishman from Helen Hironimus, 26 December 1947.

43. Letter to Helen Hironimus from Ed Fishman, 5 January 1948.

44. Letter to Billie Holiday from Ed Fishman, 5 January 1948.

45. *Downbeat*, 8 October 1947.

46. File No. 14281: USA *v.* Joe Guy, 17 September 1947.

47. Letter to Helen Hironimus from Randolph Wise, Chief US Probation Officer, 10 March 1948.

48. *Philadelphia Daily News*, 12 December 1947.

49. Letter to Joe Glaser from Helen Hironimus, 16 March 1948.

50. Letter to Helen Hironimus from Ed Fishman, 21 April 1948.

51. *Downbeat*, 4 June 1947, p. 6.

Chapter Ten

1. *Storyville*, Issue 152, p. 102.

2. Ibid.

3. Ibid.

4. Interview with author, April 1993.

5. Letter to Karl Priebe from Carl Van Vetchen, *Letters of Carl Van Vetchen*, selected and edited by Bruce Kellner, Yale University Press, New Haven, Conn., 1987.

6. Courtesy Van Vetchen Archive, The Beinecke Rare Book and Manuscript Library, Yale University Library, Yale, New Haven, Conn.

7. *Storyville*, Issue 152.

8. Paul Chevigny, *Gigs*, Routledge, New York, 1991, p. 60. Also, all details of Cabaret Card System.

9. *New York Herald Tribune*, 28 April 1948.

10. *New York Amsterdam News*, 1 May 1948.

11. Interview with author, April 1993.

12. *New York Amsterdam News*, 24 April 1948.

13. Interview with author, April 1993.

14. *New York Amsterdam News*, 29 May 1948.

15. Interview with author, April 1993.

16. *Downbeat*, 2 June 1948.

17. *Metronome*, October 1948.

18. Ibid.

19. Letter to Billie Holiday, copied to Joe Glaser from Isabelle Marks, Decca Records, 26 October 1948.

20. *Downbeat*, 1 December 1948.

21. Interview with author, April 1993.

22. *Metronome*, June 1949.

23. Interview with author, April 1993.

24. *New York Amsterdam News*, 29 May 1948.

25. Interview with author, April 1993.

26. *Ebony*, July 1949.

27. Ibid., November 1950.

28. Interview with author, April 1993.

29. Information surrounding Billie's arrest comes from FBI File 12–1720: Billie Holiday.

30. *Ebony*, July 1949.

31. Letter from Billie Holiday to Tallulah Bankhead, 12 January 1955, illustrated in Robert O'Meally, *Lady Day: The Many*

Faces of Billie Holiday, Arcade Publishing, New York, 1991, p. 173.
32. File No. 42483: People of the State of California *v.* Billie Holiday, 31 May 1949.
33. *New York Times*, 5 June 1949.
34. *San Francisco Chronicle*, 4 April 1974.
35. Interview with author, April 1993.
36. Horace Henderson interview with Tom McLusky, Jazz Oral History Project, Smithsonian Institution, courtesy Institute of Jazz Studies, Rutgers.
37. *Downbeat*, 21 October 1949.
38. Ibid., 30 December 1949.
39. Horace Henderson interview with Tom McLusky.
40. ♩ = 69; Decca ♩ = 72.
41. Interview with author, April 1993.
42. Ibid.
43. Horace Henderson interview with Tom McLusky.
44. *New York Amsterdam News*, 29 October 1949.
45. *Downbeat*, 13 January 1950.
46. Interview with author, April 1993.
47. *Tan*, February 1953.
48. Other than the Basie short, *Symphony in Black*, *New Orleans* and several television clips from the 1950s.
49. Interview with author, April 1993.

Chapter Eleven

1. *Downbeat*, 17 November 1950.
2. Anita O'Day with George Eells, *High Times, Hard Times*, Corgi Books, London, 1983.
3. *Downbeat*, 26 January 1951.
4. Jack Chambers, *Milestones 1: The Life and Times of Miles Davis*, University of Toronto Press, 1983, p. 147.
5. *Downbeat*, 26 June 1951.
6. *Philadelphia Inquirer*, 20 March 1951.
7. *Tan*, February 1953.
8. File No. A1850/1959: Surrogates Court, County of New York. Earle Warren Zaidins *v.* Louis McKay. Answering affidavit.
9. Ibid.
10. *Downbeat*, 11 January 1952.
11. Interview with Billie Holiday by Mike Wallace, November 1956. *Giants of Jazz* LP 1001.
12. *Downbeat*, 4 April 1952.
13. Interview with author, February 1994.
14. Liner notes, *The Complete Billie Holiday on Verve*, 517658–2, p. 193.
15. *Metronome*, March 1954.
16. Liner notes, *The Complete Billie Holiday on Verve*, 517658–2, p. 187.
17. *Downbeat*, April 1953.
18. Ibid., 22 October 1952.
19. *Variety*, 19 November 1952.
20. Interview with author, April 1993.
21. Ibid.
22. *Downbeat*, 4 November 1953.
23. *Boston Guardian*, 17 October 1953.
24. *Melody Maker*, 19 December 1953.
25. Interview with author, April 1993.
26. Liner notes, Verve 2610 038.
27. Interview with author, April 1993.
28. Leonard Feather has confirmed the dates of the 1954 Jazz Club USA tour as follows: 11 Jan: Stockholm; 12 Jan: Stockholm; 13 Jan: Uppsala; 14 Jan: Orerbro; 15 Jan: Gothenburg; 16 Jan: Oslo; 17 Jan: Malmo; 18 Jan: Copenhagen; 19 Jan: Hamburg; 20 Jan: Berlin; 21 Jan: Dusseldorf; 22 Jan: Cologne; 23 Jan: Amsterdam; 24 Jan: Brussels; 25 Jan: Frankfurt; 26 Jan: US Camp Baumholder; 27 Jan: Munich; 28 Jan: Stuttgart; 29 Jan: Nuremberg; 30 Jan: Rest Day; 31 Jan: The Hague; 1 Feb: Paris; 2 Feb: Geneva; 3 Feb: Zurich; 4 Feb: Basel. The dates given for the only commercially released recordings of the tour, variously given as 5 January and 23 January 1954 at Cologne, are incorrect. Indeed, Billie gave two concerts on the night of 23 January in Amsterdam, the date given in *The Complete Billie Holiday on Verve* (517 658–2) as the

Cologne date: at 8 p.m. in De Waakzaamheid in Koogaan de Zaan, ten miles north of Amsterdam, and at midnight in Amsterdam's Het Concertgebouw (thanks to Nationaal Jazz Archief, Amsterdam). The Cologne date was 22 January 1954.

29. Interview with author, April 1993.
30. Liner notes, 2610 038.
31. Max Jones, *Talking Jazz*, Macmillan, London, 1987, p. 252.
32. *Jazz Journal*, March 1954.
33. Interview with author, August 1994.
34. Liner notes, *The Complete Billie Holiday on Verve*, 517658–2, p. 188.
35. Phil Schaap Archives.
36. *Melody Maker*, 21 March 1953.
37. Burt Goldblatt, *Newport Jazz Festival*, Dial Press, New York, 1977, p. 8.
38. *Downbeat*, 25 August 1954.
39. Ibid., 3 November 1954.

Chapter Twelve

1. Keith Keller, *Oh, Jess!*, Mayan Music Corp., New York, 1989, p. 126.
2. Liner notes, *The Complete Billie Holiday on Verve*, 517658–2, p. 127.
3. *Downbeat*, 30 November 1955.
4. *Pittsburgh Courier*, 29 December 1956.
5. Interview with author, April 1993.
6. *Downbeat*, 23 January 1957.
7. Author interview with Evelyn Conway, assisted by her daughter Janice Blackwell, 21 May 1994, 31 May 1994 and 6 July 1994.
8. *New York Times*, 21 July 1956.
9. Ibid., 11 November 1956.
10. *Downbeat*, 23 January 1957; *Melody Maker*, 29 December 1956.
11. Interview with author, February 1994.
12. 'One-on-One' is how a drug is cut. One-on-One is equal proportions of drug and the compound it is cut with; Two-on-One is two

proportions of cutting compound to one of the drug and so on. In the instance Mr Waldron refers to, he was being offered a 'One-on-One' cocaine snort.

13. Interview with author, February 1994.
14. *Downbeat*, 6 February 1958.
15. Conversation with author, 21 February 1994.
16. Conversation with author, 25 April 1994.
17. *Melody Maker*, 24 August 1957.
18. Work was beginning to dry up for Billie around this period. Among her main engagements not noted in the text were:
1957, September: *Woolworths Hour* Radio Show
1957, October: Avant Garde, Hollywood
1957, November: Carnegie Hall, benefit for Morningside Community Center
1957, November: Peacock Lane, Hollywood
1958, May: Dean Martin Telethon
1958, June: Loews Sheridan Theater, New York
1958, July: Jazz Festival, Wallingford, Conn
1958, September: Town Hall, New York
1958, September: Columbia Records promotion, Plaza Hotel, New York
1959, April: Academy of Music, Philadelphia
1959, May: Jazz Seville, Hollywood
19. Interview with author, April 1993.
20. File No. 1850/1959: Surrogates Court, County of New York. Earle Warren Zaidins *v.* Louis McKay: Answering affidavit.
21. Ibid.
22. Ibid.
23. Interview with author, July 1994.
24. Ibid.
25. File No. 1850/1959: Surrogates Court, County of New York. Earle Warren Zaidins *v.* Louis McKay: Answering affidavit.

26. Ibid.
27. Ibid.
28. Ibid.
29. Ibid.
30. Ibid.
31. Interview with Ray Ellis: John Jeremy Archive. Courtesy National Sound Archive, British Library.
32. *Downbeat*, 7 August 1958.
33. *Metronome*, October 1958.
34. Interview with Ray Ellis: John Jeremy Archive. Courtesy National Sound Archive, British Library.
35. Interview with author, April 1993.
36. Joe Glaser File: Surrogates Court, County of New York. Exhibit 3: receipt signed by Billie Holiday for advance against future earnings.
37. *New York Times*, 15 September 1958.
38. *Downbeat*, 20 August 1959, p. 21.

Chapter Thirteen

1. Interview with author, March 1993.
2. Jimmy Lyons with Irma Kamin, *Dizzy, Duke, The Count and Me*, California Living Books; 1978, p. 23.
3. *The Complete Billie Holiday on Verve*, 517658–2, Disc 4, track 2.
4. *Downbeat*, 13 November 1958.
5. Liner notes, CBS 62037.
6. File No. 1850/1959: Surrogates Court, County of New York. Earle Warren Zaidins *v.* Louis McKay, Answering affidavit.
7. Postcard from Billie Holiday to Leonard Feather, courtesy Institute of Jazz Studies, Rutgers, NJ.
8. Ole Brask and Dan Morgenstern, *Jazz People*, Da Capo Press, New York, 1993, p. 17.
9. *New York Post*, 23 July 1959.
10. Interview with author, April 1993.
11. Ibid.
12. Ibid.
13. *Downbeat*, 20 August 1959, p. 21.
14. Interview with author, April 1993.
15. Unprovenanced news clipping, courtesy Free Library of Philadelphia.
16. *Boston Guardian*, undated.
17. Unprovenanced news clipping, courtesy Free Library of Philadelphia.
18. *Downbeat*, 20 August 1959, p. 21.
19. Robert O'Meally, *The Many Faces of Lady Day*, Arcade Publishing, New York, 1991, p. 180.
20. Interview with author, 1993.
21. *New York Post*, 4 June 1959.
22. File No. 1859/1959: Surrogates Court, County of New York, The Appraisal under the Estate Tax Law of the Estate of Eleanora McKay, aka Billie Holiday.
23. File No. 1850/1959: Surrogates Court, County of New York. Earle Warren Zaidins *v.* Louis McKay, Answering affidavit.
24. Ibid.: Exhibit B.
25. *Chicago Defender*, 25 July 1959.
26. File No. A1859/1959: Surrogates Court, County of New York. The Appraisal under the Estate Tax Law of the Estate of Eleanora McKay, aka Billie Holiday.
27. File No. A1850: Surrogates Court, County of New York. Earle Warren Zaidins *v.* Louis McKay. Answering affidavit.
28. Ibid.
29. File No. A1859/1959.
30. Unattached file: Surrogates Court, County of New York. Copy of contract between Louis McKay and Earle Warren Zaidins signed 17 July 1959.
31. *New York Times*, 12 February 1984.
32. Interview with author, January 1994.
33. Ibid.
34. File No. 1859/1959: Surrogates Court, County of New York. The Appraisal under the Estate Tax Law of the Estate of Eleanora McKay, aka Billie Holiday.

Epilogue

1. *Morning Call*, 10 August 1991.
2. Interview with author, May 1991.
3. Billie Holiday with William Dufty, *Lady Sings the Blues*, Penguin Books, London, 1984.
4. *Metronome*, February 1957.
5. *The Otis Ferguson Reader*, ed. Dorothy Chamberlain and Robert Wilson, December Press, Highland Park, Illinois, 1982.
6. Liner notes, *The Complete Billie Holiday on Verve*, 517658–2, p. 51.
7. *Jet*, 6 August 1959, p. 59.
8. Interview with author, 21 February 1994.
9. *East West Journal*, March 1973, p. 4.
10. Interview with author, 22 April 1993.

Discography

by Phil Schaap

Billie Holiday's discography is generally acknowledged to fall into three periods, each marked by successive associations with three record companies. Being able to categorize her production in this neat manner is unique in the world of jazz.

Her first recordings, from 1933 to 1942, are housed by Columbia Records (now SONY/CBS). From 1944 to 1950 Billie's recordings were made for Decca (now GRP/MCA). The final large block of recordings, from 1952 to 1957, was produced by Norman Granz, who consolidated them under his Verve label (now part of Polygram), which he founded in 1956.

The Columbia period, actually recorded for Brunswick Records under Teddy Wilson's name and for Vocalion under Billie Holiday's, marked the emergence of the 'Swing-Song' tradition. Unlike earlier vocalists, whose delivery often clashed with the efforts of jazz soloists, Billie took free-wheeling jazz solos, along with the instrumentalists.

The second period, the Deccas of 1944 to 1950, showcased Billie Holiday as 'chanteuse', reflecting the stardom she had achieved in cabaret. Although a number of fine instrumentalists accompany her, their occasional solos are only a backdrop to her singing, whereas the earlier work of musicians such as Lester Young and Buck Clayton was an essential contribution to the greatness of her 'Columbia' sides.

The third period is more controversial than the others. Billie's singing contains moments when her physical decline is so audible that some listeners claim they can actually hear her dying. Although many fans ignore these final recordings, others hear a maturity of interpretation beyond anything the young Billie Holiday was able to achieve. They marvel at her ability to convey her emotional message and her genius at overcoming her physical limitations. Buck Clayton, the star trumpeter of so many of her earlier recordings, was among those who proclaimed these later sides her greatest, and Buck's testimony is impressive.

Norman Granz, who was responsible for Billie's later recordings, was a fan of her earlier Swing-Song tradition and endeavoured to return her to that format, often with the same musicians. He explicitly wished to have her record the cream of the American Popular Songbook in the realm of hi-fi along with longer playing times the format offered, a concept he spread across a broader canvas when he took over the control of Ella Fitzgerald's recording career in 1955.

What is interesting to me about Billie's discography is the story it *doesn't* tell us about her career. It therefore is worth looking a little closer at what is set out here to get a greater understanding of Billie Holiday-as-performing-artist. The Swing-Song tradition represented by the greater proportion of the 'Columbia' period contains two sets of records. On the first, the Teddy Wilson Brunswicks, Billie is truly one of the gang as she takes her chorus along with the instrumentalists. The success of these sides and an apparently huge (*c.* 15,000) advance order for the still as yet unreleased 30 June 1936 session (the 'I Cried For You' date) from the jukebox industry led the parent company to launch a parallel series of sessions on the Vocalion label under Billie's own name. Here, the concept is similar to the Wilson Brunswicks, but Billie sings twice – after all, they are *her* records – and for the most part her vocals now frame a set of instrumental solos.

The Decca recordings document a genuine pop star. They offer much, much, more of Billie Holiday the 'chanteuse' of the cabaret circuit than Lady Day the jammer from Harlem. Billie's first recording for Decca was her biggest hit but was not, in fact, the dawn of a new era but the high spot of her cabaret period, a journey that had begun years before. One could argue, successfully I feel, that Lady Day was always singing jazz, even in cabaret mode, but the important point is that the acclaimed Swing-Song sides were a short-term variation that occurred only in the recording studio. Her 'Columbia' sides – the Brunswicks and Vocalions and the most famous of all her recordings – rarely represented her working situation.

In reality, Billie Holiday's singing career reflects nearly thirty years of singing with the support of instrumental backgrounds that are infrequently brought into the spotlight – a fact revealed by almost all of her live recordings. This helps explain the disappearance of the Swing-Song formula even as it reaches its pinnacle during the Lester Young 'two-of-the same-voice' period. These wonderful Swing-Songs were quickly swallowed up as she enjoyed her first success as a cabaret artist opening Café Society at the top of 1939. The final Columbia dates and the important Commodore sides produced by Milt Gabler, who would later A&R almost all her Decca sides, illustrate this point all too clearly; even when she appeared as a special feature on Norman Granz's Jazz at the Philharmonic, the perennial jam-session-as-concert, she was in fact backed discreetly by the jammers and there are no real solos.

Billie Holiday was never really a Swing-Song singer despite what might seem overwhelming recorded evidence to the contrary. The Swing-Song role came to her by force of circumstance when she got her big break with Teddy Wilson in 1935. This decided the destiny of her recorded output until she became a star in her own right. Then she quickly returned to the real Billie Holiday, a Billie Holiday who sang in front of an ensemble, big or small, that was there to provide accompaniment, with the occasional solo. She did like to jam, and there are of course moments when she sang her choruses in a jam session environment, but it was not until the Norman Granz era that she returned to the rollicking kind of jam session we tend to associate with her early years.

Finally, in introducing the discography, I am struck by the fact that most of Billie Holiday's music still remains in print. Indeed, with the possession of a handful of compact disc box-sets one can thoroughly explore Billie Holiday's recorded career. I would like to have said that, without exception, the newer compact disc issues contain the best sound quality of any issues to date. However, I know I am not alone in expressing my disappointment over the sound quality of the Sony/CBS reissues; even so, there is some consolation in the thought that while they are not good, equally they are not wholly bad.

With the era of the LP now over, it made sense to list in this discography the prime compact disc reissues (which appear in bold typeface) rather than the long playing recordings that are no longer freely available in record shops.

Phil Schaap
New York City, September 1994

ABBREVIATIONS

vo	vocal	b	bass
tp	trumpet	g	guitar
c	cornet	el-g	electric guitar
tb	trombone	bj	banjo
fl	flute	d	drums
cl	clarinet	vib	vibraphone

ss	soprano sax	xylo	xylophone
as	alto sax	arr	arranged by
ts	tenor sax	v	violin
bs	baritone sax	cond	conducted by
p	piano	mc	master of ceremonies
org	organ	orch	orchestra

27 November 1933. BH, vo; with BENNY GOODMAN AND HIS ORCHESTRA.
Charlie Teagarden, Shirley Clay (tp), Jack Teagarden (tb), Benny Goodman (cl),
Art Karle (ts), Joe Sullivan (p), Dick McDonough (g), Artie Bernstein (b),
Gene Krupa (d)
(W152568-3) *Your Mother's Son-In-Law*: Columbia 2856D; CBS 450987-2; CBS
C3K 47724 (1)

4 December 1933. BH, vo; with BENNY GOODMAN AND HIS ORCHESTRA
(same personnel 27 November 1933)
(W152575-1) *Riffin' the Scotch*: rejected/(W152575-2) *Riffin' the Scotch*: rejected

18 December 1933. BH, vo; with BENNY GOODMAN AND HIS ORCHESTRA
(same personnel 27 November 1933), Dean Kincaide (arr)
(W152650-2) *Riffin' the Scotch*: Columbia 2867D; CBS 450987-2

December 1934. BH, vo; with DUKE ELLINGTON AND HIS ORCHESTRA.
Arthur Whetsol, Freddie Jenkins, Cootie Williams (tp), Joe 'Tricky Sam' Nanton,
Lawrence Brown, Juan Tizol (tb), Otto Hardwick (cl, as), Barney Bigard (cl,
ts), Johnny Hodges (as), Harry Carney (bs), Duke Ellington (p), Fred Guy (bj),
Wellman Braud (b), Sonny Greer (d)
'Symphony in Black' – film soundtrack
Blues (Saddest Tale): CBS C3K 47724 (1)
NOTE: Soundtrack was recorded in December 1934, visuals were filmed in March
1935. Why discographers refer to this title as 'Big City Blues' is a mystery. When
introduced on film it is referred to as simply 'Blues'.

2 July 1935. BH, vo; with TEDDY WILSON AND HIS ORCHESTRA. Roy
Eldridge (tp), Benny Goodman (cl-except on d), Ben Webster (ts), Teddy
Wilson (p), John Trueheart (g), John Kirby (b), Cozy Cole (d)
a.(B17766-1) *I Wished on the Moon*: Brunswick 7501; CBS C3K 47724 (1)
b.(B17767-1) *What a Little Moonlight Can Do*: Brunswick 7498; CBS C3K
47724 (1)
c.(B17768-1) *Miss Brown To You*: Brunswick 7501; CBS C3K 47724 (1)
d.(B17769-1) *A Sunbonnet Blue*: Brunswick 7498
All on CBS 450987-2

31 July 1935. BH, vo; with TEDDY WILSON AND HIS ORCHESTRA. Roy
Eldridge (tp), Cecil Scott (cl), Hilton Jefferson (as), Ben Webster (ts), Teddy
Wilson (p), Lawrence Lucie (g), John Kirby (b), Cozy Cole (d)
(B17913-1) *What a Night, What a Moon, What a Girl*: Brunswick 7511
(B17914-1) *I'm Painting the Town Red*: Brunswick 7520
(B17915-1) *It's Too Hot for Words*: Brunswick 7511
All on CBS 450987-2

25 October 1935. BH, vo; with TEDDY WILSON AND HIS ORCHESTRA. Roy Eldridge (tp), Benny Morton (tb), Chu Berry (ts), Teddy Wilson (p), Dave Barbour (g), John Kirby (b), Cozy Cole (d)
(B18196-1) *Twenty-Four Hours a Day*/(B18197-1) *Yankee Doodle Never Went to Town*: Brunswick 7550
(B18199-1) *Eeny Meeny Miney Mo*: Brunswick 7554
(B18209-1) *If You Were Mine*: Brunswick 7554; **CBS 3K 47724 (1)**
All on CBS 450987-2

3 December 1935. BH, vo; with TEDDY WILSON AND HIS ORCHESTRA. Richard 'Dick' Clark (tp), Tom Macey (cl), Johnny Hodges (as), Teddy Wilson (p), Dave Barbour (g), Grachan Moncur (b), Cozy Cole (d)
(B18316-1) *These N' That N' Those*: Brunswick 7577; **CBS 3K 47724 (1)**
(B18318-1) *You Let Me Down*: Brunswick 7581; **CBS 3K 47724 (1)**
(B18319-1) *Spreadin' Rhythm Around*: Brunswick 7581
All on CBS 450987-2

30 January 1936. BH, vo; with TEDDY WILSON AND HIS ORCHESTRA. Gordon 'Chris' Griffin (tp), Rudy Powell (cl), Teddy McRae (ts), Teddy Wilson (p), John Trueheart (g), Grachan Moncur (b), Cozy Cole (d)
(B18612-1) *Life Begins When You're In Love*: Brunswick 7612; **CBS 460060-2; CBS C3K 47724 (1)**

30 June 1936. BH, vo; with TEDDY WILSON AND HIS ORCHESTRA. Jonah Jones (tp), Johnny Hodges (as), Harry Carney (bs*, cl), Teddy Wilson (p), Lawrence Lucie (g), John Kirby (b), Cozy Cole (d)
(B19495-2) *It's Like Reaching For the Moon*: Brunswick 7702; **CBS 4600660-2; CBS C3K 47724 (1)**
(B19496-2) *These Foolish Things**: Brunswick 7699; **CBS 4600660-2; CBS C3K 47724 (1)**
(B19498-1) *I Cried For You**: test pressing known to exist
(B19498-2) *I Cried For You**: Brunswick 7729; **CBS 4600660-2**
(B19499-2) *Guess Who?**: Brunswick 7702; **CBS 4600660-2**

10 July 1936. BH, vo; as BILLIE HOLIDAY AND HER ORCHESTRA. Bunny Berigan (tp), Artie Shaw (cl), Joe Bushkin (p), Dick McDonough (g), Pete Peterson (b), Cozy Cole (d)
(19535-1) *Did I Remember?*/(19536-1) *No Regrets*: Vocalion 3276
(19537-1) *Summertime*/(19538-2) *Billie's Blues*: Vocalion/Okeh 3288; **CBS C3K 47724 (1)**
All on CBS 460060-2

29 September 1936. BH, vo; as BILLIE HOLIDAY AND HER ORCHESTRA. Bunny Berigan (tp), Irving Fazola (cl), Clyde Hart (p), Dick McDonough (g), Artie Bernstein (b), Cozy Cole (d, speech*)
(19971-1) *A Fine Romance*/(19972-1) *I Can't Pretend*: Vocalion 3333
(19973-1) *One, Two, Button Your Shoe**/(19974-2) *Let's Call a Heart a Heart*: Vocalion 3334
All on CBS 460060-2 and CBS C3K 47724 (1)

21 October 1936. BH, vo; with TEDDY WILSON AND HIS ORCHESTRA. Irving 'Mouse' Randolph (tp), Vido Musso (cl), Ben Webster (ts), Teddy Wilson (p), Allan Reuss (g), Milt Hinton (b), Gene Krupa (d)

(B20105-1) *Easy to Love*: Brunswick 7762; **CBS 460060-2**
(B20105-2) *Easy to Love*: **CBS C3K 47724 (1)**
(B20106-2) *With Thee I Swing*: Brunswick 7768; **CBS 460060-2**
(B20107-1) *The Way You Look Tonight*: Brunswick 7762; **CBS 460060-2**
(B20107-2)*The Way You Look Tonight:* **CBS 460060-2**

28 October 1936. BH, vo; with TEDDY WILSON AND HIS ORCHESTRA (same personnel 21 October 1936).
(B20142-1) *Who Loves You?*: Brunswick 7768; **CBS 460820-2**

19 November 1936. BH, vo; with TEDDY WILSON AND HIS ORCHESTRA. Jonah Jones (tp), Benny Goodman as John Jackson (cl), Ben Webster (ts), Teddy Wilson (p), Allan Reuss (g), John Kirby (b), Cozy Cole (d)
(B20290-1) *Pennies from Heaven*: Brunswick 7789; **CBS 460820-2**
(B20290-2) *Pennies from Heaven*: **CBS C3K 47724 (1)**
(B20291-1) *That's Life I Guess*: Brunswick 7789; **CBS 460820-2**
(B20291-2) *That's Life I Guess*: **CBS C3K 47724 (1)**
(B20293-1) *I Can't Give You Anything But Love*: Brunswick 7781; **CBS 460820-2; CBS C3K 47724 (1)**

12 January 1937. BH, vo; as BILLIE HOLIDAY AND HER ORCHESTRA. Jonah Jones (tp), Edgar Sampson (cl*, as), Ben Webster (ts), Teddy Wilson (p), Allan Reuss (g), John Kirby (b), Cozy Cole (d)
(20506-1) *One Never Knows, Does One?**/(20507-2) *I've Got My Love to Keep Me Warm**: Vocalion/Okeh 3431; **CBS C3K 47724 (1)**
(20508-1) *If My Heart Could Only Talk**/(20509-2) *Please Keep Me In Your Dreams**: Vocalion 3440
All on CBS 460820-2

25 January 1937. BH, vo; with TEDDY WILSON AND HIS ORCHESTRA. Buck Clayton (tp), Benny Goodman as John Jackson (cl), Lester Young (ts)), Teddy Wilson (p), Freddie Green (g), Walter Page (b), Jo Jones (d)
(B20568-1) *He Ain't Got Rhythm*: Brunswick 7824; **CBS C3K 47724 (1)**
(B20569-2) *This Year's Kisses*: Brunswick 7824; **CBS C3K 47724 (2)**
(B20570-1) *Why Was I Born?*: Brunswick 7859; **CBS C3K 47724 (2)**
(B20571-1) *I Must Have That Man*: Brunswick 7824; **CBS C3K 47724 (2)**
All on CBS 460820-2

18 February 1937. BH, vo; with TEDDY WILSON AND HIS ORCHESTRA. Henry 'Red' Allen (tp), Cecil Scott (cl, ts), Prince Robinson (cl, ts), Teddy Wilson (p), Jimmy McLin (g), John Kirby (b), Cozy Cole (d)
(B20698-2) *The Mood That I'm In*: Brunswick 7844; **CBS C3K 47724 (2)**
(B20699-2) *You Showed Me the Way*: Brunswick 7840
(B20700-2) *Sentimental and Melancholy*: Brunswick 7844
(B20701-1) *(This is) My Last Affair*: Brunswick 7840; **CBS C3K 47724 (2)**
All on CBS 460820-2

31 March 1937. BH, vo; with TEDDY WILSON AND HIS ORCHESTRA. Cootie Williams (tp), Johnny Hodges (as), Harry Carney (bs* cl), Teddy Wilson (p), Allan Reuss (g), John Kirby (b), Cozy Cole (d)
(B20911-3) *Carelessly**/(B20912-1) *How Could You?**: Brunswick 7867
(B20913-1) *Moanin' Low*: Brunswick 7877; **CBS C3K 47724 (2)**
All on CBS 463333-2

1 April 1937. BH, vo; as BILLIE HOLIDAY AND HER ORCHESTRA. Eddie
Tompkins (tp), Buster Bailey (cl), Joe Thomas (ts), Teddy Wilson (p), Carmen
Mastren (g), John Kirby (b), Alphonse Steele (d)
(20918-1) *Where is the Sun?*: Vocalion 3543; CBS C3K 47724 (2)
(20919-1) *Let's Call the Whole Thing Off*: Vocalion 3520; CBS C3K 47724 (2)
(20920-1) *They Can't Take That Away From Me*: Vocalion 3520
(20921-1) *Don't Know If I'm Coming or Going*: Vocalion 3543; CBS C3K 47724 (2)
All on CBS 463333-2 except (20921-2) *Don't Know If I'm Coming or Going*

11 May 1937. BH, vo; with TEDDY WILSON AND HIS ORCHESTRA. Buck
Clayton (tp), Buster Bailey (cl), Johnny Hodges (as), Lester Young (ts), Teddy
Wilson (p), Allan Reuss (g), Artie Bernstein (b), Cozy Cole (d)
(B21117-2) *Sun Showers*/(B21118-2) *Yours and Mine*: Brunswick 7917
(B21119-1) *I'll Get By*/(B21120-1) *Mean To Me*: Brunswick 7903; CBS C3K
47724 (2)
All on CBS 463333-2 except (B21119-2) *I'll Get By* and (B21120-2) *Mean To Me*

1 June 1937. BH, vo; with TEDDY WILSON AND HIS ORCHESTRA. Buck
Clayton (tp), Buster Bailey (cl), Lester Young (ts), Teddy Wilson (p), Freddie
Green (g), Walter Page (b), Jo Jones (d)
(B21217-1) *Foolin' Myself*/(B21218-2) *Easy Living*: Brunswick 7911
(B21219-2) *I'll Never Be the Same*: Brunswick 7926
All on CBS 463333-2 and CBS C3K 47724 (2)

15 June 1937. BH, vo; as BILLIE HOLIDAY AND HER ORCHESTRA. Buck
Clayton (tp) Edmond Hall (cl), Lester Young (ts), James Sherman (p), Freddie
Green (g), Walter Page (b), Jo Jones (d)
(21249-1) *Me, Myself and I*: CBS C3K 47724 (2)
(21249-2) *Me, Myself and I*: Vocalion 3593; CBS 463333-2
(21250-1) *A Sailboat In the Moonlight*: Vocalion 3605; CBS 463333-2; CBS C3K
47724 (2)
(21251-1) *Born To Love*: Vocalion 3605; CBS 465190-2; CBS C3K 47724 (2)
(21252-1) *Without Your Love*: Vocalion 3593; CBS 465190-2
(21252-2) *Without Your Love*: CBS C3K 47724 (2)

30 June 1937. BH, vo; with COUNT BASIE AND HIS ORCHESTRA. Ed Lewis,
Bobby Moore, Buck Clayton (tp), Dan Minor, George Hunt (tb), Earle
Warren (as), Lester Young, Herschel Evans (ts), Jack Washington (bs), Count
Basie (p), Freddie Green (g), Walter Page (b), Jo Jones (d)
They Can't Take That Away From Me/Swing, Brother, Swing: CBS C3K 47724 (2);
A Touch of Magic DATOM 6
NOTE: Both arranged by Buck Clayton.

13 September 1937. BH, vo; as BILLIE HOLIDAY AND HER ORCHESTRA.
Buck Clayton (tp) Buster Bailey (cl), Lester Young (ts), Claude Thornhill (p),
Freddie Green (g), Walter Page (b), Jo Jones (d)
(21686-1) *Getting Some Fun Out Of Life*: Vocalion 3701
(21687-1) *Who Wants Love?*: Vocalion 3701; CBS C3K 47724 (2)
(21688-1) *Trav'lin' All Alone*/(21689-1) *He's Funny That Way*: Vocalion 3748; CBS
C3K 47724 (2)
All on CBS 465190-2

1 November 1937. BH, vo; with TEDDY WILSON AND HIS ORCHESTRA. Buck Clayton (tp), Prince Robinson (cl), Vido Musso (ts), Teddy Wilson (p), Allan Reuss (g), Walter Page (b), Cozy Cole (d)
(B21982-1) *Nice Work If You Can Get It* /(B21983-1) *Things Are Looking Up*: Brunswick 8015
(B21984-1) *My Man (Mon Homme)*: Brunswick 8008; CBS C3K 47724 (3)
(B21985-1) *Can't Help Lovin' Dat Man*: Brunswick 8008
All on CBS 465190-2

3 November 1937. BH, vo; with COUNT BASIE AND HIS ORCHESTRA. Ed Lewis, Bobby Moore, Buck Clayton (tp), Benny Morton, Dan Minor (tb), Earle Warren (as), Lester Young, Herschel Evans (ts), Jack Washington (bs), Count Basie (p), Eddie Durham (g) Freddie Green (g), Walter Page (b), Jo Jones (d), Buck Clayton (arr)
I Can't Get Started: CBS C3K 47724 (2); Touch of Magic DATOM 6

6 January 1938. BH, vo; with TEDDY WILSON AND HIS ORCHESTRA. Buck Clayton (tp), Benny Morton (tb), Lester Young (ts), Teddy Wilson (p), Freddie Green (g), Walter Page (b), Jo Jones (d)
(B22192-3) *My First Impression Of You*
(B22192-4) *My First Impression Of You*: Brunswick 8053; CBS 465190-2
(B22194-3) *When You're Smiling*: Brunswick 8070; CBS 465190-2
(B22194-4) *When You're Smiling*: Columbia 36208
(B22195-3) *I Can't Believe That You're In Love With Me*: Columbia 36335; CBS C3K 47724
(B22195-4) *I Can't Believe That You're In Love With Me*: Brunswick 8070; CBS 465190-2 (3)
(B22255-1) *If Dreams Come True*: Brunswick 8053; CBS 465190-2 (3)
(B22255-2) *If Dreams Come True*

Probably 12 January 1938. BH, vo; as BILLIE HOLIDAY AND HER ORCHESTRA. Buck Clayton (tp) Benny Morton (tb), Lester Young (ts), Teddy Wilson (p), probably Eddie Durham (el-g), Walter Page (b), Jo Jones (d)
(22281-1) *Now They Call It Swing*
(22281-2) *Now They Call It Swing*: Vocalion 3947; CBS 465190-2
(22282-1) *On the Sentimental Side*
(22282-2) *On the Sentimental Side*: Vocalion 3947; CBS 465190-2
(22283-1) *Back in Your Own Backyard*: Vocalion 4029; CBS 465190-2
(22283-2) *Back in Your Own Backyard*
(22284-2) *When a Woman Loves a Man*: Vocalion 4029; CBS 465190-2; C3K 47724 (3)
NOTE: This recording date has never been precisely pinned down. The closeness of the matrices on this date to the preceding 6 January date suggests 12 January rather than the usual 27 January date given.

11 May 1938. BH, vo; as BILLIE HOLIDAY AND HER ORCHESTRA. Charlie Shavers (tp), Buster Bailey (cl), Babe Russin (ts), Claude Thornhill (p), John Kirby (b), Cozy Cole (d)
(22921-1) *You Go To My Head*: Vocalion 4126; CBS 466313-2; CBS C3K 47724 (3)
(22921-2) *You Go To My Head*
(22922-1) *The Moon Looks Down and Laughs*: Vocalion 4126; CBS 466313-2

(22922-2) *The Moon Looks Down and Laughs*
(22923-2) *If I Were You*/(22924-2) *Forget You If I Can*: Vocalion 4151; **CBS 466313-2**

23 June 1938. BH, vo; as BILLIE HOLIDAY AND HER ORCHESTRA.
Undocumented personnel with tp, cl, ts, p, b, d plus guitar at the end of the session. Author's note: see reference 31, Chapter 6.
(23151-1) *Havin' Myself A Time*: Vocalion 4208; **CBS 466313-2**
(23151-2) *Havin' Myself A Time*: **CBS C3K 47724 (3)**
(23152-1) *Says My Heart*: Vocalion 4208; **CBS 466313-2**
(23151-2) *Says My Heart*: **CBS C3K 47724 (3)**
(23153-1) *I Wish I Had You*
(23153-2) *I Wish I Had You*/(23154-1) *I'm Gonna Lock My Heart*: Vocalion 4238; **CBS 466313-2**
(23154-2) *I'm Gonna Lock My Heart*

24 July 1938. BH, vo; with ARTIE SHAW AND HIS ORCHESTRA. Chuck Peterson, John Best, Claude Bowen (tp), George Arus, Ted Vesely, Harry Rodgers (tb), Artie Shaw (cl), Les Robinson, Hank Freeman (as), Tony Pastor, Ronny Perry (ts), Lester Burness (p), Al Avola (g), Sid Weiss (b), Cliff Leeman (d)
(OA24083-1) *Any Old Time*: Bluebird B7759; **RCA/BMG ND 86274; RCA/BMG 74321101542**

15 September 1938. BH, vo; as BILLIE HOLIDAY AND HER ORCHESTRA.
Buck Clayton (tp) Dicky Wells(tb), Lester Young (cl*,ts), 'Countess' Margaret 'Queenie' Johnson (p), Freddie Green (g), Walter Page (b), Jo Jones (d)
(23467-1) *The Very Thought Of You**: Vocalion 4457; **CBS 466313-2; CBS C3K 47724 (3)**
(23467-2) *The Very Thought Of You**: matrix known to exist
(23468-1) *I Can't Get Started*: Vocalion 4457; **CBS 466313-2**
(23468-2) *I Can't Get Started*
(23469-1) *I've Got a Date With a Dream**
(23469-2) *I've Got a Date With a Dream**/(23470-2) *You Can't Be Mine*: Vocalion 4396; **CBS 466313-2**

31 October 1938. BH, vo; with TEDDY WILSON AND HIS ORCHESTRA.
Harry James (tp), possibly Vernon Brown (tb), Edgar Sampson, Benny Carter (as), Lester Young, Herschel Evans (ts), Teddy Wilson (p), Al Casey (g), Walter Page (b), Jo Jones (d)
(B23642-1) *Everybody's Laughing*/(B23643-1) *Here It Is Tomorrow Again*: Brunswick 8259; **CBS 466313-2**

9 November 1938. BH, vo; with TEDDY WILSON AND HIS ORCHESTRA (personnel as for 31 October 1938, except Benny Morton [tb] in place of Brown)
(B23687-1) *Say It With a Kiss*: Brunswick 8270; **CBS 466313-2**
(B23688-1) *April In My Heart*: Brunswick 8265; **CBS 466313-2**
(B23688-2) *April In My Heart*
(B23689-1) *I'll Never Fail You*: Brunswick 8265; **CBS 466313-2**
(B23690-1) *They Say*
(B23690-2) *They Say*: Brunswick 8270; **CBS 466313-2**

28 November 1938. BH, vo; with TEDDY WILSON AND HIS ORCHESTRA.
Bobby Hackett (c), Trummy Young (tb), Toots Mondello (cl*, as), Ted

Buckner (as), Bud Freeman, Leon 'Chu' Berry (ts), Teddy Wilson (p), Al Casey (g), Milt Hinton (b), Cozy Cole (d)
(B23760-1) *You're So Desirable*: Brunswick 8283; **CBS CK 46180**
(B23760-2) *You're So Desirable*
(B23761-1) *You're Gonna See a Lot Of Me*: Brunswick 8281; **CBS CK 46180**
(B23761-2) *You're Gonna See a Lot Of Me*
(B23762-1) *Hello, My Darling**: Brunswick 8281; **CBS CK 46180**
(B23762-2) *Hello, My Darling**
(B23763-1) *Let's Dream In the Moonlight*
(B23763-2) *Let's Dream In the Moonlight*: Brunswick 8283; **CBS CK 46180**

17 January 1939. BH, vo; with BENNY GOODMAN AND HIS ORCHESTRA. Ziggy Elman, Chris Griffin, Cy Baker (tp), Red Ballard, Vernon Brown (tb), Benny Goodman (cl), Hymie Schertzer, Noni Bernardi (as), Jerry Jerome, Art Rollini (ts), Jess Stacy (p), Ben Heller (g), Harry Goodman (b), Buddy Schutz (d), also Martha Tilton, Johnny Mercer and Leo Watson (vo)
I Cried For You/Jeepers Creepers: **CBS C3K 47724 (3)**

20 January 1939. BH, vo; as BILLIE HOLIDAY AND HER ORCHESTRA. Charlie Shavers (tp) Tyree Glenn (tb), Chu Berry (ts), Sonny White (p), Al Casey (g), John Williams (b), Cozy Cole (d)
(23992-1) *That's All I Ask Of You*: Vocalion 4631; **CBS CK 46180**
(23992-2) *That's All I Ask Of You*
(23993-1) *Dream Of Life*: Vocalion 4631; **CBS CK 46180**

30 January 1939. BH, vo; with TEDDY WILSON AND HIS ORCHESTRA. Roy Eldridge (tp), Ernie Powell (cl*, ts), Benny Carter (as,ts), Teddy Wilson (p), Danny Barker (g), Milt Hinton (b), Cozy Cole (d)
(B24044-1) *What Shall I Say?**/(B24045-1) *It's Easy To Blame the Weather**: Brunswick 8314; **CBS CK 46180**
(B24045-2) *It's Easy To Blame the Weather**: test pressing known to exist
(B24046-1) *More Than You Know*: Brunswick 8319; **CBS CK 46180**
(B24046-2) *More Than You Know*
(B24047-1) *Sugar**: Brunswick 8319; **CBS CK 46180**

21 March 1939. BH, vo; as BILLIE HOLIDAY AND HER ORCHESTRA. Oran 'Hot Lips' Page (tp), Tab Smith (as, ss), Kenneth Hollon, Stanley Payne (ts), Kenneth Kersey (p), Jimmy McLin (g), John Williams (b), Eddie Dougherty (d)
(W24245-1) *You're Too Lovely To Last*: Vocalion 4834; **CBS CK 46180**
(W24245-2) *You're Too Lovely To Last*
(W24246-1) *Under a Blue Jungle Moon*: Vocalion 4786; **CBS CK 46180**
(W24246-2) *Under a Blue Jungle Moon*
(W24247-1) *Everything Happens For the Best*: Vocalion 4786; **CBS CK 46180**
(W24248-1) *Why Did I Always Depend On You?*: Vocalion 4834; **CBS CK 46180**
(W24249-1) *Long Gone Blues*: Columbia 37586; **CBS CK 46180**; **CBS C3K 47724 (3)**

20 April 1939. BH, vo; as BILLIE HOLIDAY AND HER ORCHESTRA. Frankie Newton (tp), Tab Smith (as), Kenneth Hollon, Stanley Payne (ts), Sonny White (p), Jimmy McLin (g), John Williams (b), Eddie Dougherty (d)
(WP24403-A) *Strange Fruit*
(WP24403-B) *Strange Fruit*: Commodore 526; **Commodore CCD 7001**

(WP24404-A) *Yesterdays*: Commodore 527; **Commodore CCD 7001**
(WP24404-B) *Yesterdays* BH, vo; as BILLIE HOLIDAY AND HER ORCHESTRA.
Kenneth Hollon (ts), Sonny White (p), Jimmy McLin (g), John Williams (b), Eddie
Dougherty (d)
(WP24405-A) *Fine and Mellow*: Commodore 526; **Commodore CCD 7001**
(WP24406-A) *I Gotta Right To Sing the Blues*
(WP24406-B) *I Gotta Right To Sing the Blues*: Commodore 527; **Commodore CCD 7001**

5 July 1939. BH, vo; as BILLIE HOLIDAY AND HER ORCHESTRA. Charlie
Shavers (tp), Tab Smith (as, ss), Kenneth Hollon, Stanley Payne (ts), Sonny
White (p), Bernard Addison (g), John Williams (b), Eddie Dougherty (d)
(W24877-A) *Some Other Spring*: Vocalion 5021; **CBS CK 46180; CBS C3K 47724 (3)**
(W24878-A) *Our Love Is Different*: Vocalion 5129; **CBS CK 46180**
(W24879-A) *Them There Eyes*: Vocalion 5021; **CBS CK 47030; CBS C3K 47724 (3)**
(W24880-A) *Swing, Brother, Swing*: Vocalion 5129; **CBS CK 47030**

13 December 1939. BH, vo; with FRANKIE NEWTON AND HIS CAFE
SOCIETY ORCHESTRA. Probably Frankie Newton (tp), Tab Smith, Sonny
Payne (as), Kenneth Hollon (ts), Kenny Kersey (p), Ulysses Livingstone (g),
John Williams (b), Eddie Dougherty (d)
I'm Gonna Lock My Heart

15 December 1939. BH, vo; as BILLIE HOLIDAY AND HER ORCHESTRA.
Buck Clayton, Harry Edison (tp), Earle Warren, Jack Washington (as), Lester
Young (ts), Joe Sullivan (p), Freddie Green (g), Walter Page (b), Jo Jones (d)
(W26341-A) *Night and Day*: Vocalion 5377; **CBS CK 46180**
(W26341-B) *Night and Day*: **CBS C3K 47724 (3)**
(W26342-A) *The Man I Love*: Vocalion 5377; **CBS CK 46180; CBS C3K 47724 (3)**
(W26343-A) *You're Just a No Account*/(W26344-A) *You're a Lucky Guy*: Vocalion 5302; **CBS CK 46180**

29 February 1940. BH, vo; as BILLIE HOLIDAY AND HER ORCHESTRA. Roy
Eldridge (tp), Jimmy Powell, Carl Frye (as), Kermit Scott (ts), Sonny White (p),
Lawrence Lucie (g), John Williams (b), Harold 'Doc' West (d)
(W26572-A) *Ghost Of Yesterday*: Vocalion 5609; **CBS CK 47030**
(W26573-A) *Body and Soul*/(W26574-A) *What Is This Going To Get Us?*: Vocalion 5481; **CBS CK 47030**
(W26575-A) *Falling In Love Again*: Vocalion 5609; **CBS CK 47030**
(W26575-B) *Falling In Love Again*

7 June 1940. BH, vo; as BILLIE HOLIDAY AND HER ORCHESTRA. Roy
Eldridge (tp), Bill Bowen, Joe Eldridge (as), Kermit Scott, Lester Young (ts),
Teddy Wilson (p), Freddie Green (g), Walter Page (b), J C Heard (d)
(W26900-A) *I'm Pulling Through*: Okeh 5991; **CBS CK 47030**
(W26901-A) *Tell Me More*/(W26902-A) *Laughing At Life*: Okeh 5719; **CBS CK 47030**
(W26902-B) *Laughing At Life*
(W26903-A) *Time On My Hands*: Okeh 5991; **CBS CK 47030**

12 September 1940. BH, vo; as BILLIE HOLIDAY AND HER ORCHESTRA.
Roy Eldridge (tp), Don Redman (as, arr), Georgie Auld (as), Don Byas, Jimmy
Hamilton (ts), Teddy Wilson (p), John Collins (g), Al Hall (b), Kenny Clarke (d)
(28617-1) *I'm All For You*: Okeh 5831; **CBS CK 47030**
(28617-2) *I'm All For You*
(28618-1) *I Hear Music*: Okeh 5831; **CBS CK 47030**
(28618-2) *I Hear Music*
(28619-1) *(It's)The Same Old Story*: Okeh 5806; **CBS CK 47030**
(28619-2) *(It's) The Same Old Story*/(28619-) *(It's) The Same Old Story*
(28620-1) *Practice Makes Perfect*: Okeh 5806; **CBS CK 47030**
(28620-2) *Practice Makes Perfect*/(28620-3) *Practice Makes Perfect*

15 October 1940. BH, vo; as BILLIE HOLIDAY WITH BENNY CARTER AND
HIS ALL STAR ORCHESTRA. Bill Coleman (tp), Benny Morton (tb), Benny
Carter (cl*, as, arr), Georgie Auld (ts), Sonny White (p), Ulysses
Livingstone (g), Wilson Myers (b), Yank Porter (d)
(28874-1) *St Louis Blues**: Okeh 6064; **CBS CK 47031**
(28874-2) *St Louis Blues**
(28875-1) *Loveless Love**: Okeh 6064; **CBS CK 47031**
(28875-2) *Loveless Love**

19 December 1940. BH, vo; with WNEW JAM SESSION. 'Hot Lips' Page (tp),
Charlie Barnet, Coleman Hawkins, Lester Young (ts), Teddy Wilson (p),
unknown (g) (b) (d)
The Man I Love

21 March 1941. BH, vo; as BILLIE HOLIDAY AND HER ORCHESTRA. Shad
Collins (tp), Leslie Johnakins, Eddie Barefield (as), Lester Young (ts), Eddie
Heywood (p), John Collins (g), Ted Sturgis (b), Kenny Clarke (d)
(29987-1) *Let's Do It*: Okeh 6134; **CBS CK 47031; CBS C3K 47724 (3)**
(29987-2) *Let's Do It*/(29987-3) *Let's Do It*
(29988-1) *Georgia On My Mind*: Okeh 6134; **CBS CK 47031**
(29988-2) *Georgia On My Mind*/(29988-3) *Georgia On My Mind*/(29988-4) *Georgia
On My Mind*
(29989-1) *Romance In the Dark*: Okeh 6214; **CBS CK 47031**
(29989-2) *Romance In the Dark*/(29989-3) *Romance In the Dark*/(29989-4) *Romance
In the Dark*
(29990-1) *All Of Me*: Okeh 6214; **CBS CK 47031; CBS C3K 47724 (3)** NOTE:
take 3
(29990-2) *All Of Me* NOTE: take 2
(29990-3) *All Of Me* NOTE: take 1; **Phontastic PHONT CD 7669**

9 May 1941. BH, vo; as BILLIE HOLIDAY AND HER ORCHESTRA. Roy
Eldridge (tp), Jimmy Powell, Lester Boone, Ernie Powell (as), Eddie
Heywood (p), Paul Chapman (g), Grachan Moncur (b), Herbert Cowans (d)
(30457-1) *I'm In a Low-Down Groove*: Okeh 6451; **CBS CK 47031**
(30458-1) *God Bless the Child*: Okeh 6270; **CBS CK 47031**
(30458-2) *God Bless the Child*
(30458-3) *God Bless the Child*: **CBS C3K 47724**
(30459-1) *Am I Blue?*: Columbia 37586; **CBS CK 47031**
(30459-2) *Am I Blue?*/(30459-3) *Am I Blue?*
(30460-1) *Solitude*: Okeh 6270; **CBS CK 47031**

June 1941. BH, vo; with MONROE'S UPTOWN HOUSE BAND inc. Floyd 'Horsecollar' Williams (as), unknown (p) (b)
I Cried For You/Fine and Mellow

7 August 1941. BH, vo; as BILLIE HOLIDAY WITH TEDDY WILSON AND HIS ORCHESTRA. Emmett Berry (tp), Jimmy Hamilton (cl), Hymie Schertzer (as), Babe Russin (ts), Teddy Wilson (p), Al Casey (g), John Williams (b), J C Heard (d)
(31002-1) *Jim*: Okeh 6369: **CBS CK 47031**
(31002-2) *Jim*
(31003-1) *I Cover the Waterfront*: Columbia 37493; **CBS CK 47031**
(31004-1) *Love Me Or Leave Me*: Okeh 6369; **CBS CK 47031**
(31005-1) *Gloomy Sunday*: Okeh 6451; **CBS CK 47031**
(31005-2) *Gloomy Sunday*: **CBS C3K 47724 (3)**
(31005-3) *Gloomy Sunday*

10 February 1942. BH, vo; as BILLIE HOLIDAY WITH TEDDY WILSON AND HIS ORCHESTRA. Emmett Berry (tp), Jimmy Hamilton (cl), Hymie Schertzer (as), Babe Russin (ts), Teddy Wilson (p), Gene Fields (g), John Williams (b), J C Heard (d)
(32405-1) *Wherever You Are*: Harmony 1075; **CBS CK 47031**
(32405-2) *Wherever You Are*
(32406-1) *Mandy Is Two*: **CBS CK 47031**
(32407-1) *It's a Sin To Tell a Lie*: Harmony 1075; **CBS CK 47031**
(32408-1) *Until the Real Thing Comes Along*: Columbia 37493; **CBS CK 47031**
(32408-2) *Until the Real Thing Comes Along*: **CBS C3K 47724 (3)**
(32408-1/2) *Until the Real Thing Comes Along*

1 June 1942. BH, vo; with LESTER AND LEE YOUNG ORCHESTRA. Probably: 'Red' Morris Mack (tp), Bumps Myers, Lester Young (ts), Jimmy Rowles (p), Red Callender (b), unknown (g), Lee Young (d)
I Hear Music/Solitude
NOTE: Norman Granz has confirmed to the author that to his best recollection this personnel seems correct.

12 June 1942. BH, vo; with PAUL WHITEMAN AND HIS ORCHESTRA inc. Skip Layton (tb)
(CAP-30-A) *Trav'lin' Light*: Capitol 116; **Blue Note CDP 7 48786-2**
NOTE: An untraced listing published in the booklet to the Billie Holiday Time-Life LP box set states that Lester Young is in Paul Whiteman's reed section for this date.

Late 1942 or early 1943. BH, vo; with HENRY 'RED' ALLEN SEXTET. Henry 'Red' Allen (tp), J C Higginbotham (tb), Don Stovall (as), Alfred Williams (p), Benny Moten (b), Alvin Burroughs (d)
Trav'lin' Light: AFRS Transcription Jubilee 17

18 January 1944. BH, vo; at FIRST ESQUIRE ALL AMERICAN JAZZ CONCERT (METROPOLITAN OPERA HOUSE JAM SESSION) ESQUIRE ALL-AMERICAN ALL-STARS. Roy Eldridge (tp) Jack Teagarden (tb), Barney

Bigard (cl), Coleman Hawkins (ts), Art Tatum (p), Al Casey (g), Oscar Pettiford (b), Sidney Carlett (d)

Do Nothin' Till You Hear From Me: V-Disc 672; **Jazz Anthology 550212; A Touch of Magic DATOM 6**

I Love My Man Billie's Blues: Navy V-Disc 28; Army V-Disc 248; **A Touch of Magic DATOM 6**

I'll Get By: V-Disc 672; **Jazz Anthology 550212; Storyville STCD 4103**

Do Nothing Till You Hear From Me: **Storyville STCD 4103**

25 March 1944. BH, vo; as BILLIE HOLIDAY WITH EDDIE HEYWOOD AND HIS ORCHESTRA. Doc Cheatham (tp), Vic Dickenson (tb), Lem Davis (as), Eddie Heywood (p, arr), Teddy Walters (g), John Simmons (b), Sidney Catlett (d)

(A4742-TK1) *How Am I To Know?*/(A4742-1) *How Am I To Know?*/(A4742-2) *How Am I To Know?*/(A4742-2/1/2) *How Am I To Know?*

(A4742-3) *How Am I To Know?*: Commodore 569; **Commodore CCD 7001**

(A4743-TK1) *My Old Flame*/(A4743-TK2) *My Old Flame*/(A4743-2) *My Old Flame*

(A4743-1) *My Old Flame*: Commodore 585; **Commodore CCD 7001**

(A4744-1) *I'll Get By*: Commodore 553; **Commodore CCD 7001**

(A4744-2) *I'll Get By*

(A4745(-TK1))*I Cover the Waterfront*/(A4745-TK2) *I Cover the Waterfront*/(A4745-TK2/(TK1)) *I Cover the Waterfront*/(A4745-1) *I Cover the Waterfront*

(A4745-2) *I Cover the Waterfront*: Commodore 559; **Commodore CCD 7001**

1 April 1944. BH vo; as BILLIE HOLIDAY WITH EDDIE HEYWOOD AND HIS ORCHESTRA. Doc Cheatham (tp), Vic Dickenson (tb), Lem Davis (as), Eddie Heywood (p, arr), John Simmons (b), Sidney Catlett (d)

(A4750-TK1) *I'll Be Seeing You*

(A4750-1) *I'll Be Seeing You*: Commodore 553; **Commodore CCD 7001**

(A4750-2) *I'll Be Seeing You*/(A4750-2/3(TK1)) *I'll Be Seeing You*

(A4751-TK1) *I'm Yours*/(A4751-2) *I'm Yours*

(A4751-1) *I'm Yours*: Commodore 585; **Commodore 7001**

(A4752-TK1) *Embraceable You*/(A4752-1) *Embraceable You*

(A4752-2) *Embraceable You*/(A4753-1)*As Time Goes By*: Commodore 7520; **Commodore CCD 7001**

(A4753-2) *As Time Goes By*

1 April session continues. BH, vo; as BILLIE HOLIDAY WITH THE EDDIE HEYWOOD TRIO. Eddie Heywood (p, arr), John Simmons (b), Sidney Catlett (d)

(A4754-TK2) *He's Funny That Way*/(A4754-1) *He's Funny That Way*

(A4755-TK1) *Lover, Come Back To Me*/(A4755-1) *Lover Come Back To Me*

(A4754-3) *He's Funny That Way*/(A4754-TK2A) *He's Funny That Way*

(A4754-2) *He's Funny That Way*: Commodore 569; **Commodore CCD 7001**

(A4755-2) *Lover, Come Back To Me*: Commodore 559; **Commodore CCD 7001**

(A4756-1) *I Love My Man (Billie's Blues)*/(A4757-1) *On the Sunny Side Of the Street*: Commodore 614; **Commodore CCD 7001**

(A4755-3) *Lover Come Back To Me*

(A4756-2) *I Love My Man (Billie's Blues)*/(A4756-3) *I Love My Man (Billie's Blues)*

24 May 1944. BH, vo; with APOLLO THEATRE HOUSE BAND.
Do Nothin' Till You Hear From Me

25 June 1944. BH, vo; as JAM SESSION WITH BILLIE HOLIDAY. Roy Eldridge, Charlie Shavers (tp), Benny Morton, Vic Dickenson (tb), Edmond Hall (cl), Ben Webster (ts), Art Tatum (p), Al Casey (g), Slam Stewart (b), Arthur Trappier (d)
Fine and Mellow/All of Me

4 October 1944. BH, vo; with TOOTS CAMARATA AND HIS ORCHESTRA. Russ Case (tp), Hymie Schertzer, Jack Cressey (as), Larry Binyon, Paul Ricci (ts), Dave Bowman (p), Carl Kress (g), Haig Stephens (b), Johnny Blowers (d), six strings, Toots Camarata (arr, cond)
(72404-A) *Lover Man (Oh, Where Can You Be?)*: Decca 23391
(72405-A) *No More*: Decca 23483
(72405-B) *No More*
All on GRP 26012

8 November 1944. BH, vo; with TOOTS CAMARATA AND HIS ORCHESTRA. Russ Case (tp), Hymie Schertzer, Jack Cressey (as), Larry Binyon, Dave Harris (ts), Dave Bowman (p), Carl Kress (g), Haig Stephens (b), George Wettling (d), six strings, Toots Camarata (arr, cond)
(72497-A) *That Ole Devil Called Love*: Decca 23391
(72498-A) *Don't Explain*/(72499-A) *Big Stuff*
All on GRP 26012

1–7 December 1944. BH, vo; with APOLLO THEATRE HOUSE BAND.
I'll Be Seeing You

17 December 1944. BH, vo; as BILLIE HOLIDAY WITH DUKE ELLINGTON AND HIS ORCHESTRA SECOND ESQUIRE ALL AMERICAN JAZZ CONCERT (THE 2ND ESQUIRE CONCERT). Rex Stewart (c), Shelton Hemphill, Taft Jordan, Cat Anderson, Ray Nance (tp), Joe 'Tricky Sam' Nanton, Lawrence Brown, Claude Jones (tb), Jimmy Hamilton (cl, ts), Johnny Hodges, Otto Hardwick (as), Al Sears (ts), Harry Carney (bs), Duke Ellington(p) Fred Guy (g), Junior Raglin (b), Hillard Brown (d), Danny Kaye, Jerome Kern (mc)
I Cover the Waterfront

12 February 1945. BH, vo; with JAZZ AT THE PHILHARMONIC. Joe Guy or possibly Howard McGhee (tp), possibly (tb), Willie Smith (as), Illinois Jacquet, Wardell Gray (ts), possibly Charlie Ventura, (ts), possibly Milt Raskin* (p), possibly Dave Barbour (g), Charles Mingus* (b), Davie Coleman (d)
Body and Soul/Strange Fruit*: **Verve 517658-2**

14 August 1945. BH, vo; as BILLIE HOLIDAY WITH BOB HAGGART AND HIS ORCHESTRA. Joe Guy (tp), Bill Stegmeyer (as), Hank Ross, Armand Camgros (ts), Stan Webb (bs), Sammy Benskin (p), Tiny Grimes (g), Bob Haggart (b, cond, arr on c and d), Specs Powell (d), Morris Leftkowitz, Frank Siefiels, George Serloff, Leo Kruczek, Charles Jaffe (v), Armaud Kaproff (viola), Toots Camarata (arr on a and b)
a.(W73006-A) *Don't Explain*: Decca 23565
b.(W73007-A) *Big Stuff*
c.(W73008-A) *You Better Go Now*: Decca 23483
d.(W73009-A) *What Is This Thing Called Love?*: Decca 23565
All on GRP 26012

15 December 1945. BH, vo; as BILLIE HOLIDAY WITH ORAN 'HOT LIPS'
PAGE AND THE APOLLO THEATRE HOUSE BAND. Oran 'Hot Lips'
Page (tp), unknown personnel.
Fine and Mellow/All Of Me
All on Storyville STCD 4103

22 January 1946. BH, vo; as BILLIE HOLIDAY WITH BILL STEGMEYER
AND HIS ORCHESTRA. Gordon Griffin, Joe Guy (tp), Bill Stegmeyer (as, cond),
Hank Ross, Bernie Kaufman, Armaud Camgros (ts), Joe Springer (p), Tiny
Grimes (g), John Simmons (b), Sidney Catlett (d), four strings
(W73300-A) *Good Morning Heartache*: Decca 23676
(W73301) *No Good Man*
(W73301-A) *No Good Man*: Decca 23676
unnumbered *Big Stuff* (false start and chatter)
unnumbered *Big Stuff*
All on GRP 26012

13 March 1946. BH, vo; as BILLIE HOLIDAY AND HER ORCHESTRA. Joe
Guy (tp), Joe Springer (p), Tiny Grimes (g), Billy Taylor (b), Kelly Martin (d)
(W73440-A) *Big Stuff*: Decca 23463; **GRP 26012**

9 April 1946. BH, vo; as BILLIE HOLIDAY WITH BILLY KYLE AND HIS
TRIO. Joe Guy (tp), Billy Kyle (p), Jimmy Shirley (g), Thomas Barney (b), Kenny
Clarke (d)
(W73497) *Baby, I Don't Cry Over You*
(W73497-A) *Baby, I Don't Cry Over You*: Decca 23957
(W73498) *I'll Look Around*
(W73498-A) *I'll Look Around*: Decca 23957
All on GRP 26012

3 June 1946. JAZZ AT THE PHILHARMONIC CONCERT.
NOTE: I now believe that Billie Holiday played two sets with different personnel
at this Jazz At the Philharmonic concert, given at Carnegie Hall on Monday, 3
June 1946. For the CD Set 'The Complete Billie Holiday on Verve 1945–
1959', I had strongly suggested that the set of 'I Cried For You' and 'He's Funny
That Way' hailed from the preceding Monday's 27/5/46 JATP concert. Both
concerts were broadcast live on WNYC, the Big Apple's municipal radio station.
A newly discovered acetate of the 3 June 1946 concert has the announcer
acknowledging Lady's just performed set. His description matches the four tune
set which I had accurately attributed to the 3/6/46 JATP event. This
Announcer then states that it is possible that Billie Holiday will come back for
another set. I believe that this clue provides the key and that Billie Holiday
did return to the Carnegie Hall stage that night for the 3 tune set with different
personnel. Hence my new listings here and in a more recent Verve CD Set of
complete JATP recordings. I had always been troubled by the absence of
Holiday's name in contemporary documents relating to the 27/5/46 concert,
but I also knew through Leonard Feather's 10/6/46 *Melody Maker* review that
both sets had already happened as his column went to bed. The WNYC
broadcast announcement on the newly uncovered 3/6/46 concert clinched a
decision to go with one date for seemingly two different concert performances.

BH, vo; with Joe Guy (tp), Georgie Auld (as), Illinois Jacquet, Lester Young and/
or maybe Coleman Hawkins (ts), Ken Kersey or Joe Springer (p), Tiny

Grimes (g), Al McKibbon or Lloyd Trotman (b), J C Heard or Eddie Nicholson (d)

NOTE: The number of saxophonists on stage and playing *and* their identities is problematic. Again using the newly uncovered acetate one can presume that Lester Young is *not* there. One can also hear an alternation of players – Georgie Auld might replace Hawkins after 'The Man I Love' – and Buck Clayton might be on stage and playing trumpet in addition to Joe Guy.

First set:

The Man I Love/Gee Baby, Ain't I Good To You/All Of Me/Billie's Blues
All on Verve 517658-2

Second set:

Buck Clayton (tp), Coleman Hawkins, Illinois Jacquet, Lester Young (ts), Joe Springer (p), Tiny Grimes (g), Al McKibbon or Lloyd Trotman (b), Eddie Nicholson (d)

I Cried For You/Fine and Mellow/He's Funny That Way
All on Verve 517658-2

NOTE: Whether this is solely a 3 June 1946 recording or both 27/5/46 and 3/6/46, it is not, apparently, Billie Holiday's Carnegie Hall debut. Photographic evidence currently on view at Carnegie Hall itself (Fall 1994) suggests that Billie Holiday sang at the 1944 Fats Waller Memorial at Carnegie Hall.

September/October 1946. BH, vo; film soundtrack of 'New Orleans'.
NOTE: Pre recording began 11 September 1946.
BH, vo; Charlie Beal (p)
(TMX27) *Do You Know What It Means To Miss New Orleans*: **Giants of Jazz GOJCD 1025**

BH, vo; with LOUIS ARMSTRONG AND HIS HOT SIX. Louis Armstrong (tp), Kid Ory (tb), Barney Bigard (cl), Charlie Beal (p), Bud Scott (g), Red Callender (b), Zutty Singleton (d)
(TMS?) *Do You Know What It Means to Miss New Orleans*/(TMX84) *Farewell to Storyville* (plus choir): **Giants of Jazz GOJCD 1025; Rare CD02**

BH vo; with LOUIS ARMSTRONG AND HIS ORCHESTRA. Louis Armstrong, Robert Butler, Louis Gray, Fats Ford, Ed Mullins (tp), Russell 'Big Chief' Moore, Waddet Williams, Nat Allen, James Whitney (tb), Don Hill, Amos Gordon (as), Joe Garland, John Sparrow (ts), Ernest Thompson (bs), Earl Mason (p), Elmer Warner (g), Arvell Shaw (b), Edmond McConney (d)
(TMX?) *The Blues Are Brewin'*: **Giants of Jazz GOJCD 1025**

7 October 1946. BH, vo; with JAZZ AT THE PHILHARMONIC. Probably Howard McGhee or Buck Clayton (tp), Trummy Young*(tb), probably Illinois Jacquet or Flip Phillips(ts), Kenny Kersey (p), Barney Kessell (g), Charlie Drayton (b), Jackie Mills (d)
Trav'lin' Light/*He's Funny That Way*: **Verve 517658-2**
NOTE: The most recent release on the Verve Complete JATP CD box set attempts a speed correction to this long issued material.

27 December 1946. BH, vo; with JOHN SIMMONS AND HIS ORCHESTRA. Rostelle Reese (tp), Lem Davis (as), Bob Dorsey (ts), Bobby Tucker (p), John Simmons (b, cond), Denzil Best (d)
(W73767-CH) *The Blues Are Brewin'*: Decca 48259

(W73768) *Guilty*/(W73768) *Guilty* (breakdown and chatter)/(W73768-CH) *Guilty*
All on GRP 26012

13 January 1947. BH, vo; with Teddy Wilson (p).
The Man I Love: **Storyville STCD 4103**

8 February 1947. BH vo; with LOUIS ARMSTRONG CARNEGIE HALL
CONCERT BILLIE HOLIDAY WITH LOUIS ARMSTRONG AND HIS
ORCHESTRA. Louis Armstrong (vo), Sidney Catlett (d), and probably Ed
Mullins, Chiefy Scott, Thomas Grinder, Bob Butler (tp), Russell 'Big Chef'
Moore, James Whitney, Alton 'Slim' Moore (tb), Arthur Dennis, Amos
Gordon (as), Lucky Thompson, Joe Garland (ts), John Sparrow (bs), Earl
Mason (p), Elmer Warner (g), Arvell Shaw (b)
(JB359) *Do You Know What It Means To Miss New Orleans*: V-Disc 760; **A Touch
of Magic DATOM 6**

BH vo; with probably Bobby Tucker (p)
(JB361) *Don't Explain*: V-Disc 771; **A Touch of Magic DATOM 6**

13 February 1947. BH, vo; with BOB HAGGART AND HIS ORCHESTRA. Billie
Butterfield (tp), Bill Stegmeyer (cl, as) Toots Mondello, Al Klink (as), Hank
Ross, Art Drellinger (ts), Bobby Tucker (p), Dan Perry (g), Bob Haggart (b,
cond), Norris 'Bunny' Shawker (d)
(W73792-CH) *Deep Song*: Decca 24138
(W73793-CH) *There Is No Greater Love*: Decca 23853
(W73794-CH) *Easy Living*: Decca 24138
(W73795) *Solitude*
(W73795-CH) *Solitude*: Decca 23853
All on GRP 26012

24 March 1947. BH, vo; with JAZZ AT THE PHILHARMONIC. Bobby
Tucker (p)
*You Better Go Now/You're Driving Me Crazy/There Is No Greater Love/I Cover the
Waterfront*
All on Verve 517658-2

7 July 1948. BH, vo; with LIONEL HAMPTON AND HIS ORCHESTRA inc.
Jimmy Nottingham, Teddy Buchner, Wendell Culley, Leo Sheppard, Duke
Garrette (tp), Lester Bass, James Wormick, Britt Woodman, Sonny Craven (tb),
Ben Kynard (cl), Bobby Plater (as), Billy Williams, John Sparrow (ts), Charlie
Fowlkes (bs), Lionel Hampton (vib), Bobby Tucker (p), Wes Montgomery (g),
Charles Mingus (b), Earl Walker (d)
I Cover the Waterfront

30 July 1948. BH, interview on Turn Back the Turntable

22 October 1948: session set up by Decca for 2pm. Musicians hired,
arrangements commissioned but BH failed to show up. Full costs of aborted
date charged to her royalty account.

10 December 1948. BH, vo; with BOBBY TUCKER AND HIS TRIO. Bobby
Tucker (p), John Levy (b), Denzil Best (d), Plus Mundell Lowe* (g), the

Stardusters* (mixed chorus of perhaps six voices including Johnny Parker who was known as 'Johnny Eager')
(W74650-CH) *Weep No More**/(W74651-CH) *Girls Were Made To Take Care Of Boys**: Decca 24551
(W74652-CH) *(I Loves You) Porgy*/(W74653) *My Man (Mon Homme)*/(W74653-CH) *My Man (Mon Homme)*: Decca 24638
All on GRP 26012

8 January 1949. BH, interview over station KQW, Los Angeles.

Unknown date 1949. BH, vo; at BABS GONZALES PARTY with unknown (p), plus other instruments at very end of each number.
That Ole Devil Called Love/I'll Be Seeing You
NOTE: The recordist and presumably one of the horns is trumpeter Ed 'Tiger' Lewis (born 14/1/25).

2 June 1949. BH, vo; with Neal Hefti (tp), Herbie Harper (tb), Herbie Stewart (cl, ts), Jimmy Rowles (p), Iggy Shevak (b), Blinkie Garner (d)
My Man
Miss Brown To You/Lover Man/I Wonder Where Our Love Has Gone/Them There Eyes/ I Love My Man (Billie's Blues)/(You Ain't Gonna Bother Me) No More/Good Morning Heartache: **Bandstand BDCD 1511**
You're Drivin' Me Crazy
Maybe You'll Be There: **Bandstand BDCD 1511**
All on Storyville STCD 4103
Strange Fruit

17 August 1949. BH, vo; with BUSTER HARDING AND HIS ORCHESTRA. Jimmy Nottingham, Buck Clayton, Emmett Berry (tp), Dickie Wells, George Mattews (tb) Rudy Powell, George Dorsey (as), Lester Young, Joe Thomas (ts), Sol Moore (bs), Horace Henderson (p), Mundell Lowe (g), George Duvivier (b), Shadow Wilson (d), Buster Harding (cond)
(W75147) *'Tain't Nobody's Business If I Do*
(W75147-CH) *'Tain't Nobody's Business If I Do*/(W75148-CH) *Baby Get Lost*: Decca 24726
All on GRP 26012

27 August 1949. BH, vo; unknown band. Radio broadcast.
The Man I Love/All Of Me/Lover Man

27 August 1949. BH, vo; with the EDDIE CONDON FLOOR SHOW with Oran 'Hot Lips' Page (tp), Horace Henderson (p), Jack Lesberg (b), George Wettling (d)
Billie's Blues (I Love My Man): **Bandstand BDCD 1511**
Keeps On a Rainin': **Bandstand BDCD 1511: Rare CD 02**
Lover Man

27 August 1949. BH, vo; with the Art Ford Television Show with Oran 'Hot Lips' Page (tp), Horace Henderson (p) and unknown (g, b, d)
Them There Eyes
Detour Ahead: **Bandstand BDCD 1511**
Lover Man
I Cover the Waterfront: **Bandstand BDCD 1511**

Billie Holiday Interviewed by Art Ford
All Of Me: **Bandstand BDCD 1511**

29 August 1949. BH, vo; with SY OLIVER AND HIS ORCHESTRA. Bernie
Privin, Tony Faso, Dick Vance (tp), Henderson Chambers, Mort Bullman (tb),
Eddie Barefield (cl, bs), George Dorsey, Johnny Mince (as), Budd Johnson,
Freddie Williams (ts), Horace Henderson (p), Everett Barksdale (g), George
Duvivier (b), Cozy Cole (d), Sy Oliver (arr, cond)
(W75203-CH) *Keeps On a Rainin'*/(W75204-CH) *Them There Eyes*: Decca 27145;
GRP 26012

3 September 1949. BH, vo; with the EDDIE CONDON FLOOR SHOW. Wild
Bill Davison (c on c and d), Cutty Cutshall (tb on c and d), Peanuts Hucko (cl
on a , c and d) Ernie Caceres (bs on c and d), Horace Henderson (p), Eddie
Condon (g on a, c and d), Jack Lesberg (b), George Wettling (d on a, c and d).
a. *Fine and Mellow*/b. *(I Loves You) Porgy*/c. *Them There Eyes*/d. *I Love My Man
(Billie's Blues)* – *Ole Miss*

8 September 1949. BH, vo; with SY OLIVER AND HIS ORCHESTRA. Lester
'Shad' Collins, Buck Clayton, Bobby Williams (tp), George Stevenson,
Henderson Chambers (tb), George Dorsey, Pete Clark (as), Budd Johnson,
Freddie Williams (ts), Dave McRae (bs), Horace Henderson (p), Everett
Barksdale (g), Joe Benjamin (b), Wallace Bishop (d), Sy Oliver (cond)
(W75241-CH) *Do Your Duty*: Decca 48259; **GRP 26012**
(W75242-CH) *Gimme a Pigfoot and a Bottle Of Beer*: Decca 24947; **GRP 26012**

30 September 1949. BH, vo; with LOUIS ARMSTRONG AND WITH SY
OLIVER AND HIS ORCHESTRA. Bernie Privin (tp), Sid Cooper, Johnny
Mince (as), Art Drellinger, Pat Nizza (ts), Billy Kyle (p), Everett Barksdale (g),
Joe Benjamin (b), Jimmy Crawford (d), Louis Armstrong, Sy Oliver (arr, cond)
(W75342-CH) *You Can't Lose a Broken Heart*/(W75343-CH) *My Sweet Hunk O'
Trash*: Decca 24785
(W75344-CH) *Now Or Never*: Decca 24947 (minus Armstrong)
All on GRP 26012

19 October 1949. BH, vo; with GORDON JENKINS AND HIS ORCHESTRA.
Bobby Hackett (tp), Milt Yaner (cl, as), John Fulton (fl, cl, ts), Bernie
Leighton (p), Tony Mottola (g), Jack Lesberg (b), Norris 'Bunny' Shawker (d),
plus five strings, Gordon Jenkins (arr, cond)
(W75421-CH) *You're My Thrill*/(W75422-CH) *Crazy He Calls Me*: Decca 24796
(W75423-CH) *Please Tell Me Now*/(W75424-CH) *Somebody's On My Mind*: Decca
24857
All on GRP 26012

Possibly late 1949. BH, vo; with PERCY FAITH ORCHESTRA
You'd Better Go Now: **Storyville STCD 4103**

8 March 1950. BH vo; with Dick 'Dent' Eckles (fl*, ts), Charles La Vere (p),
Robert 'Bob' Bain (g), Lou Butterman (b), Nick Fatool (d), David Friscina,
Joseph Quadri (v), Maurice Perlmutter (viola), Kurt Reher (cello), The Gordon
Jenkins Singers (chorus), Gordon Jenkins (arr), Fred Neff (orch manager)
(L5416-CH) *God Bless the Child**/(L5417-CH) *This Is Heaven To Me*: Decca 24972;
GRP 26012

24 May 1950. BH, vo; with APOLLO THEATRE HOUSE BAND.
You're My Thrill

August 1950. BH, vo; with COUNT BASIE AND HIS SEXTET. Clark Terry (tp),
Boniface 'Buddy' DeFranco (cl), Wardell Gray (ts), Count Basie (p), Freddie
Green (g), Jimmy Lewis (b), Gus Johnson (d)
Count Basie Universal film short – soundtrack
God Bless the Child/ Now Baby Or Never (Now Or Never)
NOTE: Marshal Royal (cl) appears on film.

25 September 1950. BH, vo; with unidentified big band on (i) and
unidentified (p) and (b) on (ii)
(i) *You Gotta Show Me*/(ii) *Crazy He Calls Me*

29 April 1951. BH, vo; with TINY GRIMES SEXTET. Unknown sax., Bobby
Tucker (p), Tiny Grimes (g), unknown (b) and (d).
(WOR1681) *Be Fair To Me*: Aladdin 3094
(WOR1682) *Rocky Mountain Blues*/(WOR1683) *Blue Turning Grey Over You*: Aladdin 3102
(WOR1684) *Detour Ahead*: Aladdin 3094
All on Blue Note CDP 7 48786-2
NOTE: The saxophonist is not Heywood Henry. He has listened to these records
with me on two separate occasions, in the 1970s and 1990s and has confirmed that
it is not his style. The player concerned does not concentrate on baritone saxophone,
Heywood Henry's main instrument, and his style is certainly not Heyward Henry's;
aurally then it is more than clear that it is not Henry and then we have the artist
himself denying he is on the session.

29–31 October 1951. BH, vo; with Buster Harding (p), John Felds (b), Marquis
Foster (d), plus guest star Stan Getz*(ts)
He's Funny That Way: **Jazz Door 1215; Rare CD02**
Billie's Blues (I Love My Man)
Ain't Nobody's Business If I Do/*You're Driving Me Crazy***: **Jazz Door 1215**
*Lover Come Back To Me**/*Billie's Blues (I Love My Man)*
*Lover Man/Them There Eyes/My Man/I Cover the Waterfront/Crazy He Calls Me/
Lover Come Back To Me/Detour Ahead/Strange Fruit/Ain't Nobody's Business If I Do/
All Of Me/(I Loves You) Porgy/Miss Brown To You*: **Jazz Door 1215**
Miss Brown To You
All on Fresh Sounds FSR-CD 151

Late spring 1952. BH, vo; with Charlie Shavers* (tp), Flip Phillips(ts), Oscar
Peterson (p), Barney Kessel (g), Ray Brown (b), Alvin Stoller (d)
(YBC764-3) *East Of the Sun**: Clef 89005
(YBC765-1) *Blue Moon**/(YBC766-3) *You Go To My Head*: Clef 89004
(YBC767-5) *You Turned the Tables On Me*/(YBC768-1) *Easy To Love**: Clef 89003
(YBC769-3) *These Foolish Things*/(YBC770-3) *I Only Have Eyes For You**: Clef
89002
(YBC771-1) *Solitude*: Clef 89005
All on Verve 517658-2

Late spring 1952. BH, vo; with Charlie Shavers*(tp), Flip Phillips(ts), Oscar
Peterson (p), Barney Kessel (g), Ray Brown (b), Alvin Stoller (d)
(YBC784-1) *Everything I Have Is Yours*

(YBC786-4) *Moonglow**
(YBC787-3) *Tenderly**: Clef 89064
(YBC788-2) *If the Moon Turns Green**: Clef 89108
(YBC789-3) *Remember**: Clef 89096
(YBC790-1) *Autumn In New York* (78 take)
(YBC790-7) *Autumn In New York*: Clef 89108 (LP take)

BH vo; with Oscar Peterson (p)
(YBC785-4) *Love For Sale*
NOTE: There is no alternative to 'Remember' on Clef 89096.

Possibly late July 1952. BH, vo; with APOLLO THEATRE HOUSE BAND
My Man

Probably 27 July 1952. BH, vo; as BILLIE HOLIDAY AND HER LADS OF
    JOY. Joe Newman* (tp), Paul Quinichette (ts), Oscar Peterson (p, org), Freddie
    Green (g), Ray Brown (b), Gus Johnson (d)
(YBC839-6) *My Man**: Clef 89089
(YBC840-4) *Lover Come Back To Me**: Clef 89037
(YBC841-3) *Stormy Weather**: Clef 89064
(YBC842-2) *Yesterdays*: Clef 89037
(YBC843-2) *He's Funny That Way**: Clef 89089
(YBC844-3) *I Can't Face the Music**: Clef 89096
All on Verve 517658-2

14 November 1952. BH, vo; at DUKE ELLINGTON 25TH ANNIVERSARY
    CONCERT with Jimmy Hamilton (cl), Ray Nance (v), Buster Harding (p), John
    Fields (b), Marquis Foster (d)
*Lover Man/My Man/Miss Brown To You/Easy Living/What A Little Moonlight Can
Do/Tenderly/Strange Fruit*
Fine and Mellow/I Cover the Waterfront/Lover Come Back To Me: **Rare CD 02**
What a Little Moonlight Can Do/My Man/Fine and Mellow

10 December 1952. BH, vo; with BUSTER HARDING AND HIS ORCHESTRA
    with Tony Scott (cl), Buster Harding (p, cond), other unknown personnel
Tenderly

16 October 1953. BH, vo; on the 'Comeback Story' with probably Carl
    Drinkard (p), Jimmy Raney (g), unknown (b), Peter Littman (d)
The Comeback Story/God Bless the Child

Late October 1953. BH, vo; with Carl Drinkard (p), Jimmy Woode (b), Peter
    Littman (d)
*I Cover the Waterfront/Too Marvelous For Words/(I Loves You) Porgy/Them There Eyes/
Willow Weep For Me/I Only Have Eyes For You/You Go To My Head*
All on Jazz Door 1215

13 January 1954. BH, interview Stockholm, Sweden.

22 January 1954. BH, vo; with JAZZ CLUB USA. BILLIE HOLIDAY WITH
    CARL DRINKARD TRIO. Carl Drinkard (p), Red Mitchell (b), Elaine
    Leighton (d), Leonard Feather (mc)

First set:
Blue Moon/All Of Me/My Man/Them There Eyes/I Cried For You/What A Little Moonlight Can Do/I Cover the Waterfront
All on Verve 517658-2 and Blue Note CDP 748786-2
Second set:

BH, vo; with JAZZ CLUB USA JAM SESSION GROUP with Boniface 'Buddy' DeFranco (cl), Red Norvo (vib), Sonny Clark, Beryl Booker (p), Jimmy Raney (g), Red Mitchell (b), Elaine Leighton (d), Leonard Feather (mc)
Billie's Blues (I Love My Man)/Lover Come Back To Me: **Verve 517658-2; Blue Note CDP 748786-2**
NOTE: I now believe 22 January to be correct following Author's research. Tape box is from Germany and Leonard Feather believes it was recorded in Cologne.

January–February 1954. BH, vo; with JAZZ CLUB USA. Various dates, personnel as 22 January date.
He's Funny That Way/All Of Me/My Man/Them There Eyes/Don't Explain/I Cried For You/Fine and Mellow/What a Little Moonlight Can Do/Nice Work If You Can Get It/Willow Weep For Me/I Only Have Eyes For You/God Bless the Child/Please Don't Talk About Me When I'm Gone/Billie's Blues (I Love My Man)/All Of Me/Willow Weep For Me

14 April 1954. BH, vo; with Charlie Shavers (tp), Oscar Peterson (p), Herb Ellis (g), Ray Brown (b), Ed Shaughnessy (d)
How Deep Is the Ocean?/What a Little Moonlight Can Do: Clef 89132
I Cried For You
All on Verve 517658-2

3 September 1954. BH, vo; with Harry 'Sweets' Edison (tp), Willie Smith (as), Bobby Tucker (p), Barney Kessel (g), Red Callender (b), Chico Hamilton (d)
BH, vo; with Bobby Tucker (p) only*
(YBC1930-2) *Love Me Or Leave Me*: Clef 89150
(YBC1931-5) *P.S. I Love You*/(YBC1932-6) *Too Marvelous For Words*/(YBC1933-7) *Softly*
(YBC1935-3) *I Thought About You**: Clef 89150
(YBC1937-4) *Willow Weep For Me*/(YBC1938-3) *Stormy Blues*: Clef 89141
All on Verve 517658-2

25 September 1954. BH, vo; as part of THE BIRDLAND ALL STARS LIVE AT CARNEGIE HALL, BILLIE HOLIDAY WITH COUNT BASIE AND HIS ORCHESTRA. Carl Drinkard (p), with Thad Jones, Reunald Jones, Wendell Culley, Joe Newman (tp), Bill Hughes, Henry Coker, Benny Powell (tb), Marshall Royal (cl, as), Ernie Wilkins (as, ts), Frank Wess (fl, ts), Frank Foster (ts), Charlie Fowlkes (bs) Freddie Green (g), Eddie Jones (b), Gus Johnson (d)
All Of Me/Ain't Nobody's Business If I Do/Lover Come Back To Me/My Man/Them There Eyes/Lover Man
All on Roulette CDS 7986602

Winter 1954. BH, vo; part of JOHNNY CARSON – TONIGHT SHOW BILLIE HOLIDAY WITH STUDIO HOUSE BAND. Billie Holiday and probably Carl Drinkard (p), remainder of personnel unknown (tp, ts, b, d), Johnny Carson (mc)

My Man
Them There Eyes/Lover Man: **Rare CD 02**

14 February 1955. BH, vo; with Charlie Shavers (tp), Tony Scott (cl), Budd
   Johnson (ts), Billy Taylor (p), Billy Bauer (g), Leonard Gaskin (b), Cozy Cole (d)
(YBC2274-4) *Say It Isn't So*/(YBC2275-5) *I've Got My Love To Keep Me Warm*/
(YBC2276-4) *I Wished On the Moon*/(YBC2277-3) *Always*/(YBC2278-2) *Every-
thing Happens To Me*/(YBC2279-2) *Do Nothin' Till You Hear From Me*/
(YBC2280-2) *Ain't Misbehavin'*
All on Verve 517658-2

6 May 1955. BH, vo; with Buck Clayton (tp), Lester Young (ts), Count
   Basie (org), Carl Drinkard (p), probably Eddie Jones (b), probably Buddy Rich (d)
Stormy Weather

22 August 1955. BH, vo; in rehearsal with Jimmy Rowles (p, vo, talk), Artie
   Shapiro (b, vo, talk)
*Nice Work If You Can Get It/Mandy Is Two/Prelude To a Kiss/I Must Have That Man/
Jeepers Creepers/Please Don't Talk About Me When I'm Gone/Moonlight In Vermont/
Misery/(I'm) Restless/Moonlight In Vermont/Everything Happens To Me/I Don't Want
To Cry Anymore/Everything Happens To Me/When You Are Away, Dear/It Had To Be
You/The Mood That I'm In/Gone With the Wind/I Got It Bad (and That Ain't Good)/
(I Don't Stand a) Ghost Of a Chance/I'm Walking Through Heaven With You/Just
Friends/The Nearness Of You/It's Too Hot For Words/They Say/I Won't Believe It Till
I Hear It From You*
All on Verve 517658-2
NOTE: This rehearsal first surfaced in 1973 when Paramount Records issued
'Billie Holiday: Songs and Conversations' (PAS-6059). More than one and a half
hours of material was whittled to a three quarter hour LP. The album was oddly
edited and the original tape thrown away. Much (some?) of the unused portions
survived as scraps on Paramount's work tapes.
 When compiling 'The Complete Billie Holiday on Verve' (Verve 517658-2) I only
undid the edits on the original LP when I could find the material's proper place
on the scrap reels. Two short fragments on the original album could not be linked
to any of the surviving tape and were held to the end of the session. Some portions
remain unissued of: *Nice Work If you Can Get It/Mandy Is Two/I Don't Want To
Cry Anymore/Gone With the Wind/They Say*

23 August 1955. BH, vo; with Harry 'Sweets' Edison*(tp), Benny Carter (as),
   Jimmy Rowles (p), Barney Kessel (g), John Simmons (b), Larry Bunker (d)
(YBC2438-1) *I Don't Want To Cry Anymore* (false starts)/(YBC2438-2) *I Don't
Want To Cry Anymore**/(YBC2439-1) *Prelude To a Kiss* (false starts)/(YBC2439-2)
Prelude To a Kiss* (incomplete)/(YBC2439-3) *Prelude To a Kiss**/(YBC2440-4) *(I
Don't Stand a) Ghost Of a Chance**/(YBC2441-1) *When Your Lover Has Gone**
(incomplete)/(YBC2441-2) *When Your Lover Has Gone** (incomplete)/
(YBC2441-3) *When Your Lover Has Gone**/(YBC2442-4) *Gone With the Wind*/
(YBC2443-2) *Please Don't Talk About Me When I'm Gone**/(YBC2444-1) *It Had
To Be You**/(YBC2445-5) *Nice Work If You Can Get It**
All on Verve 517658-2

25 August 1955. BH, vo; with Harry 'Sweets' Edison*(tp), Benny Carter (as), Jimmy Rowles (p and celeste), Barney Kessel (g), John Simmons (b), Larry Bunker (d)
(YBC2446-3) *Come Rain Or Come Shine**/(YBC2447-1) *I Got a Right To Sing the Blues**/(YBC2448-3) *What's New?*/(YBC2449-1) *A Fine Romance** (incomplete)/ (YBC2449-2) *A Fine Romance** (alternate)/(YBC2449-3) *A Fine Romance** (false starts)/(YBC2449-4)*A Fine Romance** (incomplete)/(YBC2449-5)*A Fine Romance** (incomplete)/(YBC2449-6) *A Fine Romance** (false starts)/(YBC2449-7) *A Fine Romance** (incomplete)/(YBC2449-8)*A Fine Romance**/(YBC2450-1) *I Hadn't Anyone Till You*/(YBC2451-3) *I Get a Kick Out of You**/(YBC2452-2) *Everything I Have Is Yours*/(YBC2453-3) *Isn't This a Lovely Day?**
All on Verve 517658-2

10 February 1956. BH, vo; with STEVE ALLEN SHOW HOUSE BAND.
Please Don't Talk About Me When I'm Gone/Billie interviewed by Steve Allen/*A Ghost Of a Chance*

15 February 1956. BH interviewed by Willis Conover for Voice of America.

30 May 1956. BH, vo; in rehearsal with Tony Scott (p)
Misery/Israel/Misery/I Must Have That Man/Strange Fruit/God Bless the Child/One Never Knows, Does One?/Beer Barrel Polka (Roll Out the Barrel)/Some Of These Days/ My Yiddishe Momme/Lady's Back In Town (Lady's Gonna Sing)/One Never Knows, Does One?/unknown title
All on Verve 517658-2
NOTE: This is a rehearsal for 'Lady Sings the Blues', a concert album which reprised BH's 'greatest hits' to publicize her forthcoming autobiography of the same title (each song on the album was a chapter heading in her book). Tony Scott was the musical director for the album, and like the August 1955 rehearsal with Jimmy Rowles, Scott often sings as well.

6 June 1956. BH, vo; with Charlie Shavers (tp), Tony Scott (cl, musical director, [arr]), Paul Quinichette (ts), Wynton Kelly (p), Kenny Burrell (g), Arron Bell (b), Lennie McBrowne (d)
(YBC2850-5) *Trav'lin' Light*/(YBC2851-3) *I Must Have That Man/*(YBC2853-1) *Some Other Spring*/(YBC2854-4) *Lady Sings the Blues*
All on Verve 517658-2

7 June 1956. BH, vo; with personnel as for 6 June 1956
(YBC2855-12) *Strange Fruit*/(YBC2856-1) *God Bless the Child/*(YBC2857-8) *Good Morning Heartache*/(YBC2858-1) *No Good Man*
All on Verve 517658-2

14 August 1956. BH, vo; with Harry 'Sweets' Edison (tp – except on title d), Ben Webster (ts), Jimmy Rowles (p), Barney Kessel (g), Joe Mondragon (b), Alvin Stoller (d)
a. (YBC2914-3) *Do Nothin' Till You Hear From Me/*b. (YBC2915-6) *Cheek To Cheek/*c. (YBC2916-4) *Ill Wind/*d. (YBC2917-8) *Speak Low*
All on Verve 517658-2

18 August 1956. BH, vo; with Harry 'Sweets' Edison (tp), Ben Webster (ts), Jimmy Rowles (p), Barney Kessel (g), Red Mitchell (b), Alvin Stoller (d)
(YBC2929-4) *We'll Be Together Again*/(YBC2930-3) *All Or Nothing At All*/(YBC2931-6) *Sophisticated Lady*/(YBC2932-6) *April In Paris*
All on Verve 517658-2

29 August 1956. BH, vo; with unknown (p, b, d)
Willow Weep For Me/*I Only Have Eyes For You*/*My Man*/*Please Don't Talk About Me When I'm Gone*
All on Rare CD 02

13 September 1956. BH, vo; with unknown (p, b, d)
Please Don't Talk About Me When I'm Gone/*I Love My Man (Billie's Blues)*/*My Man*

27 October 1956. BH, vo; with probably Carl Drinkard (p), unknown (b), Eddie Phyfe (d)
Nice Work If You Can Get It/*God Bless the Child*/*Please Don't Talk About Me When I'm Gone*/*Don't Explain*

8 November 1956. BH, vo; on TEX MCCLEARLY PEACOCK ALLEY TV SHOW. BH (recitation, talk) interviewed by Tex McClearly, unknown (g)

8 November 1956. BH interview, station WABD-TV by Mike Wallace.

8 November 1956. BH, vo; on STEVE ALLEN TONITE SHOW BILLIE HOLIDAY WITH STUDIO BAND DIRECTED BY SKITCH HENDERSON. Probably Carl Drinkard (p) with Studio House Band including strings.
(I Loves You) Porgy

10 November 1956. BH, vo; with Roy Eldridge*(tp), Coleman Hawkins(ts), Carl Drinkard (p), Tony Scott (p), Kenny Burrell (g), Carson Smith (b), Chico Hamilton (d)
NOTE: Tony Scott (p) replaces Drinkard on 'Lady Sings the Blues' only.
First set:
Lady Sings the Blues*/*Ain't Nobody's Business If I Do**/*Trav'lin' Light** (incomplete)/*I Love My Man (Billie's Blues)**/*Too Marvelous For Words**/*Body and Soul**/*Don't Explain*
All on Verve 517658-2

Second set:
with Buck Clayton (tp), Tony Scott (cl), Al Cohn (ts), Carl Drinkard (p), Kenny Burrell (g), Carson Smith (b), Chico Hamilton (d)
Yesterdays/*Ease Don't Talk About Me When I'm Gone*/*I'll Be Seeing You*/*My Man*/*I Cried For You*/*Fine and Mellow*/*I Cover the Waterfront*/*What a Little Moonlight Can Do*
All on Verve 517658-2
NOTE: There are five readings from Billie Holiday's autobiography 'Lady Sings the Blues' by Gilbert Millstein, who actually reads over the music on the title track. There are no solos in this concert. Most accompaniment is in a collective 'jam' style. There were two concerts, one at 8pm and one at midnight. I have been able to document the programme for each show and have come to the conclusion that the items that originally appeared on the album 'Lady Sings the Blues' (Verve V8410) probably all came from the 8pm concert. It is conceivable, however, that

for artistic and sonic reasons (the concert was not well recorded) that the issued material included songs inter-cut from the two concerts.

Late 1950s. BH, vo; with MARTHA RAYE TELEVISION SHOW HOUSE BAND. *You've Changed/My Man*

3 January 1957. BH, vo; with Harry 'Sweets' Edison (tp), Ben Webster (ts), Jimmy Rowles (p), Barney Kessel (g), Red Mitchell (b), Alvin Stoller (d) (20498-4) *I Wished On the Moon*/(20499-7) *Moonlight In Vermont*/(20500-6) *A Foggy Day*
All on Verve 517658-2

4 January 1957. BH, vo; with personnel as 3 January 1957. (20501-2) *I Didn't Know What Time It Was*/(20502-7) *Just One Of Those Things* (incomplete)/(20502-8) *Just One Of Those Things*/(20503-1) *Comes Love* (alternate take)/(20503-2) *Comes Love* (false starts)/(20503-3) *Comes Love* (false starts)/(20503-4)*Comes Love*
All on Verve 517658-2

7 January 1957. BH, vo; with personnel as for 3 January 1957. (20504-1) *Day in, Day Out*/(20505-3) *Darn That Dream*/(20506-7) *But Not For Me* /(20507-1) *Body and Soul*

8 January 1957. BH, vo; with Harry 'Sweets' Edison (tp), Ben Webster (ts), Jimmy Rowles (p), Barney Kessel (g), Joe Mondragon (b), Alvin Stoller (d) (20561-1) *Stars Fell On Alabama* (incomplete)/(20561-2) *Stars Fell On Alabama**/ (20562-1) *Say It Isn't So* (incomplete)/(20562-2) *Say It Isn't So*/(20563-1) *Our Love Is Here To Stay* (false starts)/(20563-2) *Our Love Is Here To Stay*/(20564-1) *One For My Baby* (false starts)/(20564-2) *One For My Baby* (incomplete)/(20564-3) *One For My Baby**

9 January 1957. BH, vo; with Harry 'Sweets' Edison (tp), Ben Webster (ts), Jimmy Rowles (p), Barney Kessel (g), Red Mitchell (b), probably Larry Bunker (d)
(20565-3) *They Can't Take That Away From Me*/(20566-1) *Embraceable You*/ (20567-4) *Let's Call the Whole Thing Off*/(20568-6) *Gee, Baby Ain't I Good To You?*
All on Verve 517658-2

6 July 1957. BH, vo; with Mal Waldron (p), Joe Benjamin (b), Jo Jones (d), Willis Connover (mc)
Nice Work If You Can Get It/Willow Weep For Me/My Man/Lover Come Back To Me/ Lady Sings the Blues/What a Little Moonlight Can Do
All on Verve 517658-2

5 December 1957. BH, vo; with Doc Cheatham (tp), Vic Dickenson (tb), Lester Young, Ben Webster, Coleman Hawkins (ts), Mal Waldron (p), Danny Baker (g), Jim Atlas (b), Jo Jones (d)
Fine and Mellow: **CBS C3K 47724-3**

8 December 1957. BH, vo; with Roy Eldridge, Doc Cheatham (tp), Vic Dickenson (tb), Lester Young, Ben Webster, Coleman Hawkins (ts), Gerry Mulligan (bs), Mal Waldron (p), Danny Barker (g), Milt Hinton (b), Osie Johnson (d)

TV soundtrack: 'Seven Lively Arts: The Sound of Jazz'
Fine and Mellow

19 February 1958. BH, vo; with RAY ELLIS AND HIS ORCHESTRA with Mel Davis, Billy Butterfield, Bernie Glow (tp), Urbie Green (tb), Gene Quill (as), George Ochner, Milton Lomask, Emmanuel Green, Harry Atzmann, David Sarcer, Samuel Rand, Leo Kauczeck, Harry Melnikoff, Harry Hoffman, David Newman (v), Sid Brecher, Richard Dichler (viola), David Soyer, Maurice Brown (cello), Janet Putman (harp), Mal Waldron (p), Barry Galbraith (g), Milt Hinton (b), Osie Johnson (d), unknown choir, Ray Ellis (arr, cond)
(CO60460-1) *You Don't Know What Love Is*/(CO60461-1) *I'll Be Around*/ (CO60462-1) *For Heaven's Sake*/(CO60466-1) *I'm a Fool To Want You*/(CO60466-2) *I'm a Fool To Want You*/(CO60463-1) *But Beautiful*
(CO60464-1) *For All We Know*: **CBS C3K 47724-3**
(CO60465-1) *It's Easy To Remember*
All on CBS 4508832

20 February 1958. BH, vo; with RAY ELLIS AND HIS ORCHESTRA. Urbie Green, Tom Mitchell, J J Johnson (tb), Ed Powell, Tom Pashley, Romeo Penque, Phil Bodner (reeds), George Ochner, Eugene Bergen, Max Cahn, Felix Giglio, Harry Katzmann, David Sarcer, Samuel Rand, Leo Krucleck, Harry Hoffman, David Newman (v), Sid Brecher, Richard Dichier (viola), David Soyer, Maurice Brown (cello), Janet Putman (harp), Bradley Sinney (xylo), Mal Waldron (p), Barry Galbraith (g), Milt Hinton (b), Don Lamond (d), unknown choir, Ray Ellis (arr, cond)
(CO60467-1) *I Get Along Without You Very Well*/(CO60468-1) *Glad To Be Unhappy*: **CBS 4508832**
(CO60469-1) *You've Changed*: **CBS C3K 47724-3: CBS 4508832**
(CO60470-1) *The End Of a Love Affair*
(CO60470-21) *The End Of a Love Affair*: **CBS 4508832**
(CO60471-1) *Violets For Your Fur*: **CBS 4508832**
NOTE: The 19 February and 20 February sessions were released on the album 'Lady in Satin'. This was originally released in both stereo and mono versions, although the former did not include 'The End Of a Love Affair'. Billie did not know the song and had great difficulty interpreting it. In the event a backing track was mixed to mono and Billie later sang over it. For the CD re-issue an unmixed backing track and a tape of Billie singing with just a rhythm section were married-up to produce a stereo version of 'The End Of a Love Affair', although Billie's vocal had to be slowed fractionally.

29 May 1958. BH, vo; with Mal Waldron (p) and unidentified backing group
You've Changed/I Love My Man (Billie's Blues)/When Your Lover Has Gone

10 July 1958. BH, vo; with Buck Clayton*(tp), Tyree Glenn (tb), Georgie Auld (ts), Mal Waldron (p), Mary Osborne (g), Vinnie Burke (b), Osie Johnson (d)
*What a Little Moon Light Can Do/Foolin' Myself/It's Easy To Remember**

17 July 1958. BH, vo; with Buck Clayton*, Charlie Shavers(tp), Tyree Glenn*(tb), Georgie Auld (ts), Harry Shepherd (vib), Mal Waldron (p), Mary Osborne (g), Vinnie Burke (b), Osie Johnson (d)
Moanin' Low/Don't Explain/When Your Lover Has Gone**

28 July or 9 September 1958. BH, vo; with Mal Waldron (p), Buck Clayton (tp), unknown (b and d)
When Your Lover Has Gone/Don't Explain

26 September 1958. BH, vo; with Buck Clayton (tp); Georgie Auld or Coleman Hawkins*(ts), Mal Waldron (p), Milt Hinton (b), Don Lamond (d)
I Wished On the Moon*/Lover Man: Verve 517658-2

Probably Fall 1958. BH, vo; with PERCY FAITH ORCHESTRA
You Better Go Now/Them There Eyes

5 October 1958. BH, vo; with Mal Waldron (p), Eddie Khan (b), Dick Berk (d). Plus guest stars: Boniface 'Buddy' DeFranco (cl), Benny Carter (as), Gerry Mulligan* (bs)
Ain't Nobody's Business If I Do/Willow Weep For Me/When Your Lover Has Gone/God Bless the Child*/I Only Have Eyes For You*/Good Morning Heartache*/Them There Eyes*/Fine and Mellow*/What a Little Moonlight Can Do*/Trav'lin' Light*/Lover, Come Back To Me*
All on Blackhawk BKH 50701-CD

12 November 1958. BH, vo; with Mal Waldron (p), Paul Rovere (b), Kansas Fields (d)
Billie's Blues (I Love My Man)

Between 22–25 February 1959. BH, vo; with PETER KNIGHT directing the CHELSEA AT NINE HOUSE BAND with Mal Waldron (p)
(I Loves You) Porgy/Please Don't Talk About Me When I'm Gone/Strange Fruit

3–4 March 1959. BH, vo; with RAY ELLIS AND HIS ORCHESTRA. Jimmy Cleveland*(tb), Romeo Penque (as, ts and bass cl), Hank Jones (p, celeste), Kenny Burrell (g), Joe Benjamin (b), Osie Johnson (d), Janet Putnam (harp), plus four strings. Ray Ellis (arr, cond)
(59XY435) *All the Way*/(59XY436) *It's Not For Me To Say*/(59XY437) *I'll Never Smile Again**/(59XY438-1) *Just One More Chance**
All on Verve 517658-2

4–5 March 1959. BH, vo; with RAY ELLIS AND HIS ORCHESTRA with Harry 'Sweets' Edison*(tp), Jimmy Cleveland (tb), Gene Quill (as), Hank Jones (p), Barry Galbraith (g), Milt Hinton (b), Osie Johnson (d), unknown (harp), plus 12 strings and harp. Ray Ellis (arr, cond)
(59XY439) *When It's Sleepy Time Down South**/(59XY440-2) *Don't Worry 'Bout Me*/(59XY441) *Sometimes I'm Happy**/(59XY442) *You Took Advantage Of Me**
All on Verve 517658-2
NOTE: Dick Hyman replaced Hank Jones (p) on either 4–5 March Session or the 11 March session.

11 March 1959. BH, vo; with RAY ELLIS AND HIS ORCHESTRA with Harry 'Sweets' Edison, Joe Wilder (tp), Billy Byers (tb), Al Cohn (ts), Danny Bank (bs), Hank Jones (p), Barry Galbraith (g), Milt Hinton (b), Osie Johnson (d), Ray Ellis (arr, cond)
(59XY445)*There'll Be Some Changes Made*/(59XY456) *'Deed I Do*/(59XY457) *All Of You*/(59XY458) *Baby, Won't You Please Come Home*
All on Verve 517658-2

NOTE: I continue to be troubled by the sound of Billie's voice on the March 11 session and 'Baby Won't You Please Come Home' in particular. At the time these were recorded in three-track stereo. Billie was in the booth on one track and the orchestra on the other two. To me it sounds as if her voice was speeded up on the mix to be in tune with the band. When I became involved in 'The Complete Billie Holiday On Verve' I queried this with musicians, who felt it had been done. When I put it to Ray Ellis, he at first thought this was a possibility, as he had done such things on pop dates. Later, however, he stated that no speeding up of Billie's voice had been done on the MGM album.

Mid April 1959. BH, vo; with Mal Waldron (p), Champ Jones (b), Roy Haynes (d)
Nice Work If You Can Get It/Willow Weep For Me/When Your Lover Has Gone/Billie's Blues (I Love My Man)/Too Marvelous For Words/Lover, Come Back To Me
All on Jazz Door 1215

25 May 1959. BH, vo; Mal Waldron (p) and group inc. Tony Scott (cl) and Jo Jones (d)
I Can't Get Started/Ain't Nobody's Business If I Do

283

Appendix 1

MARTHA MILLER ≠ UNKNOWN
(c 1850–1930)

SUSSIE HARRIS ≠ CHARLES FAGAN
(c 1850–1930)   (1869/70–1931)
≠
UNKNOWN(s) (1)
= m c 1896–7
JAMES HARRIS (2)

also known as:
SADIE HARRIS
JULIA HARRIS
SARAH GOUGH
SADIE GOUGH
SADIE HOLIDAY

ROBERT MILLER = EVA HARRIS (2)
(1876–?)   (1886–?)

GEORGE   MAGGIE
(c 1897–?)   (c 1899–?)

SARAH JULIA HARRIS
(1895–1945)
≠
CLARENCE HOLIDAY (1)
(1898–1937)
= m 28 September 1920
PHILIP GOUGH (2)
(1893–?)
= m 20 October 1920

JENNY (1)
(c 1885–1909)
=

CHARLES   DOROTHY   MARTHA
(1916–94)   (1919–70s)   (1921–2)
=   ≠
EDITH (1)   UNKNOWN (1)
=   =
HATTIE (2)   MEL SHERIDAN (2)
             EDWARD PRESTON (3)
             (d 1970s)

CHARLES

ELEANORA HARRIS   also known as: ELEANORA FAGAN,
(1915–59)   ELEANORA GOUGH,
= m 25 August 1941   ELEANORA MONROE,
JAMES NORMAN MONROE (1)   ELEANORA McKAY,
(1911–94)   ELEANORA GOUGH McKAY,
= m 28 March 1957   BILLIE HOLIDAY
LOUIS McKAY (2)
(1909–81)

EVELYN
(1906–94)
= m 24 November 1924
MATTHEW CONWAY
(b 1901)

JANICE ELEANORA
(b 1929)
= m 1948
ALBERT BLACKWELL

SYLVIA   MELROSE   ANNETTE

PAMELA   VALERIE   CHARLES ROBERT LEONARD ELAINE BARBARA-JEAN
(1949–87) (b 1954) all born in 1940s

KEY
= : married
≠ : not married
(1) (2) etc : 1st relationship, 2nd relationship etc.

Billie Holiday (1) Harris family tree

Appendix 2

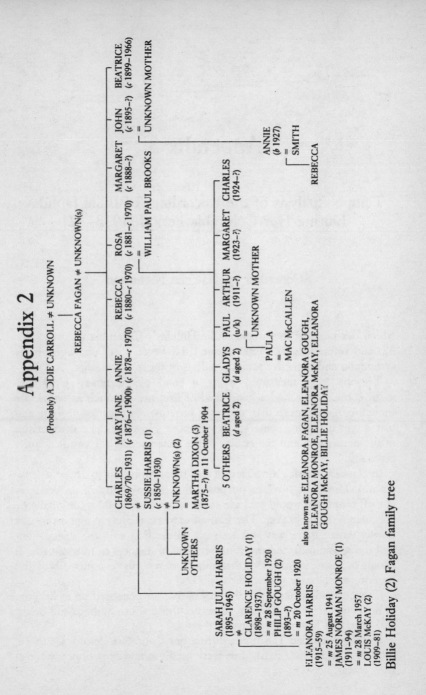

(Probably) ADDIE CARROLL ≠ UNKNOWN

REBECCA FAGAN ≠ UNKNOWN(s)

CHARLES (1869/70–1931) ≠

MARY JANE (c 1876–c 1900) b

ANNIE (c 1878–c 1970)

REBECCA (c 1880–c 1970)

ROSA (c 1881–c 1970) =

MARGARET (c 1888–?)

JOHN (c 1895–?) =

BEATRICE (c 1899–1966)

SUSSIE HARRIS (1) (c 1850–1930) ≠

UNKNOWN(s) (2) =

MARTHA DIXON (3) (1875–?) m 11 October 1904

WILLIAM PAUL BROOKS

UNKNOWN MOTHER

UNKNOWN OTHERS

5 OTHERS

BEATRICE (d aged 2)

GLADYS (d aged 2)

PAUL (u/k)

ARTHUR (1911–?) =

MARGARET (1923–?)

CHARLES (1924–?)

ANNIE (b 1927) =

SMITH

UNKNOWN MOTHER

PAULA = MAC McCALLEN

REBECCA

SARAH JULIA HARRIS (1895–1945) ≠

CLARENCE HOLIDAY (1) (1898–1937) = m 28 September 1920

PHILIP GOUGH (2) (1893–?) = m 20 October 1920

ELEANORA HARRIS (1915–59) = m 25 August 1941

JAMES NORMAN MONROE (1) (1911–94) = m 28 March 1957

LOUIS McKAY (2) (1909–81)

also known as: ELEANORA FAGAN, ELEANORA GOUGH, ELEANORA MONROE, ELEANORA McKAY, ELEANORA GOUGH McKAY, BILLIE HOLIDAY

Billie Holiday (2) Fagan family tree

Appendix 3

Tempo Analysis of the Recordings of Billie Holiday During Her Columbia Period (1933–42)

Compiled by Malcolm Nicholson

Much has been written about Billie Holiday's Columbia years (1933–42) and references to tempo abound. However, I am unaware of any systematic and objective tempo analysis of these recordings.

Tempos were measured using a good old-fashioned clockwork metronome. It has had a good deal of use; not as much as some, although certainly more than others. Consequently vagaries of wear and tear might make for some small variances. However, as a comparison of the perception and the reality of the tune speeds, the result is quite revealing.

In classical music, 'slow' tempi can be anything up to 76 bpm (sostenuto). However, for jazz purposes this is something of an arbitrary cut-off point and would exclude some tempi that would traditionally be considered 'slow' in jazz. The Columbia years represent a point in jazz history where there was still a strong connection with the dance-floor and the music reflected the requirements of dancers in tune speeds. It should be borne in mind that the majority of recordings under discussion here were made for the jukebox market.

Consequently I have included tunes that are recorded up to 80 bpm in the slow category. Medium tunes are those above 80 bpm and below 120 bpm and fast, those above 120 bpm.

Holiday recorded 158 tunes during her Columbia Period. Of these, fifty-eight were fast, eighty-five were medium and only fifteen were at slow tempi.

She did not record any slow tunes prior to April 1939, when she recorded 'Strange Fruit'. By then she had already recorded 125 tunes. Thus chronologically and numerically her recorded output up to this point had been completed without a single slow tune.

Between 1939 and 1942 Holiday recorded a total of fourteen slow tunes. During the eighteen months between the 'Strange Fruit' session and her last date in 1940, 23 per cent of the songs she recorded were at slow tempi, a total of five songs in all. During the eleven-month period from the next session in March 1941 to her last Columbia session in February 1942, 56 per cent of the songs she recorded were at slow tempi, a total of nine songs in all. Thus the greater proportion and number of slow tunes were recorded between 1941 and 1942, some distance from the success of 'Strange Fruit'.

One final point of interest is that at no point during the period under discussion did Holiday record a tune as slow as 'Strange Fruit' (56 bpm). The slowest tempi to approach this occurred during the 1941–2 period, again some distance from the success of 'Strange Fruit': 'Gloomy Sunday' (59 bpm) from August 1941, 'Until the Real Thing Comes Along' (66 bpm) and 'Mandy Is Two' (67 bpm), both from 1942.

Malcolm Nicholson
London, September 1994

TEMPO ANALYSIS - THE COLUMBIA YEARS 1933-42		SPEED	SLOW	MEDIUM	FAST
YEAR 19-	TUNE	BPM	40-79	80-119	120+
33	YOUR MOTHERS SON-IN-LAW	192			■
33	RIFFIN' THE SCOTCH	176			■
34	BLUES (SADDEST TALE)	88-96		■	
35	I WISHED ON THE MOON	106		■	
35	WHAT A LITTLE MOONLIGHT CAN DO	268			■
35	MISS BROWN TO YOU	150			■
35	A SUNBONNET BLUE (& A YELLOW STRAW HAT)	152			■
35	WHAT A NIGHT WHAT A MOON WHAT A GIRL	202			■
35	I'M PAINTING THE TOWN RED	114		■	
35	IT'S TOO HOT FOR WORDS	198			■
35	TWENTY FOUR HOURS A DAY	212			■
35	YANKEE DOODLE NEVER WENT TO TOWN	175			■
35	EENY MEENY MINEY MO	260			■
35	IF YOU WERE MINE	111		■	
35	THESE N' THAT N' THOSE	108		■	
35	YOU LET ME DOWN	100		■	
35	SPREADIN' RHYTHM AROUND	182			■
36	LIFE BEGINS WHEN YOURE IN LOVE	174			■
36	ITS LIKE REACHING FOR THE MOON	102		■	
36	THESE FOOLISH THINGS	96		■	
36	I CRIED FOR YOU	152			■
36	GUESS WHO	184			■
36	DID I REMEMBER?	148			■
36	NO REGRETS	134			■
36	SUMMERTIME	100		■	

TEMPO	ANALYSIS - THE COLUMBIA YEARS 1933-42	SPEED	SLOW	MEDIUM	FAST
YEAR 19-	TUNE	BPM	40-79	80-119	120+
36	BILLIES BLUES	110		▓	
36	A FINE ROMANCE	125			▓
36	I CANT PRETEND	114		▓	
36	ONE, TWO BUTTON YOUR SHOE	172			▓
36	LETS CALL A HEART A HEART	104		▓	
36	EASY TO LOVE	156			▓
36	WITH THEE I SWING	172			▓
36	THE WAY YOU LOOK TONIGHT	174			▓
36	WHO LOVES YOU?	162			▓
36	PENNIES FROM HEAVEN	112		▓	
36	THATS LOVE I GUESS	115		▓	
36	I CAN'T GIVE YOU ANYTHING BUT LOVE (BABY)	118		▓	
37	ONE NEVER KNOWS - DOES ONE?	82		▓	
37	I'VE GOT MY LOVE TO KEEP ME WARM	130			▓
37	IF MY HEART COULD ONLY TALK	110		▓	
37	PLEASE KEEP ME IN YOUR DREAMS	174			▓
37	HE AIN'T GOT RHYTHM	174			▓
37	THIS YEARS KISSES	114		▓	
37	WHY WAS I BORN	144			▓
37	I MUST HAVE THAT MAN	94		▓	
37	THE MOOD THAT I'M IN	96		▓	
37	YOU SHOWED ME THE WAY	104		▓	
37	SENTIMENTAL & MELANCHOLY	104		▓	
37	MY LAST AFFAIR	92		▓	
37	CARELESSLY	108		▓	
37	HOW COULD YOU?	150			▓
37	MOANIN' LOW	88		▓	
37	WHERE IS THE SUN?	80		▓	
37	LET'S CALL THE WHOLE THING OFF	102		▓	
37	THEY CAN'T TAKE THAT AWAY FROM ME	86		▓	
37	I DON'T KNOW IF I'M COMING OR GOING	88		▓	
37	SUN SHOWERS	126			▓
37	YOURS AND MINE	118		▓	
37	I'LL GET BY	112		▓	
37	MEAN TO ME	104		▓	
37	FOOLIN' MYSELF	94		▓	
37	EASY LIVING	86		▓	
37	I'LL NEVER BE THE SAME	84		▓	
37	ME, MYSELF & I	152			▓
37	A SAIL BOAT IN THE MOONLIGHT	112		▓	
37	BORN TO LOVE	120			▓
37	WITHOUT YOUR LOVE	120			▓
37	GETTING SOME FUN OUT OF LIFE	110		▓	
37	WHO WANTS LOVE?	134			▓
37	TRAV'LIN' ALL ALONE	162			▓
37	HE'S FUNNY THAT WAY	100		▓	
37	NICE WORK IF YOU CAN GET IT	160			▓
37	THINGS ARE LOOKING UP	90		▓	
37	MY MAN	100		▓	
37	CAN'T HELP LOVIN' DAT MAN	88		▓	
38	MY FIRST IMPRESSION OF YOU	104		▓	
38	WHEN YOU'RE SMILING	188			▓
38	I CAN'T BELIEVE THAT YOU'RE IN LOVE WITH ME	106		▓	
38	IF DREAMS COME TRUE	170			▓
38	NOW THEY CALL IT SWING	156			▓
38	ON THE SENTIMENTAL SIDE	86		▓	

TEMPO	ANALYSIS - THE COLUMBIA YEARS 1933-42	SPEED	SLOW	MEDIUM	FAST
YEAR 19-	TUNE	BPM	40-79	80-119	120+
38	BACK IN YOUR OWN BACK YARD	164			▓
38	WHEN A WOMAN LOVES A MAN	86		▓	
38	YOU GO TO MY HEAD	90		▓	
38	THE MOON LOOKS DOWN AND LAUGHS	100		▓	
38	IF I WERE YOU	130			▓
38	FORGET IF YOU CAN	96		▓	
38	HAVING MYSELF A TIME	108		▓	
38	SAYS MY HEART	124			▓
38	I WISH I HAD YOU	106		▓	
38	I'M GONNA LOCK MY HEART	156			▓
38	THE VERY THOUGHT OF YOU	98		▓	
38	I CAN'T GET STARTED	96		▓	
38	I'VE GOT A DATE WITH A DREAM	100		▓	
38	YOU CAN'T BE MINE (& SOMEONE ELSES TOO)	118		▓	
38	EVERYBODY'S LAUGHING	120			▓
38	HERE IT IS TOMORROW AGAIN	152			▓
38	SAY IT WITH A KISS	158			▓
38	APRIL IN MY HEART	112		▓	
38	I'LL NEVER FAIL YOU	142			▓
38	THEY SAY	110		▓	
38	YOU'RE SO DESIRABLE	104		▓	
38	YOU'RE GONNA SEE A LOT OF ME	112		▓	
38	HELLO, MY DARLING	102		▓	
38	LET'S DREAM IN THE MOONLIGHT	106		▓	
39	THAT'S ALL I ASK OF YOU	104		▓	
39	DREAM OF LIFE	102		▓	
39	WHAT SHALL I SAY?	112		▓	
39	IT'S EASY TO BLAME THE WEATHER	140			▓
39	MORE THAN YOU KNOW	100		▓	
39	SUGAR(THAT SUGAR BABY O' MINE)	167			▓
39	YOU'RE TOO LOVELY TO LAST	88		▓	
39	UNDER A BLUE JUNGLE MOON	92		▓	
39	EVERYTHING HAPPENS FOR THE BEST	94		▓	
39	WHY DID I ALWAYS DEPEND ON YOU?	106		▓	
39	LONG GONE BLUES	96		▓	
39	SOME OTHER SPRING	88		▓	
39	OUR LOVE IS DIFFERENT	90		▓	
39	THEM THERE EYES	198			▓
39	SWING, BROTHER, SWING	192			▓
39	NIGHT & DAY	96		▓	
39	THE MAN I LOVE	88		▓	
39	YOU'RE JUST A NO ACCOUNT	95		▓	
39	I GOTTA RIGHT TO SING THE BLUES	110		▓	
39	YESTERDAYS	76	▓		
39	STRANGE FRUIT	56	▓		
39	FINE & MELLOW	78	▓		
39	YOU'RE A LUCKY GUY	158			▓
40	GHOST OF YESTERDAY	80		▓	
40	BODY & SOUL	80		▓	
40	WHAT IS THIS GOING TO GET US?	106		▓	
40	FALLING IN LOVE AGAIN (CAN'T HELP IT)	126			▓
40	I'M PULLING THROUGH	72	▓		
40	TELL ME MORE AND MORE, AND THEN SOME	74	▓		
40	LAUGHING AT LIFE	192			▓
40	TIME ON MY HANDS	76	▓		
40	I'M ALL FOR YOU	74	▓		

TEMPO	ANALYSIS - THE COLUMBIA YEARS 1933-42	SPEED	SLOW	MEDIUM	FAST
YEAR 19-	TUNE	BPM	40-79	80-119	120+
39	I HEAR MUSIC	166			
39	THE SAME OLD STORY	83			
40	PRACTICE MAKES PERFECT	154			
40	ST LOUIS BLUES	112			
40	LOVELESS LOVE	110			
41	LETS DO IT	146			
41	GEORGIA ON MY MIND	80			
41	ROMANCE IN THE DARK	154			
41	ALL OF ME	112			
41	I'M IN A LOW - DOWN GROOVE	82			
41	GOD BLESS THE CHILD	76			
41	AM I BLUE?	80			
41	SOLITUDE	70			
41	JIM	80			
41	I COVER THE WATERFRONT	70			
41	LOVE ME OR LEAVE ME	93			
41	GLOOMY SUNDAY	59			
42	WHEREVER YOU ARE	154			
42	MANDY IS TWO	67			
42	IT'S A SIN TO TELL A LIE	154			
42	UNTIL THE REAL THING COMES ALONG	66			
	TOTALS	158	15	85	58
	PERCENTAGE OF TOTAL		9%	54%	37%

Appendix 4

Analysis of the Live Recordings by Billie Holiday
1948–59

Compiled by Malcolm Nicholson

Examining live recordings is necessarily an inexact science, as new, previously unknown material can often surface quite unexpectedly.

To establish an absolute at a given moment in time, I used the May 1985 discography by Akira Yamato from the Japanese Box Set *Billie Holiday On Verve, 1946–59* (Verve OOMJ–3480/9), to which I added *Billie Holiday At Monterey 1958* (Blackhawk BKH50701–1), a body of work that subsequently became commonly available on both vinyl and CD.

From the year Holiday came out of prison until her death, the discography lists some forty-eight separate live recording dates during which a total of 193 tunes were recorded. These vary from airshots with just one or two recordings to major events like the *Lady Sings the Blues* concert of November 1956.

Of the 193 songs recorded, ninety-seven tracks permutate ten different songs, and these comprise about 50 per cent of her live recordings.

This would seem to suggest that contemporary reports about the predictability of her repertoire were well founded, though it must be emphasized that these recordings are snapshots only.

However, the number and variety of songs is sufficient to be statistically relevant. The ten most recorded 'live' songs from 1948 to 1959 in Akira Yamato's May 1985 discography (amended as indicated) are:

Song	Number of Recordings
'Billie's Blues'	15
'My Man'	13
'Them There Eyes'	12
'Lover Man'	10
'Lover Come Back To Me'	9
'What A Little Moonlight Can Do'	9
'I Cover the Waterfront'	8
'Fine and Mellow'	7
'Willow, Weep For Me'	7
'All of Me'	7
Total	97

Some interesting points: 50 per cent of these tunes are medium tempo, 30 per cent slow tempo and now only 20 per cent are fast. Of these, only 'Willow, Weep For Me' was first recorded later than 1944 (an airshot 1953, studio 1954), while 50 per cent were first recorded in the 1930s. Note that, perhaps surprisingly, 'Strange Fruit' is not among the ten.

Malcolm Nicholson
London, September 1994

LIVE BROADCASTS 1948 - 59

TUNE 19-	48	49	50	51	52	53	54	55	56	57	58	59	TOTAL
(YOU AINT GONNA BOTHER ME)NO MORE		1											1
A GHOST OF A CHANCE									1				1
AINT NOBODY'S BUSINESS IF I DO				2			1		1		1	1	6
ALL OF ME	1	2		1			3						7
BILLIES BLUES		3		2			4	1	2		2	1	15
BLUE MOON							1						1
BODY & SOUL									1				1
CRAZY HE CALLS ME				1									1
DETOUR AHEAD		1		1									2
DONT EXPLAIN	1								2		2		5
EASY LIVING					1				1				2
FINE & MELLOW	1	1			2		1		1	1			7
FOOLIN MYSELF											1		1
GOD BLESS THE CHILD						1			2		1		4
GOOD MORNING HEARTACHE		1									1		2
HE'S FUNNY THAT WAY				1			1						2
I COVER THE WATERFRONT	2	1		1	1	1	1		1				8
I CRIED FOR YOU							2		1				3
I LOVE YOU PORGY		1		1		1			2			1	6
I ONLY HAVE EYES FOR YOU						1			2		1		4
I WISHED ON THE MOON											1		1
I WONDER WHERE OUR LOVE HAS GONE		1											1
I'LL BE SEEING YOU		1							1				2
ITS EASY TO REMEMBER											1		1
KEEPS ON A RAININ'		1											1
LADY SINGS THE BLUES									1	1			2

292

TUNE 19-	48	49	50	51	52	53	54	55	56	57	58	59	TOTAL
LOVER COME BACK TO ME				2	1		3			1	1	1	9
LOVER MAN		4		1	1		1	1	1		1		10
MAYBE YOU'LL BE THERE		1											1
MISS BROWN TO YOU	1	1		2	1				1				6
MOANIN LOW											1		1
MY MAN		1		1	2		3	1	4	1			13
NICE WORK IF YOU CAN GET IT									1	1		1	3
PLEASE DON'T TALK ABOUT ME WHEN I'M GONE									5			1	6
SOLITUDE	1												1
STORMY WEATHER							1						1
STRANGE FRUIT	1			1	1				1			1	5
TENDERLY					2								2
THAT OLE DEVIL CALLED LOVE		1											1
THE MAN I LOVE		1											1
THEM THERE EYES		3		1		1	3	1	1		2		12
TOO MARVELLOUS FOR WORDS						1			1			1	3
TRAV'LIN LIGHT									1		1		2
WHAT A LITTLE MOONLIGHT CAN DO					2		3		1	1	2		9
WHEN YOUR LOVER HAS GONE											4	1	5
WILLOW WEAP FOR ME						1			3	1	1	1	7
YESTERDAYS									1				1
YOU BETTER GO NOW											1		1
YOU GO TO MY HEAD						1							1
YOU'RE DRIVING ME CRAZY		1		1									2
YOU'RE MY THRILL			1										1
YOU'VE CHANGED									1		1		2
TOTAL NO. OF TUNES RECORDED PA	8	27	1	19	14	8	27	5	41	7	26	10	193
TOTAL NO. CONCERTS RECORDED PA	2	6	2	1	3	2	5	3	12	3	6	3	48
AVERAGE NO TUNES PER SESSION	4	5	1	19	5	4	5	2	3	2	4	3	4.02
YEAR 19-	48	49	50	51	52	53	54	55	56	57	58	59	

Appendix 5

List of Compositions Composed or Co-composed by Billie Holiday

'Fine and Mellow', words and music by Billie Holiday, published by E. B. Marks

'God Bless the Child', words and music by Billie Holiday and Arthur Herzog, published by E. B. Marks

'Left Alone', words by Billie Holiday, music by Mal Waldron, published by E. B. Marks

'Who Needs You?', words and music by Billie Holiday, published by E. B. Marks

'Long Gone Blues', words and music by Billie Holiday, published by E. B. Marks

'Say I'm Yours Again', words by Morgan, music by Billie Holiday, published by E. B. Marks

'Preacher Boy', words and music by Billie Holiday and Burns, published by E. B. Marks

'Please Don't Do It Here,' words and music by Billie Holiday and Buster Harding, published by E. B. Marks

'Tell Me More, and More and Then Some', words and music by Billie Holiday, published by E. B. Marks

'Billie's Blues', words and music by Billie Holiday, published by JATP Publishing Co.

'Lady Sings the Blues', words by Billie Holiday, music by Herbie Nichols, published by Northern Music Inc.

'Don't Explain', words by Billie Holiday, music by Arthur Herzog, published by Northern Music Inc.

'Stormy Blues', words and music by Billie Holiday, published by Travis Music Co.

'Somebody's On My Mind', words by Billie Holiday, music by Arthur Herzog, published by International Music, Inc.

'Close Dem Eyes My Darlin'', words and music by Billie Holiday and Morgan, published by International Music, Inc.

'Lost at the Crossroads of Love', words and music by Billie Holiday, unpublished

'Everything Happens for the Best', words and music by Billie Holiday and Tab Smith, publisher unknown

'Our Love is Different', words and music by Billie Holiday, Sonny White, R. Conway and B. Alba, publisher unknown

Appendix 6

On 16 August 1995 new information was released for the first time ever from Billie Holiday's FBI file, numbered 12–1720, after an appeal under the Freedom of Information Act. It reveals a letter sent to Edgar Hoover, Director of the FBI, from Tallulah Bankhead, who, in response to a telephone conversation she had had with Hoover, clearly believed he had interceded on Holiday's behalf in the matter of her arrest for possessing drugs on 22 January 1949. Bankhead's father was a congressman, to whom she refers obliquely in her letter. Holiday's file, of which two pages still remain classified, gives no indication of what Hoover may or may not have done to help Holiday. However, he did reply to Bankhead on 11 February 1949 as follows:

> Dear Tallulah,
> I have received your letter of February 9 and was very glad to hear from you. Your kind comments are greatly appreciated and I trust you will not hesitate to call on me at any time you think I might be of assistance to you. Hoping to see you in the not too distant future.
>
> Sincerely,
> J. Edgar Hoover

Hotel Elysee
60 East 54th Street
New York, N. Y.
February 9, 1949

J. Edgar Hoover
Federal Bureau of Investigation
Washington, D. C.

Dear Mr. Hoover:

I am ashamed of my unpardonable delay
in writing to thank you a thousand times for the kindness,
consideration and courtesy, in fact all the nicest
adjectives in the book, for the trouble you took re
our telephone conversation in connection with Billie Holiday.

I tremble when I think of my audacity
in approaching you at all with so little to recommend me
except the esteem, admiration and high regard my father
held for you.   I would never have dared to ask him or you
a favor for myself but knowing your true humanitarian spirit
it seemed quite natural at the time to go to the top man.
As my Negro mammy used to say - "When you pray you pray to
God don't you?".

I have met Billie Holiday but twice in
my life but admire her immensely as an artist and feel
the most profound compassion for her knowing as I do the
unfortunate circumstances of her background.   Although my
intention is not to condone her weaknesses I certainly
understand the eccentricities of her behaviour because she
is essentially a child at heart whose troubles have made her
psychologically unable to cope with the world in which she
finds herself. Her vital need is more medical than the
confinement of four walls.

However guilty she may be, whatever penalty
she may be required to pay for her frailties, poor thing,
you I know did everything within the law to lighten her
burden.   Bless you for this.

Kindest regards,

Tallulah Bankhead

Tallulah Bankhead

RECORDED - 92   12-17   - 3

Index

Bali Club, Washington, 170
Ball and Chain, Miami, 207
Bandstand, Philadelphia, 208
Bank, Danny, 220
Bankhead, Tallulah, 174
Barker, Danny, 43
Barnes, Mae, 192
Barnet, Charlie, 117, 124
Barrymore, Lionel, 142
Bascomb Brothers, 140
Basie, Count: Young's work, 50, 80, 86, 87, 210; band's New York opening, 81–2; auditions BH, 83–4; BH joins band 84–5; rhythm team, 88; BH's work with band, 85, 90, 92–7, 229; relationship with BH, 97–8, 118, 119; BH split, 97–8; Famous Door party, 105; Verve, 130; Strand Theater season, 169; movie short, 181–2; Harding's work, 186; *Comeback* appearance, 192; Newport tribute, 196; *Birdland All-Stars*, 197
Baskette, Jimmy, 59
Bauza, Mario, 92
Bedford Ballroom, 80
Beiderbecke, Bix, 87, 89, 178
Bell, Aaron, 205
Benjamin, Ben, 218
Bently, Gladys, 43
Berg, Billy, 128, 171, 172–3, 180
Berigan, Bunny, 74, 77–9, 152, 229
Berk, Dick, 217
Bernstein, Artie, 50
Bernstein, Leonard, 149
Berry, Chu, 46, 50–1
Bert, Eddie, 144
Best, Denzil, 176
'Big Stuff', 149
Bigard, Barney, 135
Birdland, Chicago, 204
Birdland, New York, 197, 220, 221
Billie Holiday, 220
Billie Holiday Sings, 188
'Billie's Blues', 78, 151, 177, 196, 207
Black, Ivan, 111

Blackhawk Restaurant, San Francisco, 208, 217
Blackmon, Ted, 44
Blakey, Art, 180, 183
Bledsoe, Jules, 47
Block, Sandy, 117
Blowers, Johnny, 141
Blue Note, Chicago, 179, 190
Blue Note, Le, Paris, 218
Blue Rhythm Band, 57
'Blues Are Brewin', The', 153, 154
Blues Are Brewin', The, 155
Boatner, Edward, 180
Bodenheim, Maxwell, 111
'Body and Soul', 120, 143, 151, 181
Bon Bon, 107
Boogie-Woogie, Cleveland, 128
Booker, Beryl, 193, 194
'Born to Love', 88
Boston Arena, 197
Bradley, Nita, 101
Bradshaw, Tiny, 60
Brady, Anna, 52
Breadbar, Rudy, 155
Brooklyn Academy of Music, 180
Brooks, Dudley, 129
Brown, Ray, 188, 196, 210
Brown Derby, 75, 154
Brubeck, Dave, 202
Brunis, George, 70
Brunswick Records, 61, 62–3, 74, 77, 85, 102
Bryant, Marie, 131
Bryant, Willie, 44, 66, 70, 96, 108, 111
Bushkin, Joe, 70, 74, 77

Café Society, New York, 108–12, 116–18, 121–2, 133, 178
Café Society, San Francisco, 173
Café Society, Los Angeles, 123
Caldwell, Happy, 79
Callender, Red, 129, 153
Calloway, Cab, 36, 44, 55, 57
Camarata, 140
Camel Caravan (radio programme), 111